Comparative Syntax and Language Acquisition

This important work explores the key linguistic issues of syntactic theory, comparative syntax, and the study of language acquisition. Written by Luigi Rizzi, one of the discipline's leading authorities, some of the essays collected here have already been profoundly influential in their field. Others are published here for the first time, and present important new directions for linguistic research.

This study is centred on four major topics:

- the theory of principles and parameters, with special reference to the properties and functioning of the pronominal systems
- the theory of locality
- the detailed study of syntactic configurations, leading to a refined cartography of structural positions
- the theory-conscious comparative study of language acquisition and language development.

This book represents an essential text for any linguist with a particular interest in syntax and language acquisition.

Luigi Rizzi is a professor of linguistics at the University of Siena, Italy. He was previously associate professor at MIT and professor at the University of Geneva. He is the author of *Issues in Italian Syntax* and *Relativized Minimality*.

Routledge leading linguists
Series editor Carlos Otero

Essays on Syntax and Semantics
James Higginbotham

Partitions and Atoms of Clause Structure
Subjects, agreement, case and clitics
Dominique Sportiche

The Syntax of Specifiers and Heads
Collected essays of Hilda J. Koopman
Hilda J. Koopman

Configurations of Sentential Complementation
Perspectives from Romance languages
Johan Rooryck

Essays in Syntactic Theory
Samuel David Epstein

On Syntax and Semantics
Richard K. Larson

Comparative Syntax and Language Acquisition
Luigi Rizzi

Comparative Syntax and Language Acquisition

Luigi Rizzi

LONDON AND NEW YORK

First published 2000
by Routledge
2 Park Square, Milton Park, Abingdon, Oxon, OX14 4RN

Simultaneously published in the USA and Canada
by Routledge

711 Third Avenue, New York, NY 10017

Reprinted 2001 (twice)

Transferred to Digital Printing 2005

Routledge is an imprint of the Taylor & Francis Group

First issued in paperback 2012

© 2000 Luigi Rizzi

Typeset in Baskerville by Wearset, Boldon, Tyne and Wear

All rights reserved. No part of this book may be reprinted or reproduced or utilized in any form or by any electronic, mechanical, or other means, now known or hereafter invented, including photocopying and recording, or in any information storage or retrieval system, without permission in writing from the publishers.

British Library Cataloguing in Publication Data
A catalogue record for this book is available from the British Library

Library of Congress Cataloging-in-Publication Data
Rizzi, Luigi, 1952–
  Comparative syntax and language acquisition / Luigi Rizzi
  p. cm.
  Essays, seven of which were previously published in various sources, 1986–1997.
  Includes bibliographical references and index.
  Contents: Introduction–Null objects in Italian and the theory of pro–Three issues in Romance dialectology–Some notes on Romance cliticization–On chain formation–On the anaphor-agreement effect–Argument-adjunct (a)symmetries–Direct perception, government, and thematic sharing–Residual verb second and the Wh criterion–The fine structure of the left periphery–Early null subjects and root null subjects–Remarks on linguistic theory and language development: the case of root infinitives.

  1. Grammar, Comparative and general–Syntax. 2. Language acquisition. I. Title

P291 .R57 2000
415–dc21   99 058192

ISBN 978-0-415-21549-7 (HB)

ISBN 978-0-415-64684-0 (PB)

To Adriana, Marco and Leonardo

Contents

Original publication details ix

1 Introduction 1

PART I
Principles and parameters in the pronominal systems 17

2 Null objects in Italian and the theory of *pro* 19
3 Three issues in Romance dialectology 80
4 Some notes on Romance cliticization 96

PART II
Locality 123

5 On chain formation 125
6 On the anaphor–agreement effect 158
7 Argument/adjunct (a)symmetries 174
8 Direct perception, government and thematic sharing 189

PART III
Cartography 211

9 Residual verb second and the Wh Criterion 213
10 The fine structure of the left periphery 241

PART IV
Acquisition 297

11 Early null subjects and root null subjects 299

12 Some notes on linguistic theory and language development: the case of root infinitives 320

References 340

Author index 357

Subject index 362

Original publication details

Chapter 2 'Null objects in Italian and the theory of *pro*' is reprinted from *Linguistic Inquiry*, 17: 501–57 by permission from MIT Press.

Chapter 5 'On chain formation' is reprinted from H. Borer (ed.) *The Syntax of Pronominal Clitics, Syntax and Semantics* 19, 1986: 65–95, by permission from Academic Press.

Chapter 6 'On the anaphor–agreement effect' is reprinted from *Rivista di Linguistica* 2,1, 1990: 27–42 by permission from *Rivista di Linguistica*, Pisa.

Chapter 9 'Residual verb second and the Wh Criterion' is reprinted from A. Belletti and L. Rizzi (eds) *Parameters and Functional Heads*, 1996: 63–90, by permission from Oxford University Press.

Chapter 10 'The fine structure of the left periphery' is reprinted from L. Haegeman (ed.) *Elements of Grammar*, 1997: 281–337 by permission from Kluwer Academic Publishers.

Chapter 11 'Early null subjects and root null subjects' is reprinted from T. Hoekstra and B. Schwartz (eds) *Language Acquisition Studies in Generative Grammar*, 1994: 151–76 by permission from John Benjamins Publishing Company.

Chapter 12 'Some notes on linguistic theory and language development: the case of root infinitives' is reprinted from *Language Acquisition*, 3,4, 1993/94: 371–93 by permission from Lawrence Erlbaum.

1 Introduction*

The essays collected in this volume are articulated around four major research topics: the parametric approach to comparative syntax, with special reference to the properties of the pronominal systems; the theory of locality in a representational approach; the fine-grained study of structural representations, leading to a detailed cartography of syntactic configurations; and the theoretically-conscious study of language acquisition and language development. The essays have been written at different times over a period of about fifteen years. Rather then presenting them chronologically, I have opted for organizing the presentation in four sections corresponding to the major research lines mentioned above. In this introductory section, I would like to outline the theoretical context of each topic, review some of the results achieved, and discuss and speculate on possible developments.

1 The theory of parameters and comparative syntax

Up until the mid-seventies, particular grammars were conceived of as systems of rules meeting some general constraints, but fundamentally specific to individual languages. For instance, French causatives differed from English causatives in that French syntax had certain transformational rules of causative formation (Kayne 1975) which English lacked, certain Italian verbs allowed clitic climbing and other phenomena disallowed in Contemporary French because Italian syntax had a restructuring rule missing in Contemporary French (Rizzi 1976, 1978a), etc. Universal Grammar (UG), the abstract theory of the human language faculty, was conceived of as a grammatical metatheory constraining the form and functioning of particular grammars (Chomsky 1973). On the one hand, UG defined the *format* for possible grammatical rules; in terms of the cognitive interpretation of UG as a theory of the initial cognitive state, it then defined the 'search space' for grammatical construction, the space of grammatical possibilities within which the language learner had to build

---

* Thanks are due to Marco Nicolis and Manola Salustri for editorial help.

the particular rule system generating the language he or she was exposed to. On the other hand, UG defined the *functioning* of rule systems through such principles as A over A, Subjacency and other theoretical entities intended to cover the locality phenomena referred to as Island Constraints (Ross 1967) and other empirical generalizations.

Two major advances took place in the course of the seventies which led to a radically different picture around the end of the decade. The first was theoretical. The sharpening of general conditions on rules made it possible to drastically simplify the rule systems: in particular, the complex trasformational rules of previous generative descriptions could be reduced to extremely simple rule schemata such as 'move category', or 'delete category', with overgeneration controlled by a very tight system of conditions operating on rule application, or on the output (Chomsky 1976; Chomsky 1980; Chomsky and Lasnik 1977). The second advance was empirical. The first large-scale attempts, within the generative tradition, to carefully describe large fragments of languages different from English revealed a fundamental underlying uniformity, much deeper than an approach to individual grammars as language-specific rule systems would have led one to expect (see much of the work on Romance syntax inspired by Kayne 1975 and the earlier essays collected in Kayne 1984). At the same time, relational grammarians were able to show that argument changing processes in a wide variety of languages could be reduced to a small number of universal laws expressed in terms of grammatical relations (see, for example, the essays collected in Perlmutter 1983a).

These advances led to the Principles and Parameters approach. The possibility of reducing (aspects of) cross linguistic variation to the fixation of parameters was already hinted at, as an abstract possibility, in Chomsky (1975, republished as Chapter 5 of Chomsky 1977b: 157); it was then discussed in connection with a concrete case in Chomsky (1980) (written in 1978), and fully developed for the first time in a series of seminars at the Scuola Normale Superiore of Pisa in the spring of 1979, then systematized in Chomsky (1981). Within this approach, Universal Grammar ceases to be a higher order entity with respect to particular grammars, and is conceived of as an integral component of them.

The grammar of a language consists of a lexicon and a computational component specifying some choice points, or parameters; the computational component is universal, except for the fixation of the parameters; the computational component of a particular grammar, then, is UG plus a set of parametric values. This simple approach to language uniformity and language variation quickly manifested an extraordinary heuristic value: it prompted a wealth of research on different language families bringing to light new phenomena, and permitting a better grasp of known generalizations.

The first concrete case discussed in terms of the parametric approach was related to the theory of locality. It was proposed that the reported cross-linguistic variation in the extractability from a Wh Island and other embedded domains could be accounted for by assuming that the set of bounding nodes, or Subjacency barriers, could vary in part from language to language (see Rizzi 1978b, republished as 1982, Chapter 2, the reassessment in Chomsky 1986b, and the discussion in Lightfoot 1989 and in various comment papers in the same issue of *Behavioral and Brain Sciences*). In retrospect, the locality case clearly was not an ideal case to start with in the exploration of parametric theory: the relevant cross-linguistic differences are subtle, involving degrees of marginality rather than clear-cut distinctions, and substantial individual variation, as is to be expected given the rarity of the critical evidence in the primary linguistic data.

1.1 Parametric properties of the pronominal systems

It is not surprising that comparative research quickly turned to more robust patterns of cross-linguistic variation to put to test the explanatory and heuristic power of the parametric approach. Pronominal systems offered just such a testing ground. On the one hand, the option of not pronouncing an understood pronominal subject in certain languages offered an obvious case of cross-linguistically variable choice, giving rise to a sharp grammatical bifurcation and with the relevant triggering evidence densely attested in the primary data. On the other hand, the Null Subject option quickly appeared to enter into a network of non-trivial relations with other major syntactic properties, which could be revealed and to some extent explained by the parametric approach (Rizzi 1982, Chapter 4 and the essays collected in Jaeggli and Safir 1989, among many other references).

Three of the essays collected in this volume directly deal with the parametrization involved in the pronominal systems. Chapter 2, 'Null objects in Italian and the theory of *pro*' (written in 1984/85 and first published in 1986) is an attempt to define an approach to the licensing and interpretation of the null pronominal element *pro* in the context of the general theory of null elements. The initial empirical observation is that null pronominals can occur not only in subject position, but also, in some languages, in object position (and possibly in other structural configurations), so that a comprehensive theory of this element must express its relative distributional freedom across languages, and the relevant parametrization. The basic theoretical idea which grounds the approach to *pro* is that for each kind of null element Universal Grammar must provide at least two kinds of specifications: it must specify the conditions under which the null element is *formally licensed*, i.e., the structural contexts in which it is allowed to occur; and the way in which it is *identified*, i.e. how its content is recovered from the structural environment. So, PRO is formally licensed by the PRO theorem (ultimately by the Binding Theory), or by the assignment of a special null Case (as in the Chomsky–Lasnik approach presented in the first chapter of Chomsky 1995), and it is identified by the

Theory of Control, which assigns an argumental antecedent to it, or, by default, assigns arbitrary interpretation. The various kinds of traces are formally licensed by the Empty Category Principle (or by its head-government component in the sense of Rizzi 1990a), and identified by being chain-connected to an antecedent. What about *pro*? Previous work on the Null Subject Parameter had highlighted the relevance of the verbal inflection in the licensing and interpretation of subject *pro*. Generalizing this observation to the occurrence of *pro* in other positions, Chapter 2 states the licensing principle in terms of a local relation with a designated kind of head (the class of the licensers being parametrized), with the identification provided by the featural content of the licensing head.

Chapter 3, 'Three issues in Romance dialectology', was presented at the GLOW workshop on the syntax of dialects (Venice, 1987) and has never been published elsewhere. Building on Rizzi (1986), the chapter extends the analysis in terms of the Null Subject Parameter to some Northern Italian Dialects which have the peculiarity of requiring (in some varieties, and for some person–number specifications) a subject clitic in finite clauses, while retaining other peculiarities of Null Subject Languages such as free subject inversion, free Wh extraction of embedded subjects, etc. In fact, there are good reasons for analysing such obligatory subject clitics as expressing functional heads of the inflectional system rather than as genuine fillers of the subject DP position. This research witnesses, with much previous and subsequent work (see, for example, the papers collected in Benincà 1989, 1994; Belletti 1993), the renewed interest for the study of dialects which was raised by the introduction of the parametric approach: dialectology deals with systems which are very close structurally and diachronically, which should then provide particularly favourable opportunities for teasing apart the primitive lines of bifurcation differentiating possible grammatical systems. I thought it was worthwhile to publish this text here essentially in the original form (in spite of the fact that it is little more than an annotated handout), as some of the points raised in the Venice talk were taken up in the literature; in particular, the chapter provides one of the first pieces of evidence in favour of an IP system consisting of distinct inflectional heads; moreover it provides a straightforward argument for the assumption that *pro* is licensed in preverbal subject position in Italian, rather than in postverbal position.

Chapter 4, 'Some notes on romance cliticization', was presented at the Durham meeting of the 'Clitics' group of the Eurotyp Project (European Science Foundation, October, 1993), and has never been published elsewhere. It addresses some of the basic issues raised by the analysis of Romance cliticization in terms of the ideas and technology of the first version of the Minimalist Program (Chomsky 1993). Special emphasis is put on the conditions which determine the enclitic or proclitic position in different Romance varieties.

2 Aspects of locality

Locality has been one of the classical topics of generative grammar ever since the sixties, and the study of locality conditions has been much developed within principles and parameters and minimalist models. Different kinds of locality are in focus in some of the essays collected here.

Chapter 5, written in 1982 and first published in 1986, studies locality effects in argument chains. The leading theoretical motivation in the background is an attempt to provide an empirical argument in favour of the view that chains are read off from S-structure (or possibly LF) by a chain formation algorithm; more generally, the argument supports a representational approach to chain formation and locality. The fundamental empirical fact is the following generalization: anaphoric clitics in different Romance languages can be bound by deep subjects, but not by derived subjects in such constructions as passive and raising (Kayne 1975; Burzio 1981, 1982); the incompatibility is also by and large found with unaccusatives and adjectival constructions, but with somewhat less sharp results. The relevant configuration can be naturally excluded if there is a chain formation algorithm reading chains off from representations. If such an algorithm restricts chain links to connect a position to its closest binder, then the incompatibility of anaphoric clitics with derived subjects is predicted: in a configuration like (1) in which t is the trace of the derived subject, the clitic, as an anaphor, will have to be bound by the subject; the derived subject, in order to be properly interpreted, will have to be chain connected to its trace in a Theta position; but then the chain formation algorithm will not be able to skip the anaphoric position, and the structure will eventually lead to a violation of the Theta Criterion:

(1) * DP ... si ... t ...

The incompatibility is less straightforwardly expressible in a derivational view of chains because the key notion of 'closest binder' cannot be naturally appealed to in that approach.

This simple argument is apparently incompatible with the VP-internal Subject Hypothesis, developed a few years later (Kuroda 1988; Koopman and Sportiche 1985, 1991), according to which all subjects start VP internally and always move to the Spec of inflectional positions for Case (or other feature checking) reasons. Under this hypothesis, all sentences involving reflexive clitics would give rise to configuration (1) because the surface position of the subject is always non-thematic. It should be noted, though, that if one adopts the approach proposed for independent reasons in footnote 17, the bulk of this approach becomes consistent with the VP-internal subject hypothesis: if the relevant intervener is not the clitic itself but the clitic trace, we will normally have intervention with passive, raising and unaccusative predicates, but not with deep subjects, as desired. See Vikner and Sprouse (1988) for a different restatement of this analysis in terms compatible with the VP Internal Subject Hypothesis, and for an analysis of the difference between Romance and Germanic reflexives in this respect. See also Belletti and Rizzi (1988), Roberts (1991a) for the weaker intervention effects determined by non-clitic anaphors with Psych Verbs and other constructions.

Some elements of this approach to A-chains are preserved, at least as underlying intuitions, in the general approach to locality known as Relativized Minimality, which was developed a few years later (Rizzi 1990a). According to this approach, a local relation cannot hold between two elements X and Y in the following configuration:

(2) ...X...Z...Y...

if the element Z has some properties in common with X (basically, if Z potentially enters into the same local relation with Y), and Z intervenes between X and Y. A proper formalization of this principle was shown to hold of the different kinds of chains and of other types of local relations, such as the local relations which must hold for a head and a maximal projection for Case licensing and other sorts of licensing processes (Rizzi, op. cit.). Chapter 7 'A/A' (A)symmetries', presented at the 1991 NELS Conference and first circulated in the proceedings, assumes the general architecture of the Relativized Minimality approach and addresses an apparent important exception to the locality effects in A'-chains: the extractability of argument Wh phrases from Wh Islands and other Weak Islands in the sense of Cinque (1990) and Rizzi (1990a). This essay develops an approach based on a procedure assigning referential indices to thematic arguments, under the assumption that bearers of such indices can enter into non-local binding relations, thus bypassing Relativized Minimality; this approach is then tested against some special cases of argument A' chains which surprisingly obey strong locality on a par with adjunct A' chains: partial Wh movement and further movement of clefted constituents.

Another classical domain for the study of locality is the theory of binding, and in particular the exact characterization of the local environments in which binding principles must be satisfied. Chapter 6, 'On the anaphor–agreement effect', written in 1989 and first published in 1990, deals with the systematic impossibility of nominative anaphors, or more precisely, the non-occurrence of anaphors locally construed with Nominative assigning agreement. The solution envisaged involves a particular sharpening of the definition of the local domains for principles A and B, which derives the anaphor–agreement effect and also extends to certain cases of disjoint reference induced by subjunctive. The approach proposed here is modified and extended in important respects in Burzio (1992) and Woolford (1999).

One case of syntactic process involving highly local configurations is the assignment of Thematic Roles, often assumed to take place under sisterhood uniquely. Chapter 8, 'Direct perception, government and thematic sharing', written in 1990 and circulated as a working paper in 1993, addresses the special case of Theta assignment in the infinitival complement of perception verbs, whose exceptional properties are particularly revealing for the study of locality on Theta assignment. The analysis also leads to a study of the structural peculiarities of the clausal complements of perception verbs, which naturally introduces the next topic.

3 Left-peripheral constructions and cartographic studies

The study of the fine-grained structure of syntactic representations has become one of the central research topics of syntactic theory in the last decade. In the first version of the Principles and Parameters approach, an important role was attributed to the node Infl (see Chomsky 1981), understood as the head of the clause providing the expression of tense and responsible for the Case marking of the subject in tensed clauses. Advances in the investigation of this and other functional heads led researchers to the hypothesis that the generator of structure is in fact fully provided by X-bar theory: all structural configurations are headed, and the only way to produce structure consists in starting from a head (lexical or functional) which projects a phrase in accordance with the fundamental X-bar schema and which can recursively take other phrases as specifiers and complements. So, clauses are IPs, and are generally embedded within a phrase projecting the complementizer, CP (Chomsky 1986b); nominal expressions in the general case are projections of the determiner, DPs (Abney 1987), etc.

As soon as this perspective was established in the mid-eighties, it also became obvious that functional structures were more complex than had been initially assumed. The case of inflection was paradigmatic. First of all, the number of morphosyntactic properties to be expressed in the assumed inflectional position (tense, aspect, modality, agreement, ...) quickly expanded under the pressure of a wealth of empirical studies; the single inflection node looked more and more like an empty container for a disparate collection of properties, which strongly reduced the plausibility of the single inflection approach. Secondly, it soon became obvious that a principled account of syntactic positions of verbal elements, arguments and modifiers in the clause required many more positions of heads and specifiers than those provided by a unique X-bar schema. The natural move was to postulate distinct inflectional nodes, each expressing an elementary morphosyntactic property, and combining with the others to form a rich inflectional space. Many indications emerged around the mideighties in favour of this line of inquiry (among them, the analysis of subject clitics in Chapter 3). But the real catalyzer for this development was provided by Jean-Yves Pollock's essay on verb movement (Pollock 1989). Pollock showed that by postulating distinct inflectional heads it was possible at the same time to provide a revealing analysis of form–position correlations in the verbal systems, thus grounding the study of verbal morphology on principles of syntactic organization, and provide enough room in the structure to lay the foundations of a principled account of adverbial positions. Pollock's results gave rise to a wealth of research on the fine structure of the IP, which culminated in Guglielmo Cinque's detailed cartography of the functional structure of the sentence (see Cinque 1999). It was only natural to extend this line of inquiry to other categories.

Chapter 10, 'The fine structure of the left periphery', written in 1995 and first published in 1997, offers an attempt to study the cartography of the complementizer system along the same general guidelines. Some adaptation to the peculiarities of this part of the structure is required, of course. Considerations of inflectional morphology are inevitably of more limited scope and relevance than for the study of the inflectional system. So, positions can be detected directly, on the basis of word order considerations, and indirectly, through subtler interactions with principles of structural organization and well-formedness. On the basis of positional considerations, a richly articulated structure is proposed for Italian and extended, with limited parametrization, to other languages:

(3) Force   Topic*   Focus   Topic*   Finiteness   IP

Each position is defined by a head, which may or may not be phonetically realized. Each head may license a specifier position which can function as the landing site of movement to the left periphery. So a focalized constituent will move to the Spec of the focal head, etc. The presence of the system of licensing heads is highlighted in some cases in an indirect manner. Consider for instance the fact that a preposed adverbial phrase can substantially improve a *that-t* violation, and is incompatible with I to C movement in English:

(4) a ?This is the man who I think that next year t will win the elections
    b *Will next year he win the elections?

Assuming that the left peripheral position occupied by the preposed adverbial is licensed by a head X,

(5) ... [next year X [...

we can provide natural explanations of facts like (4): the presence of X can be deemed responsible for the satisfaction of the ECP on the subject trace in (4)a, and for the ill-formedness of (4)b as a violation of the Head Movement Constraint, ultimately of the ECP under Relativized Minimality.

Neither effect would be expected if the preposed adverbial was simply adjoined to the IP, as in traditional accounts. This kind of indirect detection of the system of heads constituting the left periphery offers clear evidence in favour of a restrictive theory of syntactic configurations, excluding free adjunction as a structural option and fundamentally favouring bi-uniqueness between specifiers and licensing heads.

But how are positions licensed by heads in the A' system? Chapter 9, 'Residual verb second and the Wh Criterion', written in 1991 and first published in 1996, introduces the licensing principle which is then fully exploited in the analysis of the left periphery. Suppose that the Wh feature, generated under Tense (in some languages) and characterizing the clause as an interrogative must meet a 'Wh Criterion', i.e. must be in a Spec-Head configuration with a Wh phrase on the appropriate level of representation. This then provides the functional motivation for the inversion (I to C) processes taking place in interrogatives and related constructions in many languages. This principle can be naturally extended to other constructions involving movement to the left periphery, thus providing a fundamental tool for the exploration of the C system. An extension of this principle to negative constructions, hinted at in the chapter, has been fully developed in Haegeman (1995); an extension to a larger class of cases of feature licensing is proposed in Sportiche (1996). The criterial approach bears an obvious resemblance to the feature checking approach, developed by Chomsky (1993, 1995) for the Case-agreement system, which also involves a local Spec-head configuration; the main difference is that the criterial approach has been developed for interpretable features of the A' system, which plausibly don't disappear from representations, but require local licensing in Spec-head configurations (see Friedemann 1995 for an attempt to translate the criterial approach in terms of feature checking).

4 Syntactic theory and language acquisition

Ever since the late fifties, language acquisition has been a central topic of the research program of generative grammar. So much so that the notion of 'explanatory adequacy', the fundamental level of empirical adequacy defined in the theoretical literature of the sixties, was defined in terms of the acquisition problem: a linguistic analysis reaches the level of explanatory adequacy when it correctly describes the relevant fragment of the speaker's competence and is selected by the theory of the language faculty over potential competitors on some precise formal grounds. In other words, a descriptively adequate analysis is explanatory (in the relevant technical sense) when it comes with a reasonable account of how that fragment of competence was acquired by the speaker on the basis of his innate language faculty and of the experience he was exposed to in early childhood (see the first chapter of Chomsky (1965) and references quoted there for relevant discussion).

In spite of so much emphasis on acquisition, relatively little attention was paid, in this research program, to the actual course of language development until relatively recently. It was rather common among theoretical linguists to consider the study of what the learner actually knows and does with language in early childhood as fundamentally irrelevant for the linguist's main endeavour, the study of UG-constrained systems. It is not difficult to understand the reason for this apparent lack of interest. The study of adult competence systems with the methodology of grammaticality judgements had quickly revealed extremely rich and sophisticated systems of knowledge, knowledge very largely underdetermined by the linguistic evidence available in childhood. Such 'poverty of stimulus' considerations made it possible, and necessary, to formulate detailed hypotheses on the initial cognitive state, thus permitting rapid progress in the construction of plausible models of UG. The actual description of language development did not seem to be able to add much to the clear results which could be achieved by idealized, instantaneous models of language acquisition. Moreover, the simple and effective methodology of grammaticality judgements seemed difficult or impossible to apply with young children, and the empirical basis for the concrete study of development was then largely limited to the much less revealing analysis of natural production corpora. It was also widely believed that the early production might not bear directly on the study of UG constrained systems, either because performance limitations make it an unfaithful reflection of the underlying systems of knowledge, or because early systems are fundamentally impoverished, and qualitatively different from adult systems due to some fundamental lack or immaturity of computational capacities in the early stages. On top of that, the model of the adult grammar as a system of language specific rules did not provide a natural basis for a revealing comparison with the early systems, nor plausible mechanisms for understanding development.

The perspective has changed rather radically from the mid-eighties on. It is not accidental that a new growth of interest for the study of language development came shortly after the introduction of parametric models. Such models recreated a taste for linguistic comparison by providing an effective tool for expressing local divergencies among fundamentally uniform systems. It was only natural to try them out for comparing adult and early grammatical systems. Hyams' (1986) analysis of early subject drop was extremely influential in showing the promise and feasibility of a parametric approach to language development. Previous work on language development had showed that children pass through a phase in which they can selectively omit subjects, even if their target language is not a Null Subject Language. Hyams' hypothesis was that perhaps the initial setting of the Null Subject Parameter (or, in the theory of Chapter 2, the licensing of *pro* in a local environment with Infl) is positive: children acquiring a Null Subject Language simply keep the initial fixation, compatible with the evidence they are exposed to; children acquiring a non Null Subject Language must refix the parameter on the negative value on the basis of evidence conflicting with the initial fixation; this requires time, whence the observed developmental effect, with an initial Null Subject stage and the shift to a non Null Subject system, generally at some point in the course of the third year of life, or slightly later. This simple approach convinced many theoretical linguists that language development could become a serious testing ground for parametric models, thus expanding the empirical basis and the explanatory potential of the theory of UG.

Another factor which raised the theoretical interest of development studies was connected to important advances in the theory of the morphology/syntax interface. Of particular significance was the discovery and analysis of form–position dependencies, particularly in the domain of verb syntax, as mentioned in Section 3. The more refined understanding of the morphology/syntax interface which resulted from this trend enhanced the relevance of the study of natural production corpora: certain dependencies between verb form and verb position (in many languages inflected verbs move higher than uninflected verbs in the inflectional field, or even to the C system in V2 constructions, etc.) are very frequently observable, virtually in every sentence in some cases; therefore, simple techniques of quantitative analysis of natural production corpora permit us to go a long way in revealing the underlying grammatical knowledge. So, much progress was possible in determining the early knowledge of verbal morpho-syntax in French, German and many other languages (see Pierce 1992; Poeppel and Wexler 1993; Weissenborn 1994; Wexler 1994, among many other references) through corpus analysis. At the same time, skilful experimental techniques have made it possible to tap into early grammatical knowledge through grammaticality and interpretive judgements, elicited production, etc. (Crain 1992). In the course of the nineties, the study of development has thus become an integral part of the general endeavour pursued through theoretical and comparative research. One important finding, which has been progressively corroborated in the course of the decade, is the fundamental validity of the continuity hypothesis: early systems are UG constrained systems, essentially of the same nature as adult grammars. The limited points of discontinuity may be due to maturation in some cases, but still within the guidelines set by UG ('UG constrained maturation', in the sense of Borer and Wexler 1987). Even though the questions on the role and properties of maturational processes are far from settled, there is a general consensus that continuity is the overwhelming factor. If so, a direct comparison between adult and early systems is both legitimate and informative on the nature and properties of UG.

4.1 Early null subjects and root infinitives

Chapter 11, 'Early null subjects and root null subjects', written in 1991–2 and first published in 1994, addresses the problem of early subject drop in the acquisition of a non NSL. The basic idea is to study the fine structural properties of such early null subjects and compare them with the properties found in adult Null Subject Languages. Clear structural differences emerge: early null subjects are by and large restricted to the initial position of the clause, so that, for instance in Early English, declaratives (6)a–b freely alternate, while question (7)b, with a post-Wh subject position, is not a possible variant of (7)a:

(6)a Dis goes here.
 b ___ goes here.

(7)a Where dis goes?
 b *Where ___ goes?

No such restriction is found in adult Null Subject languages: for instance, the Italian equivalent of (7)b (*Dove va?*) is fully acceptable on a par with the equivalent of (6)b. The conclusion that is reached is that early subject drop is a fundamentally different phenomenon from the positive setting of the Null Subject Parameter: the former is restricted to the specifier of the root, the initial position of the clause, the latter is possible whenever the subject is in a local environment with the appropriate licensing inflection, regardless of whether the position is initial or not. The next observation is that children acquiring Null Subject Languages show an early mastery of Null Subject licensing with the property of the target language: for instance, there are plenty of post-Wh null subjects in natural production corpora of learners of Italian.

The conclusion is that the Null Subject Parameter is correctly fixed early on: children acquiring English fix it negatively from the onset of the syntactically relevant production (as is shown by the non-occurrence of (7)b), and children acquiring Italian fix it positively; in this respect, the Null Subject Parameter is no exception to the other best studied parameters, which also appear to be fixed very early on in development (Pierce 1992; Wexler 1994). On top of the negative fixing of the Null Subject Parameter, Early English (as well as the early phases of other non NSLs) has the option of dropping the subject in the specifier of the root, as in (6)b, an option that is grammatically independent from the Null Subject Parameter; reflexes of this option are also found in some adult varieties or registers, as is to be expected under continuity assumptions.

The chapter is then devoted to investigating the nature of this special grammatical option, the characteristics of the null element involved, the licensing conditions and the cause of development. In a nutshell, the basic idea can be summarized as follows. The specifier of the root, the highest position in the syntactic tree, is exempted from the identification requirement normally applying to null elements in all other positions (as alluded to in Section 1), hence it can freely host a null element which remains unidentified clause-internally, and receives an interpretive content in discourse. Suppose now that early systems have the option of truncating the initial part of the structure, for example, omitting the CP system; hence, the main subject position of a declarative like (6)b can be the specifier of the root in an early system, and can freely host a null element.

Let me go back to some of these points in the context of the presentation of the following chapter, and focus for a moment on some results achieved after the completion of Chapter 11. The conjecture that early null subjects are by and large inconsistent with post-Wh environments, originally put forth on the basis of some marginal remarks on Early English in Valian (1991), was then confirmed for Early French (Crisma 1992; Levow 1995), Early Dutch (Haegeman 1996a), and Early German (see the discussion in Hamann 1997). As for Early English, the non-occurrence of null subjects in contexts like (7)b was confirmed by Roeper and Rohrbacher (1994) and Bromberg and Wexler (1995) on corpora different from Valian's. These authors also showed that in non-inflected post-Wh contexts (*Where ___ go(ing)?*) null subjects could occur quite frequently in Early English. This led to the natural conclusion that a second kind of null subject is possible in uninflected environments in early systems (say, a PRO subject), not restricted to the specifier of the root, much as in adult embedded infinitives. See Rizzi (1998) for detailed discussion of this independent grammatical option, and for various slight modifications and updates of the ideas presented in Chapter 11. See also Haegeman (1996b) and Hamann (1997) for discussion of cases of apparent non-initial early null subjects, and an analysis in terms of the theory of the C system presented in Chapter 10.

Chapter 12, 'Some notes on linguistic theory and language development: the case of root infinitives', was written in 1993 and first published in 1994. The topic addressed is another major property of early systems: around the age of two, children freely produce main declaratives with the verb in the infinitival form, an option generally precluded in the corresponding target systems. We illustrate this construction with examples in French, a language in which infinitives are morphologically marked by a special suffix (examples from the CHILDES database, see MacWhinney 1999; on Philippe's corpus see Suppes, Smith and Léveillé 1973):

(8) a Voiture partir. (Grégoire 1;11)
 'Car leave.'
 b Michel dormir là. (Philippe 2;2)
 'Michel sleep there.'

The first question to ask is: why are such structures generally ruled out in adult systems? If clauses contain a *tense variable* located in the T node in the inflectional system, this variable will have to be fixed in some way, in order to comply with Chomsky's (1986a) principle of Full Interpretation. Consider the relevant cases in Adult French structures:

(9) a Les enfants jouaient+T au ballon.
       'The children played soccer.'
    b J'ai vu les enfants T jouer au ballon.
       'I saw the children play soccer.'
    c *Les enfants T jouer au ballon
       'The children play soccer.'

The most straightforward device is the one normally used in finite clauses: in (9)a the T variable is locally bound (essentially in the checking configuration, in the sense of Chomsky 1995) from the verbal morphology after V movement to the I system in the overt (or, in other languages, covert) syntax; in embedded infinitival clauses like (9)b this device is not available due to the lack of appropriate verbal morphology, still the tense variable can be fixed by binding from the superordinate tense specification in the main clauses. But in root infinitival clauses like (9)c neither device is available: that is why root infinitives tend not to exist in adult grammars (except for special cases discussed in Chapter 12). Why are they freely possible in (some) early systems then? We must assume here some kind of local discontinuity between early and adult systems. We have already assumed a local discontinuity, the availability of truncated structures in the early systems, to account for the early null subject phenomenon. As early null subjects and root infinitives are by and large co-extensive phenomena in language development (see below), it was reasonable to try to relate root infinitives to the same underlying grammatical option.

The proposal in Chapter 12 is that there is no reason to limit the truncation option introduced in Chapter 11 to the higher layers of the clausal structure. Truncation can involve lower layers as well, in particular the projection of the clausal structure can stop within the inflectional system leaving out the TP layer (and everything above it); when this happens no position for the tense variable is specified in the truncated clausal structure, hence a (truncated) root infinitive does not contain any unbound variable and complies with the principle of Full Interpretation. Once the truncation option ceases to be available, and clauses must be projected up to the CP system, the free generation of root infinitives is lost, and indeed it is generally missing in adult systems.

The truncation analysis provides a simple explanation for a number of structural properties of root infinitives, in particular the incompatibility with Wh constructions, with weak pronominal subjects and with functional verbs (auxiliaries, modals, etc.): if root infinitives involve truncation under T, it is expected that properties licensed by the structural layers from T upward will not be found.

Under the proposed analysis, both root null subjects and root infinitives are related to the same underlying property of early grammatical systems, the option of truncating main clauses at different structural layers lower than the CP system. It is then expected that the two phenomena should disappear about simultaneously in development (or possibly with root infinitives disappearing slightly earlier than root null subjects, as they require a 'deeper' truncation). The existence of a developmental correlation has in fact been substantiated in more recent work by Haegeman (1996b), Rasetti (1999) and Hamann and Plunkett (1997) on Early Dutch, French and Danish, respectively. These authors show that root infinitives tend to disappear at about the same time as (or slightly earlier than) early null subjects in finite environments, thus supporting the prediction of the truncation approach. Other consequences of this hypothesis are explored in various essays collected in Friedemann and Rizzi (2000); for the implications of the truncation approach in second language acquisition see Prévost (1997) and White and Prévost (2000).

Under this approach, the study of language acquisition and development is fully congruent and complementary to modern comparative syntax, both domains being part of the same endeavour. On the one hand, the modest points of discontinuity between early and adult systems provide new variations on the fundamental research theme, the study of UG constrained systems, thus making accessible to inquiry aspects of UG which may be concealed in adult systems. On the other hand, the very goal of capturing development introduces new empirical demands and challenges to the explanatory capacity of UG models. Comparative acquisition studies can thus add novel empirical dimensions to syntactic theory and the comparative syntax of adult languages, an enrichment which may shed much light on the same fundamental object of inquiry.

PART I
Principles and parameters in the pronominal systems

2 Null objects in Italian and the theory of *pro**

One of the central concerns of current syntactic research is the characterization of the mapping relating lexical meaning and syntactic form. An important facet of this comprehensive issue is the syntactic status of 'understood' or 'implicit' arguments: does an 'understood' thematic role, inherent in the lexical meaning of a verb, always correspond to a structural slot in syntactic representations? If not, under what conditions can the mismatch between meaning and form be tolerated? The concrete case that this article addresses is illustrated by the following pairs in English and Italian:

(1) a This leads (people) to the following conclusion.
    b Questo conduce (la gente) alla seguente conclusione.
(2) a This sign cautions (people) against avalanches.
    b Questo cartello mette in guardia (la gente) contro le valanghe.
(3) a John is always ready to please (people).
    b Gianni è sempre pronto ad accontentare (la gente).

Consider the variants in which the parenthesized direct object is omitted. We must choose between two *a priori* possible candidates for the structures of the relevant VPs:

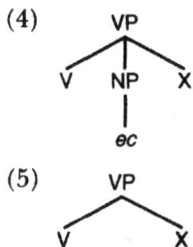

(4)
(5)

* Thanks are due, for useful discussion, to the students and visitors who attended my Fall 1984 course at MIT, and to M. Baker, A. Barss, A. Belletti, L. Burzio, G. Chierchia, G. Cinque, D. Everett, J. Grimshaw, J. Guéron, J. Higginbotham, K. Johnson, R. Kayne, B. Levin, M. R. Manzini, W. O'Neil, T. Roeper, M. Saito, E. Torrego; and, for editorial assistance, to M. Carracino.

Example (4) claims that the missing object is structurally realized as a phonetically null element; (5) claims that the object is missing in the more radical sense of a total absence of structure. Different components of the Government–Binding Theory give rise to different expectations as to what should turn out to be the empirically correct structure. Consider the Projection Principle, the hypothesis that categorial structure reflects thematic structure at all syntactic levels (Chomsky 1981, 1982b). Of course, the exact prediction of the Projection Principle for the question at hand will depend on the specific formal characterization that we choose. If we make the reasonable initial assumption that the intuitive characterization is literally correct, the consequences for (1)–(3) are straightforward. The missing object is understood as part of the lexical meaning of *lead*, *caution*, and *please*; moreover, given our favoured theory of θ-roles, we can even name the role that it receives, that is, the same that the overt object *people/la gente* would receive. Therefore, we would be led to expect that (4) is correct, with the object position presumably filled by a zero generic pronoun close in meaning to arbitrary PRO.

If we look at the problem from the viewpoint of another major component of the Government–Binding Theory, the theory of null elements, we are led to the opposite conclusion. The fact is that the standard theory of null elements does not seem to provide any possible null filler for the object position in (4): it cannot be a trace because there is no antecedent; nor a variable because there is no (visible) operator (on null operators, see below); nor PRO because it is governed by V; nor *pro* because it is not locally construed with a 'strong' agreement. One could reasonably argue that if there is no possible filler for the object position, the position cannot exist; hence, (5) is correct. Therefore, there appears to be a tension between the Projection Principle and the typology of null elements in this domain. How is this tension to be resolved?

I would like to argue that this indeterminacy cannot be fully resolved at the level of Universal Grammar because different particular grammars can resolve it differently. More specifically, even two rather close grammatical systems like English and Italian differ in the relevant respect in that (5) is the only possible structural representation of the English examples, whereas Italian allows (4) as a possible representation. If this is correct, various theoretical questions arise immediately:

a   Which is the type of the null object in Italian?
b   Which is the parameter differentiating Italian and English?
c   How is the standard theory of null elements to be qualified to accommodate the Italian case?
d   How is the Projection Principle to be qualified to accommodate the English case?

In trying to answer these questions, I will elaborate a theory of *pro* that departs substantively from standard assumptions. But before I address the theoretical questions, a rather extensive discussion of the empirical material is in order.

1 Empirical evidence

In this section I will give five arguments supporting the conclusion that Italian and English differ as suggested. Four have the same essential structure: the understood object in Italian is syntactically 'active' in that it can act as a controller, as a binder, and as a subject of predication for adjunct and argument small clauses, whereas the null object in English appears to be syntactically 'inert' in the same environments. The fifth argument involves the different productivity of the null object option in the two grammatical systems. The section will conclude with a brief analysis of the English case.

1.1 Control

Consider the following paradigm in English:

(6) a This leads people to the following conclusion.
    b This leads to the following conclusion.
    c This leads people [PRO to conclude what follows].
    d *This leads [PRO to conclude what follows].

The ungrammaticality of (6)d instantiates a constraint that appears to be generally operative in English: a direct object controller cannot be omitted. This descriptive constraint, known as 'Bach's generalization' (Bach 1979), has been traced back to principles of control theory (Bresnan 1982; Chierchia 1984) or binding theory (Koster 1984). I will not take a specific stand on the correct deduction; for the purposes of this discussion it is sufficient to assume that the following version of Bach's generalization is descriptively correct (but see the Appendix for further discussion):

(7) In object control structures the object NP must be structurally represented.

The ungrammaticality of (6)d then follows from (7) in conjunction with the hypothesis that no structurally represented zero object is possible in English – that is, no structural position is specified between the verb and the control clause in (6)d, and the representation of the VP is (5).

Things are different in Italian. There is no gap in the paradigm corresponding to (6):

(8) a Questo conduce la gente alla seguente conclusione.
   b Questo conduce ___ alla seguente conclusione.
   c Questo conduce la gente a [PRO concludere quanto segue].
   d Questo conduce ___ a [PRO concludere quanto segue].

In general, an object controller can always be phonetically missing in Italian, provided that the sentence has a generic time reference:

(9) a Il bel tempo invoglia a [PRO restare].
       'The nice weather induces ___ to stay.'
   b L'ambizione spesso spinge ___ a [PRO commettere errori].
       'Ambition often pushes ___ to make mistakes.'
   c Un generale può costringere a [PRO obbedire ai suoi ordini].
       'A general can force ___ to obey his orders.'
   d In questi casi, di solito Gianni invita ___ a [PRO mangiare con lui].
       'In these cases, generally Gianni invites ___ to eat with him.'

If the time reference is specific, the acceptability degrades:

(10) a *?Alla fine della vacanza il bel tempo ha invogliato a [PRO restare].
        'At the end of the vacation the nice weather has induced ___ to stay.'
    b *Alle cinque il generale ha costretto ___ a [PRO obbedire].
        'At five the general forced ___ to obey.'

This state of affairs suggests the following interpretation. Bach's generalization is exceptionless and holds in Italian as well as in English. Italian, contrary to English, has a possible null filler of the object position in such sentences as (9)a–d. This filler is interpreted as a generic, arbitrary pronoun, and because of its meaning requires generic time reference; like any other NP in the correct structural configuration, this element can function as a controller, thus meeting the requirement of Bach's generalization.[1]

1.2 Binding

The second argument refers to a less controversial module of the system, the theory of binding. The understood object with arbitrary interpretation can be the antecedent of an anaphor:

(11) a La buona musica riconcilia ___ con se stessi.
        'Good music reconciles ___ with oneself.'
    b Un bravo psicanalista può restituire ___ a se stessi.
        'A good psychoanalyst can give back to oneself.'

Se stessi (literally *themselves*) is the third person plural reflexive, which can occur with ordinary third person plural antecedents, and with arbitrary PRO:

(12) a Loro parlano di se stessi.
 'They speak about themselves.'
 b Non è chiaro [come [PRO parlare di se stessi]].
 'It is not clear how to speak about oneself.'

This element appears to be in the domain of principle A of the binding theory both in the specific and in the arbitrary interpretation. For instance, in the latter interpretation, if there is no available antecedent *se stessi* cannot be rescued by any sort of pragmatic or discourse control even in generic statements:

(13) a *La buona musica piace a se stessi.
 'Good music pleases oneself.'
 b *Un bravo psicanalista può dare aiuto a se stessi.
 'A good psychoanalyst can give help to oneself.'

Taking the binding principle and the definition of the binding relation literally, we must conclude that a structurally represented binder exists in (11), and the only possible candidate, given the interpretation, is a null filler of the object position. A similar option does not exist in English, as is suggested by the unacceptability of the glosses.[2]

1.3 Adjunct small clauses

The understood object can be modified by an adjunct small clause in Italian:

(14) a Un dottore serio visita ___ nudi.
 'A serious doctor visits ___ nude ([+pl]).'
 b Di solito, Gianni fotografa ___ seduti.
 'In general, Gianni photographs ___ seated ([+pl]).'
 c Di solito, quel famoso pittore ritrae ___ vestiti di bianco.
 'In general, that famous painter portrays ___ dressed ([+pl]) in white.'

In all of these cases the small clause could not modify the subject, because of the mismatch in number (of course, if the subject is plural, the structure becomes ambiguous). Where does the plural agreement on the adjective come from? We have already seen it on the reflexive, and we normally find it on adjectives predicated of arbitrary PRO:

(15) È difficile [PRO essere sempre allegri].
 'It is difficult to be always happy.'

It appears to be the case that arbitrary interpretation in Italian is grammatically specified as plural, a specification that shows up both with arbitrary PRO and with arbitrary null objects.[3]

In English an understood object cannot be modified by an adjunct small clause, as is shown by the fact that the glosses of (14)a–c (abstracting away from the agreement specification on the adjective) are unambiguous, with the small clause modifying the subject. This contrast follows again from the assumption that the missing object is structurally represented in Italian but not in English, in conjunction with one of the current analyses of adjunct small clauses. If adjunct small clauses are bare APs (Schein 1981; Williams 1983), the contrast is ultimately reduced to Williams's Predication Principle, subsuming the extended clause of Chomsky's Extended Projection Principle: if every predicate requires a structurally represented 'subject' (that is, a noun phrase in a local configuration), this requirement can be met by the structurally represented understood object in Italian, but not by the structurally missing understood object in English. If adjunct small clauses have PRO subjects (that is, the structure is [PRO AP], as proposed in Chomsky 1981 and Stowell 1983), then 'modification of the object' amounts to object control, and this argument becomes a variant of the one given in Section 1.1: object control requires a structurally represented controller, which is possible in (14) but not in the corresponding English examples.[4]

1.4 Argument small clauses

The fourth related difference between English and Italian involves, not configurational objects, but verb-governed subjects of argument small clauses. Argument small clauses selected by causative verbs in Italian can take null subjects having exactly the same interpretive and formal properties as the null objects discussed so far:

(16)a Questa musica rende [___ allegri].
       'This music renders ___ happy([+pl]).'
    b Certe medicine rendono [___ più intelligenti/giovani/calmi].
       'Certain drugs render ___ more intelligent/young/calm([+pl]).'
    c Il comportamento di Gianni lascia [___ sconcertati/stupiti/
       meravigliati]
       'Gianni's behaviour causes-to-remain ___ disconcerted/puzzled/
       astounded ([+pl]).'

The other major class of verbs taking argument small clauses, the epistemic class, does not allow this option:

(17) *Il governo ritiene [___ allegri].
     'The government believes happy.'

This is an important contrast, to which we shall return. Let us focus on causative small clauses for the time being. The option shown in (16) does not exist in English, as the ungrammaticality of the glosses indicates. This follows again from the nonavailability of the appropriate null filler for a V-governed NP position in English: whatever theory of argument small clauses one adopts, if there is no subject available for the adjectival predicate, the structure is ruled out by the Predication Principle.

1.5 Productivity

Apart from these important differences in the syntactic behaviour of understood objects, Italian and English already differ in the productivity of the null object option. The possibility of a missing object with arbitrary interpretation appears to be highly restricted in English and to have the kind of idiosyncratic restrictions typical of lexical processes: near synonyms can differ in allowing a missing object or not, with important variations from speaker to speaker. For instance, the following contrast holds for some speakers:

(18)a ?An unpopular law can incite ___ against the government.
  b *An unpopular law can push ___ against the government.

On the contrary, in Italian the possibility of a null object appears to have the productivity of a true syntactic option, comparable to the possibility of having an arbitrary null subject in infinitives. There is a systematic exception, which will be addressed in Section 5; however, since it can be stated in general terms by referring to certain properties of thematic grids, it will not undermine the conclusion that the licensing of arbitrary null objects in Italian is syntactic in nature.

1.6 Null objects in English

Before giving a detailed analysis of the Italian case, I would like to sketch a possible approach to the English case. Given the very restricted character of the option illustrated by (1)a, etc., we cannot simply assume that the projection of an object θ-role is optional. If, as seems plausible, the general case is the obligatoriness illustrated by (18)b, what appears to be required to deal with such examples as (1)a is a lexically governed device preventing the syntactic projection of an understood θ-role. The θ-grid of a verb (the set of θ-roles that the verb assigns; see Stowell 1981) has often been naturally assimilated to a valence structure that requires proper saturation (Rothstein 1983; Higginbotham 1985). Intuitively, a θ-role is saturated when it is associated with some referential content – that is, when we can understand 'who does what' in the situation referred to. Standard saturation is done in the syntax, through the Projection Principle (which creates the appropriate structural slots for the saturators) and the θ-Criterion (which ensures that the structural slots are filled by the proper saturators). Adopting the formalism of Stowell (1981), we will assume that a θ-role is automatically coindexed with the structural position projected from it; the θ-Criterion then operates as a well-formedness condition on the substantive nature of the filler of this position, which must be an 'argument', in the required sense. For instance, the lexical representation (19)a would project the syntactic representation (19)b, which would then be checked by the θ-Criterion:

(19)a Please: (... experiencer ...)
   b

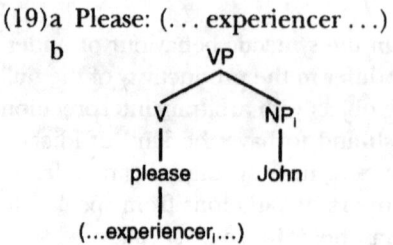

The previous discussion suggests that saturation can also be done in the lexicon, before the application of the Projection Principle. Consider the following rule:

(20) Assign *arb* to the direct θ-role,

where *arb* is a cover term for the feature specification identifying the set of properties generally referred to as 'arbitrary interpretation': [+human, +generic, ±plural], etc.;[5] and where 'direct θ-role' is meant to single out the direct object θ-role, the only θ-role that a verb directly θ-marks for (not compositionally, or through the selection of an autonomous θ-marker, as presumably happens for subject and prepositional object θ-roles, respectively). We can think of this rule as a lexically governed process applying in the lexicon, prior to the Projection Principle. Its application amounts to saturating the internal θ-role in the lexicon: the carrier of this θ-role will be understood as having the properties defining *arb*: [+human, +generic], etc. We can now think of the Projection Principle as operating solely on lexically unsaturated θ-roles. For example:

(21) Categorial structure reflects *lexically unsaturated* thematic structure at all syntactic levels.

This is rather natural if the Projection Principle is seen as (part of) the syntactic mechanism of saturation. If (20) saturates the object θ-role in the lexicon, there is no structurally projected position; the θ-role is 'understood' because it still is part of the lexical meaning, which is unaffected, but it remains syntactically 'inert'. That is, the lexical representation

(22)a, derived through a lexically governed application of rule (20), projects the syntactic representation (22)b:

(22)a Please: (... experiencer$_{arb}$ ...)

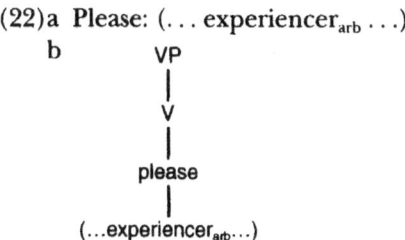

b

    VP
    |
    V
    |
  please
    |
(...experiencer$_{arb}$...)

In summary, a θ-role can be saturated either in the syntax, through the Projection Principle, or in the lexicon. The Projection Principle operates on θ-roles that have not been previously saturated by lexical rules like (20). If a θ-role is saturated in the lexicon, it is not projected; hence, it never reaches the syntax, and it appears to be inert in this component. This is our initial characterization of the English case.[6,7]

2 Some properties of arbitrary null objects

2.1 Relevance of principle B

The first part of this section tries to determine the syntactic status of the arbitrary null object in Italian, and the second part is devoted to a more systematic characterization of its interpretation.

We have already informally characterized the null object as a generic pronoun. The next step is to integrate this hypothesis, at a more formal level, into the current typology of null elements: what is the status of the null object with respect to the features [±pronominal, ±anaphoric]? As an initial attempt, we can try to use the binding principles as a diagnostic. The specification of the null object with respect to [±anaphoric] can be easily determined. In all relevant examples it is governed by V; hence, it receives a governing category. If it were [+anaphoric], binding principle A would require a close enough antecedent for it. In all the examples we have considered so far, however, it has no antecedent at all; hence, the null object is [–anaphoric]. This rules out trace and PRO as possible types.

At this point our informal characterization of the null object as a generic pronominal element would imply [–anaphoric, +pronominal], hence *pro*. As such, it would be in the scope of binding principle B, and we would expect the following state of affairs: the pronominal object should allow referential linking to a c-commanding NP outside its governing category (GC), but not inside:

(23)a NP$_i$ ... [$_{GC}$ ... *pro*$_i$ ...]
   b *[$_{GC}$ ... NP$_i$ ... *pro*$_i$ ...]

A complicating factor is that the null object always has arbitrary interpretation; hence, the referentially linked NP itself should be arbitrary. Does it make sense to expect different kinds of referential dependencies to hold between different occurrences of *arb* interpretation? It is possible to get the flavour of the relevant judgement through the following illustration:

(24) a John$_i$ hopes [PRO$_j$ to win the race].
   b John$_i$ hopes [that PRO$_j$ winning the race] will be easy].
   c It is difficult [PRO$_{arb'}$ to hope [PRO$_{arb''}$ to win the race]].
   d It is difficult [PRO$_{arb'}$ to hope [that [PRO$_{arb''}$ winning the race] will be easy]].

(24)a is a context of obligatory control; hence, $i = j$ necessarily. In (24)b control is free; hence, j = *arb*, or $j = i$ (it is irrelevant here whether or not the latter relation is mediated through some sort of control of the implicit experiencer of *easy* by *John*). In (24)c–d we find exactly the same range of interpretations, even if the controller is itself an occurrence of arbitrary PRO. (24)c is unambiguous, with *arb'* = *arb''*. (24)d appears to be as ambiguous as (24)b: the two occurrences of PRO can be understood as referring either to the same group of people (*arb'* = *arb''*) or to two distinct groups (*arb'* ≠ *arb''*) (that this is real ambiguity, not simply vagueness, will be shown in a moment).

We find the same ambiguity in structures instantiating (23)a in Italian:

(25) a È un'illusione [PRO$_{arb'}$ sperare [che un buon pranzo possa riconciliare ___$_{arb''}$ con se stessi]].
   'It is an illusion [PRO to hope [that a good meal can reconcile ___ with oneself]].'
   b È difficile [PRO$_{arb'}$ sperare [che il governo possa autorizzare ___$_{arb''}$ a [PRO vivere cosi]]].
   'It is difficult [PRO to hope [that the government can authorize ___ [PRO to live like that]]].'

(25)a can mean 'It is an illusion for x to hope that a good meal can reconcile x with x' (hence, *arb'* = *arb''*), or 'It is an illusion for x to hope that a good meal can reconcile y with y' (hence, *arb'* ≠ *arb''*); (25)b can mean 'It is difficult for x to hope that the government can authorize x to live like that' (hence, *arb'* = *arb''*), or 'It is difficult for x to hope that the government can authorize y to live like that' (hence, *arb'* ≠ *arb''*). This is exactly what we would expect given the hypothesis that the null object is pronominal: it can be referentially linked to another NP, provided that the latter is outside the governing category. It is possible to show that the two interpretations that can be detected in (25) are a real case of ambiguity, not simple vagueness intrinsic in arbitrary interpretation: if PRO is in the governing category of the null object, the two occurrences of *arb* must be understood as referring to two separate groups of people. This is shown by the following contrast:

(26) a In questo dipartimento, [PRO$_{arb'}$ temere [che il capo possa costringere ___$_{arb''}$ a [PRO lavorare]]] è ingiustificato.
'In this department, [PRO to fear [that the boss can force ___ [PRO to work]]] is not justified.'
b In questo dipartimento, [PRO$_{arb'}$ costringere ___$_{arb''}$ a [PRO lavorare]] è difficile.
'In this department, [PRO to force ___ [PRO to work]] is difficult.'

(26)a, on a par with (25)a–b, can be interpreted with $arb' = arb''$ (that is, the set of people who fear and the set of people who can be forced can be the same); but (26)b allows only the interpretation $arb' \neq arb''$ (that is, it cannot mean '... to force oneself to work is difficult'). We thus have an instance of disjoint reference between occurrences of arbitrary interpretation, and both predictions of the *pro* hypothesis abstractly represented in (23) are fulfilled.

Incidentally, this array of facts is relevant for the choice of a specific formal characterization of *arb* interpretation. A common assumption (tacitly adopted in the representations I have used so far) is that *arb* interpretation is characterized through a designated referential index *arb*, a special case of ordinary referential indices. If this were correct, we would expect all the elements carrying this index to be understood as coreferential in a given structural representation, as elements carrying the same referential index generally are. But this is not the case: we have seen that different arbitrary NPs are understood, in different configurations, either as obligatorily coreferential (see (24)c), as free in reference (see (24)d, (25), (26)a), or as disjoint (see (26)b). We thus find all the types of referential dependencies that can obtain between nonarbitrary NPs. We should then conclude that an arbitrary element carries the usual referential index, which allows its referential dependencies with other positions to be characterized in the familiar way. Hence, statements like $arb' \neq arb''$ would reduce to the more familiar $i \neq j$. Arbitrary interpretation should then be characterized, not by an index, but directly by the collection of features [+human, +generic, ±plural], etc., which are inherent properties of certain nominal elements (German *man*, French *on*, Italian *si*, etc.) or are assigned through rule (20). In what follows we will keep the notation NP$_{arb}$, which is perspicuous enough in the present context. But the reader should bear in mind that this notation is an abbreviation for the following more adequate representation:

(27) NP$_i$

$$\begin{bmatrix} +\text{human} \\ +\text{generic} \\ \pm\text{plural} \\ \cdot \\ \cdot \\ \cdot \end{bmatrix}$$

2.2 Pronoun versus variable

Does the preceding argument establish that the null object is *pro*? The alternative, which has not yet been ruled out, is that it is a variable ([−pronominal, −anaphoric]). This hypothesis should postulate a phonetically null operator that would bind the null object intrinsically carrying *arb* interpretation. This alternative could reproduce the correct result achieved by the *pro* hypothesis through the auxiliary assumption that such an arbitrary null operator can have scope over the clause immediately containing the variable (that is, it is not forced to take maximal scope, like the null operator introduced in work by Huang and Raposo that will be discussed in a moment). (23)a–b would then become (28)a–b:

(28)a NP$_{arb'}$ ... [OP$_{arb''}$ ... $e_{arb''}$ ...]
  (arb' = arb", or arb' ≠ arb")
 b [OP$_{arb''}$ ... NP$_{arb'}$ ... $e_{arb''}$ ...]
  (arb' ≠ arb")

That is to say, (25) and (26)a are possible with the referentially linked reading because the variable would be free in the scope of its operator, whereas (26)b would be excluded in the relevant reading as a case of strong crossover (binding principle C violation). Therefore, the apparent sensitivity of the null object to binding principle B could be mimicked by the hypothesis that it is a variable bound by a zero operator in the appropriate position; hence, such contrasts as the one in (26) do not discriminate yet between the *pro* hypothesis and the operator-variable hypothesis.

Still, the latter hypothesis is not plausible from the perspective of what is known about null operators and their properties. First of all, familiar cases of null operators moved in the syntax appear to move to Comp, where they cannot co-occur with other (overt or null) operators. This appears to be true for the discourse-bound null operator in Portuguese. Raposo (1986a) gives the following contrast:

(29)a [OP [a Joana viu *ec* na televisão ontem à noite]].
  'Joana saw (him) on TV last night.'

b *[Quando OP [é que o João vai oferecer *ec* à Maria t]]?
   'When is João going to offer (it) to Maria?'
   c *[Para qual dos filhos OP [é che a Maria comprou *ec* t]]?
   'For which of his children did Maria buy (it)?'

If the null object referring to some entity salient in discourse in (29)a is a variable bound by a discourse-bound null operator, the ill-formedness of (29)b–c is naturally to be attributed to the mutual exclusiveness of the null operator and a Wh-element in Comp (see also Campos 1986 for an extension to Spanish).⁸ The same point is shown by purpose clauses. Chomsky (1980) points out that a maximum of two gaps are possible in this construction, and, if there are two, one is necessarily the subject:

(30)a John bought the dog [for Bill to give ___ to Mary].
   b John bought the dog [for Bill to give bones to ___].
   c *John bought the dog [for Bill to give ___ to ___].
   d John bought Bill the dog [___ to give ___ to Mary].
   e *John bought Bill the dog [___ to give ___ to ___].

A gap in subject position involves a PRO filler; a gap in object position must involve a variable bound by a null operator, which is in turn bound by an NP of the main clause. The ungrammaticality of (30)c,e shows that there can be at most one null operator. This can be naturally traced back to the assumption that null operators are moved to Comp, and at most one null operator can occur per Comp, exactly as in the case of overt Wh-operators.

Finally, the same constraint can be found in parasitic gap constructions. Consider the following contrast:

(31)a ?Which student did you tell t [that we can help *e*]?
   b *Which student did you tell t [who can help *e*]?

Assuming that parasitic gaps are bound by null operators somehow licensed by the overt operators (Chomsky, class lectures, Fall 1983, Fall 1984; see also Chomsky 1986b), this contrast follows if null operators necessarily move to Comp and cannot co-occur with overt operators.⁹

Now, in structures involving arbitrary null objects in Italian it is perfectly possible to have overt operators in Comp:

(32)a Quale musica riconcilia ___ con se stessi?
   'Which music reconciles ___ with oneself?'
   b Non so [che cosa le sue parole possano indurre ___ a [PRO concludere t]].
   'I do not know [what his words can lead ___ [PRO to conclude t]].'

This fact is not surprising for the *pro* hypothesis: the licensing conditions for *pro*, whatever they are, could hardly be affected by the presence of a Wh-element in Comp. However, it would represent an anomaly for the operator-variable hypothesis, since the null operator binding the arbitrary object would differ from other familiar instances of null operators in that it would allow co-occurrence with another (wh) operator.

2.3 Against a mixed analysis

One could object that the operator-variable hypothesis can be made compatible with such facts as (32) through the assumption that the null operator involved in this construction differs from the null operators of (29), (30) and (31) in that it is moved to its scope position not by Wh movement in the syntax, but by QR at LF, on a par with other non-Wh quantifiers. In this case the well-formedness of (32) would not be problematic: Wh-elements in Comp can co-occur, at LF, with quantifiers having scope over the same S (May 1985). A *priori*, this version of the operator-variable hypothesis is not unappealing, because it seems to give for free what, at first sight, is a plausible logical form for the structures with null objects. These structures, and arbitrary interpretation in general, could be viewed as instances of universal quantification over a pragmatically identified domain. In fact, the two sentences (33)a and (33)b appear to be roughly synonymous, and one might reasonably propose that they share the same logical form (33)c:

(33)a Questa decisione rende [tutti felici].
    'This decision makes [everyone happy].'
  b Questa decisione rende [___ felici].
    'This decision makes [___ happy].'
  c For all x, this decision makes [x happy]

(See Epstein 1984 and Lebeaux 1984 for a similar assumption on related cases in English.) This hypothesis would still have to deal with the characterization of the status of the null object at S-Structure, prior to movement. One could consider an extension of Epstein's proposal: the null object is *pro*, licensed at S-Structure in a way to be determined, but it carries the inherently quantificational meaning of *arb*, and it is then moved to its scope position at LF. The *pro* hypothesis and the operator-variable hypothesis would thus be combined. But is (33)c the correct logical form for (33)b? There are reasons to believe it is not, in spite of the fact that (33)a seems to be a sufficiently accurate paraphrase. In certain environments the putative universal quantification associated with the null object patterns differently from genuine cases of quantification. Consider, for instance, the interaction with negation. A quantified NP in subject position of a small clause cannot have scope over a negation on the main verb:

(34) a Questa decisione non rende [molti cittadini felici].
'This decision doesn't make [many citizens happy].'
 b Questa decisione non rende [solo Gianni felice].
'This decision doesn't make [only Gianni happy].'

In these examples the only possible interpretation is *not Q*, and *Q not* is excluded: (34)a can mean 'Not for many *x*, this decision makes *x* happy', but it cannot mean 'For many *x*, this decision doesn't make *x* happy'; (34)b can mean 'Not only for *x* = Gianni, this decision makes *x* happy', but it cannot mean 'Only for *x* = Gianni, this decision doesn't make *x* happy'.[10] Let us now compare the roughly synonymous (33)a and (33)b. Under negation they pattern in opposite ways:

(35) a Questa decisione non rende [tutti felici].
'This decision doesn't make [everyone happy].'
 b Questa decisione non rende [___ felici].
'This decision doesn't make [___ happy].'

Example (35)a can only mean 'Not for all *x*, this decision makes *x* happy'; hence, the universal quantifier expectedly patterns with the other quantifiers of (34). On the contrary, the interpretation of (35)b would correspond to a structure with wide scope of the universal quantifier: 'For all *x*, this decision doesn't make *x* happy.' This anomalous behaviour of the null object with respect to all other instances of quantified NPs casts serious doubts on the assimilation of (33)a–b at LF that is suggested by (33)c. In fact, the flavour of universal quantification does not necessarily imply an operator-variable structure at LF; it can be conveyed, for instance, by a generic NP that presumably does not undergo QR. The following is, in turn, roughly synonymous with (33)a–b:

(36) Questa decisione rende [la gente felice].
'This decision makes [people happy].'

Moreover, under negation null objects and generic NPs pattern alike, as opposed to quantified NPs:

(37) Questa decisione non rende [la gente felice].
'This decision doesn't make [people happy].'

Example (37) is synonymous with (35)b, not with (35)a. It appears that generic NPs pattern with referential NPs in their interaction with negation: the interpretation of *la gente* in (37) is not affected by negation any more than the referential NP *i miei genitori* 'my parents' would be in the same environment. The fact that the zero objects (in fact, verb-governed subjects) of (33)b and (35)b pattern alike reinforces our informal characterization of them as generic pronouns and further decreases the plausibility of the operator-variable hypothesis.[11]

2.4 Properties of arb

Let us have a closer look at the interpretation of the null object. I have mentioned the fact that it shares the three basic properties of arbitrary PRO: [+human, +generic, +plural]. I have suggested that the second property is responsible for the fact that the null object can occur only in sentences with generic time reference. This requirement appears to hold for all the structures that motivate the postulation of a null object position:[12]

(38) a *Mario ha costretto a partire.
         'Mario forced to leave.'
      b *Il concerto di ieri ha riconciliato con se stessi.
         'Yesterday's concert has reconciled with oneself.'
      c *Il medico sta visitando nudi.
         'The doctor is visiting nude.'
      d *Il concerto ha reso allegri.
         'The concert rendered happy.'

The [+plural] specification has already been discussed in Section 1.3, footnote 3. Notice that such examples as *La musica riconcilia ___ con se stessi* show not only that the null object is plural, but also that it is masculine and third person: these are the features manifested by the reflexive. We can therefore conclude that, in addition to the number specification, which varies across languages, the set of φ-features of *arb* is completed by the default specifications of person and gender. The [+human] nature of arbitrary PRO can be seen in the peculiar interpretation of structures like (39)a, which can mean '... how people can roll down the hill', but not '... how stones can roll down the hill'. The same can be shown to hold for the null object (or V-governed subject): (39)b can mean '... render people more efficient', but not '... render machines more efficient':

(39) a It is unclear [how [PRO to roll down the hill]].
      b Certe innovazioni tecniche rendono [*pro* più efficienti].
         'Certain technical innovations render [*pro* more efficient (([+pl]))].'

This is, among other things, relevant for the correct understanding of what arbitrary interpretation is. The necessarily human interpretation of PRO in (39)a might be analysed as a consequence of control by the implicit experiencer of *unclear*, which obviously must be human, rather than as an intrinsic property of arbitrary interpretation. But this analysis cannot extend to (39)b, which therefore suggests that the 'intrinsic' approach is correct.[13]

Here again *pro* can refer only to people, not to stones, and still there is no implicit argument (experiencer, goal, or other) available as a controller in the main clause. Therefore, the necessary human interpretation cannot be treated as a property inherited from the controller, and must be an intrinsic property of *arb*.

3 On licensing and interpreting *pro* in object position

3.1 Formal licensing

The evidence discussed in the preceding section suggests that the arbitrary null object belongs to the type *pro*. The parameter differentiating English and Italian can therefore be viewed as involving the licensing conditions of *pro*: an occurrence of this element in verb-governed position is allowed in Italian but not in English. Standard assumptions on the theory of *pro* do not seem to suffice in this case: if *pro* were restricted to occur in local construal with 'strong agreement' (see Chomsky 1982b for discussion), it should be excluded in object position both in Italian and in English (and in any language lacking object agreement). Therefore, the standard view of the '*pro* module' must be modified.

The minimal contribution that is to be expected from a theory of a null element is that it should specify (a) the conditions that formally license the null element (the conditions that allow it to occur in a given environment) and (b) the way in which the content of the null element (minimally, its φ-features) is determined, or 'recovered', from the phonetically realized environment. In the standard approach to *pro*, formal licensing and 'recovery' of the content are unified, both being performed through government by 'strong Agr(eement).' But this unification is surprising in the broader context of the standard typology of null elements: in the theories of the other types of null elements, formal licensing and 'recovery' are generally kept separate. Trace and variable are formally licensed (in part) by the Empty Category Principle (ECP), and their feature content is recovered through formation of an A- or A'-chain with an antecedent or an operator, respectively. PRO is formally restricted to occur in ungoverned contexts, and its content is recovered through the theory of control, which designates an antecedent for it (or assigns *arb* interpretation). In all three cases formal licensing appears to involve some kind of (positive or negative) government relation, and the recovery procedure involves some kind of binding relation, in an extended sense. The government requirements of these three types of null elements are sometimes stated as a single principle, the Generalized Empty Category Principle (GECP; see Chomsky 1981: 274).[14]

In the spirit of these considerations I would like to propose the following first approximation to the licensing principle for *pro* – that is, the *pro* subcase of the GECP:

(40) *pro* is governed by X_y^0.

(40) means that *pro* is licensed by a governing head of type *y*, where the class of licensing heads can vary from language to language. For instance, the defining property of null-subject languages can be looked at as a particular setting of the parameter of (40): in Italian, Spanish, etc., but not in English, French, etc., a governing Infl capable of assigning nominative Case is a member of X_y^0. The licensing of *pro* in object position can now be viewed as another instantiation of the licensing schema: in Italian V belongs to the licensing class, in English it does not. We would then conclude that the class X_y^0 includes both Infl and V in Italian, whereas it is empty in English, a grammatical system that does not license any occurrence of *pro*. Other cases are to be expected. For instance, French is not a null-subject language, but it allows *pro* in object position on a par with Italian. Moreover, Zribi-Hertz (1984) gives interesting evidence in support of the claim that *pro* can occur as a prepositional object in French; therefore, in this grammatical system $X_y^0 = \{V, P\}$.[15] In short, the licensing schema for *pro* contains a multivalued parameter; in principle, we may expect natural languages to vary from a maximally restrictive setting (no head is a possible licenser) to a maximally liberal setting (every head is a possible licenser).[16]

This is a first approximation to the formal licensing schema. Notice that in the spirit of the previous discussion (40) treats on a par occurrences of *pro* with different interpretations (definite pronominal, arbitrary, expletive), exactly as the PRO Theorem treats on a par arbitrary and controlled PRO. The next step is to determine how different occurrences of *pro* get their content from the structural environment; that is, we must deal with the analogue of control theory for *pro*.

3.2 Interpretation

How is *pro* assigned a content? As for the other cases of null elements, we can assume that it is freely assigned φ-features, and possibly other specifications, but such inherent 'content' must be fully recoverable from the overt linguistic context through some kind of binding relation, in an extended sense of the term: the feature specification on an empty category is licit only when it matches the specification of the designated binder. The natural intuitive idea behind most analyses of the null-subject parameter is that the content of *pro* in subject position is recovered through the rich agreement specification. I would like to incorporate this idea, in a more general form, into the following convention:

(41) Let X be the licensing head of an occurrence of *pro*: then *pro* has the grammatical specification of the features on X coindexed with it.

According to (41), the peculiar binding relation responsible for the recovery of *pro*'s content is binding from (features on) the local head. Head binding is then the abstract equivalent of control, and of A- or A'-chain formation. In the case of *pro* in subject position, the application of (41) is straightforward. The licensing head, Infl, has features of agreement, and features of tense and mood. Only the former are coindexed with the *pro* subject. Through (41) *pro* is allowed to have specifications of person, gender and number (φ-features), which allow it to function as a definite pronoun.[17] In Italian (and in other familiar cases of null-subject languages) there is one case in which *pro* in subject position of a tensed clause does not function as a (referential or expletive) definite pronoun: in impersonal *si* sentences it is interpreted as arbitrary:

(42) pro_{arb} si_{arb} dorme troppo.
 'People sleep too much.'

Here *pro* is linked to the arbitrary subject clitic *si* under Infl, which allows *pro* to have the usual specifications associated with *arb*: [+human, +generic, +plural].[18]

In Italian, *arb* interpretation is the exceptional case for *pro* in subject position; but, as we have seen, it is the norm in object position. In order to deal with this case, we must assume some procedure for the assignment of *arb* (free assignment would be descriptively inaccurate for reasons to be discussed in the following sections). I have already introduced such a procedure in discussing the English case; recall the discussion of (20), repeated here:

(43) Assign *arb* to the direct θ-role.

This rule was introduced as a lexically governed process applying on θ-grids in the lexicon. Can it be assumed to be operative in the syntax as well, and without lexical restrictions, as the Italian case would require? Borer (1984) has suggested that there are rules (certain affixation processes in her discussion) that can apply freely in the lexicon or in the syntax. If they apply in the lexicon, they feed the Projection Principle and affect its application; if they apply in the syntax, they are fed by the Projection Principle and therefore operate on structural representations already formed. The former type of application has the characteristic modalities of lexical processes (e.g., lexical government). The latter type of application obeys the Projection Principle; hence, it cannot introduce structural distortions and modifications of the argument structure, and it has the other characteristic properties of syntactic processes (e.g., lack of lexical government). This approach provides a neat, principled characterization of the relationship between lexical and syntactic processes: for instance, lexical and syntactic passive involve the same rule of *-en* affixation, the familiar differences being reduced to principled reasons.

I would like to adopt this approach, assuming that rule (43) can apply in both components. If it applies in the lexicon, we have the result that appears to be needed for the English case: the object θ-role is saturated before the Projection Principle applies and therefore is not projected to a syntactic position. If (43) applies in the syntax, the Projection Principle has already projected the object position. The features defining *arb* interpretation must now be transferred onto the object position. This is done automatically in the system I have proposed. From the viewpoint of the *pro* module as conceived here, a coindexed slot in the θ-grid of a verb is the analogue of a coindexed Agr under Infl:

(44) pro_i Infl   V pro_j
           | |
        Agr_i θ_j

In general, there is one important difference between the two cases. A slot in a θ-grid does not have any intrinsic content (no φ-features in particular); hence, in the preceding representation θ_j is generally unable to assign any content to (or recover any content of) *pro*. But if (43) applies, assigning *arb*, the θ-slot acquires some intrinsic content: the usual specifications associated with *arb*: [+human, +generic, +plural], etc. A *pro* with such a content is then sanctioned through procedure (41), in a way that is fully parallel to the sanctioning of a definite pronominal (or arbitrary) interpretation to a subject *pro*.[19]

Let us summarize the properties of the proposed system, and the various options that it allows. I have introduced

a a theory of *pro* that consists of
   i   licensing schema (40) containing a parameter, and
   ii convention (41) for the recovery of the content of *pro*;
b a rule of arbitrary interpretation that is unordered with respect to the Projection Principle; that is, it can apply both in the syntax and in the lexicon.

Suppose that rule (43) applies in the lexicon. Then the object θ-role is saturated prior to the Projection Principle, and a well-formed structure can be projected without a structurally represented object position; this modality of application represents a partial formalization of the intuitive notion 'optional object' and is available in both English and Italian. Suppose now that rule (43) applies in the syntax (hence, after the Projection Principle has projected the object position). In Italian this gives rise to a well-formed structure: the object position can be filled by a licit occurrence of *pro*, which receives arbitrary interpretation through convention (41). In English this option is excluded by the negative setting of the licensing parameter.[20]

In conclusion, similarities and differences between English and Italian follow from a simple system of principles and parameters. The fact that both Italian (in general) and English (with some verbs) allow *arb* interpretation of an 'understood object' follows from the fact that both systems have rule (43). The fact that the understood object can be syntactically active in Italian but not in English follows from the different setting of the parameter in the licensing schema (40). The fact that both the structurally represented and the structurally missing understood object share the same interpretation follows from the assumption that rule (43) can apply both in the lexicon and in the syntax. The lexically restricted character of the option in English follows from the fact that, because of the negative setting of the parameter in (40), rule (43) gives a well-formed result only when it applies in the lexicon, where the characteristic modality of application is through triggering by lexical government. Finally, the whole class of facts is fully compatible with the Projection Principle, which is minimally qualified to the effect that it now refers to lexically unsaturated θ-roles, not just to θ-roles, saturation in the lexicon being understood as a partial characterization of the notion 'optional argument'. And the Italian facts are fully compatible with the theoretical typology of empty categories, now incorporating a more structured theory of *pro*.[21]

3.3 Relevance of Case

The arbitrary null object of Italian has been shown to interact with several syntactic processes. There is an important limitation, though: it cannot undergo NP Movement and, more generally, it cannot occur in passive sentences. This limitation will require a qualification of the licensing schema. Consider the following pair:

(45) a Gianni fotografa ___ nudi.
    'Gianni photographs ___ nude.'
   b ___ vengono fotografati ___ nudi.
    '(They) are photographed ___ nude.'

(45)b cannot be interpreted as the passive counterpart of (45)a: the null derived subject cannot be arbitrary and must be interpreted as referring to a specific set of people. What prevents movement of pro_{arb}? At first sight, the problem appears to be trivially solved by a natural assumption on the level of representation at which the *pro* module applies. The case of *pro* in subject position requires that it apply at (or not earlier than) S-Structure: in any sentence with a derived subject *pro* meets the conditions for its licensing and interpretation no earlier than this level. If the *pro* module applies at S-Structure, then it applies on the following representation for (45)b:

(46) *pro* Infl vengono fotografati *e* nudi.

Here *pro* is licensed by the governing Infl and, through convention (41), can have content that matches the agreement specification. It thus becomes a definite pronoun, and there is no way for it to receive *arb* interpretation: in the present approach the content of *pro* is determined in a strictly local fashion, through the specification of the governing head, and the governing head at the relevant level, Infl, allows only the definite pronominal interpretation.[22]

But there is another potential S-Structure representation for (45)b that must be ruled out. This is a structure in which *pro*$_{arb}$ is left in object position and enters into a chain with the preverbal subject position filled by an expletive *pro*:

(47) *pro* Infl vengono fotografati *pro*$_{arb}$ nudi.

The option of being left in object position is clearly available for a lexical NP in these structures, as is shown by the well-formedness of the following sentence:

(48) *pro* Infl ne è stato fotografato [uno *e*] nudo.
 'Of-them has been photographed one nude.'

As the extraction of the clitic pronoun *ne* shows, the logical object is in object position in this structure (see Burzio 1981, 1986 and Belletti and Rizzi 1981 for discussion). Notice that in (47) the conditions on licensing and interpretation seem to be met: the first occurrence of *pro* is licensed by Infl and receives the interpretation of an expletive pronoun (see Rizzi 1982, Chapter 4 for discussion). The second occurrence should be licensed by the verb and interpreted as arbitrary through (43) and (41). Still, the relevant interpretation is impossible; hence, (47) must be ruled out. This appears to require a revision of the proposed licensing schema.

My previous work on the null-subject parameter suggests that the licensing of *pro* in subject position is coextensive with the domain of nominative Case assignment: *pro* is possible not only in finite clauses but also in the nonfinite clauses in which nominative Case can be assigned to the subject (see Rizzi 1982, Chapters 3 and 4 for details). Capitalizing on this observation, we can revise the licensing schema, assuming that the crucial licensing relation is not just government, but Case assignment by a designated head:

(49) *pro* is Case-marked by X_y^0.

Structure (47) is now correctly excluded: the passive past participle does not assign Case; hence, the second occurrence of *pro* is not licensed.[23] Notice that, as far as the *pro* module is concerned, it is irrelevant whether or not the chain of the second occurrence of *pro* (including the first occurrence) has Case: licensing and interpretation of *pro*, as viewed here, are strictly local and solely involve the relation with a governing (and Case-marking) head. A Case provided through chain formation is inconsequential for the licensing of *pro*.[24,25]

3.4 Learnability

We must still consider how the parameter in (49) can be fixed by the language learner. Assuming that the decision to add a given head to the class of licensers is always justified by the primary data,[26] the problem reduces, as usual, to understanding how a negative setting can be justified. How do learners of English determine that Infl and V are not licensers of *pro* in their grammatical system? Notice that Berwick's (1982) Subset Principle appears to give the right result in this case: assuming that a given head is a licenser of *pro* amounts to increasing the set of well-formed structures that the system can produce; hence, according to the Subset Principle, assuming that a given head is *not* a licenser represents the unmarked decision, the one the language learner adopts in the absence of evidence to the contrary. I would like to rephrase this result in slightly different terms. Suppose that every option that Universal Grammar offers is inherently marked: that is, an option offered by Universal Grammar is adopted by the language learner only if its adoption is justified by the primary data. In the present case Universal Grammar allows for the possibility that every head (perhaps, every Case-marking head) is a licenser; but the language learner will assume that a given head is a licenser only when confronted with justifying evidence, directly or in the indirect way suggested in footnote 26. This rather natural assumption gives the desired result in this case, and, in general, it appears to provide the right markedness hierarchy for different values of parameters of Universal Grammar that are naturally characterizable as involving the presence versus the absence of an optional property.[27]

4 A consequence: null expletive subjects of small clauses

4.1 Non-arguments

The idea of separating formal licensing from assignment/recovery of the content of *pro* makes a prediction. If the sanctioning of *arb* interpretation to the object θ-role is not built into the licensing procedure of object *pro*, and if the two processes are independent, as I have proposed, then we should expect a double dissociation. A *priori*, we should be able to find both of the following cases:

(50) a Cases of arbitrary 'understood objects' not involving *pro*;
 b Cases of V-licensed *pro* not involving *arb* interpretation.

We already have an example of (50)a: English structures like *John always warns against this type of mistake.* Can we find examples of (50)b? If the suggestion of footnote 26 concerning clitic structures is correct, then clitic 'traces' would be instances of V-licensed *pro* whose content is recovered through the clitic chain (presumably another case of head binding if the clitic is attached to the verb in the syntax). Since an analysis of clitics goes beyond the limits of this article, I would like to consider a simpler case in more detail. Consider a case of V-licensed *pro* in a structure not involving clitics, and where *arb* assignment does not apply. Then *pro* could not have any content sanctioned through head binding. 'A pronominal without any content' appears to be a sufficiently accurate description of a familiar entity that natural languages may resort to: an expletive. Under this set of assumptions, the second expected type of dissociation reduces to the existence of a V-governed expletive *pro* (see Section 6.2 for a precise formulation of this argument). Does such a case exist? *A priori*, there are two possible V-governed environments to look at:

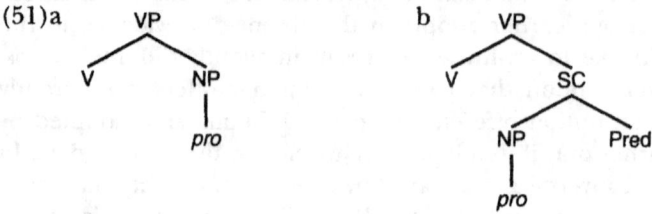

An expletive *pro* in (51)a is independently excluded by the usual conspiracy between the θ-Criterion and the Projection Principle: if the verb does not assign an object θ-role, then the position cannot be projected, and configuration (51)a cannot arise; if the verb does assign an object θ-role, then the position is projected, but the θ-role is assigned to a nonargument, and the θ-Criterion is violated. Therefore, (51)a does not allow us to check the prediction (but see footnote 31). Consider now (51)b, where *pro* is licensed by V through the transparent boundaries of the small clause. Here the subject NP position is required by the extended clause of the Extended Projection Principle (or by the Predication Principle); therefore, it is there irrespective of the thematic properties of the main verb, and the conspiracy does not arise. But then in (51)b an expletive *pro* subject should be possible, provided that the predicate of the small clause does not assign any external θ-role. The expectation is fulfilled: the subject position can contain a null expletive in structures with an extraposed sentential complement:

(52) Gianni ritiene [*pro* probabile [che Mario venga]].
    'Gianni believes likely that Mario comes.'
(53) Il tuo comportamento ha reso [*pro* improbabile [che Mario venga]].
    'Your behaviour rendered unlikely that Mario comes.'

This is the second type of dissociation: *pro* is licensed by the main verb through government and Case marking, but it is not θ-marked (but see the discussion of the next section). Therefore, *pro* cannot have *arb* interpretation, nor can it have any other content (which, because of convention (41), would be contingent on the existence of some coindexed features in the licensing head). Still, the structure is possible with the contentless *pro* functioning as an expletive. The corresponding structures in English are ungrammatical, as the glosses show (they become grammatical if the overt expletive *it* is inserted). This follows from the proposed system: because of the negative setting of the parameter, *pro* is not licensed in this (or in any other) environment in English, and therefore an overt expletive is the only option here.

In conclusion, Italian has both a syntactically 'active' null arbitrary object and a null expletive subject of small clauses, whereas English lacks both. In the present terms this is a linguistically significant generalization that can be reduced to a unique primitive difference between the two grammatical systems: the different setting of the licensing parameter for *pro*.[28]

4.2 Quasi arguments

An expletive pronoun can be found in three basic environments: in construction with an extraposed sentential subject, in construction with a postverbal subject NP, and with atmospheric (or 'temporal') predicates. We have discussed the first case; let us now consider the remaining two. A 'temporal' adjectival predicate can (and must) have a *pro* expletive subject in tensed clauses, but not in small clauses:

(54) a *pro* è presto.
    '(It) is early.'
  b *pro* è troppo tardi per tornare.
    '(It) is too late to come back.'
(55) a *Considero [*pro* presto].
    'I consider (it) early.'
  b *Ritengo [*pro* troppo tardi per tornare].
    'I believe (it) too late to come back.'

Since Italian does not have overt expletives available in this case, there is simply no way to fix these structures (which are more or less acceptable in English with an overt expletive). In the terminology of Chomsky (1981), an expletive construed with an extraposed sentential complement is a 'non-argument', whereas an expletive subject of a predicate like those in (54) is a 'quasi argument'. The question is then why a V-licensed *pro* subject of a small clause can function as a non-argument, but not as a quasi argument. A natural answer is available in the system proposed here if we adopt Chomsky's view that 'quasi arguments' really are special cases of arguments, receiving atmospheric or temporal θ-roles and being in the domain of the θ-Criterion on a par with referential arguments. This view is substantiated by the observation that quasi arguments, like real arguments, can act as controllers:

(56) It rained for days without [PRO stopping].

If quasi arguments are true arguments (which simply happen to be nonreferential), the ungrammaticality of (55)a–b follows: the subject position of the small clause is not θ-marked by the governing verb; therefore, convention (41) cannot apply to sanction *arb* or any other content of *pro*. A pronominal without any content can only function as a non-argument (see Section 6.2); therefore, if the embedded predicate assigns a θ-role to it, the structure is ruled out by the θ-Criterion. The structures of (55) are then ruled out on a par with, for example, (57):

(57) *Considero [*pro* intelligenti].
     'I consider intelligent.'

(57) and (55)a–b differ from (51)b in that the embedded predicate assigns an external θ-role, which gives rise to a θ-Criterion violation. The parallel behaviour of arguments and quasi arguments, as opposed to the behaviour of non-arguments, supports the hypothesis that 'quasi argument' is simply a label for arguments that are nonreferential.

4.3 Subject inversion

The third *a priori* possible case of null expletive concerns subject inversion structures. When subject inversion applies, the expletive in preverbal subject position is clearly a nonargument; hence, an expletive *pro* in V-governed subject position of a small clause should be possible. Indeed, subject inversion can take place within small clauses:

(58)a Ritengo [suo fratello più intelligente].
      'I believe his brother more intelligent.'
   b Ritengo [___ più intelligente suo fratello].
      'I believe more intelligent his brother.'

But this fact is less significant for our purposes than the possibility of (51)b: in fact, NP subject inversion in small clauses is not excluded in English either. Consider the following contrast between a postpredicate sentential subject and a postpredicate subject NP:

(59)a *I consider *ec* desirable that John wins.
    b I consider *ec* desirable the perspective that John wins.

Given our analysis, the empty category in (59)b cannot be *pro*, because of the negative setting of the relevant parameter in English. There must be a different well-formed representation for this example, not available for (59)a. (59)b is obviously reminiscent of 'Heavy NP Shift structures': in fact, the acceptability degrades if the NP is made less heavy (e.g. *the solution*). On the other hand, no comparable degradation is found in the corresponding Italian example, a difference that we should bear in mind. Pursuing the assimilation of (59)b to Heavy NP Shift, we are led to assume the following representation:

(60) I consider [ec_i desirable] NP_i.

(60) is well-formed without requiring *ec* = *pro*. *ec* can be trace or variable: it is properly governed by the main verb, and it is bound in the required sense by the right-peripheral NP.[29] The next question is, Why isn't this kind of representation available for (59)a? We will assume with Koster (1978a) that 'sentential subjects don't exist', as is suggested by the impossibility of the 'intraposed' version of (59)a:

(61) *I consider that John wins desirable.

In current terms, this amounts to saying that the Predication Principle requires an NP and is not satisfied by an S'. Even so, base generation of the following structure would not be excluded:

(62) I consider [[$_{NP}$ ec_i] desirable] S'_i.

Still, this structure must be ruled out, given the ill-formedness of (59)a. How does it differ from (60)? The ECP requirement is met in the same way through proper government by the main verb, but the binding requirement (whatever type of binding is operative in Heavy NP Shift structures) is not met: it is natural to assume that, in addition to coindexing and c-command, the binding relation (at least in the restrictive sense of A- or Ā-binding) involves categorial matching between the binder and the bindee. This requirement is met in (60), but not in (62). Therefore, a well-formed representation (not involving *pro*) can be associated with (59)b, but not with (59)a, as required.[30]

In conclusion, the contrast between Italian and English with nominal subject inversion does not emerge as clearly as it does with extraposed sentential subjects, because nominal subject inversion in small clauses can also involve a structural representation not requiring *pro*, hence available in English. Still, a contrast with Italian can be detected here as well: the inverted subject must be 'heavy' in English, but not in Italian. This follows from the fact that the only available representation in English involves Heavy NP Shift, whereas Italian also allows a representation with expletive *pro* and inverted subject, corresponding to the one available in tensed clauses, which does not involve any heaviness requirement.[31]

4.4 Diachronic evidence

In this section I have proposed a unitary treatment of the fact that Italian allows null arbitrary objects that are syntactically 'active' and null expletive subjects of small clauses, whereas English lacks both options. The history of English provides interesting diachronic evidence that this approach captures a genuine generalization: both options were syntactically productive in earlier stages of the language.[32] In Old English, Middle English, and Early Modern English an arbitrary null object could function as a controller (examples from Visser 1969, 1342ff.):[33]

(63) a *1340 Ayenbite p. 104, 33*: thet uerste ... *somoneth to worthsipie* god
  b *c1425 tr. Chauliac's Grande Chirurgie I b/a*: Som tyme forsoth it is suych thing that hastieth that yt *compelleth for to leue* the particule vncured (MMED)
  c *1443 Pecock, Reule Crystien Rel. (EETS) 173*: Thou *apprisist and chargist* as myche *to queeme and fulfille* the desijr of thi freende how myche eny man in this world *apprisith and chargith to perfoorme and fulfille* the desijr of his freend
  d *1532–3 St. Th. More, Wks (1557) 826 E7*: When he *commaunded to receiue* the man ... into the church again, in what church *commaunded* he *to receiue* him?
  e *1649 Milton, Tenure of Kings (ed. Garnett) p. 72*: He had not otherwise *forbid to molest* them
  f *1725 Pope, Tr. Odyssey (World Classics) IX p. 133*: I then *advised to fly*
  g *1748 James Thompson, Castel of Indolence II, VIII, 7*: all the gods ... That *teach to tame* the soil and rule the crook

Similarly, Visser notices that expletive *it* in subject position of small clauses has become obligatory in contemporary English (with the exception of a few frozen expressions like *find fit, think proper, make clear*, etc., in which the V+A combination is felt to be 'an indivisible semantic whole' (Visser 1963: 476), whereas it was optional in previous stages. For instance, discussing the type *I have seen it proved that ...*, Visser remarks, 'Nowadays heralding *it* is always used in this type of construction. In Middle English and in early Modern English it is occasionally done without' (p. 467); and, discussing the type **We found very difficult to go there*, he points out, 'In early stages of the language this does seem to have been the usual form of this construction. ... In later English, however, it became more usual to insert a heralding *it* before the predicative adjunct, ... Consequently nowadays the preponderant type is 'He considered *it* impossible to execute that plan' ... (p. 475). The following are some examples (pp. 467ff.):

(64) a *a1398 Trevisa, Barth. 192a/a*: They *countede grete worshepe* to folowe here forfadres in clothinge, in tonge, and in lyflode (MMED)
 b *1530 St. Th. More, Wks. (1557) 868 G6*: I haue euer *accompted my deuty* to forbeare all suche maner of vnmannerly behauioure
 c *1534 St. Th. More, Wks (1557) 1244 H15*: I *see very clerely proved* that it can be done none otherwise
 d *1668 Dryden, Secret Love (Scott/Saintsb.)Pref. 421*: This is what I *thought convenient* to write by way of preface to 'The Maiden Queen'
 e *1673 Dryden, The Assignation (ScottlSaintsb.) Dedic. 372*: I can make *my boast* to have found a better Maecenas (Sod.)

The parallel loss of these two options in transition to contemporary English strongly suggests a unified analysis, and it can be immediately captured in the terms I have proposed: in the course of the development of Modern English, V ceased to be a member of the licensing class for *pro*. Whether this modification came about as a primitive change, or was the consequence of other changes in the grammatical system, is an important question that I cannot address here (also see footnote 26 for relevant discussion). I simply note that the observed development follows a rather familiar pattern. What was a fully productive syntactic option in previous stages of the language became a limited lexical option: the possibility of an understood object with arbitrary interpretation was restricted to the (lexically governed) saturation of the internal θ-role in the lexicon via rule (20); the possibility of a null expletive subject of a small clause was restricted to a few idiomatic V+A expressions, presumably stored as such in the lexicon. This case then appears to be another instance of the common diachronic process involving the lexicalization of a syntactic option when the syntactic licensing conditions cease to exist.[34]

5 Two types of small clauses and the affectedness constraint

5.1 Causative and epistemic small clauses

We have seen in Section 1.4 that argument small clauses selected by causative verbs allow an arbitrary *pro* subject, but small clauses selected by an epistemic verb do not:

(65) a Talvolta la stampa lascia [___ perplessi].
   'Sometimes the press causes-to-remain puzzled.'
 b Questo esercizio mantiene [___ sani].
   'This exercise keeps healthy.'
 c Certe decisioni possono rendere [___ più responsabili].
   'Certain decisions can render more responsible.'
(66) a *Talvolta la stampa ritiene [___ perplessi].
   'Sometimes the press believes puzzled.'

b *Spesso il medico considera [___ sani].
  'Often the doctor considers healthy.'
c *Ultimamente il governo crede [___ più responsabili].
  'Lately the government believes more responsible.'

On the other hand, we have seen in the preceding section that both classes allow an expletive *pro* subject:

(67) Il comportamento di Gianni ha reso [___ improbabile [che Maria rimanga]].
  'Gianni's behaviour rendered unlikely that Maria stays.'
(68) Gianni ritiene [___ improbabile [che Maria rimanga]].
  'Gianni believes unlikely that Maria stays.'

This fact has been attributed to the possibility of licensing an expletive *pro* through V-government (Case marking), which holds in both cases. The contrast between (65) and (66) is still to be explained. The impossibility of (66)a–c already follows from the current analysis, given plausible additional assumptions, as was shown in Section 4.2. If the main verb does not θ-mark the subject position of the small clause, as is usually assumed, an occurrence of *pro* can be formally licensed, but *arb* interpretation cannot be sanctioned, being contingent upon θ-marking via rule (43) and the 'recovery' convention (41). Therefore, *pro* in this position is left without content and can only have the role of a non-argument expletive, which can occur in a well-formed structure only if the predicate of the small clause assigns no external θ-role, as in (67) and (68). In other words, structures (66)a–c are ruled out by the θ-Criterion, because the θ-role assigned by the embedded predicate is assigned to a non-argument. But why are sentences (65)a–c well-formed? This question now reduces to the following: How can *arb* interpretation be assigned to the subject of the small clause in these cases?

The first solution that comes to mind consists in capitalizing on a semantic difference that appears to distinguish the causative construction from other types of subordination. It is intuitively plausible to look at the subject of the causative clause as an argument of the causative verb, as well as of the embedded predicate: the subject of the causative clause is (or more precisely, can be) 'acted upon' by the subject of the causative verb in order to bring about a certain result. This intuition is given formal status in Rouveret and Vergnaud's (1980) analysis of the French causative construction, according to which, in a sentence like (69), the embedded subject becomes an argument of the complex predicate *faire* + *acheter* formed through a reanalysis process:

(69) Jean a fait acheter le livre a Marie.
  'Jean made Marie buy the book.'

If a similar kind of thematic reanalysis is also triggered by causative predicates taking small clauses, the acceptability of (65)a–c can be accounted for: the embedded subject becomes a θ-marked argument of the complex predicate V+A, which licenses *pro* and can sanction *arb* interpretation, as a verb generally does for its object. No such mechanism would be available in (66)a–c on the assumption that the reanalysis process is restricted to causatives; the contrast would then be explained.

But this analysis is unsatisfactory for two reasons. First, the syntactic facts that motivated postulating a thematic reanalysis, having mainly to do with the distribution of clitics, would require a similar analysis for perception verbs, which behave like causative verbs in the relevant respects. Since perception verbs can take small clause complements (as in (70)a), one would expect them to allow arbitrary null subjects, on a par with causative verbs. But this expectation is incorrect:

(70) a La stampa estera vede [la gente tranquilla].
 'The foreign press sees people calm.'
 b *La stampa estera vede [___ tranquilli].
 'The foreign press sees calm.'

The second and more straightforward reason for the inadequacy of this analysis is that there are independent motivations to assume that a reanalysis process between the main verb and the small clause predicate takes place with epistemic verbs as well. The basic evidence (this volume, Chapter 5) is that a clitic pronoun can be extracted from the small clause predicate not only with causative verbs, but also with epistemic verbs:[35]

(71) a Ne ritengo [Gianni responsabile *ec*].
 'I of+it believe Gianni responsible.'
 b ?Gli ritenevo [Maria più affezionata *ec*].
 'I to+him believed Maria more affectionate.'

In general, clitics cannot be extracted from clauses; in particular, they cannot be extracted from the verbal complements of epistemic verbs. Consider the following contrast:

(72) a La sola persona che *gli* ritengo [___ ancora fedele *ec*] è Gianni.
 'The only person that I to+him believe still loyal is Gianni.'
 b *La sola persona che *gli* ritengo [___ aver parlato *ec*] è Gianni.
 'The only person that I to+him believe to have spoken is Gianni.'

The locality condition on the clitic-trace relation is usually assumed to be provided by principle A of the binding theory, whence the ill-formedness of (72)b. Why is the clitic extractable from the small clause in (72)a, etc., across the opacity-creating (trace of the) subject? In Chapter 5, I propose that these structures can undergo a reanalysis process creating a complex predicate V+A, of which the embedded subject is an argument. This was expressed in terms of Rouveret and Vergnaud's (1980) cosuperscripting formalism for reanalysis. The intuition behind this formalism is that elementary governors, lexical heads, can sometimes combine to form complex governors, but the process does not (necessarily) involve a modification in the tree structure – that is, the complex governor does not (necessarily) become a syntactic constituent. Superscripts are used to encode the relation 'A is a member of complex governor B', which cannot be read off a nonannotated tree structure (also see Manzini 1983b; Baker 1985). For instance:

(73) ... ritengo' [... fedele' ec...]

The trace of the clitic is now governed by the complex governor V'+A'; hence, the embedded subject can be 'bypassed' in the assignment of the governing category, and no violation of principle A arises. The same conclusion holds if Borer's (1983) approach to clitics is adopted. But if this is correct, then not only in (65), but also in (66) the embedded subject becomes a θ-marked argument of the complex predicate V'+A'; therefore, appeal to reanalysis does not suffice to account for that contrast. I believe that the reanalysis approach to small clauses is essentially correct in general (see Chomsky 1955/1975 for an early account along these lines, and the discussion of Chomsky 1986a) and provides a simple characterization of the well-formedness of (72)a, etc. It remains to be determined why θ-marking by the complex predicate does not suffice to permit *arb* interpretation in (66), although it does in (65).

5.2 *Affectedness*

In fact, this distinction is plausibly a subcase of a general exception to the possibility of having an arbitrary null object, which can be stated in terms of θ-theory. If we look at the distribution of arbitrary null objects from the viewpoint of θ-theory, we realize that they can always occur when the verb assigns a θ-role different from theme. A limited illustration follows (as usual, the attribution of a given case to a given thematic label is sometimes intuitively clear and sometimes rather arbitrary):

(74) *Experiencer*
 Talvolta Mario colpisce/spaventa/preoccupa/impressiona/
 meraviglia ___ .
 'Sometimes Mario strikes/frightens/worries/impresses/amazes ___.'
(75) *Bene(male)factive*
 Talvolta il direttore promuove/aiuta/punisce/ringrazia/premia ___
 senza ragione.

'Sometimes the director promotes/helps/punishes/thanks/rewards ___ without reason.'

(76) *Goal (in control structures)*
In queste condizioni, difficilmente il direttore potrebbe indurre/convincere/persuadere/costringere ___ a lavorare di più.
'In these conditions, it is unlikely that the director can induce/convince/persuade/force ___ to work harder.'

(77) *Source and goal*
Un insuccesso può privare ___ della sicurezza nei propri mezzi.
'A failure can deprive ___ of the confidence in one's means.'
Un successo può dotare ___ di maggior entusiasmo.
'A success can endow ___ with more enthusiasm.'

(78) *Location*
Prima di operare, il chirurgo copre ___ con un panno bianco.
'Before operating, the surgeon covers ___ with a white cloth.'

As for direct objects plausibly characterizable as themes, we must distinguish two classes. With some verbs, the arbitrary null object is possible, with other verbs it is not:

(79) *Theme₁*
Gianni fotografa/ritrae/visita ___ nudi.
'Gianni photographs/portrays/visits nude.'

(80) *Theme₂*
*Gianni incontra/trova/vede/sente ___ arrabbiati.
'Gianni meets/finds/sees/hears ___ angry.'
*Gianni conosce ___ giovani.
'Gianni meets ___ young.'

Compare:

(81)a Gianni li incontra/trova/vede/sente ___ arrabbiati.
   'Gianni them meets/finds/sees/hears ___ angry.'
  b Gianni li ha conosciuti ___ giovani.
   'Gianni them met ___ young.'

Notice moreover that whereas psychological verbs with θ-structure *theme ___ experiencer* generally allow an arbitrary null object (see (74)), psychological verbs with structure *experiencer ___ theme* generally do not:

(82) *?Spesso Gianni teme/detesta/apprezza/disprezza/ammira ___ .
'Often Gianni fears/hates/appreciates/despises/admires ___ .'

In other words, the theme of psychological verbs appears to be a 'Theme₂'.

This distinction between two classes of themes is not completely isolated: similar distinctions manifest themselves in the grammar, along parallel lines. It has been shown (Anderson 1977; Rappaport 1983) that the class I have called 'Theme$_1$' allows passivization in NPs, whereas the class 'Theme$_2$' does not:

(83) a the portrait/picture of John
     b John's portrait/picture
(84) a the sight of John
     b the knowledge of physics
     c the fear of the earthquake
     d the contempt of money
(85) a *John's sight
     b *physics' knowledge
     c *the earthquake's fear
     d *money's contempt

Fiengo (1980) and Keyser and Roeper (1984) point out that the same distinction tends to show up in the middle construction: Theme$_1$ allows middle formation, whereas Theme$_2$ does not:

(86) a John portrays easily.
     b John photographs easily.
(87) a *John sees easily.
     b *The earthquake fears easily.
     c *Money despises easily.

Theme$_2$ would thus appear to be a syntactic natural class, in that it rules out a number of syntactic options otherwise available. Can this class be naturally characterized in semantic terms? It has been suggested that there is a semantically natural distinction to be drawn. The carriers of some θ-roles appear to be necessarily affected by the process (or state) referred to by the verb in that the process (or state) necessarily implies some modification (or involvement) of their physical or psychological state. This is clearly the case when the θ-role is different from theme: an experiencer, a bene(male)factive, a source, a goal, or a location is always affected in this sense. On the other hand, a theme can be unaffected in certain cases: the object of a process of perception (vision, etc.) or the theme of someone's psychological state (fear, etc.) is not necessarily affected by the process (of course, it *could* be affected, but this is not implied by the meaning of the verb). This is, according to Anderson (1977) and Fiengo (1980), the natural semantic distinction defining the class 'Theme$_2$': certain syntactic processes appear to be inapplicable to the carriers of unaffected θ-roles (see also Jaeggli 1984). Notice that in order to properly characterize the admissible cases, we must assume that the natural language metaphysics classifies the voluntary reproduction of an object through painting or photography as a process affecting the object, whereas the simple perception of an object would be classified as non-affecting. In this and many other borderline cases it is not conceptually obvious why the affectedness constraint should have exactly the domain that is empirically justified, while in many other cases this notion appears to provide the natural conceptual basis for the required syntactic distinction. But whether or not this particular way of looking at 'affectedness' is the correct defining property of the natural class, the fact that concerns us more directly is that there *is* a natural syntactic class: a direct object corresponding to an unaffected θ-role cannot undergo passivization in NPs, nor can it undergo middle formation, nor can it be a null object with arbitrary interpretation in Italian.[36]

The contrast between the different classes of small clauses can now be reconciled with the independent evidence that the reanalysis process applies uniformly. Consider:

(88) a Gianni rende [*pro* felici].
    'Gianni renders happy.'
  b *Gianni vede [*pro* felici].
    'Gianni sees happy.'
  c *Gianni ritiene [*pro* felici].
    'Gianni believes happy.'

Even if, on independent grounds, we have to assume that in all these cases *pro* is θ-marked by the complex predicate V+*felici*, it is intuitively clear that the subject of the small clause is affected by the process referred to by the complex predicate in (88)a, but not in (88)b–c: it is directly or indirectly 'acted upon' by the main subject, and the process involves some modification of its physical or psychological state in (88)a; but it is simply the content of someone else's perception process or psychological state in (88)b–c. Therefore, arbitrary *pro* is ruled out by the affectedness constraint in (88)b–c, on a par with simple structures like (80).[37]

We can now determine in which component of the proposed system the affectedness constraint applies. It cannot be operative on the formal licensing of *pro*: epistemic predicates must have the ability to license a null expletive *pro*. Therefore, it must be operative on the rule of *arb* interpretation. This is rather natural: the rule has been stated as operating on θ-grids; hence, its sensitivity to the nature of the θ-role involved is not surprising. Restricting the rule of *arb* interpretation to affected θ-roles correctly characterizes the data introduced in this section.[38]

Of course, several important questions remain: What do arbitrary objects have in common with passive in NPs and the middle construction? Why does the affectedness constraint single out these three processes, and why is it not operative in minimally different structures like clitic constructions (presumably involving V-governed *pro*) and ordinary sentential passive? I cannot adequately address these important issues here. But it is worthwhile to close this section by stressing that the affected-unaffected distinction appears to be of higher syntactic relevance than most distinctions offered by θ-theory. The fact that it cuts across the class of 'themes' suggests that this label identifies a spurious collection. This conclusion is not particularly undesirable or surprising, given that the label 'theme' is less intuitively unitary and conceptually well defined than other labels in θ-theory.

6 Some typological speculations

6.1 A typology and its language-specific counterpart

The theory of *pro* that I have proposed involves a parametrized licensing schema and a 'recovery' convention: *pro* is allowed to occur through government (Case assignment) by a head belonging to a language-specific set of licensers, and its content is recovered through nonstandard binding by (features on) the licensing head.

A quick survey of a larger sample of grammatical systems suggests a number of readjustments, which I will only hint at in rather speculative terms.

In a variety of languages that do not allow null referential subjects in tensed clauses a null expletive is possible (see Safir 1985 on German; Pollock 1986 on subjunctive clauses in French; Platzack 1987 on the insular Scandinavian languages; Travis 1984 on several cases). A reasonable working hypothesis (explicitly proposed by Pollock) is that these null expletives are instances of *pro*, which thus appears to be allowed in some grammatical systems with a reduced range of uses. A further typological distinction is necessary, according to Travis's classification: in some languages *pro* can only function as a non-argument (*pro seems that S*); in other languages it can function as a non-argument and as a quasi argument (*pro is raining*). The first case is illustrated by German and the second by Yiddish in Travis's classification (Icelandic and Faroese are like Yiddish, according to Platzack 1987). Restricting our attention to Infl-licensed occurrences of *pro*, we thus find the following cases:

(89) a no occurrence *of pro* (English)
    b *pro* = non-argument (German)
    c *pro* = non-argument and quasi argument (Yiddish)
    d *pro* = non-argument, quasi argument, and referential argument (Italian)

The distinction between (89)a and the other cases can be described by the parameter in the licensing schema, as before. The other distinctions are not immediately representable in the system proposed here, as formulated so far. Some revision is in order. A full-fledged analysis of (89) would require a detailed discussion of the different types, which is beyond the bounds of this article. I will deal with the problem indirectly, through the observation that the cross-linguistic typology of the possible uses *of pro* is reproduced in different constructions of a single grammatical system. Italian has structures instantiating its basic typological case, resulting from its particular way of fixing the relevant parameters, and structures instantiating the other cases of (89); in other languages such structures result from a different assignment of values to the parameters, but in Italian they arise from the peculiar properties of certain constructions. I will briefly analyse the Italian facts and use the results to motivate a conjecture on the nature of the cross-linguistic parameter.

All the relevant types of complements are selected by epistemic verbs. The first type is a tensed complement. It instantiates the basic typological status of Italian, (89)d, with *pro* functioning as a referential argument, quasi argument, and non-argument:

(90) a Ritengo [che *pro* sia simpatico].
'I believe that (he) is nice.'
  b Ritengo [che *pro* sia troppo tardi per S].
'I believe that (it) is too late for S.'
  c Ritengo [che *pro* sia probabile che S].
'I believe that (it) is likely that S.'

The complementary case is provided by infinitival structures introduced by the complementizer *di*: only a controlled PRO is licit in subject position (see (91)), and *pro* is never licensed, under any interpretation, because of the lack of Case (see the final version of the licensing principle (49)):

(91)   Ritengo [di PRO essere simpatico].
'I believe to be nice. = I believe that I am nice.'
(92) a *Ritengo [di *pro* essere simpatico].
'I believe (him) to be nice.'
  b *Ritengo [di *pro* essere troppo tardi per S].
'I believe (it) to be too late for S.'
  c *Ritengo [di *pro* essere probabile che S].
'I believe (it) to be likely that S.'

This is the (trivial) language-internal equivalent of the typological case (89)a.

The third case, corresponding to (89)b, arises in Italian in the following way. We have already seen that epistemic verbs can take small clauses, and a *pro* subject can function as a non-argument but not as a quasi argument and a referential argument:

(93) a *Ritengo [*pro* simpatico].
   'I believe (him) nice.'
   b *Ritengo [*pro* troppo tardi per S].
   'I believe (it) too late for S.'
   c Ritengo [*pro* probabile che S].
   'I believe (it) likely that S.'

The final case, (89)c, arises in Italian in the marked infinitival construction in which the auxiliary moves to Comp and nominative Case is assigned to the subject (see Rizzi 1982, Chapters 3 and 4). Here both the non-argumental and quasi-argumental uses are possible, and only the referential use is excluded:

(94) a *Ritengo [essere *pro* simpatico].
   'I believe to be (he) nice.'
   b Ritengo [essere *pro* troppo tardi per S].
   'I believe to be (it) too late for S.'
   c Ritengo [essere *pro* probabile che S].
   'I believe to be (it) likely that S.'

6.2 Analysis

Let us start from the last case. In previous work, in order to keep the generalization that nominative Case is assigned through Agr, I assumed that the Aux-to-Comp construction involves an abstract Agr specification under Infl, which combines with an auxiliary and moves to Comp, from where nominative Case can be assigned (for details, see Rizzi 1982, Chapter 4, app. 2). The Agr specification is obviously weak here: it is not realized morphologically on the verb, which keeps the infinitival form (but it is morphologically realized in the corresponding Portuguese construction), and only the gender and number specification can be marked on the past participle in compound tenses, or on the postcopular adjective. It is natural to assume that the person specification, which is never morphologically manifested, is not there at all. The abstract agreement of these infinitival structures is then 'weak' in the precise sense that it lacks the person specification. We can capitalize on this difference between (90) and (94) to account for the reduced range of interpretations of *pro* through the following rather natural assumption:

(95) An NP is referential only if it has the specification of person and number.

pro cannot receive the person specification in (94)a through head binding by weak Agr; hence, it is restricted to nonreferential uses.[39]

How does (93) differ from (94)? Our analysis of (93) was that *pro* cannot acquire any content through head binding because it is not θ-marked by the licensing head.[40] It is a null element specified as [–anaphoric, +pronominal, +accusative] and having no other specification, no licit φ-features in particular. The intuitive idea assumed in the discussion of (54)–(57) was that such a contentless element could not carry any θ-role, either referential or 'atmospheric'. The acceptability of (94)b shows that the lack of the person specification is not the decisive factor. For concreteness, I will identify the discriminating specification in the number feature, stating the relevant principle in the following somewhat arbitrary form:

(96) An NP is argumental only if it has the specification of number.[41]

Principles (95)–(96) provide a partial characterization of the status that an NP can have within θ-theory. The rather natural claim is that non-arguments, quasi arguments, and referential arguments are hierarchically ordered with respect to the required richness of their content expressed in terms of φ-features. The system now precisely characterizes the contrast among (90), (93), and (94). In all three cases *pro* is formally licensed, but in (93) the argumental uses are excluded by the lack of the number specification (in fact, of any specification), and in (94) the referential use is excluded by the lack of the person specification; only in (90) does *pro* have the full range of interpretations allowed by the rich agreement specification under the recovery convention and principles (95)–(96).[42]

This language-specific analysis suggests a conjecture on the cross-linguistic parameters responsible for the different cases of (89). Our system acquires the necessary flexibility if we assume that not only the licensing principle, but also the recovery procedure (41), is parametrized. Suppose that recovery of φ-features through head binding is an option that different grammatical systems can exploit to different degrees. Some systems can choose not to use it at all: such systems will allow occurrence of *pro* through the positive setting of the licensing parameter, but argumental uses of *pro* will be systematically ruled out by (96). This corresponds to case (89)b. Other systems can choose to exploit the recovery component only in part – that is, by recovering only one φ-feature specification of *pro*. If the only recovered specification is the number feature, formally licit occurrences of *pro* will be restricted to nonreferential uses through principle (95). This corresponds to case (89)c.[43] Other systems choose to exploit the recovery component fully; if they have rich Agr, a formally licit *pro* will be available for all referential and nonreferential uses. This corresponds to case (89)d.

In conclusion, the typology illustrated in (89) can be accounted for through minimal assumptions on the parametrization of the system. The distinction between (89)a and (89)b–d follows from the licensing parameter. The distinctions (89)b versus (89)c–d and (89)c versus (89)d follow from a trivial parametrization of the recovery component in interaction with principles (95)–(96), which determine the status of NPs with respect to θ-theory: recovery through head binding is an option of Universal Grammar that different grammatical systems can reject or adopt, fully or in part.

6.3 Chinese

There is a fifth important typological case to be added to (89). Huang (1984) has shown that *pro* can occur in subject position in Chinese; his arguments and analysis naturally extend to Japanese and Korean. Since there is no Agr specification in these languages, our system would lead us to expect that *pro* should be restricted to the non-argumental use, there being no possible recovery of φ-features through head binding. But this is incorrect: *pro* can function as a quasi argument and as a referential argument in these languages. Therefore, a further revision is apparently in order.

Huang makes the interesting claim that the basic typological generalization concerning *pro* in subject position is that it is possible only in languages with strong Agr or no Agr at all – hence in Italian and Chinese, but not in English. He then elaborates a theory of *pro* based on this generalization. As far as I can see, there is no natural way to represent Huang's generalization in the system I have proposed. The main reason is that, for this system, the licensing property of a given head (Infl, for instance) does not depend on its feature specification (whether or not it has Agr). In fact, there are empirical problems as well: if (89) is the correct partial typology, *pro* is possible in languages with weak Agr; moreover, as Sten Vikner points out (personal communication), mainland Scandinavian languages generally do not manifest any Agr specification on verbs, and still they do not allow *pro* to occur (see also Platzack 1987). Thus, there are both empirical and theoretical reasons for exploring a different approach to the Chinese type.

Mamoru Saito has pointed out (personal communication) that φ-features do not seem to play any role in the grammar of another language of the relevant type, Japanese. Suppose this extends to the whole type (but see Choe 1985 for a different view). This is perhaps an independent factor differentiating grammatical systems: Universal Grammar offers the option of using φ-features, and some grammatical systems take it, whereas others do not. If this is correct, it is natural to assume that (95)–(96) operate only in grammatical systems that take the option of using φ-features: within a grammatical system that does not, they cannot be operative; otherwise, the system would disallow argumental and referential NPs. Then we obtain the correct result: if a language uses φ-features (as is always the case when there is some form of Agr), (95)–(96) are operative, and the *pro* module works as described in Section 6.2. If a language does not have Agr and, more importantly, does not use ϕ-features in general, principles (95)–(96) are vacuous, and any licit occurrence of *pro* can be used as non-argumental, quasi-argumental, and referential.[44] (For relevant discussion see also Oshima 1985: 20.)

7 Conclusion

The basic empirical observation of this article is that Italian allows null V-governed NP positions carrying arbitrary interpretation or functioning as expletives, whereas contemporary English lacks both options; diachronic evidence supports the view that this correlation is not accidental. Some evidence that the V-governed NP is filled by *pro* has suggested a revision of the current theoretical assumptions concerning this element; in particular, it appears to be necessary to separate the formal licensing of *pro* from the procedure through which its content is recovered from the phonetically realized environment. In sum, the basic reason for this conclusion, internal to Italian, is that *pro* is *always* licit in positions governed and Case-marked by Infl or V, regardless of whether the licensing head has an overt feature specification recovering the feature content of *pro*. This specification is only relevant to determine the possible use of *pro* as a referential definite pronoun, an arbitrary pronoun, a quasi argument, or a non-argument.

I have proposed that *pro* is formally licensed through Case assignment by a designated head. The membership of the set of licensing heads defines a parameter whose values range from the empty set (no licensing head, hence no occurrence of *pro* is allowed by the grammatical system, which is probably the case of contemporary English) to, in principle, the set including all the Case-assigning heads. I have discussed in detail different cases of V-licensing, and I have hinted at well-motivated and familiar cases of Infl-licensing and at a plausible case of P-licensing. This licensing principle involves a government relation, as the other subcases of the Generalized Empty Category Principle (GECP) do. Since it involves a positive government relation, one might wonder whether it could be collapsed with the Empty Category Principle (ECP) proper, the subcase of the GECP concerning trace and variable, which also involves a positive government requirement. This does not seem to be feasible because the structural requirements of the ECP are weaker in some respects and stronger in others. The ECP does not require Case assignment, whereas reference to Case appears to be crucial for *pro* (see the discussion of Section 3.3). On the other hand, a Case-assigning Infl in null-subject languages licenses *pro*, but it does not suffice for the ECP (this is the conclusion suggested by the evidence presented in Rizzi (1982, Chapter 4), if it is reconsidered from the perspective of the *pro* analysis of the null-subject parameter). Similarly, prepositions appear to be able to license *pro* in French, but they do not qualify as proper governors for the ECP: P-stranding is not allowed in that grammatical system.

In addition to the formal licensing principle analogous to the ECP and the PRO Theorem, the theory of *pro* specifies a procedure to 'recover' the feature specification of the null element from the phonetically realized environment, the partial analogue of control theory and A/A' chain formation. The strategy that appears to be operative in Italian is that the 'recovery' is done through (nonstandard) binding from the licensing head. *pro* in subject position in a null-subject language can function as a definite pronoun through 'binding' from the Agr specification of the licensing Infl, which recovers and sanctions the necessary φ-features (see Bouchard 1983 for a discussion of this issue in a broader theoretical context). The same analysis is plausibly extendable to object *pro* 'bound' by a clitic on the licensing V. Subject and object *pro* can have *arb* interpretation sanctioned through 'binding' from the impersonal subject clitic (*si* in Italian) and an *arb* slot in a θ-grid, respectively. If the 'recovery' procedure fails to apply, the system still sanctions an occurrence of *pro*, but it can only function as a contentless element, an expletive pronoun. If we restrict our attention to V-licensed *pro*, the usual conspiring effect of the Projection Principle and the θ-Criterion will limit this option to the subject position of small clauses, the only V-governed position that can be nonthematic in Italian (but see footnote 31).

A quick cross-linguistic survey has suggested the speculative hypothesis that the recovery component is also parametrized. Languages can choose to fully exploit the recovery option offered by head binding, or to use it in part, or not to use it at all. This parameter interacts with the richness of Agr (more generally, with the richness of the feature specification of the licensing head) and with principles (95)–(96) to determine three typological cases: if no content is recovered, *pro* will be restricted to non-argumental use; if only the number specification is recovered, *pro* will be restricted to nonreferential uses; if both person and number are recovered, it will have the full range of uses. Languages not using φ-features seem to be immune from principles (95)–(96); hence, in these systems *pro* has the full range of interpretations in spite of the fact that the recovery procedure is not operative.

All the possible values of the parameters postulated in this speculative discussion can be reasonably determined on the basis of the primary data. The assumption that a given head is a possible licenser must be justified by positive evidence – that is, the primary data must contain sentences with gaps that can only be *pros*, whereas the assumption that a given head is not a licenser is the unmarked assumption, in the terms discussed in Section 3.4. As for the possible values of the 'recovery' procedure, the decision to recover some specifications of *pro* through head binding must be justified by positive evidence,[45] whereas the decision not to adopt the head-binding option represents the unmarked case.

Appendix: dative *pro* and dative control

A1 *Dative pro*

The final version of the licensing principle was formulated in terms of Case, and I gave examples of nominative and accusative *pro*. In this appendix, I will consider the licensing capacity of dative Case assignment. The question is whether in structures like (97) not only the understood theme but also the understood goal can be structurally represented as *pro*.

(97) Gianni presenta volentieri ___ ___ .
    'Gianni introduces willingly.'

Much of the previous evidence appears to be unavailable here: in general, a dative, even when overt, cannot license an adjunct small clause, cannot be the subject of an argument small clause, and can function as the binder of an anaphor only in a marginal way:[46]

(98) a *Gianni le ha parlato malata.
      'Gianni to+her spoke sick([+fem]).'
   b *Gianni le ritiene [___ AP].
      'Gianni to+her believes [___ AP].'
   c ??Ho descritto se stesso a Gianni.
      'I described himself to Gianni.'
   d ?Gli ho descritto se stesso.
      'I to+him described himself.'

On the other hand, a dative can function nonmarginally as a controller, and we have already seen that a dative controller can be dropped in both Italian and English (footnote 1). Let us postpone the discussion of this fact.

If ordinary datives do not seem to provide clear-cut evidence, there is one construction that provides a more reliable testing ground. In the causative construction the standard Case pattern is that the subject of the causative clause is marked accusative if the embedded verb is intransitive, and dative (through the dative preposition/Case marker *a*) if the verb is transitive:

(99) a Gianni fa cantare Maria.
      'Gianni makes sing Maria.'
   b Gianni fa cantare l'inno nazionale a Maria.
      'Gianni makes sing the national anthem to Maria. = Gianni makes Maria sing the national anthem.'

Both accusative and dative subjects can nonmarginally bind anaphors, license adjunct small clauses, and, of course, function as controllers if the embedded verb is a subject-control verb (in the following examples the embedded subject is cliticized to the causative verb):

(100) a Lo psicanalista lo fa parlare di se stesso.
  'The psychoanalyst him makes speak about himself.'
 b Gianni la fa cantare seduta.
  'Gianni her makes sing seated ([+fem]).'
 c Un buon consiglio la può far riuscire a superare le difficoltà.
  'Good advice her can make manage to overcome the difficulties.'
(101) a L'orgoglio gli fa nascondere la verità a se stesso.
  'Pride to+him makes hide the truth from himself.'
 b Gianni le fa cantare l'inno nazionale seduta.
  'Gianni to+her makes sing the national anthem seated ([+fem]).'
 c Gianni le fa promettere di rispettare la legge.
  'Gianni to+her makes promise to obey the law.'

Both an accusative and a dative subject can be null and receive arbitrary interpretation in all these cases:

(102) a Lo psicanalista fa parlare di se stessi.
  'The psychoanalyst makes speak about oneself.'
 b Il generale fa cantare seduti.
  'The general makes sing seated ([+pl]).'
 c Un buon consiglio può far riuscire a superare le difficoltà.
  'Good advice can make manage to overcome the difficulties.'
(103) a Talvolta l'orgoglio fa nascondere la verità a se stessi.
  'Sometimes pride makes hide the truth from oneself.'
 b Il generale fa cantare l'inno nazionale seduti.
  'The general makes sing the national anthem seated ([+pl]).'
 c Il generale fa promettere di rispettare la legge.
  'The general makes promise to respect the law.'

On the basis of the usual assumptions, (102) argues for a structurally represented accusative *pro*, and (103) for dative *pro*. This shows that the licensing principle includes dative Case assignment.[47]

A2 Dative control

Let us now consider control. We have already seen that in English dative control contrasts with object control in that a dative controller can be omitted (examples adapted from Roeper 1985):

(104) a John shouted/said/gave the order (to Bill) to leave.
 b John told/ordered *(Bill) to leave.

In Italian there is also a detectable difference between null direct and null indirect controlling objects: a null direct object controller can occur only in sentences with generic time reference, whereas a null dative controller is not so restricted:

(105) a Il generale può costringere (i soldati) ad obbedire.
   'The general can force (the soldiers) to obey.'
   b Il generale può ordinare (ai soldati) di partire.
   'The general can order (to the soldiers) to leave.'
(106) a Il generale ha costretto *(i soldati) ad obbedire.
   'The general forced (the soldiers) to obey.'
   b Il generale ha ordinato (ai soldati) di partire.
   'The general ordered (to the soldiers) to leave.'

A third difference between the two types of null controllers is that in Italian a null object can have only the arbitrary interpretation, whereas a null dative controller can also be pragmatically bound, most naturally by a salient group of people including the speaker ('we'):

(107) a Il sergente può costringere ___ a prepararsi/*ci in cinque minuti.
   'The sergeant can force ___ to prepare oneself/*ourselves in five minutes.'
   b Il sergente ha ordinato di prepararsi/ci in cinque minuti.
   'The sergeant ordered to prepare oneself/ourselves in five minutes.'

A fourth property differentiating null objects and null datives is that the null dative that is able to control in English cannot function as a binder:

(108) a John said something to them about themselves/each other.
   b *John said something about themselves/each other/oneself.
   c John said [PRO to speak about oneself/?themselves/?each other].

Example (108)a illustrates binding by an overt dative; (108)c shows that an understood dative can control (and, at a marginal level, can indirectly bind an anaphor through the controlled PRO);[48] (108)b illustrates the fact that a null dative cannot (directly) bind an anaphor.

The same fact emerges in a slightly more complex way in Italian. We have already seen (in (103)a) that a null dative can bind, and we have concluded that it can be structurally represented in Italian. This is true for the null dative with arbitrary interpretation occurring in generic statements. If we consider statements with specific time reference, however, the pragmatically interpreted understood dative behaves as in English: it keeps the ability to control, but it loses the ability to bind, under any interpretation:

(109) Lo psichiatra ha detto [di PRO parlare di se stessi/noi stessi].
'The psychiatrist said to speak about themselves/ourselves.'
(110)a ?Lo psichiatra gli ha restituito se stesso.
'The psychiatrist to+him gave back himself.'
b *Lo psichiatra ha restituito se stessi/noi stessi.
'The psychiatrist gave back themselves/ourselves.'

On the other hand, if the time reference of (110)b is made generic, the sentence improves:

(111) ??Un buono psichiatra può restituire se stessi.
'A good psychiatrist can give back oneself.'

We can thus summarize the observed facts in the following way:

a   Italian has an understood null dative with *arb* interpretation that has the same formal and interpretive properties of the null direct object; in particular, it can control and bind.
b   Both Italian and English have an understood null dative that is not restricted to generic contexts, can be pragmatically interpreted, and can function as a controller, but not as a binder.

The syntactic status of case a is clear: it involves another instance of V-licensed *pro*, which receives *arb* interpretation and can control and bind like any other structurally represented position.[49] The remaining question is, What is the syntactic status of case b?

The fact that the understood dative of case b cannot bind immediately suggests that it does not correspond to a structurally represented position. The contrast between binding and control suggests that the structural requirements associated with the former are weaker than those associated with the latter. Of course, we cannot weaken the requirements on control too much; otherwise, our account of the contrast in (6)–(8), which crucially relied on the obligatory presence of a structural controller, would be lost. In fact, from the perspective of the discussion in Section 1, the existence of case b is surprising. The simple approach to implicit arguments that proved successful there was that either an implicit argument is structurally represented and can control and bind (like the null object in Italian), or it is not structurally represented and does not have any syntactic manifestation (like the null object in English). Now, however, we must integrate case b of null datives, which appears to split the battery of our tests and is intermediate in the obvious sense that it has only a partial syntactic manifestation.

A3 Analysis

An adequate solution to this problem would require a detailed study of the theory of control, a task that cannot be undertaken here. Let us simply sketch the lines of a possible solution. We will assume that control theory crucially involves θ-grids, in that a control verb has a member of its θ-grid lexically designated as the controller (For possible refinements, see Ruzicka 1983; Koster 1984; Melvold 1985.) Control is a syntactic process, consisting of the coindexing of PRO with the designated θ-role; therefore, the designated θ-role must be visible in the syntax, when the control module applies. It is not unreasonable to assume that if a θ-role is saturated in the lexicon, it is not syntactically visible; hence, in particular, it cannot act as a controller. This allows us to keep our original account of the ungrammaticality of (6)d in a slightly different form; if the object θ-role is saturated in the lexicon, it cannot control; if it is not, it can control, but the position is obligatorily projected by the Projection Principle, and there is no appropriate null filler in English, whence the ill-formedness of (6)d. This approach differs from the original discussion in Section 1 simply in that the obligatoriness of the direct object controller is not stated as a primitive principle (see (7)) but follows from the interplay of control theory, the Projection Principle, and the assumption that a θ-role saturated in the lexicon is not visible for syntactic processes. On the other hand, the obligatory structural representation of a binder still follows directly from the formal definition of the binding relation. We thus introduce an asymmetry between binding and control that should provide enough flexibility to capture the intermediate behaviour of indirect objects.

The desired result is the following. Contrary to a direct object θ-role, an indirect object θ-role can fail to be structurally projected even if it is not lexically saturated. Being lexically unsaturated, it is syntactically visible and can act as a controller. Since it fails to be structurally projected, the problem of filling the position does not arise; hence, the option is available in English as well. This option meets the requirements of the theory of control, but not the stronger requirements of the theory of binding, which demands a structurally represented position.

If this approach is on the right track, the difference between direct and indirect objects would ultimately reduce to the fact that the Projection Principle functions differently in the two cases. The hypothesis that direct objects have a peculiar status in this respect is not implausible. Consider the following structure:

(112)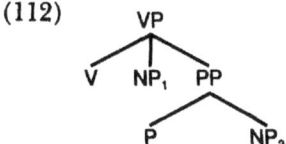

It can be argued that a verb directly θ-marks only the direct object in (112). Then NP_2 is θ-marked not directly by the verb, but by its local governor P. Still, in some sense NP_2 clearly is an argument of the verb, an intuition that can be given formal content by having the corresponding θ-role listed in the θ-grid of the verb. This suggests that another distinction is to be added to the generally assumed distinction between internal and external θ-roles: within the internal θ-roles, θ-grids should single out the direct θ-role, directly θ-marked by the verb, from the indirect θ-roles, indirectly θ-marked by the verb through the selection of an autonomous θ-marker (preposition or inherent Case).[50] Suppose further that when a head directly θ-marks for a given θ-role, the corresponding structural position must be projected, whereas the selection of an autonomous θ-marker is, in the unmarked case, optional; that is, in (110) NP_1 cannot be omitted, nor can NP_2 if P is there, but the whole PP can be omitted. This captures the fact that objects of verbs and prepositions tend to be obligatory, whereas PPs tend to be optional.[51]

Consider now the control case. If there is an object θ-role, and it is not saturated in the lexicon, the object position must be there; no object position implies no syntactically available θ-role for control. This captures the ungrammaticality of (6)d. On the other hand, there can be a syntactically available indirect object θ-role not corresponding to a structural position: this happens when the verb has in its grid the corresponding (indirect) θ-role, but it takes the option of not selecting the autonomous θ-marker, the preposition/inherent dative marker *a*. The resulting 'floating' θ-role can receive a referential content through *arb* interpretation, and apparently can also be pragmatically interpreted. Moreover, being visible in the syntax, it can function as a controller; not corresponding to a structural position, however, it cannot function as a binder. This accounts for the well-formedness of (104)a, (106)b, (108)c, and (109) and for the ill-formedness of (108)b and (110)b. The analysis of this appendix has the significant theoretical implication that binding and control involve different structural requirements (hence cannot be (fully) assimilated) and that the theoretical typology of implicit arguments cannot be reduced to the presence versus lack of structural representation: at least one intermediate case must be allowed.

Notes

1 Bresnan (1982) mentions *signal* as a possible exception to Bach's generalization in English (as in i–ii): but *signal* also takes an indirect object (as in iii):

  i Mary signalled Tom to leave.
  ii Mary signalled ___ to leave.
  iii Mary signalled to Tom to leave.

Therefore, the possibility of dropping the controller can be related to the latter structure. Indirect object control appears to contrast rather systematically with direct object control with respect to the possibility of dropping the controller; see the Appendix for a possible analysis, and Roeper (1985) for relevant discussion. Another apparent problem for Bach's generalization is raised by *help*, which apparently allows the dropping of a direct object controller (Mohanan 1983):

iv I helped Bill (to) solve the problem.
v   I helped (to) solve the problem.

I will tentatively suggest that, in spite of the optional presence of *to*, *help* can select a bare VP in these cases; hence, there is no subject position to be controlled in v. This analysis, reminiscent of Burzio's (1981, 1986) proposal for one causative construction in Romance, is supported by the fact that the VP can contain a trace in vi but not in vii:

vi a John helped Bill (to) get nominated.
    b John helped Bill (to) go away.
vii a *John helped (to) get nominated.
    b *John helped (to) go away.

Sentences viia–b are excluded by the bare VP hypothesis because the trace in the passive or unaccusative construction does not have the required structural binder.

2 The contrast is not as minimal as in (6)–(8) because the corresponding verbs in English do not allow a missing understood object, irrespective of the presence of an anaphor in the structure. Minimal pairs are difficult to find because of the idiosyncratic nature of the missing object option in English, which itself constitutes an important difference between this language and Italian (see below). Still, relevant contrasts can be detected, at least at the level of relative acceptability:

i   ??This can incite against the government.
ii *This can incite against oneself.

The additional deviance of ii can be attributed to the binding theory violation resulting from the lack of a structural binder for the anaphor. This follows from the binding theory in conjunction with the assumption that no structurally represented zero object is possible in English. Notice that in Italian the null object can also function as a binder in the reciprocal construction (see Belletti 1982):

iii Un buon pranzo può riconciliare ___ gli uni con gli altri.
    'A good meal can reconcile ___ with each other.'

3 Trigo (1985) points out that in Spanish both instances of arbitrary interpretation can occur with singular agreement, as has often been stated, but there is a difference between the two cases: arbitrary null objects require singular agreement, whereas arbitrary PRO can also occur with plural agreement. This appears to be essentially correct for plural agreement in Italian: the plurality requirement on the null object appears exceptionless:

i   *Questi dottori visitano ___ nudo.
    'These doctors visit ___ nude ([+sg]).'

On the other hand, the adjective modifying PRO in sentences like (15) can be singular if the statement is pragmatically understood as concerning one individual (typically the speaker or the hearer):

ii In una situazione di questo genere, è difficile [PRO essere sempre allegro].
'In a situation of this kind, it is difficult to be always happy ([+ sg]).'

Notice that this option is found in structures in which the arbitrary interpretation is (arguably) induced by control from an arbitrary implicit experiencer of the main predicate (i.e. *It is difficult for someone...*), but not in structures where the arbitrary interpretation of PRO must be primary, there being no potential implicit controller in the main clause (Manzini 1983a):

iii Lucia ha detto a Maria [come [PRO essere sempre allegri/*allegro]].
'Lucia told Maria how to be always happy ([+masc, +pl])/*happy ([+masc, +sg]).'

This suggests the following account. True arbitrary interpretation is intrinsically plural in Italian, whence i and iii for object and subject, respectively. An implicit experiencer differs from a PRO subject and a null object in that it also admits some sort of pragmatic control from a salient element in discourse in addition to true arbitrary interpretation: this is the case represented in ii, where the pragmatically controlled null experiencer in turn controls PRO.

4 In fact, quite independently of the specific approach to small clauses that is chosen, it is possible to show that null objects in Italian can control not only in argument clauses, but also in adverbial clauses, like the following causal clause:

i Un tribunale equo condanna ___ solo per [PRO aver commesso crimini accertati].
'A fair tribunal convicts ___ only for committing verified crimes.'

5 Where the value of the number specification is a parameter. Presumably, *arb* also includes default specifications of person and gender; see Section 2.3 for more detailed discussion.

6 This approach provides a partial formal characterization of the notion 'optional argument': an optional argument is an argument (more precisely, a θ-role) saturated in the lexicon. Restricting our attention to apparent cases of optionality of the direct object (nominal or clausal), there are two other major cases, which are often referred to as 'unspecified object deletion' and 'null complement anaphora', respectively:

i John ate ___ .
ii I know ___ .

In the first case the missing object is interpreted as somehow canonical or prototypical: Gruber (1965) notes that i could not appropriately describe a situation in which John ate marbles; Susan Fisher points out (personal communication) that i is more appropriate if John ate lunch than if he ate a bite of someone else's sandwich. On the other hand, Haegeman (1985) notices that pragmatic considerations affect the interpretation of the understood object: if we are discussing the progress of patients who were unable to eat before, *They are eating* may simply refer to their eating anything, even if they are not taking meals. In cases of null complement anaphora the interpretation of the missing object appears to be definite and anaphoric to some linguistic (or pragmatically salient) element. Attempting an extension of our proposal for *arb* interpretation, we could suggest that an internal θ-role can be saturated in the lexicon not only by *arb* but also either by a lexically designated constant identifying the canonical object of a given verb (in which case the saturated θ-role would function like a cognate object, with the interpretation affected in part by pragmatics) or by a referential index (in which case the saturated θ-role would function like a definite pronoun). All these processes are lexically governed: near synonyms often contrast (*incite* vs. *push*, *eat* vs. *devour*, *know* vs. *prefer*). If this approach proves feasible, apparent cases of optionality of the direct object can be reduced to saturation in the lexicon in one of the ways indicated. Other cases could be real instances of optionality of the object θ-role or, perhaps more appropriately, of different lexical entries.

7 Guglielmo Cinque points out (personal communication) that there are no examples of the type **People often talk to ___*, in spite of the fact that there are syntactic reasons to assume V+P reanalysis, with the object of P behaving syntactically like the object of the complex 'verb' (Hornstein and Weinberg 1981; Kayne 1984, Chapter 3). This suggests that (20) cannot be fed by V+P reanalysis. The necessary ordering follows, given our assumption that (20) applies only in the lexicon in English, if V+P reanalysis can apply only in the syntax. Cinque's observation can therefore be construed as evidence for the syntactic nature of reanalysis.

8 Guglielmo Cinque points out (personal communication) that the effect is particularly clear in German:

i [OP [Habe ich *ec* schon gesehen]].
'I have already seen (it).'
ii *[Wer OP [hat *ec ec* schon gesehen]]?
'Who has already seen (it)?'

Also see Ross (1982) for discussion.

9 Richard Kayne points out (personal communication) that (31)b improves if the embedded Wh-element binds a nonsubject:

i ??Which student did you tell t [what you were planning to say *e* about *e*]?

A possible interpretation of the decreasing acceptability of (31)b could be that the presence of the null operator in Comp prevents antecedent government of the subject variable by *who* (the exact implementation of this idea depends on the structure of Comp that is assumed) – whence an ECP violation in (31)b, in addition to the doubly filled Comp effect. But Kayne notices a similar contrast in cases of extraction from Wh-islands:

ii a *What don't you know who should do?
b ??Who don't you know what you should say about?

This contrast could not be treated in the same way (unless the extracted Wh-element is assumed to move obligatorily through the embedded Comp).

10 In this respect, the subject position of a small clause differs from a true object position. Compare, for instance, (34)a with i:

i Questa decisione non aiuta molti cittadini.
'This decision doesn't help many citizens.'

(34)a allows only the *not many* reading, whereas i is ambiguous between *not many* and *many not*. Some quantifiers have the lexical property of ruling out the *not* Q interpretation, for instance *diversi* 'several':

ii Questa decisione non aiuta diversi cittadini.
  'This decision doesn't help several citizens.'

So, ii contrasts with i in that it is nonambiguous: it can only mean 'For several x, x = citizens, this decision doesn't help x' (see Lasnik 1972). As expected, the structure corresponding to (34)a is ungrammatical:

iii *Questa decisione non rende [diversi cittadini felici].
  'This decision doesn't make [several citizens happy].'

The interpretation *not* Q is excluded by the lexical property of *diversi*, and the interpretation Q *not* is ruled out by whatever structural property of the subject of small clauses is operative in (34), etc. Therefore, iii cannot receive a proper interpretation.

11 Further evidence supporting the *pro* hypothesis is given in footnotes 24 and 28; also see footnote 38. Dotson Smith (1984) argues on independent grounds that certain Italian constructions involve *pro* in object position.

12 But notice that the English verbs allowing an understood arbitrary object do not homogeneously require a generic time reference:

 i Yesterday John pleased *(everyone).
 ii Yesterday John warned (everyone) against this mistake.

If an example like ii also involves *arb* interpretation, as I have argued, then the generic time reference requirement must be a function of *arb* and lexical meaning, interacting in a more complex way than is suggested in the text.

13 The same point can be made on the basis of the 'primary' instances of *arb* interpretation of PRO introduced in footnote 3:

 i John told Mary [how [PRO to roll down the hill]].

14 A standard assumption is that the statement of the GECP concerning PRO is derivable from the theory of binding (the 'PRO Theorem'), whereas the statements concerning trace and variable are a primitive principle (ECP proper). If this is correct, my proposal for the *pro* module, involving a primitive government requirement, is fully parallel to the standard approach to trace and variable only.

15 A rough generalization that seems to emerge from Zribi-Hertz (1984) is that *pro* is allowed by polysyllabic prepositions and is impossible with monosyllabic prepositions (some monosyllabic prepositions can be made to allow *pro* through a process of *de-* prefixation, which makes them bisyllabic: *dedans, dessus, dessous*). Suppose that monosyllabic prepositions obligatorily cliticize to their complements in French. Then we can keep the fully general claim that P is a licenser in French: cases of *P pro* with monosyllabic prepositions will be excluded by the lack of a phonetically realized target of the obligatory cliticization.

16 How the parameter can be actually set by the language learner will be discussed in Section 3.4.

17 Notice that the formulation of (41) is neutral between an assignment procedure (copying of features from the licensing head) and a recovery procedure (the only specifications that *pro* can have are those that match the specifications on the head, hence are recoverable from it). For concreteness, in general I will phrase the discussion as if (41) were a recovery procedure, but without attaching any empirical import to this decision.

18 The most plausible S-Structure position of *si* is not under Infl but in the VP. In fact, it follows other complement clitics, for example, the locative clitic *ci*:

i Ci si dorme troppo.
'People there sleep too much.'

For the sake of our discussion it is sufficient to assume that *si* is connected to the Agr slot under Infl through chain formation (or simple coindexing) at the level of representation where convention (41) applies.

Suñer (1982), Jaeggli (1985) and Otero (1985) analyse another case in which a subject *pro* can have arbitrary interpretation. This case, which has slightly different properties, will not be discussed here.

19 We are now crucially assuming that *arb* interpretation is defined by a collection of features and not by a designated referential index, an assumption already motivated in Section 2.1. We have assumed that an object NP position is automatically coindexed with the θ-slot in the governing verb from which it is projected. We are now assuming that *arb* can be assigned by (43) to a θ-slot in the syntax, after a D-Structure representation has been projected and the positions have been indexed. This is not problematic if *arb* is a collection of features, whereas it would involve some complication (e.g., a reindexing procedure) if *arb* were a referential index. We thus have internal reasons, in addition to the more forceful empirical reasons discussed in Section 2.1, for rejecting the view that *arb* is a special referential index.

20 This system excludes *pro* as a possible object filler in English, but it does not necessarily exclude applications of (43) in the syntax in English. These could give a well-formed result if there existed a licit filler of the object position that did not give rise to a semantic clash with arbitrary interpretation. Whether or not such a case exists is immaterial for our discussion, which solely concerns arbitrary *pro*.

21 Cinque (1984) and Obenauer (1984) argue that *pro* can be sanctioned and interpreted as a variable through local operator binding. If this possibility is to be allowed, it would seem to require an independent statement, not naturally collapsible with our principles of licensing and recovery.

22 Unless, of course, Infl contains or is construed with the impersonal *si*. In this case a passive sentence having the interpretation of (45)a is possible:

i *pro* si viene fotografati *e* nudi.
'People are photographed nude.'

This is consistent with the view that the interpretation of *pro* is solely determined by the local governing head: it is clear that the arbitrary interpretation in i is locally determined by *si*, and not transmitted from the verb-governed trace.

23 Belletti (1986) argues that passive past participles keep the ability to assign an inherent partitive Case, which is responsible for the definiteness effect found in constructions with a postverbal subject. If this is correct, then partitive Case lacks the licensing property referred to in (49). Alternatively, there could be an intrinsic incompatibility between *arb*, which is close to universal quantification, and the inherent semantic content associated with partitive Case. Jacqueline Guéron points out (personal communication) that if this is correct, then representations like (47) would be ruled out by the semantic clash, and no reference to Case would be needed. This conclusion would hold if partitive Case assignment obligatorily applied to postverbal NPs. Belletti explicitly argues against this conclusion.

24 Notice that the object position of a passive sentence is a possible site for a variable resulting from syntactic or LF movement of the operator:

  i Quanti ne sono stati fotografati ___ nudi?
     'How many of + them have been photographed ___ nude?'
  ii Ne sono stati fotografati molti nudi.
     'Of + them have been photographed many nude.'

If the arbitrary null object involved an operator-variable structure, there would be no reason to expect it to behave differently from these standard cases.

25 In Rizzi (1982, Chapter 4) I suggested that the licensing Infl of null-subject languages is specified [+pronominal]. This assumption is made particularly plausible by the northern Italian dialects in which Agr is phonetically spelled out as a clitic pronoun (see Rizzi 1986 and this volume, Chapter 3, and references cited there). If this is also correct for other types of occurrences of *pro*, then we could assume that the language-specific set of licensers is defined by the assignment of the feature [+pronominal] to designated Case slots in Case-assigning heads: for instance, in null-subject languages the nominative slot in Infl is [+pronominal]; in null-object languages the accusative slot in the Case grid of a verb is [+pronominal]; etc. Assuming the formalization of Case assignment of Chomsky (1986b), the licensing principle would then be that *pro* can occur when it is coindexed with a [+pronominal] Case slot in its governing head. This elaboration, which would make formal licensing closer to the recovery procedure, has no immediate consequences for the discussion in the text and will not be pursued here.

26 This is rather straightforwardly plausible for Infl, given the frequency of structures like *Arriva* 'is arriving' in null-subject languages. Less straightforward is the determination that V is a licenser, given the rather exotic nature of the crucial syntactic evidence (i.e. the facts discussed in Section 1). One possible additional clue is offered to the language learner by the full productivity and frequency of the structures with an understood arbitrary object. Alternatively, the assignment of V to the licensing class could be justified by some other more salient clue available in the primary data. A natural candidate seems to be the presence of clitics: if the trace of (nonanaphoric) clitics is *pro* (Sportiche 1983), the presence of these elements implies that the local head, the verb, is a licenser. The possibility of arbitrary *pro* would then be, in a sense, parasitic on the existence of clitics. Notice that the presence of clitics can be at most a sufficient, not a necessary, condition for V-licensing and *pro arb*: the primary data might offer other salient clues justifying the same conclusion (for instance, Cole 1985 shows that Hindi allows arbitrary object *pro* but lacks object clitics).

27 It follows from this set of assumptions that English represents the unmarked case for the null-subject parameter, the assumption that Infl is a licenser for *pro* being the marked option. This is not necessarily inconsistent with Hyams' (1983) observation that the actual acquisition of English involves an initial stage in which the grammatical system is assumed to be a null-subject language (but see Chapter 11 for a different interpretation of the acquisition facts). This observation simply means, in present terms, that the initial access to the primary data of English justifies the adoption of the marked value. This is by no means logically impossible. Consider, for instance, the following abstract possibility. The initial access is constrained by severe working memory limitations that involve the dropping of various grammatical morphemes (including pronouns) from the initial linguistic representations; this justifies the initial adoption of the marked value. A subsequent, more refined access to the

primary data allowed by an improved memory capacity eliminates the justification for the marked choice; hence, the parameter is reset on the unmarked value. This purely speculative hypothesis is simply meant to suggest that there is no inherent contradiction in assuming that a marked option is chosen before its unmarked counterpart in the actual acquisition process: abstract hypotheses about properties of Universal Grammar give rise to specific predictions about the actual course of acquisition only if paired with explicit assumptions about the actual capacity to access the primary data at different stages of acquisition.

28 The existence of this generalization was originally conjectured by Richard Kayne in a talk at MIT, Fall 1981. Notice that if a genuine generalization exists (see also the diachronic evidence given in Section 4.4), this provides further evidence against the empty operator-variable analysis for the arbitrary case. This analysis could not be extended to cover the expletive case, since variables are intrinsically argumental, in the strong sense that they appear to be restricted to range in the domain of referential arguments (see Chomsky 1981: 327 for relevant discussion). For instance, a variable can be assigned the value of the referential argument *the train*, but not of weather *it* (examples due to Barry Schein):

i ?The train was running too fast [OP [PRO to consider [*e* likely [*e* to stop]]]].
ii *It was raining too heavily [OP [PRO to consider [*e* likely [*e* to stop]]]].

The contrast disappears in control structures:

iii The train was running too fast [PRO to stop in five minutes].
iv It was raining too heavily [PRO to stop in five minutes].

It appears that PRO must be controlled by an argument (it does not matter whether it is a referential argument or a nonreferential 'quasi argument'), whereas a variable can be assigned a value only through a referential argument. An operator-variable structure is therefore excluded *a fortiori* for cases like (52), because of the non-argument status of the element involved. Therefore, the operator-variable analysis for arbitrary objects could not provide a uniform account of the two cases (this argument does not apply to the 'mixed' analysis hinted at in Section 2.2).

29 Whether it is trace or variable depends on what is assumed for ordinary cases of Heavy NP Shift, a question that does not concern us directly here.

30 I leave open the question of the exact formal status of the relation involving an expletive and an extraposed sentential complement, noticing that this relation cannot be simple binding, because of the lack of categorial matching. The contrast in (59) can be reproduced with exceptional Case-marking structures:

i *I consider *ec* to be desirable that S.
ii I consider *ec* to be desirable the perspective that S.

The same analysis holds. Of course, the contrast disappears in tensed clauses:

iii *I consider that *ec* is desirable that S.
iv *I consider that *ec* is desirable the perspective that S.

The impossibility of iv and the contrast with ii naturally suggests an account in terms of the ECP; but this implies that the rightward-moved subject cannot count for antecedent government. This result can be achieved if it is assumed that antecedent government (in fact, government in general) can only take place from a head position. Therefore, a *Wh*-element or trace in Comp (a head position) can antecedent-govern a trace in subject position, but an NP right-adjoined to S or S' (a nonhead position) cannot antecedent-govern; hence, iv is ruled out by the ECP (the desired result follows more straightforwardly from a conjunctive formulation of the ECP, as in Rizzi 1990a).

31 Luigi Burzio points out (personal communication) that the proposed analysis should integrate another difference between the two languages; rightward movement of nonheavy object NPs is much more natural in Italian than in English. In fact, the following parallelism does not seem accidental:

i a Ho invitato *ec* [a partecipare] il presidente.
  b *I invited *ec* [to participate] the president.
ii a Considero [*ec* più intelligente il presidente].
  b *I consider [*ec* more intelligent the president].

The natural conclusion seems to be that ia is well-formed because Italian has a possible null filler for the empty object position, an expletive *pro*. The analysis of (51)a–b is then to be revised to the effect that null expletives should now be allowed to occur in θ-positions vacated by movement (a revision that is independently supported by the possibility of inverting thematic subjects in null-subject languages: *pro ha telefonato Gianni*). Overt expletives would still be restricted to θ-positions, perhaps because, on a par with other lexical material, they can be inserted only at D-Structure, where θ-positions must be filled by arguments (Burzio 1986). If this is correct, then the whole adjacency parameter on Case assignment (Stowell 1981) could reduce to the *pro* parameter. Contrasts like the following one

iii a Gianni vede spesso Maria.
  b *Gianni sees often Maria.

could be dealt with by assuming that accusative Case assignment requires adjacency in Italian as well, but in Italian the object can be moved to the right of the adverb, leaving behind an expletive *pro*. In English, because of the negative setting of the *pro* parameter, the only available device to obtain this order of constituents would be Heavy NP Shift, restricted to heavy objects.

32 Thanks to Bob Ingria for pointing out the possible diachronic implications of my analysis and to Wayne O'Neil for useful discussion of the issue.

33 Some of these verbs could involve a dative controller (e.g. *advise, forbid, teach*). Therefore, when such verbs are involved, the possibility of a null controller could be related to the general option of dropping a dative controller (see footnote 1 and the appendix), and the corresponding examples would not support the *pro* hypothesis. Notice that in such examples as (63)d–f the time reference is specific, a possibility that is available in Italian only for null dative controllers, whereas null direct object controllers require a generic time reference. The conjecture that in previous stages of English true instances of null direct object controllers also required generic time reference is consistent with the data reported in the text, but I have not been able to check its general validity (also see footnote 8). Notice that previous stages of English also allowed a missing arbitrary subject of a causative clause:

i 1429 *Charter in Flasdiek, Mitteleng. Originalurkunden* 75: He ... shall
   discontinue or *make discontinue*, and defect or *make defect* ... the foresaid taile

ii *1560 Peter Whitehorn, Machiavelli's Arte of Warre (1573) 71*: Many times the saying backe, backe hath *made to ruinate* an armie

This construction could involve another instance of V-governed *pro* (in this case in subject position of the causative clause); alternatively, it could arise from the selection of a bare VP, a marked option generally unavailable in Modern English (but see footnote 1 on *help*), but available in the Romance languages (Burzio 1981, 1986; Zubizarreta 1985) and in other Germanic languages (Coopmans 1985).

34 Some speakers find a difference in the degree of ill-formedness of examples like i and ii, ii being better than i:

i *John can force ___ to leave.
ii *John considers ___ clear that Bill is lying.

This difference can be interpreted as follows. Sentence i could only have a structural representation involving V-licensed *pro*, an option not available in contemporary English; ii could also involve a 'Heavy NP Shift' type representation (see the discussion of Section 4.3), which could be made available by relaxing the categorial matching requirement on binding (that is, allowing an S' to bind a null NP). We could then attribute the marginal improvement of the relative grammaticality of ii for some speakers to the marginal availability of this alternative structural option.

35 These examples, often marginal for some lexical choices, generally improve when the main verb is made string-adjacent to the adjective through movement of the embedded subject:

i Ne ritengo [___ responsabile *ec* Gianni].
  'I of+it believe responsible Gianni.'
ii Gliela ritenevo [___ più affezionata].
  'I to+him her believed more affectionate.'

This suggests that reanalysis preferentially applies under string adjacency.

36 Notice that there is no intrinsic incompatibility between *arb* interpretation and unaffected θ-roles:

i Il governo ritiene [la gente stupida].
  'The government considers people stupid.'
ii È spiacevole [PRO$_{arb}$ essere temuti].
  'It is unpleasant to be feared.'

The semantically very close generic NP *la gente* is possible in contexts where the null object is excluded, and PRO$_{arb}$ can receive an unaffected θ-role.

37 It is worth pointing out in this connection that reanalysis must be optional. If it were obligatory, the subject position would become a θ-marked argument of the complex predicate in such examples as (67); hence, an expletive would be excluded from this position. (I assume that an expletive *pro* can occur in a θ-position only when the latter is vacated by movement, as in ia and iia of footnote 31; this possibility does not concern extended chains involving expletives and sentential complements base-generated in extraposed position.) We must assume that when an expletive *pro* appears, reanalysis has not applied. This makes an interesting prediction: an expletive *pro* in subject position should be incompatible with clitic extraction from the small clause (which requires reanalysis). The prediction appears to be correct:

76 *Principles and parameters in the pronominal systems*

    i Gli è difficile ___ [fare questo].
       'It to+him is difficult ___ to do that.'
    ii *Gli ritengo [*pro* difficile ___ [fare questo]].
       'I to+him believe difficult ___ to do that.'

The experiencer of *difficile*, which can be cliticized as a dative in ordinary copular structures like i, cannot be extracted from the small clause across the expletive *pro* subject.

38 Contextual conditions can partially override the affectedness constraint in some cases. This happens when the group referred to by arbitrary *pro* is somehow characterized as affected in the immediate linguistic context. Compare the following examples:

    i *In questo paese, talvolta la polizia trova ___ nudi sulla spiaggia.
       'In this country, sometimes the police find ___ nude on the beach.'
    ii ?In questo paese, un giudice può condannare ___ severamente, se la polizia trova ___ nudi sulla spiaggia.
       'In this country, a judge can convict ___ heavily if the police find ___ nude on the beach.'

The significant improvement of ii might recall parasitic gaps, hence indirectly lending support to the operator-variable analysis. But this conclusion would be incorrect because the improvement effect also holds across discourse, in configurations in which parasitic gap structures are not allowed:

    iii A: È vero che in questo paese un giudice può condannare ___ facilmente per atti osceni?
        'Is it true that in this country a judge can convict ___ easily for obscene behaviour?'
        B: ?Sì, per esempio questo può avvenire se la polizia trova ___ nudi sulla spiaggia.
        'Yes, for instance this can happen if the police find ___ nude on the beach.'

39 Notice that the corresponding construction in Portuguese involves an inflected infinitive with an overtly marked person specification. Agr is not weak in this case; hence, principle (95) should allow a referential interpretation of *pro*. In fact, the equivalent of (94)a is grammatical in Portuguese (Raposo 1987).

40 If reanalysis does not apply. If reanalysis applies, the rule of *arb* interpretation is inapplicable since the assigned θ-role is 'unaffected' (and *arb* interpretation would be incompatible in any event with the 'atmospheric' θ-role of (93)b).

41 This principle has consequences that go beyond the facts at issue. For instance, consider the fact that some languages can use locatives as expletives, but such locatives can only function as non-arguments: for instance, in English, *There arrived a man*, but **There was raining* (note also Dutch *er*, which has a more extended range of uses than English *there* but still does not extend to quasi arguments). This follows from principle (96) and the assumption that quasi arguments are special kinds of arguments, given the natural additional assumption that locatives lack (intrinsic) φ-features, an intrinsic number specification in particular.

    Notice that (95)–(96) define necessary, not sufficient, conditions for argumenthood and referentiality: for instance, English *it* can function as non-argument and quasi argument in spite of the fact that it has a full specification of φ-features.

42 The case of P-licensed *pro* in French, discussed in Zribi-Hertz (1984), appears to involve a definite pronominal (referential) interpretation, but the licensing preposition does not seem able to recover any feature specification of *pro*. Still, it is not inconceivable that the interpretation is somehow related to θ-marking, hence to the head-binding option. Consider the following contrasts:

i a On est parti avec ma voiture.
'We left with my car.'
b Je me suis retrouvé avec [ma voiture à réparer].
'I ended up with my car to repair.'
ii a On est parti avec *pro*.
b *Je me suis retrouvé avec [*pro* à réparer].

The contrast is possibly to be attributed to the fact that *pro* is not a θ-marked complement of the preposition in ib, but the subject of the small clause. If the definite pronominal interpretation of iia is contingent upon θ-marking by the licensing head, it is conceivable to try to extend the proposal for *arb* assignment to this case.

An alternative possibility is suggested by the fact that the P-licensed *pro* is restricted to nonhuman interpretation (that is, it alternates with the overt *lui/elle/eux*, restricted to human interpretation: iia can mean 'with my car', but not 'with my best friend'). This automatically excludes first and second person; hence, the feature of person (third) is determined by default. We thus come close to fulfilling principle (95); however, the determination of the feature of number remains mysterious.

Also see Tuller (1982) on an apparent case of V-licensed *pro* that is formally and interpretively very close to the P-licensed *pro* of French, and Chung (1984) on a more complex case of V-licensed *pro*.

43 Notice that the choice of person as the only recovered specification would give a result indistinguishable from (89)b since *pro* could never function as an argument, because of (96).

How much can be recovered depends in part on the richness of Agr, in the obvious sense that, if a weak Agr lacks a feature specification, this specification is unrecoverable through head binding. The Italian example (94)a illustrates this case. Thus, the actual richness of Agr puts an upper bound on the possible values of the recovery parameter. Within this upper bound, choices would seem to be arbitrary. For instance, German appears to have a richer Agr specification than Faroese, yet the latter instantiates (89)c and the former (89)b (in present terms, German chooses no recovery option, and Faroese chooses recovery of number). According to Milsark (1985), Finnish and Estonian appear to have an equally rich Agr specification, with the verbal conjugation fully differentiated for person and number. Still, the former instantiates (89)d and hence chooses to fully exploit the recovery option, whereas the latter excludes referential uses of *pro* and hence, in present terms, does not recover the person specification. I will leave open the question of whether a tighter relation can be found between richness of Agr and the fixing of the recovery parameter, in addition to the obvious 'upper bound' effect.

I will also leave open the further problems raised by Hebrew (Borer 1983) and Irish (McCloskey and Hale 1984), where the referential use of *pro* appears to be possible for some choices of person and number and impossible for others (the 'analytic paradigms' of Irish).

44 A problem left open by this approach is that an embedded *pro* subject in Chinese, Japanese and Korean appears to be restricted to corefer with the closest superordinate subject (see Huang's 1984 Generalized Control Rule).

Mamoru Saito observes (personal communication) that in Japanese this local A-binding effect is more properly characterized as a preference strategy than as a strict grammatical principle. If this is correct, and the effect can be adequately dealt with as a processing strategy, the decision of not specifying it within the *pro* module would seem to be appropriate. Local A-binding effects on embedded *pro*s appear to be operative in other language types as well; see Torrego (1985).

45 That is, by the occurrence of structures with quasi-argumental and referential *pro*s. The decision to recover features of both person and number is correctly characterized as more marked than the decision to recover number alone by Berwick's (1982) Subset Principle. The assumption made in Section 3.4 concerning optionality also gives the correct result if the recovery of each φ-feature is an independent option. Remember that the recovery of person alone gives rise to a system empirically indistinguishable from one with no recovery at all, as a result of the operation of principle (96) and the intrinsic hierarchization of referentiality and argumenthood (something that is not argumental cannot be referential).

46 Ruwet (1982) notices that in French a dative appears to have a subject-like behaviour in a peculiar epistemic construction:

i Je lui croyais beaucoup d'intelligence.
   'I to+him believed a lot of intelligence.'

Still, this type of structure is not relevant for the question at hand because, even if a *pro* dative were possible in general, its occurrence here would be excluded by the affectedness constraint.

47 Burzio (1981) notices the following contrast:

i Gianni ha fatto telefonare.
   'Gianni made telephone.'
ii *La pioggia ha fatto arrivare in ritardo.
   'The rain made arrive late.'

His interpretation is as follows. In addition to a full sentential complement, *fare* can take a bare infinitive VP. This possibility exists with the intransitive *telefonare*, but not with the unaccusative *arrivare*, because the VP would contain an unbound empty category:

iii ... fare [$_{VP}$ arrivare *ec* ...]

But notice that ii becomes acceptable if the time reference is generic:

iv Talvolta la pioggia fa arrivare in ritardo.
   'Sometimes the rain makes arrive late.'

This fact is interpretable in terms of the analysis I have proposed: if the time reference is generic, representation iii is well-formed with *ec* = *pro* licensed by the (accusative Case-assigning) complex predicate *fare+arrivare*.

48 Mark Baker points out (personal communication) that the variants of (108)c with *themselves* and *each other*, impossible out of context, become quite acceptable if the null goal of *say* is salient in the discourse context, whereas (108)b cannot be salvaged by discourse factors. This recalls the pragmatic interpretability of the null dative in the Italian example (107)b and is expected given the analysis to be developed below.

49 In order to allow *arb* interpretation to be assigned to the null indirect object, we must generalize rule (41) to the effect that it should now apply to any internal θ-role, not just to the direct object θ-role. Of course, this is a welcome consequence.
50 As a matter of implementation, I will assume here that dative is an inherent Case selected by V in the sense just discussed, and realized through the preposition *a*, which is phonetically overt just in case the NP is phonetically overt. Notice that in this system objects and datives differ with respect to the Projection Principle in the way indicated, but not with respect to the *pro* module. *pro* is licensed by a Case-marking V, regardless of whether the assigned Case is structural or inherent; and *arb* can be assigned through the θ-grid of V, regardless of whether V directly θ-marks for the relevant θ-role or selects an autonomous θ-marker (here an inherent Case).
51 This system can express the fact that certain PPs are obligatory by allowing obligatory selection of the independent θ-marker, perhaps a marked option induced by the meaning of certain verbs. Obligatoriness of NP and PP complements would then be different in nature. This is supported by the fact that the two types of obligatoriness behave differently in some cases: Guglielmo Cinque (talk, Scuola Normale Superiore, 1983) has noticed that obligatory PPs can be omitted in question–answer pairs, whereas direct objects must be retained:

   i   Q: Che cosa hai messo sul tavolo?
       'What did you put on the table?'
       A: Ho messo i libri.
       'I put the books.'
   ii Q: Dove hai messo i libri?
       'Where did you put the books?'
       A: *Ho messo sul tavolo.
       'I put on the table.'

3 Three issues in Romance dialectology

In this chapter I would like to address three theoretical issues which are raised by the comparative study of some Romance languages and dialects:

1   What is the status of subject clitics in Romance? How does this affect the analysis of the Null Subject Parameter?
2   The Northern Italian Dialects seem to provide a good case of subject clitic doubling. A major difference between subject and object clitic doubling is that the former seems to systematically violate Kayne's generalization, a major property of the latter. Where does this difference stem from?
3   Recent studies have shown that the Verb Second parameter and the Null Subject parameter interact in an interesting way in some languages. How is this interaction to be expressed?

In the following discussion, I will rely extensively on the very important work that has been done in the 1980s on the Northern Italian Dialects, in particular by Benicà, Brandi, Cordin, Renzi and Vanelli in a series of papers that have brought Romance dialectology back to the fore of modern comparative syntax.

1 Subject clitics and IP positions

It has been argued in various papers (Brandi and Cordin 1981; Kayne 1984, Chapter 10; Rizzi 1986) that the notion subject clitic is syntactically spurious in Romance. A subject clitic, at least in non-inverted constructions, occupies the canonical subject NP position in Standard French, whereas it is the spell-out of the agreement features generated under INFL in the Northern Italian Dialects (henceforth NID). So, two sentences like (1) and (2), in spite of superficial similarities, differ structurally as indicated in (3) and (4):

(1) French: Il mange.
(2) Trentino: El magna.

(3)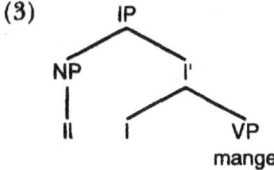

(4)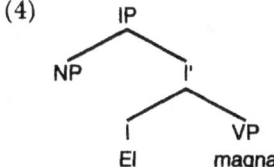

It is only at the PF level that the two pronouns have the identical status of clitics attached to the inflected verb. The important syntactic consequence of this hypothesis is that the NID are Null Subject Languages (NSL) like Italian and Spanish, their peculiar property being that the Agr specification under the inflection licensing *pro* is spelled out independently from the V morphology. French is a non-Null Subject Language, like English and the Continental Scandinavian Languages, its peculiar property being that the overt subject NP, when realized as an unstressed pronominal, is cliticized onto the inflected verb at PF.

This hypothesis, put forth in the references quoted, seems to be essentially correct. Still, I will claim that the status of the clitics in the dialects requires an important refinement with respect to representation (4). Let us first have a look at the reasons which justify the basic hypothesis expressed in (3) versus (4). There are at least six differences that have been argued to support this hypothesis; of these, the first three distinguish French from many but not all of the dialects; the other three seem to neatly discriminate French (here I basically summarize, and expand on, the arguments given in Rizzi 1986):

1 The paradigm of subject clitics in many NID has a typical gapped look: for some person and number specification the clitic is obligatory, for others it may be optional, or may not exist. Out of the 27 dialectal varieties with uncontroversial subject clitics taken into account in Renzi and Vanelli's (1982) survey study, 16 have at least one obligatory gap in the clitic paradigm; of the remaining 11 cases which do not have obligatory gaps, five varieties have fully optional subject clitics for some choice of person and number. So, only six out of 27 varieties appear to have obligatory subjects for all persons and numbers. Moreover, speakers of some such varieties seem to consider the specifications of Is, Ip and IIp subject clitics a matter of strong preference rather than of strict obligatoriness. The largely predominant pattern in NID thus seems to be involve a Scl paradigm with obligatory or optional gaps. In French, of course, there is

no gap, and subject pronouns are equally obligatory for all person and number specifications. This state of affairs is immediately understood, given (3)–(4): Agr may have an obligatory, optional or zero spell-out depending on its feature specification in (4), whereas in (3) a 'gap in the clitic paradigm' would amount to admitting a structure with a null subject position, an option normally illicit in a non-NSL.

2   In many NID the clausal negation is expressed by a preverbal clitic, which may or may not be doubled by a negative adverb. We find three major cases: the negative clitic always precedes the subject clitic (Romagnolo), it always follows the subject clitic (Trentino), it may precede or follow the subject clitic depending on the person and number specification of the latter.

(5) Romagnolo: (Maria) la n ve brisa.
                 'Maria she not comes' (neg. adv)!
(6) Trentino: (La Maria) no la parla.
                 'Maria she not speaks.'
(7) Fiorentino: a (La Maria) la un parla.
                  'Maria she not speaks.'
                b (Te) t'un parli.
                  'You you not speak.'
                c (Te) un tu parli.
                  'You not you speak.'

So, the major observed oscillation in the position of the negative clitic is that it may precede or follow the subject clitic and generally precedes other clitics (in some varieties the negative clitic may even follow object clitics, as pointed out by M. Parry; we will not address this case here):

(8) NP (neg) Scl (neg) cl, ... cl V

If the negative clitic and the subject clitic belong to the same clitic cluster (under Infl in (4)), we will expect this restricted variability as a possible reordering within the cluster. If French has structure (3) and the negative clitic is always under Infl, the order Neg-Scl is correctly excluded:

(9) French: Il ne parle pas.
               'He not speaks.' (neg. adv.)

This ordering criterion separates French from NID such as Trentino and Fiorentino, but fails to distinguish French and the NID in which Scl always precedes the negative clitic, eg., Romagnolo (as in (5)).

3   In many NID the subject clitic is obligatory, whether or not the subject position is filled by an overt NP (e.g., *el* in (4) is obligatory whether or not

the subject NP is overt); so, these are real cases of doubling; in French, given (3), we expect doubling to be impossible. Hence a structure like (10)a must be a case of Left Dislocation; this view is supported by the ungrammaticality of (10)b: quantified NPs, in general, cannot be left-dislocated:

(10)a Jean (,) il n'a rien dit.
　　　'Jean (,) he hasn't said anything.'
　　b * Personne (,) il n'a rien dit.
　　　'Nobody (,) he hasn't said anything.'

In fact, if QR applies from a representation like (11), the trace left in the dislocated position is in an A' position, hence the quantified expression is left without a variable at LF and the structure is ruled out:

(11) *Personne [$_{IP}$ [il] n'a rien dit]]

Cases superficially analogous to (10)b are possible in some of the dialects:

(12)a Piemontese: Gnun l'a dit gnent.
　　　　　　　　'No-one he has said anything.'
　　b Fiorentino: Nessuno l'ha detto nulla.
　　　　　　　　'No-one he has said anything.'

Given a structure like (13), corresponding to (4), QR can apply leaving a well-formed variable in subject position, therefore these cases are possible:

(13) [$_{IP}$ [nessuno] l'ha detto nulla]]

Again, this property fails to distinguish French from some of the dialects, at least at first sight. Benincà reports that in Padovano the same contrast holds as in French (10). Nevertheless, Padovano patterns with NID and against French in other crucial respects:

(14) Padovano: a Giorgio vien.
　　　　　　　　'Giorgio comes.'
　　　　　　　b El vien.
　　　　　　　　'He comes.'
　　　　　　　c * ___ vien.
　　　　　　　　'Comes.'
　　　　　　　d ___ piove.
　　　　　　　　'Rains.'
　　　　　　　e ___ vien Giorgio.
　　　　　　　　'Comes Giorgio.'

French: a' Jean vient.
         b' Il vient.
         c' *___ vient.
         d' *___ pleut.
         e' *___ vient Jean.

(14)d–e show that when the preverbal subject position is not referential, the clitic is omitted in Padovano but not in French. Following Benincà, I will assume that Padovano is a NSL whose Scl occupies the inflectional position in (4), and differs from other dialects in the conditions on spell-out of Agr as a Scl: Agr is spelled out only if it licenses a referential *pro*. So, it is not spelled out when it licenses no *pro* at all (as in (14)a), or a non-referential *pro* (as in (14)d–e). This implies that the Padovano equivalent of (10) must be a LD structure as in French (even though for different reasons: in French the Scl already occupies the subject NP position, so the overt NP must occupy the next available position, the topic in the complementizer system; in Padovano, if the subject clitic is expressed, the subject NP position must be filled by (referential) *pro*, under our assumptions, so that the overt NP must be a topic), hence the Padovano equivalent of (10)b is excluded on a par with the French case.

As I said, properties 1–3 fail to distinguish French from some the NID. So, each of these properties, taken individually, is not criterial to distinguish languages with subject clitics of type (3) or (4) (even though hypothesis (3)–(4) retains an explanatory value here, in that it makes the clustering of the properties of French non-arbitrary).

The following three properties distinguish French from all the NID I know of.

4   Kayne (1984) reports that French subject clitics are marginally acceptable in isolation in quasi-metalinguistic contexts like (15):

(15) French A: Ils ont tout mangé.
                'They have eaten all.'
             B: ? Qui ça, ils?
                'They who?'

This seems to be generally impossible in the dialects. For instance, in Padovano (Benincà, p.c.)

(16) Padovano A: I riva.
                 'They arrive.'
              B: I chi?
                 'They who?'

(cf. the possibility of B with an overt pronominal NP: *lori chi?* 'They who?')

This contrast is amenable to (3)–(4): in French Scl's are bound elements only at PF, whereas they are bound elements in a deeper syntactic sense in the NID; it is not surprising then that producing such elements in isolation leads to a much stronger violation in the latter case.

5   In French, a single subject clitic tolerates what looks like a conjunction of VPs. This is impossible in the dialects, which require a repetition of the clitic:

(17) French: Elle chante et danse.
                'She sings and dances.'
(18) Trentino: La canta e *(la) balla.

If true conjunction of VPs is excluded here (possibly because the verb must move to Infl in the relevant cases), we would be left with sentential conjunction with ellipsis, hence with representations (19):

(19)a [[elle Infl chante] et [___ Infl danse]]
    b *[[___ [la] canta] e [___ [___] balla]].

(19)a is a well-formed case of subject ellipsis in the second conjunct; (19)b should involve ellipsis of Infl without ellipsis of the inflected verb, an option excluded by reasonable assumptions on the theory of ellipsis, as argued in Rizzi (1986).

6   In French, untriggered inversion is restricted to certain verb classes (optimal with unaccusative verbs) and shows the definiteness effect (both properties are violated in (20)a); the NID have free inversion, on a par with standard Italian:

(20)a French: *Il me l'a donné Marie.
                   'There gave it to me Marie.'
    b Fiorentino: E me l'ha dato la Maria.
                   'There gave it to me Maria.'

This is expected if free inversion comes with the cluster of properties determined by the Null Subject Parameter (Rizzi 1982), and the NID, but not French, are genuine NSLs. The same conclusion is supported by the fact that Wh extraction of the subject gives rise to *that-t* violations in French, but not in the NID, nor in Standard Italian, another property related to the NSP in Rizzi (op. cit.).

In spite of these pieces of supporting evidence, there are some indications that an analysis like (3)–(4), with the sharp structural distinction it introduces, is simplistic in other respects. One indication is that both French and some of the NID exhibit inversion of the inflected verb and the Scl in interrogatives:

(21) a French: Avec qui est-elle partie?
        'With whom has she left?'
     b Trentino: Con chi è-la nada via?
        'With whom has she gone away?'

In both cases, we have reasons to believe that the inversion is determined by movement of the inflected verb to Comp: in varieties in which the Wh phrase can co-occur with the element corresponding to English *that*, inversion is incompatible with *that*:

(22) Québec French: a Qui que tu as vu?
        'Who that you have seen?'
     b Qui as-tu vu?
        'Who have you seen?'
     c *Qui qu'as-tu vu?
        'Who that have you seen?'
(23) Romagnolo: a Chi ch t'è vest?
        'Who that you have seen?'
     b Chi è-t vest?
        'Who have you seen?'
     c *Chi ch è-t vest?
        'Who that have you seen?'   (Poggi 1983)

This is immediately explained if inversion is determined by movement of the verb to C, where it competes with the normal filler of that position. So, there are reasons to believe that the inversion process is basically uniform in the relevant NID and in French, an instance of movement of the inflected verb to C.

The problem is this. The verb moves to Infl in examples like (4), as in standard Italian (Roberge 1986). Then Infl with its content moves to C in interrogatives like (21)b and (23). Now, if the Scl is in Infl, and the verb normally raises to this node in declaratives, creating a complex inflection [Scl+V], how can further raising of this complex inflection to C determine the observed inversion? All things being equal, one would expect the order of the two elements internal to Infl to remain constant under further movement of Infl to C.

These observations lead us to conclude that more than one inflectional position must be postulated. Clausal structures like (4) involve a recursive inflectional projection, essentially on the model of complex VPs consisting of combinations of simple verbal projections each headed by a single auxiliary or verb. So, we have a higher inflectional head which is the spell-out of Agr as a Scl, and a lower inflectional head which expresses +Agr, +T and is the usual landing site of V movement (with the moved verb carrying along complement clitics if there are some, as in (24)).

(24)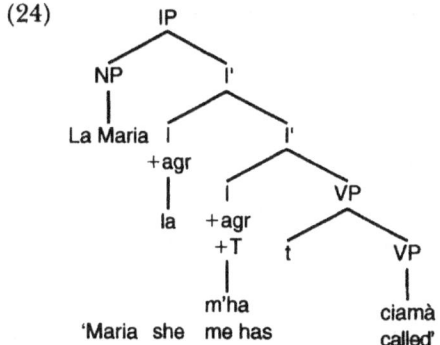

Suppose now that an interrogative must be formed, hence the inflected verb must move to C from the lower inflection (for the reasons to be discussed in Chapter 9). Due to the ECP, it cannot skip the higher Infl, already filled by the subject clitic. Then it must adjoin to this node: if adjunction is to the left, this determines the inverted order; then the complex inflection created in this way [V+Scl] moves to C (as for the fact that the lexical subject cannot occur in the canonical subject position in such inverted structures, see Chapter 9 and references quoted there for a possible explanation in terms of Case Theory).

This analysis may also provide the beginning of an explanation for the following surprising fact. While in French a negation does not affect inversion in interrogatives, in some NID it does: negative interrogatives must remain uninverted:

(25) a Ne part-il pas?
      'Not leaves he (neg. adv.)?'
    b A qui ne l'as-tu pas envoyé?
      'To whom not it have you (neg. adv.) sent?'
(26) Fiorentino: *A chi un l'ha'-tu mandato?
      'To whom not it have you sent?'
(27) Romagnolo: Ve-t veia?
      'Do you go away?'
(28) Romagnolo: Te n ve brisa veia?
      'You don't go away?'
(29) Romagnolo: *N ve-t brisa veia?
      'Don't you go away?'   (Poggi 1983)

Suppose that in these varieties the negative clitic is defined by the syntactic property of belonging to the higher inflectional node and by the PF property of being a proclitic. Then, if on its way to C the inflected verb is forced to adjoin to the higher Infl, and adjunction is to the left, this derivational procedure offers no way to satisfy the PF property of negation (it would always end up in enclitic position). The problem does not arise in French if the verb substitutes into the inflectional head which carries the negative clitic, preserving the negative element in proclitic position, and then moving with it to C.

2 Subject and object clitic doubling

The co-occurrence of Scl and subject NPs in argument position can be looked at as a particular case of the well-known and extensively studied phenomenon of clitic doubling. As has been frequently noticed, e.g. in Roberge (1986), there is a very important asymmetry between subject and complement clitic doubling. Object clitic doubling quite generally obeys the following statement, known as 'Kayne's generalization' ever since Jaeggli (1982):

(30) An object NP may be doubled by a clitic only if there is an independent Case marker for this NP.

The generalization is illustrated by the following examples:

(31)a RP Spanish: Lo vimos *(a) Juan. (Jaeggli 1982)
'We him saw to Juan.'
b Hebrew: beit-a *(šel) ha-mora. (Borer 1984)
'house-her of the teacher.'
c Lebanese: Hkit ma?-o *(la) Karim. (Aoun 1981)
'Talked-I with him to Karim.'
(32) Italian: *Lo abbiamo visto Mario.
'We him saw Mario.'

In River Plate Spanish, Modern Hebrew and Lebanese Arabic, doubling is possible in the relevant constructions (in VPs, NPs and PPs, respectively) when the independent prepositional case assigner is available for the doubled argument; Standard Italian has no Case assigner available for a direct object, hence doubling is excluded.

Still, statement (30) clearly does not hold for subject clitic constructions in the NID and, as Roberge (op. cit.) argues, in some French varieties which pattern with NID as far as the status of subject clitics is concerned, such as Pied Noir French. The latter case is particularly relevant, as Roberge points out, because it has both subject and object clitic doubling, and only object doubling obeys (30).

I would like to suggest that this asymmetry should be derived from an independent fact about subject and object clitics:

(33)a There are expletive subject clitics.
b There are no expletive object clitics.

This asymmetry would seem to be a trivial consequence of the Projection Principle: object positions, contrary to subject positions, must be θ-marked, hence there are no object expletives. In fact things are more complex. Cases like the following, in which the expletive object clitic would correspond to an expletive subject of a small clause in an environment of accusative Case marking, are not ruled out by current formulations of the Projection Principle (the point is illustrated with French examples):

(34) a *Je le crois [t probable que IP].
    'I it believe likely that IP.'
   b *Cela l'a fait [t sembler que IP].
    'This it made seem that IP.'
   c *Cela l'a fait [t pleuvoir].
    'This it made rain.'

The fact that the ill-formedness of (34) is related to the presence of a non-argumental (or quasi-argumental) object clitic, is supported by the observation that these examples become possible if the object clitic is dropped, presumably with a non-argument (or quasi argument) *pro* subject licensed in the way suggested in Chapter 2. So, the inherent argumenthood of object clitics seems to be a fact independent from the Projection Principle. It is conceivable that (33) could still be related directly or indirectly to a suitably sharpened definition of the Projection Principle, but I will not pursue this possibility here, and will just assume that (33) holds of (Romance) clitics.

Once this fact is noticed, the relation between (33) and the observed fact that subject clitics do not obey (30) becomes obvious. I will assume that a chain is a formal object, possibly including different syntactic positions (under the approach developed in Chapter 5), involving exactly one argument and made visible by a Case feature (under the visibility approach developed in Chomsky 1981). An overt subject and a subject clitic in the NID can form a well-formed chain at S-structure (and at LF) because the subject clitic can be an expletive under (33)a, so that the relevant chain will contain exactly one argument, the lexical subject, and will be made visible by nominative Case.

(35) Maria la parla.
    'Maria she speaks.'
    Chain: (Maria, la)

In cases like (32) a similar chain structure for the object would not be possible: the object clitic is an argument under (33)b, so we would end up with an ill-formed chain containing two arguments.

What about the well-formedness of examples like (31)? Given (33), we are led to conclude that two chains are involved here, each one containing exactly an argument, and each one licensed by an independent Case (whence Kayne's generalization):

(36) Lo vimos a Juan.
 'We him saw to John.'
 Chains: (lo), (a Juan)

The outstanding problem with this analysis is why the Theta Criterion is satisfied by (36), as we end up with two argument chains and one Theta role.

The problem is not unprecedented: a very close analogue, at a rather abstract level, is offered by *Easy to please* constructions, which, under the line of analysis initiated in Chomsky (1977a), also involves two argument chains (the lower one including the variable bound by a null operator), each one made visible by an independent Case, and associated to a single Theta role:

(37) John is [t easy [Op [PRO to please t']]].
 Chains: (John, t), (Op, t')

This kind of construction supports Chomsky's (1986a) proposal of a procedure of chain composition: at Logical Form, two chains independently meeting well formedness constraints and visibility requirements (i.e., each containing exactly one argument, each associated to a Case), and in an appropriately local configuration, can be composed. If the Theta Criterion applies only at LF (as a subcase of Chomsky's principle of Full Interpretation), after chain composition, all the arguments of the composed chain will be associated to a Theta role, as required. This analysis immediately extends to (31). The fact that (30) does not hold of subject doubling is derived from (33), as desired.

3 Interactions between null subjects and V-2

Vanelli, Renzi and Benincà (1985) have made the important observation that the Null Subject Parameter and the Verb Second (V-2) Parameter interact in an important way in some languages. Taking up and rephrasing in modern theoretical terms traditional observations in Romance philology, they notice that Old French and the NID in the medieval stages observed the V-2 constraint in main clauses; moreover, the licensing of a null subject in Spec IP was contingent upon the previous creation of a V-2 configuration: i.e., subject drop was possible in (38)a, but not in b (subject in Spec of C position), nor in c (lack of V-2 in an embedded environment):

(38) Old French: a Et ton nom revoel (ge) savoir.
 'And your name want (I) to know.'

b Ge revoel savoir ton nom.
'I want to know your name.'
c ... que ge revoel savoir ton nom.
'... that I want to know your name.'

So, the licensing of null subjects is restricted in this system to the Spec of IP, and to the case in which I has been moved to C in a V-2 configuration.

Building on these observations, Adams (1987) proposed a radical approach to express the link between V-2 and null subjects. Suppose that *pro* is licensed by the appropriate head in the canonical government configuration in the sense of Kayne (1984, Chapter 8) (from left to right in the relevant cases). So, an application of V-2 puts Infl in the required licensing position in Old French. If V-2 has not applied, or it has applied but the subject has been moved to the Spec of C, the licensing environment is not met, and a subject *pro* cannot occur. This analysis can be extended to the licensing of subject *pro* in non-V-2 languages like Modern Italian or Spanish, Adams observes. These languages possess so-called 'free subject inversion', so it may be the case that *pro* is licensed in postverbal position, where it can be canonically governed by Infl from left to right.

In spite of its elegance, this analysis is problematic in several respects. First of all, the idea that *pro* is licensed under canonical government from Infl is both too strong and too weak. All things being equal, it would incorrectly predict the possibility of (at least non-argument) *pro* in modern English and French in constructions in which the inflected verb has moved to C:

(39) a Does it/*pro seem that IP?
b Semble –t-il/*pro que IP?

Moreover, in Modern German, non-argument *pro* appears to be licensed in Spec-IP, no matter whether V-2 has applied or not:

(40) a Es wurde [t getanzt t].
'It was danced.'
b Gestern wurde [*pro* getanzt t].
'Yesterday was danced.'
c ... dass [*pro* getanzt wurde].
'... that was danced.'

In none of these cases does the theory relying on *pro* licensing under canonical government from Infl make the right predictions. In addition to that, there is evidence that in Languages like Italian *pro* is licensed in preverbal, not in postverbal position. Consider for instance the following control paradigm:

(41) a [PRO essendo stanco] Gianni è andato via.
  'Being tired, Gianni left.'
 b *[PRO essendo stanco] è andato via Gianni.
  'Being tired, left Gianni.'
 c [PRO essendo stanco] *pro* è andato via.
  'Being tired, (he) left.'

(41)a–b show that a preverbal but not a postverbal subject is able to control into a clause initial adjunct. (41)c is a structure with a null subject. It is well-formed, which shows that *pro* patterns with overt preverbal subjects with respect to control.

A similar kind of argument is provided by Q-float:

(42) a Tutti i soldati sono andati via.
  'All the soldiers have left.'
 b I soldati sono tutti andati via.
  'The soldiers have all left.'
 c Sono andati via tutti i soldati.
  'Have left all the soldiers.'
 d * Sono tutti andati via i soldati.
  'Have all left the soldiers.'
 e *pro* sono tutti andati via.
  '(They) have all left.'

The contrast (42)a–d shows that preverbal subjects, but not postverbal subjects, are compatible with Q-float from the subject: evidently, the floated quantifier must be c-commanded by the NP it is construed with and postverbal subjects are too low in the structure to license floated quantifiers (a result that immediately follows under Sportiche's 1988a theory of Q-float). (42)e shows that a null subject is consistent with Q-float, a fact which, given the premises, strongly supports the view that *pro* is in preverbal subject position.

In conclusion, *pro* appears to be licensed in preverbal position in Italian, in a Spec-head configuration with the licensing Infl, not in a canonical government configuration.

Going back to the interactions of V-2 and the licensing of *pro*, some Rhaeto-Romance varieties offer a case which is almost the mirror image of Old French. Let us illustrate the point with Gardenese, following the analysis of Benincà (1985–6): in this variety, in embedded clauses null subjects are licensed for some person and number specifications, as in (43)a; in main V-2 clauses, the pronoun is always expressed in initial position (as in (43)b), and also in third position (as in (43)c), except with 2s subjects which are dropped in this environment:

(43) Gardenese: a i ... that (pron) left.   (1s, 1p, 2p)
        a ii ... that pron left.   (2s, 3s, 3p)

b   Pron left yesterday.
c i Yesterday left Pron.   (1s, 3s, 1p, 2p, 3p)
c ii Yesterday left ___ .   (2s)

So, the option of a null subject is considerably reduced in V-2 environments. If case cii can be analysed as involving incorporation of the 2s pronoun into I in C (rather then genuine licensing of *pro*), it is arguable that V-2 destroys the environment for *pro* licensing here. A similar conclusion appears to be justified at least for another Rhaeto-Romance dialect. According to Haiman (1988), the Puter dialect freely allows null subjects in embedded clauses:

(44) Puter: ... cha cernins la via comoda.
       '...that (we) choose the easy way.'

but in post V-2 environments in main clauses only the second person admits a zero form; otherwise, a pronoun cliticized onto the verb is obligatory. Again, V-2 appears to drastically reduce the null subject options in this language.

In conclusion, it appears that all the possible interactions between V-2 and the licensing of null subjects are attested across languages. In some cases, V-2 creates the environment for the licensing of *pro*, in others it destroys the environment, and in other cases still, V-2 leaves things unaffected. More precisely, we have found the following:

I   V-2 creates the environment for *pro*: Old French, Medieval stages of MID.
II   V-2 destroys the environment for *pro*: Gardenese, Puter (at least for certain grammatical specifications).
III *Pro* is licensed whether or not V-2 applies: German (only non-argument *pro*), Icelandic (only non-argument and quasi argument *pro*: Platzack 1987).
IV   *Pro* is not licensed whether or not V-2 applies: English, Continental Scandinavian.

Building on Sportiche's (1988b) approach to Case, it is possible to slightly modify the theory of *pro* presented in Chapter 2 by assuming that a given head may be a formal licenser for *pro* either in a Spec-head configuration, or in a government configuration (understanding now 'government' as 'local c-command', hence a relation not including Spec-head), the choice between the two configurations being a binary parameter to be fixed for each licensing head (see Roberts 1993a for a detailed approach along these lines). The observed state of affairs is now expressible as follow: if Infl is a licenser under government, we will have *pro* only when the government configuration is created by V-2, as in case I; if Infl is a licenser under

Spec-head uniquely, V-2 will destroy the licensing configuration, as in case II; if C is a licenser under government, the licensing of *pro* in Spec IP will be possible no matter whether V-2 has applied or not, as in III (and in this case *pro* will typically be non referential, as the licensing C is normally not endowed with overt identifying features, under the theory of Chapter 2); if neither C nor Infl is a licenser, we will have case IV, no occurrence of subject *pro*.

In spite of all the observed variation, there is one fact that remains quite solid in the varieties considered: *pro* is not licensed in initial position in V-2 structures:

(45) German: *pro wurde [t getanzt t].
 'Was danced.'

Notice that we cannot simply say that V-2 cannot be satisfied by a null element: other types of null elements in Spec of C can clearly satisfy the V-2 constraint, e.g. an intermediate Wh trace, as in (46) (a case of embedded V-2, example from Haider 1986) or the discourse bound null operator (Huang 1984), as in (47):

(46) Welches Problem, meinte er damals, [t wurde [niemand loesen koennen]]?
 'Which problem thought he then would nobody solve can?'
(47)a OP hab' [t ihn schon gesehen t].
 '(I) have him already seen.'
 b OP hab' [ich t schon gesehen t].
 '(Him) have I already seen.'

The absence of *pro* licensing in environment (45) could be an accident of the sample of languages we have considered, in which case there is nothing to add. We can describe this fact by assuming that none of the systems considered admits a licensing C in the Spec-head configuration. But suppose the fact is not accidental: could there be a reasonable approach excluding (45) in a principled manner? It is a fact that only empty categories in A position allow a natural classification in terms of the features +-anaphoric, +-pronominal: we don't seem to find the equivalents of PRO, NP-t or variable in A' position, the only relevant distinction in the A' system apparently being the one between intermediate trace and null operator, as in (46)–(47). Then, if the Spec of C is, in general, an A' position, and *pro* is defined as –anaphoric, +pronominal (Chomsky 1982b), *pro* may simply not be definable in this position (but see Chapters 10 and 11 for various complications).

Conclusions

1 Subject clitics are generated under an inflectional head in the NID; in order to account for Subject clitic inversion in interrogatives we must postulate that they occupy an inflectional position distinct from and higher than the one reached by the inflected verb in declarative clauses.
2 The fact that Subject clitic doubling in the NID does not obey Kayne's generalization can be related to the fact that subject clitics, contrary to object clitics, can be expletives.
3 V-2 interacts in various ways with the licensing of *pro* subjects. In some cases it creates a licensing environment, in others, it destroys a licensing environment, in others still, the application of V-2 does not affect the licensing of *pro*. In language like Italian, *pro* is licensed in preverbal subject position. All these properties can be made to follow from a simple extension of the licensing theory presented in Chapter 2.

4 Some notes on Romance cliticization*

The study of Romance cliticization must, at least, deal with the following four questions:

1   What is the categorial status of clitics?
2   What makes clitics move?
3   What is the landing site of cliticization?
4   What determines encliticization and procliticization?

These questions are obviously interrelated: a proper understanding of the inherent constitution of clitics may shed light on the causal force triggering cliticization and on the surface position of clitics; the identification of the landing site, in interaction with assumptions on verb movement, may account for the choice of the enclitic versus proclitic position, etc.

In this chapter, I would like to briefly touch upon questions 1 and 2, and then address in more detail questions 3 and 4, putting special emphasis on the last.

1 Clitics as V-related determiners

The central theoretical problem raised by Romance clitics is the mismatch between form and interpretation. Interpretively, they appear to function as definite pronouns, hence express arguments at LF; on the other hand, they do not occupy a plausible argument position in the pronounced representation, where they seem to be attached to the string of inflectional heads which defines the configurational structure of the sentence. The tie to arguments is not purely interpretive: it is further strengthened by the fact that Romance clitic systems often are formally close to determiner systems, the formal markers of arguments. For instance, in French, accusative pronominal clitics are identical to definite articles; in Italian the feminine forms are identical and the masculine forms close or identical:

---

* This paper was prepared for a meeting of the Eurotyp Group on Clitics, The European Science Foundation. 15–17 October, 1993, Durham Castle.

(1)

	French			Italian	
	Det	Cl		Det	Cl
Masc	le	le	Masc Sing	il/lo	lo
Fem	la	la	Fem Sing	la	la
Plur	les	les	Masc Plur	i/gli	li
			Fem Plur	le	le

This resemblance makes it plausible to formally identify clitics as definite D°s, an identification that is further supported by the fact that (accusative) clitics express definite arguments; but the identification cannot be complete because of the existing formal mismatches between the two series and the fact that clitics morphologically encode more information than determiners: determiners are invariable for Case, while clitics typically manifest Case distinctions (four-way distinctions in Italian (Accusative, Dative, Genitive, Locative: *lo/la/li/le, gli/le, ne, ci*) and French: (*le/la/les, lui, en, y*)). Moreover clitic systems morphologically manifest person features (Italian *mi, ti, lo*; French *me, te, le*) and the distinction between pronouns and anaphors (*lo, si; le, se*) while determiners do not.

Assuming that Romance clitics (or, possibly, a subset of them) are somehow special determiners, what makes them move to a verbal landing site? The feature-checking system of the Minimalist Program (Chomsky 1993) offers promising concepts and technology to precisely address this question (in the following discussion we omit refinements made possible by the distinction between interpretable and uninterpretable features, subsequently introduced in Chomsky 1995, Chapter 4).

In the system of Chomsky (1993), inflectional heads such as AgrS, T, etc., have a dual function: they check morphological features of tense and agreement on the verb moving to them as a head, and Phi features and Case features of DPs moving to their specifiers (definiteness or specificity may also be properties subjected to a similar checking procedure, see Corver and Delfitto 1993; Sportiche 1996). The feature checking system is plausibly to be extended to the internal structure of the nominal system, e.g., in a DP like the following:

(2)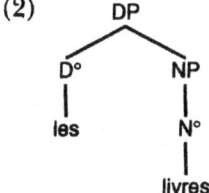

The features morphologically expressed on D and/or on N presumably are to be checked, or mutually licensed, by having N move to D, possibly at S-structure in some languages and at LF in others (for discussion see Longobardi 1994; Siloni 1996, 1997), possibly with the mediation of a richer functional structure in the DP (Cinque 1995, Chapter 10). Consider now the case in which a determiner remains lexically defective, i.e., it does not take an NP complement:

(3)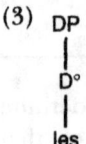

Here D could not have its features checked DP-internally, hence it should move to find a checker elsewhere in the structure. This may be, in essence, what a clitic is (Abney 1987). More precisely, we will say that Romance determiners are either N-related or V-related; N-related determiners enter representations such as (2) and have their Phi features checked by a nominal head; V-related determiners enter representations such as (3) and have their features checked by a verbal head; a clitic is a V-related determiner (if Corver and Delfitto 1993 are correct in assuming that clitics enter a representation like (2) but with a null pronominal NP, their property of 'V-relatedness' would either be a primitive, or should be derived from the impossibility of having the null pronominal NP check the D features DP-internally). Nothing excludes this possibility in Chomsky's (1993) system, as far as we can see: in his discussion, verbal inflectional heads check features morphologically expressed on verbs in local head–head configurations and features morphologically expressed on nominal expressions in Spec/head configurations, but nothing enforces this particular pairing between kinds of features and checking configurations; in particular, nothing excludes checking of a nominal feature by a verbal head in a local head–head configuration.[1,2]

Why is the clitic forced to move syntactically? Two approaches have been explored in the literature. The first (Belletti 1994) exploits the *richness* of the clitic in morphosyntactic features with respect to other nominal expressions. The clitic is endowed with strong, overtly realized grammatical and Case features, which are plausibly to be checked in the overt syntax according to Chomsky's (1993) system. In this view, the same nominal features may be strong or weak depending on the bearer: they are weak in N-related determiners and strong in V-related determiners, which must move syntactically. The second approach assumes that nominal features in the DP system are uniformly weak for both N-related and V-related determiners, and exploits the arguable *poverty* of the DP headed by the clitic to explain syntactic movement. In Chomsky's system, auxiliaries in English move in the syntax to AgrS even if the corresponding features are weak in this language. The reason is that auxiliaries, being semantically empty, are not visible in the LF component, hence they are forced to move in the overt syntax to ensure proper checking. Suppose that the relevant divide is not 'being provided with semantic content' (a rather slippery notion, hardly compatible with the fact that modals pattern with aspectual auxiliaries), but is rather 'being endowed with lexical content': only elements endowed with lexical content are accessible to LF movement. So auxiliaries and modals in English must move in the syntax to check their verbal features because they are not endowed with lexical content, hence they cannot undergo LF movement. Friedemann (1992: footnote 8) has extended this analysis to the obligatory syntactic movement of bare quantifiers in French, as opposed to quantifiers endowed with a lexical restriction:

(4)a Jean a mangé tout le gâteau.
   'Jean has eaten all the cake.'
  b Jean a tout mangé.
   'Jean has all eaten.'

Analogous proposals have been developed in Corver and Delfitto (1993) and in a preliminary version of Cardinaletti and Starke (1994) for the case of cliticization. In the terms of the background sketched out in this paragraph, one could think that the V-related determiner in the defective structure (3) must move out of its XP in order to have its features checked in the syntax, LF movement not being available because of the lack of lexical content. We will not try to choose here between the approaches based on richness and on poverty; let us simply note in passing that they are not strictly inconsistent with each other, in that they refer to richness and poverty of different properties (of feature specification and phrase structure realization, respectively), so that it may be possible to reconcile them.

2 On the landing site problem

In this section I would like to mention some empirical problems arising for the traditional approach to the landing site of cliticization, and then reconsider the issue based on the background sketched out in 1.

The traditional assumption about the landing site of clitics, spelled out in Kayne (1975) and much subsequent work, is that Romance clitics adjoin to the verb. This captures the obviously correct fact that Romance clitics basically are verbal clitics, they don't attach to nouns, adjectives or prepositions. Still, this approach has to face several problems:

1 In compound tenses and passive sentences, clitics attach to the aspectual or passive auxiliary, not to the lexical verb in the participial form. This holds for Italian and many other Romance varieties (some notable

exceptions are Piedmontese, (Kayne 1991; Valdôtain, Roberts 1993b; Romanian, Dobrovie-Sorin 1994; and more systematically Brazilian Portuguese, Bianchi and Figueiredo-Silva 1993):

(5)a Gianni lo ha messo sul tavolo.
 'Gianni it has put on the table.'
 b * Gianni ha messolo sul tavolo.
 'Gianni has put it on the table.'

Italian is particularly significant in this respects in that it shows that there is no intrinsic incompatibility between the participial form and cliticization: in participial clauses (Belletti 1990, Chapter 3; Belletti 1994), clauses headed by a verb in the participial form with no auxiliary verb, the clitic can attach to the participle:

(6) Messolo sul tavolo, Gianni è uscito.
 '(Having) put (past part) it on the table, Gianni left.'

So, the traditional approach cannot simply be salvaged by excluding the participial form from the class of verbal landing sites (e.g. by attributing it a quasi-adjectival character).

2 Clitics can generally attach to infinitival verbs, but there are some special infinitival environments which resist cliticization.

2.1 Infinitives embedded under the causative verb (cf. Guasti 1993 and references cited there):

(7)a Gianni lo farà scrivere a Piero.
 'Gianni it will make write to Piero.'
 b *?Gianni farà scriverlo a Piero.
 'Gianni will make write it to Piero.'

If the landing site of cliticization was any verbal form, this restriction would not be expected.

2.2 Analogously, in the somewhat special cases in which passive can apply across a restructured complex (only with aspectual verbs, and at a rather literary level: see Rizzi 1982), the clitic cannot remain on the embedded verb:

(8)a La chiesa fu cominciata a costruire sulla collina nel 1736.
 'The church was begun to build on the hill in 1736.'
 b La chiesa vi fu cominciata a costruire nel 1736.
 'The church there was begun to build in 1736.'

c *La chiesa fu cominciata a costruirvi nel 1736.
   'The church was begun to build there in 1736.'

2.3 We find the same restriction in the *Easy to please* construction:³

(9) a Questi fiori sono difficili da sistemare sul tavolo.
       'These flowers are difficult to range on the table.'
    b *?Questi fiori sono difficili da sistemarvi.
       'These flowers are difficult to range there.'
    c E' difficile sistemarvi questi fiori.
       'It is difficult to range there these flowers.'
(10) a Questo teorema è difficile da spiegare agli studenti.
       'This theorem is difficult to explain to the students.'
     b *?Questo teorema è difficile da spiegargli.
       'This theorem is difficult to explain to him.'
     c E' difficile spiegargli questo teorema.
       'It is difficult to explain to him this theorem.'

3   The previous examples show that some verbal forms/structures are not suitable landing sites for clitics. A problem of the opposite kind for the traditional approach is raised by the Romance varieties in which the clitic clearly is not attached to the verb, as some non-verbal material intervenes:

(11) Nu'l mai văd.   (Romanian)
     'I not him anymore see.'
(12) N'en pas parler.   (Literary French)
     'of+it not to+speak.'

An extreme case of intervention is possible in Galician (Uriagereka 1995; see also Rouveret 1992 on literary Portuguese), which allows the subject NP to intervene between a clitic and the inflected verb in some environments:

(13) Cantas veces a Pedro veu!
     'How many times her Pedro saw!'

If all and only verbal forms were suitable landing sites for clitics, neither the restrictions of problems 1 and 2 nor the options of problem 3 would be expected. Restricting cliticization to a subset of verbal forms would not account for problem 3. Moreover, this approach would offer no insight as to what factors determine the attachment of the clitic to the left or to the right of the verbal form in different environments. A more promising revision of the traditional approach is to take advantage of the current assumptions on the articulated clausal structure along the following lines:

(14) The landing site of the clitic is a V-related functional head.

Where V-related means possessing features to be checked by the verb, in the sense of Chomsky (1993) (or in the extended projection of the verb, in the sense of Grimshaw 1991). (14) accounts for the fact that it is not the case that any verb is a possible landing site for cliticization, but only a verb associated with some functional head; the statement 'V-related' captures the correct part of the traditional account, i.e. the fact that Romance clitics are essentially verbal clitics. (11), (12) and (13) are also consistent with this approach if the verb has not raised to the relevant functional head in the syntax, but it will at LF, along the lines of Chomsky (1993).

However, (14) is still insufficient. Given a Split-Infl type approach, the verb in the infinitival or participial form is not a pure lexical category, but is already a complex form arising from the association of a lexical category with a functional head, the infinitival inflection -r (Raposo 1986b; Kayne 1991), or the participial head -t-, which in turn combines with its own agreement morpheme (Belletti 1990).

So, the landing site must be expressed in a more selective manner than (14). In order to further narrow down the identification of the relevant functional head, let us focus on some properties of the three infinitival constructions disallowing cliticization. They do not (easily) allow a clausal negation to occur (compare (15)a, c, e) with the nearly synonymous constructions (15)b, d, f which permit negation):

(15) a Il medico ha fatto (??non) uscire Gianni.
  'The doctor made (not) go out Gianni.'
 b Il medico ha fatto sì che Gianni non uscisse.
  'The doctor made so that Gianni didn't go out.'
 c L'altare fu continuato a (*non) restaurare per più di un secolo.
  'The altar was continued (not) to restore for more than one century.'
 d Continuarono a non restaurare l'altare per più di un secolo.
  'They continued not to restore the altar ... '
 e Questo problema è facile da (*non) capire.
  'This problem is easy to (not) understand.'
 f E' facile non capire questo problema.
  'It is easy not to understand this problem.'

They are also incompatible with an embedded aspectual auxiliary (this property is not testable in the case of restructuring complexes undergoing passivization because aspectual verbs are already incompatible with an embedded aspectual auxiliary).

(16) a *?La fretta mi ha fatto aver già finito dopo un minuto.
  'The haste made me have already finished after one minute.'

b La fretta ha fatto sì che io avessi già finito dopo un minuto.
  'The haste made so that I had already finished after one minute.'
c *Questo problema è difficile da aver già risolto dopo un minuto.
  'This problem is difficult to have already solved after one minute.'
d E' difficile aver già risolto questo problema dopo un minuto.
  'It is difficult to have already solved this problem after one minute.'

This suggests the following approach: infinitival verbs in the causative construction, in passivizable restructuring complexes, in the (Italian) *Easy to please* construction, as well as participles in complex tenses, head impoverished clausal structures disallowing negation, aspectual auxiliaries and not providing a landing site for cliticization. If we assume that functional projections of the clausal system are hierarchically organized as follows (Belletti 1990; Chomsky 1991),

(17)
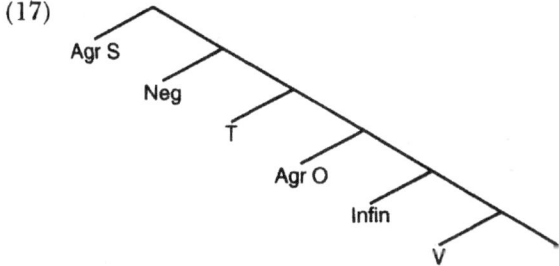

then the absence of negation suggests that the relevant structures start at a level lower than the NegP. The absence of aspectual auxiliaries may suggest that the structure starts at a level lower than T, if aspectual auxiliaries are intimately connected with T (have obligatory T-features, as in Guasti 1993, and this volume, Chapter 12).

As for the AgrO projection, the possibility of passivization in (8) may be interpreted as showing that AgrO is not present in these structures: assuming that AgrO is responsible for accusative case assignment or checking (Chomsky 1993), if it were present in (8) we would have a case-marked NP-trace, in violation of the chain condition (or economy). Guasti (1993: 54) argues along similar lines that the infinitival complement embedded under the causative verb lacks AgrO; she shows, in particular, that the causative verb is directly responsible for case assignment of the embedded object. This would not be expected if the embedded structure were endowed with an autonomous AgrO projection. Even though direct evidence of this sort is not available for the *Easy to please* construction, nothing forces us to postulate an AgrO projection there either. So, it seems reasonable to conjecture that the lack of AgrO may be a general property of the infinitival constructions disallowing cliticization. On the other hand, these constructions plausibly contain an Infin projection (Kayne 1991), as they display infinitival morphology which presumably requires a licenser. What the evidence reviewed establishes so far is that Infin is not a suitable landing site for clitics, the landing site must be a functional projection higher than Infin in (17).

Starting now from the top of (17) in the effort to narrow down the landing site of cliticization, we observe that French infinitives provide evidence that the landing site must be lower than AgrS: clitics can be adjacent to a verb which has not raised to AgrS, as is shown by its respective order with *pas*, the Spec of NegP:

(18) Ne pas le connaître ...
      'To not it know ...'

Moreover, if Pollock is right in interpreting alternations like (19)a–b as involving optional movement of the lexical verb to a functional head lower than NegP, in terms of (17) his proposal becomes: the lexical verb may move to T (as in (19)b) or stay in AgrO (as in (19)a):

(19)a Souvent lui donner des cadeaux.
       'To often to him/her give presents.'
    b Lui donner souvent des cadeaux.
       'To to him/her give often presents.'

But then the possibility of (19)a suggests that the clitic can remain lower than T. Independent evidence that clitics can survive in a position lower than T is offered by language acquisition. Around the age of two, children learning French typically use infinitives as root declaratives (*Papa manger gâteau*, 'Daddy eat cake'), a construction which involves a truncated structure not including T°, as argued in Chapter 12. Now, judging from Friedemann (1992), object clitics appear to be possible in root infinitives (we find in natural production corpora utterances like *Les mettre dans le garage*, 'Them put into the garage'), hence, their landing site must be lower than T.

In conclusion, the landing site is higher than Infin and lower than T in (17). We than conclude that in the core Romance case clitics move to AgrO.

This conclusion is fully natural from the theoretical perspective sketched out in Section 1. If the triggering force of clitic movement is the checking of its features in the overt syntax, and accusative Case is checked in the AgrO projection (Chomsky 1993), then, at least for accusative clitics, the landing site should be AgrO (as in Belletti 1994). On the other hand, if we assume that accusative Case can only be checked in a Spec-head configuration (as in Friedemann and Siloni 1997), then the picture is slightly more complex: the accusative clitic and the DP it heads must move to the specifier of AgrO, for Case checking; from there the clitic can cliticize via head movement to the next higher head:

(20)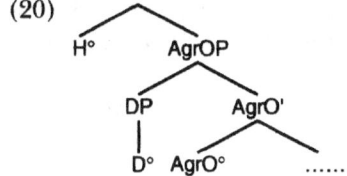

What is H°? Under usual assumptions on the hierarchical order of projections (e.g., (17)), the natural candidate would be T°; but in a feature checking approach it would be natural to think that the host head of cliticization can bear the features that the clitic manifests, hence is an Agr-type head (Haegeman 1991; Belletti 1994). Moreover, we have found empirical reasons for assuming that clitics do not have to go as high as T. So, we may think that AgrO can undergo a recursion upwards (as Agr nodes seem to be allowed to in other cases: see, on AgrS, Chapter 3 of this volume, Belletti 1990; Cardinaletti and Roberts 1991) and this extra Agr node is the landing site of cliticization (Haegeman 1991 motivates an extensive use of Agr recursion to provide landing sites for clitics in West Flemish. Sportiche's 1996 approach also involves a sequence of Agr-like heads expressed by the clitics). As a pure mnemonic label, we will call it Agr_{cl}. As for clitic clusters, we will make the simplifying assumption that more than one clitic can attach to this head (but see Laenzlinger 1993, 1998 for relevant discussion).

Consider now participial heads and projections. Following Belletti (1990), we will assume that the structure of the participial phrase selected by the aspectual auxiliary is the following:

(21)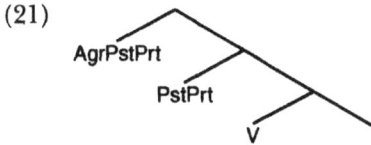

Following Friedemann and Siloni (1997), we do not identify AgrPstPrt with AgrO (see also Uriagereka 1995): the latter, the head responsible for accusative Case assignment, is a higher functional projection associated with the aspectual auxiliary in compound tenses (see the reference quoted for detailed empirical evidence). So, a structure involving a compound tense like (5) has a representation combining (17) (with V = aspectual auxiliary and no Infin, as we are considering a finite clause) and (19), which is selected as a complement by the auxiliary.

The ungrammaticality of (5)b shows that, in addition to Infin and V, PstPrt and AgrPstPrt are also V-related heads which don't function as landing sites for clitics. Under the Friedemann and Siloni (1997) proposal on the position of AgrO, this is expected: the participial phrase selected by an aspectual auxiliary lacks AgrO, so that it offers no landing site for the clitic in the normal case. As for past participial (small) clauses like (6),

Belletti (1990, 1994) argues that they contain an AgrO layer in Italian, as is shown by the fact that accusative Case is assigned, so that the possibility of cliticization is expected.

If the normal cliticization site seems to be provided by a recursion at the AgrO level, certain 'exceptional' Romance varieties allowing a larger set of cliticization sites can now be described in a concise manner as allowing the special Agr_{cl} head as a recursion of Agr nodes different from AgrO. So, the varieties allowing cliticization to the past participle in ordinary clauses (e.g., Piedmontese) would involve recursion at the Agr Past Part layer;[4] combining Uriagereka (1995), Shlonsky (1994) and Starke (1993), we could think that the Western varieties allowing clitics in pre-subject position (see (13)) involve recursion at the level of Agreement in the C system (Starke 1993 claims that AgrC is the normal landing site for clitics in Slovac).

3 Enclisis and proclisis

In Italian, clitics immediately precede finite verbs (in indicative, subjunctive and conditional forms) and immediately follow non-finite verbs (in infinitives, gerunds, past participles):

(22) a La conosco. (ind)
  'I her know.'
 b ... che la conosca. (subj)
  '... that I her know.'
 c La conoscerei. (cond)
  'I her would know.'
(23) a Conoscerla. (inf)
  'to know her.'
 b Conoscendola. (ger)
  'knowing her.'
 c Conosciutala. (part)
  '(having) known her.'

Affirmative imperatives take enclitic forms (this generalization appears to hold very systematically across the different Romance varieties, see Rooryck 1992), while negative imperatives are the only forms allowing both the enclitic and proclitic position:

(24) a Prendilo!
  'Take it!'
 b Non prenderlo!
  'Don't take it!'
 c Non lo prendere!
  'Don't it take!'
(25) a Prendiamolo!
  'Let's take it!'

b Non prendiamolo!
     'Let's not take it!'
   c Non lo prendiamo!
     'Let's not it take!'
(26)a Prendetelo!
     'Take(2pl) it!'
   b Non prendetelo!
     'Don't take(2pl) it!'
   c Non lo prendete!
     'Don't it take(2pl)!'

Kayne (1991) proposes to derive the enclitic position in the following manner: the clitic does not have the option to right-adjoin, a possibility that is excluded in principle (see also Kayne 1994 for relevant discussion); its only option is to be left-adjoined to some inflectional head I (T or Agr); the non-finite verb skips that head and moves further (*e* is the verbal trace in (27)):

(27) ...V...cl+I...[e]...

this gives the V cl order. The verb and the clitic do not form a constituent in this analysis; following a suggestion due to Esther Torrego, Kayne observes that this analysis explains why encliticization is not possible with finite forms (in Italian and other central Romance varieties): the verb must pick up the finite morphology of tense and Agr, hence the verb cannot skip the head which the clitic is attached to (whether this is T or Agr is not crucial here).

I would like to keep the essence of this analysis while modifying it in one important respect. I believe there is clear evidence that the non-finite verb and the enclitic form a syntactic constituent.

1   On the one hand, Benincà and Cinque (1990) show that there is a higher degree of cohesion between the verb and the enclitic than between the proclitic and the verb: semantically close verbs hosting a clitic can be coordinated with proclisis, but not with enclisis:

(28)a Gianni lo legge e rilegge infinite volte.
      'Gianni it reads and rereads infinite times.'
   b *Per leggerlo e rileggere infinite volte.
     'To read it and reread infinite times.'
   c *Per leggere e rileggerlo infinite volte.
     'To read and reread it infinite times.'

The only possibility with enclisis is to repeat the clitic in both conjuncts:

(29) Per leggerlo e rileggerlo infinite volte.
     'To read it and reread it infinite times.'

Moreover, proclitics may sometimes be coordinated under special conditions, but enclitics cannot. I agree with Benincà and Cinque (op. cit.) that even proclitics generally disallow conjunctive coordination in Italian; but Sportiche (1997) noticed that disjunctive coordination of proclitics is quite acceptable in French and a clear improvement is detectable in Italian; so, with respect to disjunctive coordination, there is a sharp asymmetry between encliticization and procliticization:

(30) a ? Chiunque abbia lanciato questo appello, lo o la dobbiamo aiutare.
 'Whoever sent this appeal, we him or her must help.'
 b *Chiunque abbia lanciato questo appello, dobbiamo aiutarlo o la.
 'Whoever sent this appeal, we must help him or her.'

Benincà and Cinque assume that the clitic and its verbal host form a syntactic constituent in both cases, but only in the cases of enclisis are the verb and the clitic syntactically fused to form a single word (as is also witnessed by the graphic convention); so, (28)b–c and (30)b are ruled out by the coordinate structure constraint applying on the fusion (incorporation) operation.[5]

2   Moreover, clear syntactic evidence that the verb and the enclitic form a unit is that the clitic is carried along by the auxiliary in the so-called Aux-to-Comp construction (Rizzi 1982):

(31) Avendola Gianni restituita al direttore, ...
 'Having it Gianni given back to the director.'

That the Aux actually moves to C here is suggested by the complementarity with an overt non-finite complementizer, which is consistent with the unmoved control structure (32)c:

(32) a Ritengo esser lui una brava persona.
 'I believe to be he a good guy.'
 b *Ritengo di esser lui una brava persona.
 'I believe of to be he a good guy.'
 c Ritengo di PRO essere una brava persona.
 'I believe of PRO to be a good guy.'

That the subject actually occupies the highest subject position (and not some lower A-position) is suggested by the fact that it precedes negative adverbials typically occurring in the Spec of the NegP (Belletti 1990) and sentence adverbials of the *probably/certainly* type:

(33) a Non avendo Gianni mai / più trovato la soluzione, ...
 'Not having Gianni ever / anymore found the solution, ...

b Avendo Gianni probabilmente / certamente trovato la
soluzione, ...
'Having Gianni probably / certainly found the solution, ...

The contrast between the acceptability of (31) and the sharp ungrammaticality arising if the clitic is stranded in post subject position

(34) **Avendo Gianni la restituita al direttore.
'Having Gianni it given back to the director, ...'

is not expected under hypothesis (27) (unless some auxiliary hypotheses are made and/or the construction is reanalysed: see Kayne 1991: footnote 27, who also observes that the impossibility of (34) is fully general in Romance, see below).

Under usual assumptions, (27) is excluded by the Head Movement Constraint (ultimately, by the ECP under Relativized Minimality), and this appears to be the empirically correct result. So, we will abandon (27) while trying to retain the spirit of Kayne's approach (encliticization arises when the verb jumps past the cliticization site).

Consider the following empirical generalization, which we believe is consistent with the observed cases:

(35) Generalization: We have enclisis only if
   i the verb is morphologically complete under the cliticization site, and
   ii the verb must move at least as far as the cliticization site.

Clause ii holds by necessity: If no rightward/downward movement of the clitic is allowed (perhaps under a general ban against such movements: Kayne 1994), then the order V-cl implies that the verb has moved (leftward, upward) at least as far as the cliticization site. Clause i is less obvious; we say that a verbal form is *morphologically complete* at a given point of the checking procedure if all its morphologically overt affixes have already been checked, or licensed; otherwise, it is morphologically incomplete. So, given the representation in (17), repeated here, and the assumption that the landing site of clitics in Italian is at (a recursion of) AgrO in (36),

(36)
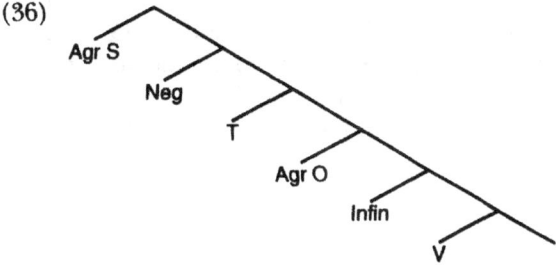

we observe that the infinitival verb fulfils both conditions for enclisis: the infinitival verb is morphologically complete when it reaches AgrO (the infinitival inflection has already been checked at the Infin level); moreover, infinitival verbs in Italian must raise as high as AgrS (in spite of the lack of any overt agreement morphology: Belletti (1990), and Chapter 12), past the cliticization site, hence both conditions are met and we have encliticization. The same holds for participial clauses under Belletti's (1993) analysis, where the verb is morphologically complete already at AgrPrt, a position lower than AgrO, and must move further; the gerundival construction is amenable to the same analysis if the gerundival inflection is checked in a position identical or close to the position of the infinitival inflection (on the special present participial construction see Appendix II). In finite clauses, on the other hand, the verb is morphologically complete only at AgrS (where the overt subject agreement affix is checked); as in this case, morphological completeness is reached past the cliticization site, we do not have enclisis here, in accordance with generalization (35).

Positive imperatives seem to challenge generalization (35): they manifest overt subject agreement, so that the verb should be morphologically complete only under AgrS, apparently past the cliticization point, and under generalization (35) we would expect such structures to pattern with finite forms and disallow enclisis, contrary to fact. On the other hand, (positive) imperatives clearly involve an impoverished structure with respect to ordinary finite clauses: they disallow ordinary clausal negation (as witnessed by the fact that negative imperatives quite generally require special suppletive morphology, Zanuttini 1991, 1997), they cannot occur with subject clitics in Northern Italian Dialects, etc. Moreover, Kayne and Zanuttini argue that imperatives do not include the tense projection. If T is essential to select Agr_{cl}, then the impoverished imperative IP does not provide an IP internal landing site for clitics. But then, why are clitics allowed to appear at all in imperatives? Imperatives plausibly involve movement of V to the C system (presumably for reasons akin to V to C movement in main questions, as discussed in Chapter 9, that is, for the licensing of a (null) operator under some kind of Imperative Criterion); then, we may think that imperatives exploit an IP-external landing site for clitics in the C system, the natural candidate being (the usual recursion of) AgrC.

If this line of analysis is on the right track, then the cliticization site here is higher than the layer at which the verb is morphologically complete (AgrS), hence we now expect encliticization under (35). So, the general encliticization in positive imperatives is not exceptional, once the impoverished structure of the construction is recognized.

Consider now the contrast between positive and negative imperatives, starting from the French case:

(37)a Mange-le.
　　　'Eat it.'

b Ne le mange pas.
      'Don't it eat.'
   c Mange-le pas.
      'Don't eat it.'

One may think that the negative head *ne* licenses T (somehow in the spirit of Zanuttini 1991), which in turn licenses AgrO recursion, and hence provides a 'lower' site for cliticization, making procliticization possible (and necessary, if cliticization must be to the closest available site in French) as in (37)b; the zero variant of *ne* does not seem to have this licensing capacity, though. Hence clitic movement to the C system is the only possibility in (37)c (possible in some varieties of colloquial French), with encliticization in accordance with (35).

Negative imperatives in Italian are more complex. First of all, the paradigm of negative imperative is peculiar: the second person singular form is morphologically identical to the infinitive (*Non mangiare!*), while the first and second person plural forms are inflected, and identical to the positive imperative (as well as to the indicative forms: (*Non mangiamo!*, *Non mangiate!*)). All the forms allow both the enclitic and the proclitic position of the clitic:

(38) a Non prenderlo!
        'Don't take it!'
     b Non lo prendere!
        'Don't it take!'
(39) a Non prendiamolo!
        'Let's not take it!'
     b Non lo prendiamo!
        'Let's not it take!'
(40) a Non prendetelo!
        'Don't take(2pl) it!'
     b Non lo prendete!
        'Don't it take(2pl)!'

(38)b is striking, as it is the only case of a morphologically infinitival verb taking a proclitic in Italian, but also (39)b and (40)b are unexpected, as the (morphologically identical) corresponding positive imperatives disallow procliticization:

(41) *Lo prendiamo!
       'Let's it take!'
(42) *Lo prendete!
       'It take(pl)!'

Irrelevantly examples (41)–(42) are well-formed as declaratives. Consider first the contrast between (39)b, (40)b and (41)–(42). It recalls the corresponding contrast in French, and is amenable to the same analysis: in (41)–(42) the only possible landing site for the clitic is in the C system, outside the impoverished imperative IP, which gives encliticization under (35); on the other hand, negation licenses an occurrence of T which provides (through AgrO recursion) a landing site for the clitic lower than AgrS, the level at which the inflected imperative form becomes morphologically complete in our sense. This determines the option of procliticization in (40)–(41) under (35). But why do we also have the enclitic option of (39)a and (40)a (disallowed in French)? (38) raises the symmetric problem: the infinitive-like verb presumably becomes morphologically complete at the Infin layer, lower than the cliticization site, hence the enclitic variant (38)a is the expected form under (35). But why do we also find the proclitic option (38)b (disallowed in ordinary Italian infinitives)?

A simple possibility that comes to mind to deal with both the unexpected cases is to relate them to the very special morphological shape of the negative imperative paradigm, the only paradigm in the Italian verbal morphology which includes both infinitive and inflected forms. Suppose that all the members of a given paradigm are normally checked in the same structural position(s); then, the negative imperative paradigm is unique in that it has two possible checking sites, Infin and AgrS, justified by 2nd singular (infinitive-like) and 2nd/3d plural (inflected) forms, respectively, but both available to the whole paradigm. Depending on which site each form chooses, we will have either encliticization (if the Infin position is selected) or procliticization (if the AgrS position is selected), under generalization (35).[6]

We may account for encliticization with finite verbs in Western Romance languages along similar lines: according to Uriagereka (1995) the landing site for clitics in these varieties is (can be) a functional head higher than AgrS, which the verb may move to depending on different factors. We have identified this head in a recursion of AgrC, the agreement head of the C system (Shlonsky 1994). If the verb moves to it, our conditions for encliticization are met, since the verb is morphologically complete at AgrS, a position lower than AgrC:

(43) Ouvimo-lo.
'(We) hear it.'

The proposed generalization also accounts for a striking asymmetry between subject clitics and complement clitics in the Northern Italian Dialects with respect to I to C movement in interrogatives: in many varieties subject clitics invert, while object clitics never invert: (examples from Fiorentino adapted from Brandi and Cordin 1989; see also the discussion in Chapter 3):

(44)a Quando se'-tu arrivato?
'When have you arrived?'

b Quando ci se'-tu andato?
   'When there have you gone?'

In Chapter 3 it was proposed that the dialects systematically exploit AgrS recursion, with the subject clitic attached to the higher AgrS (possibly, heading it) and the verbal morphology of agreement licensed in the lower AgrS. So, at S-structure we would have:

(45)

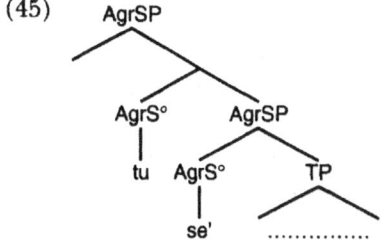

In direct questions, the verbal AgrS° moves to C° for familiar reasons having to do with the mutual licensing of Wh features and operators (see Chapter 9). Here the conditions for encliticization of the subject clitic are met: the verb is morphologically complete under the cliticization site (higher AgrS) and must move past it, to C°. On the other hand, if object clitics are involved in direct questions, the conditions for enclisis are not met: the finite verb is not morphologically complete at the cliticization site of object clitics (at the AgrO layer), hence, encliticization will not be available no matter whether the verb stops at AgrS (as in declaratives) or at C (as in questions, such as (44)b).

Consider now the asymmetry between main questions and imperatives, e.g., in French:

(46)a Le manges-tu?
     'It eat you? = do you eat it?'
   b Mange-le!
     'Eat it!'

Putting aside the status of the subject clitic (which in French is controversial: Rizzi 1986; Friedemann 1995; and Chapter 3), we observe that the object clitic is proclitic in the question and enclitic in the imperative. Under the proposed analysis, the contrast cannot depend on a different landing site for V-movement, as both constructions ultimately involve movement of the verb to C. Rather, the contrast reduces to a difference in the landing site for the clitic in the two cases: AgrO in the question, and AgrC in the imperative, due to the impoverished IP structure of the latter. This difference gives the contrast in (46), under (35).

4 Explaining the generalization

In order to express the observed empirical generalization, we now need a device to formally differentiate 'morphologically complete' verbal forms (i.e., verbal forms in which all the overt affixes have been properly checked) and 'incomplete verbal forms' (in which some affixes remain to be checked).

A possible formal distinction exploits the two modes of incorporation envisaged in Rizzi and Roberts (1989), which I will formally characterize following Roberts (1993a) in essence. Suppose that functional heads checking morphologically expressed affixes on a verbal form match the bar level of the affix: as the affix is less than a word (less than an H°), it is of bar level −1; hence the checking head is also an H^{-1}; this kind of checking exploits the modality known as 'substitution into a subcategorized slot': H^{-1} is morphologically subcategorized for a V slot, and verb incorporation involves substitution of the verb into this slot. So, we have:

(47)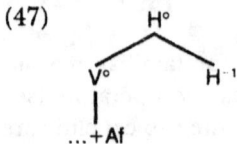

This corresponds to the case in which the verbal form still is 'morphologically incomplete', in the terms of the previous informal discussion. From the point in which the verbal form becomes morphologically complete, i.e., all its overt affixes have been checked, I will assume that its further incorporation into higher V-related heads (for abstract feature checking, e.g., movement of the Italian infinitive verb to AgrS in the absence of overt agreement morphology) will involve adjunction in the general case, as here H matches a property of the whole V category, rather than of a particular affix in it (but see below on French infinitives):

(48)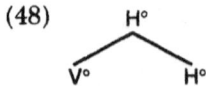

It seems natural to assume that, as soon as the head has started going up with the adjunction mode, it cannot revert to substitution, such a mixed chain would instantiate a kind of improper head movement. That is, (49)a is a well-formed chain, (49)b is improper head movement:

(49) a Adj Adj Adj Subs Subs Subs
     b *Adj Adj Subs Adj Subs Subs

This implies that, as long as a verb has overt morphological affixes to check, it will be forced to pass through a given head via substitution, no matter whether it actually checks features against this head (e.g., even if a finite verb in Romance does not have to check any morphological feature of AgrO, it will have to incorporate via substitution into AgrO in order to be able to later incorporate via substitution under T and AgrS without incurring an improper movement).

Consider now cliticization. We will continue to assume, with Kayne (1991, 1994), that clitics can only adjoin to the left, so, for H = the appropriate landing site of clitics, we can only have:

(50)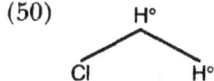

If, in the particular language/construction we are looking at, the verbal form is incomplete at this point (e.g., in finite forms in Italian, with landing sites for clitics in the recursive AgrO, and with a verbal form possessing morphological specifications of tense and subject agreement to check), the verb will be forced to incorporate using the substitution mode (regardless of whether or not the verb has morphologically realized features to check against H°), otherwise improper movement would arise; therefore, we will get the following configuration:

(51)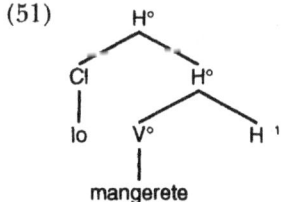

H° will keep moving as a whole to higher heads, and in the end we will get procliticization.

On the other hand, suppose that the verb is morphologically complete under the cliticization site. In Italian, for example, the infinitival verb, which has already checked its Infin morphology when it moves to the cliticization site H°. But then, under our assumptions, both the clitic and the verbal form should be adjoined to H°, which should *a priori* give rise to (52)a–b, depending on whether the verb or the clitic adjoins first:

(52)a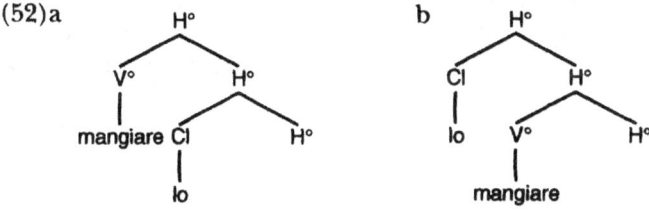

116 Principles and parameters in the pronominal systems

Under this analysis, explaining why the enclitic form is required in these cases boils down to finding a way to exclude (52)b and have (52)a as the only legitimate form. Various possibilities come to mind. Consider the following one. The clitic has to check against H whatever features make its movement to H compulsory (see Sections 1–2). On the contrary, V arguably has no feature to check here, it must move through H simply in order not to violate the Head Movement Constraint (ECP) on its way to higher functional heads. So, the checking is blocked in (52)b by the intervention of V between Cl and H (arguably a case of Relativized Minimality), while no problem arises in (52)a. The higher degree of cohesion in the case of enclisis may be related to the fact that there is an X° category including the verb and not the clitic in (51), H, but there is no category including one element and not the other in (52)a. Here, both cl and V are attached to a segment of H, given the segment-category distinction of May (1985) and Chomsky (1986b).

A further sharpening is suggested by Kayne's (1993) hypothesis that only one adjunction per head is possible. If this is correct, then, both (52)a and b are out, and the only possibility is that either the clitic adjoins to H and the verb adjoins to the clitic, or the verb adjoins to H and the clitic adjoins to the verb:

(53)a   b

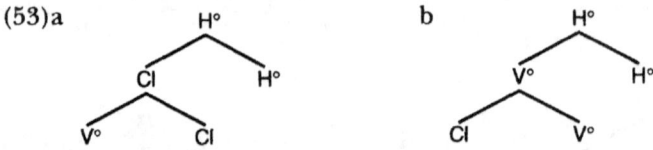

(53)b is ruled out for the same reason as before. This alternative has the advantage that it expresses more straightforwardly the higher degree of syntactic fusion in enclitic position.[7,8]

Conclusion

The reader can now check that this system accounts for the generalized encliticization found in non-finite forms in Italian, the generalized encliticization found in positive imperatives across Romance (through the auxiliary assumption of the impoverished IP), various idiosyncrasies found in negative imperatives, the encliticization of subject clitics versus procliticization of object clitics in questions in Northern Italian Dialects, the different behaviour of object clitics (e.g., in French) in questions and imperatives, both involving I to C movement but triggering procliticization and encliticization, respectively.

It should be noticed that the conditions of generalization (35) are necessary but not sufficient for encliticization. This is so because when a verbal form is morphologically complete, the language or construction may start exploiting the adjunction mode for further raising, which will ultimately produce encliticization, but it does not have to: presumably nothing excludes that a language/construction may still use the substitution mode (47) for raising of the verbal form even past the 'completion point'. We have to leave this option open to account for two classes of cases:

1 Non-finite forms in French (and other Romance varieties: Kayne 1991) involve procliticization:

(54)a Ne pas le manger.
   'Not it to eat.'
  b Ne pas l'avoir mangé.
   'Not it to have eaten.'
  c Ne l'avoir pas mangé.
   'It to have not eaten.'

One could try to account for (54)a–b by assuming that the verb does not reach the cliticization site here (hence condition i of (35) is not met), but this would be insufficient for (54)c, in which the auxiliary optionally moved to AgrS appears to 'push up' the clitic, and still we have procliticization. So, we seem to have to assume for this case that French has the option of using (47) (and (51)) even past the 'completion' point.[9]

2 In some Northern Italian Dialects (e.g., Piedmontese) direct questions keep subject clitics in proclitic position, while presumably involving I to C (as is suggested by the fact that a lexical subject cannot intervene between the Wh element and the subject clitic). Here again, presumably, the verb is allowed to raise to the higher AgrS of (the equivalent of) (45) via substitution, in spite of the fact that it is already morphologically complete.

Appedix I: another generalization

Consider the fact that no Romance languages apparently allows

(55) *V   NP   cl ...

with the subject NP intervening between a preposed V and the clitic, while some (the Western Romance varieties) allow

(56) Cl ... NP ... V

(Kayne 1991, Uriagereka 1995).
   Similarly, Benincà and Cinque (1990) have observed that the following

configuration with a (non-clitic) adverb intervening between a preposed verb and the clitic seems generally disallowed

(57) *...V...Adv...cl

while proclitics can be separated from verbs by (non-clitic) adverbs in some varieties (see above).

(58) ...Cl...Adv...V

These two observations seem to constitute another significant generalization, which we can phrase as follows:

(59) If the verb moves to a position past the landing site of the clitic, it carries the clitic along.

This follows from two theoretical assumptions:

1 Clitics are V-related (they attach to a head that the verb inevitably passes through).
2 If the verb moves to a given functional head, then further excorporation of the verb is not allowed (possibly because of the ECP, Roberts 1991b).

That is, if in the following representation X is the landing site of the clitic and Y is the final position that V must reach,

(60) ...Y...Cl+X...V...

V must move through X because X must be V-related to support the clitic (itself V-related), but then V must carry the clitic (and its support X) to its final destination Y because of the ban on excorporation.

Notice that this generalization is massively violated by Germanic weak pronouns, which are never carried along by the inflected verb moving to C in V-2 constructions. Then, either such elements are not V-related clitics, or they are not clitics at all, in the Romance sense.

Appendix II: on present participles in Italian

Present participles have a very restricted use in Italian: they can only be used in reduced relatives, and at a very special stylistic level, typical of bureaucratic/legal documents:

(61)a Tutte le persone facenti parte di questa associazione...
       'All the people belonging to this association...'

b Tutte le persone ottemperanti alle disposizioni di legge ...
    'All the people obeying the legal dispositions ...'
  c Tutte le persone richiedenti l'autorizzazione entro i termini previsti ...
    'All the people asking for the authorization before the deadline ...'

In spite of such restrictions, one can have fairly clear intuitions at least on some structural properties of the construction. Cliticization is by and large allowed, most naturally with prepositional clitics, and only in the enclitic position:

(62) a Tutte le persone facentine parte ...
      'All the people belonging to it ...'
    b Tutte le persone ottemperantivi ...
      'All the people obeying it ...'

This case seems to be a counterexample to the proposed generalization: the present participle agrees with the understood subject (the head of the reduced relative) in number: *facente vs facenti*. So, a sort of AgrS seems to be involved here; moreover, the structure seems to be more complete in this case than with past participial clauses: negation is allowed (with typical NegP material as the adverb *più*)

(63) Tutte le persone non facenti più parte di questa associazione ...
      'All the people not belonging anymore to this association ...'

and even an aspectual auxiliary appears to be tolerable:

(64) ?Tutti i candidati aventi già inviato una domanda di partecipazione ...
      'All the candidates having already sent an application ...'

So the structure seems to be problematic: If there is an overt AgrS and a (recursive) AgrO which can function as the landing site of clitics, one would expect this case to behave like finite structures and only allow procliticization, as the verbal form would not be morphologically complete at the cliticization site.

One possible solution is to observe that Agr here differs from finite subject agreement in that it only contains number, not person specification and is presumably not involved in any form of nominative licensing. As such, it is clearly closer to the adjectival agreement expressed, e.g., in passive participles (as well as in various adjectival constructions). If the analogy with passive participle is a valid one, this instance of number agreement would be checked in a low position in the tree, arguably lower than Agr_{cl}, which would make it possible to maintain generalization (35) as is.

Notes

1 The fourth possibility, checking a verbal feature by a verbal head in a Spec-head configuration may also be instantiated: if Kayne (1994) is right in predicting that heads always precede complements in the basic position, the VP I order that many languages manifest may be derived by moving the VP to the Spec of some inflectional head to check V-features phrasally, so to speak.
2 As for clitics that do not manifest person, number and gender features, such as *ne* and *ci* in Italian, we can assume that they manifest at least a Case feature (genitive and locative, respectively) which must be checked in the V-system. We do not attempt here to integrate the verbal clitics of Slavic languages (see Starke 1993).
3 Notice that the weak pronoun *loro* (Cardinaletti 1991) is allowed to occur in the *Easy to please* construction

    i Il problema è difficile da spiegare loro.
       'The problem is difficult to explain to them.'

This is consistent with Cardinaletti's analysis, according to which *loro* is licensed by a lower head than the cliticization site.
4 We will not address the question here of whether the AgrO layer plays a role in accusative assignment in such systems; we will also omit discussing the difference between systems in which cliticization onto the participle is incompatible with past participle agreement (Roberts 1993b) and systems in which it is not (Kayne 1991).
5 The high degree of fusion manifested by enclisis is also witnessed by the obligatory elision of the final vowel of the infinitive as in ie, which is optional when followed by local syntactic material (as in ic–d and, slighty less naturally in the less local case ib), and excluded elsewhere (as in ia):

  i a Partir*(e) sarebbe un errore.
        'To leave would be a mistake.'
    b Toglier?(e) lo zucchero.
        'To take away the sugar.'
    c Metter(e) via lo zucchero.
        'To put away the sugar.'
    d Dar(e) loro i soldi.
        'To give them the money.'
    e Metter(*e)lo via.
        'To put it away.'

Obligatory elision in ie is possibly akin to the obligatory word-internal elision in cases like *stabile, stabil(*e)mente* ('stable, stably'), *regolare, regolar(*e)mente* ('regular, regularly').
6 A different approach is proposed in Kayne (1992), who argues that negative imperatives in Italian involve a null modal, which the clitic may climb to, thus giving rise to the unexpected proclitic order. Kayne argues for this analysis on the basis of the following cross-dialectal generalization: while standard Italian allows both options on a par, Italian dialects and regional varieties may manifest a strong preference for one or other option, and this correlates with restructuring/clitic climbing:

  i a Voglio mangiarlo.
        'I want to eat it.'
    b Lo voglio mangiare.
        'I it want to eat.'

Varieties preferring ia tend to prefer (38)a and vice versa. If (38)b involves clitic climbing to a higher null modal, the case (under representation iib) is fully parallel to ib, and varieties lacking/disfavouring restructuring will lack/disfavour both.

ii a Non M mangiarlo!
    b Non lo M mangiare!

It should be noticed, though, that the null modal approach is not naturally extendable to the cases of pro-/en-clitic options of the inflected negative imperative (39)–(40), as one would not expect a modal to select an inflected verbal form in Italian. An independent problem for the null modal approach is that overt restructuring modals can be followed by negative adverbs sitting in the Spec of NegP (see iiia), but one does not find the same possibility with the assumed null modal iiib: the only possible position for such adverbs in negative imperatives is after the overt verb iiic:

iii a Non lo voglio più mangiare.
      'I don't it want anymore to eat.'
    b *Non lo più mangiare!
      'Don't it anymore eat!'
    c Non lo mangiare più!
      'Don't it eat anymore!'

We will not attempt here to reconcile the approach presented in the text with the generalization observed by Kayne.

7 The verb ends up in a root–suffix configuration with the clitic in (53)a (an intuition expressed by Belletti 1994, among others), a configuration generally disallowing coordination of the root or of the suffix:

i a *Mangiava-mo o –te ? (cf. Mangiavamo o mangiavate ?)
     'We ate or you ate?'
   b *Pensava- e ripensava-mo a questa storia. (cf. pensavamo e ripensavamo . . .)
     'We thought and rethought about this story.'

Notice that some prefixes differ from suffixes in that they allow coordination: *bi- o tri-sillabico*, *il trattamento pre- o post-operatorio*, etc. This may be similar to the observed behaviour of proclitics.

8 It should be noticed that the checking via adjunction or substitution that we have postulated must be kept separate from Chomsky's distinction between checking of strong and weak features. For instance, the infinitival verb in Italian must raise as far as AgrS in the syntax (Belletti 1990), hence it has strong AgrS features in Chomsky's sense; still, these strong features are abstract, not morphologically expressed (they do not participate in the morphological completeness of the verbal form, in our sense), so that they are checked via adjunction, which gives rise to encliticization.

9 Even in a case like (54)c, the French structure would differ from the corresponding Italian structure in that the verbal form is substituted into AgrS, not adjoined to it as in Italian, etc. This difference should be sufficient to express Kayne's (1991) comparative generalization concerning the cross-linguistic cooccurrence of encliticization in infinitives and the possibility of *if* complementizer with infinitives.

Part II
Locality

5 On chain formation*

1 Introduction

The notion of *chain*, originally introduced in Chomsky (1982a), has acquired an important role in the theory of grammar known as the Government and Binding Theory (Chomsky 1981, especially Chapter 6; and 1982b). A chain can be intuitively characterized as a device to concisely represent properties of the transformational derivation at S-structure. As a first approximation, the chain associated to a phrase moved n times consists of the phrase itself and its n traces. For instance, in the following S-structure the NP *John* is assigned the chain ($John_i$, e'_i, e''_i):[1]

(1) John$_i$ seems [e'_i to have been arrested e''_i].

If we move from the intuitive level to the precise characterizations and uses of this notion in the recent literature, two rather different views emerge:

1 The *derivational* characterization: every phrase is provided with a 'memory' which keeps track of every application of 'move α' which the phrase undergoes. In this conception, chains are built in the course of the transformational derivation, and inevitably are faithful representations of derivational properties (for instance, this interpretation is suggested in Chomsky 1982b: 68).

2 The *representational* characterization: chains are read off from S-structures (and/or other syntactic levels), hence chain formation is a mechanism independent from 'move α', and in principle chains do not necessarily reflect derivational properties.

Under reasonable assumptions on the chain-formation algorithm, for examples like (1), the two characterizations give identical results, but

* I would like to thank Adriana Belletti, Denis Bouchard, Luigi Burzio, Guglielmo Cinque, Richard Kayne, and Jean-Roger Vergnaud for helpful comments.

more complex cases can be found in which they diverge. In this study I argue for the representational characterization of chains, showing that the dissociation between 'move α' and chain formation has desirable empirical consequences. In particular, it permits an explanatory account of various problems of Romance syntax which have resisted satisfactory analysis so far.

2 Chains and the θ-Criterion

Adopting the representational view, we need a formal definition which can function as an algorithm to read chains off from S-structures (and other levels). A minimal characterization, undoubtedly to be completed with other specifications, is the following:

(2) $C = (a_1 \ldots a_n)$ is a chain iff, for $1 \leq i < n$, a_i is the local binder of a_{i+1}.

α is a *binder* of β iff, for α, β = any category, α and β are co-indexed, and α c-commands β; α is the local binder of β iff α is a binder of β and there is no γ such that γ is a binder of β, and γ is not a binder of α. In short, what (2) amounts to is that a chain is a sequence of co-indexed positions such that each of them (but the last) is the closest antecedent of the following one.[2]

The theoretical relevance of the notion *chain* emerges in connection with the 'Thematic (θ) Criterion'. This is the well-formedness condition which ensures biuniqueness between the thematic roles assigned in a given structure and certain expressions having, in some intuitive sense, semantic content: referential NPs, pronominals including PRO, variables, clitics, overt anaphors, and clauses. These elements are referred to as *arguments*; *nonarguments* are all sorts of expletives and NP/cl traces. Chomsky (1981: 335) defines the θ-Criterion as follows:

(3) θ-Criterion: Given the structure S, there is a set K of chains $K = \{C_i\}$, where $C_i = (a^i_1 \ldots a^i_n)$, such that:
 i if α is an argument of S, then there is a $C_i \in K$ such that $a = a^i_j$ and a θ-role is assigned to C_i by exactly one position P;
 ii if P is a position of S marked with θ-role R, then there is a $C_i \in K$ to which P assigns R, and exactly one a^i_j in C_i is an argument.

What (3) essentially amounts to is very simple: there is biuniqueness between θ-roles and chains containing exactly one argument. Since a chain containing exactly one argument can be viewed as an abridged representation of the full syntactic manifestation of that argument, the ultimate content of the θ-Criterion is that there must be biuniqueness between θ-roles and arguments, as was directly stated in more 'archaic' formulations of this principle (e.g., Chomsky 1981: 36).

Let us briefly discuss a few examples showing how the system works:

(4) a John$_i$ seems [e'_i to have been arrested e''_i].
  b John$_i$ wants [PRO$_i$ to be arrested e_i].

Implicit in our definition is that chain formation is free: any sequence of elements meeting (2) can be a chain, and no maximality is stipulated. Consider now (4)a: this structure has only one θ-position, the object position of the verb *to arrest* (the 'theme'),[3] the subject position of the embedded passive and of the raising verb being non-θ positions (θ̄-positions), as is usually assumed. For terminological convenience, we will use the term *chain structure* to refer to a set of chains associated to a given level of representation by free chain formation. This process, applying on the S-structure of (4)a, can give any of the following chain structures:

(5) a (John), (e'), (e'')
  b (John, e'), (e'')
  c (John), (e', e'')
  d (John, e', e'')

We can now think of the θ-Criterion as a filter applying on chain structures: if no chain structure associated to a given sentence (more exactly, to a given level of syntactic representation of a sentence) fulfils the requirements of θ-Theory, then the sentence is ruled out. (5)a–c are ruled out by the θ-Criterion: in all of them an argument (*John*) belongs to a chain which is not assigned a θ-role, and a θ-role ('theme') is assigned to a chain (the one containing e'') which does not contain an argument. On the contrary, (5)d meets the biuniqueness requirement, and the sentence is well-formed with this chain structure.[4]

As for (4)b, the structure contains two θ-positions, the subject position of *to want* ('experiencer') and the object position of *to arrest* ('theme'). Chain formation gives again four options:

(6) a (John), (PRO), (e)
  b (John, PRO), (e)
  c (John), (PRO, e)
  d (John, PRO, e)

It is easy to see that (6)a,b,d are ruled out by the θ-Criterion. In (6)a there is an argument (PRO) which belongs to a chain which is not assigned a θ-role, and a θ-role is assigned to a chain which does not contain an argument (e). In (6)b the two θ-roles are assigned to two chains, neither of which contains exactly one argument: the first contains two arguments, the second contains none, (6)d is similarly excluded, and only (6)c fulfils the biuniqueness requirement.

Consider now:

(7)a *John seems [that Bill was arrested e].
   b John said [that Bill was arrested e].

(7)a contains only one θ-position, the object position of *to arrest*, and there is no chain structure giving a well-formed result: in particular, (John), (Bill, e) is excluded since an argument, *John*, belongs to a chain which does not receive a θ-role. On the contrary, (7)b has two θ-positions, the subject of *to say* and the object of *to arrest*, and the sentence is well-formed with chain structure (John), (Bill, e).

Adapting a core GB assumption, in fact enforced by Chomsky's Projection Principle, we can say that the θ-Criterion is a well-formedness condition operating on chain structures read off from all syntactic levels of representation: D-structure, S-structure, Logical Form (LF). The mapping from D-structure to the corresponding chain structure is trivial, since at this level all chains have length one. Chain structures corresponding to S-structure and LF can contain chains of arbitrary length, as a consequence of the fact that 'move α' can indefinitely reapply on its output. The triviality of the mapping from D-structures to chain structures suggests that the two notions should be identified. Remember that the identification is essentially done in one direction by the derivational characterization of chains: chains at D-structure are substructures of the D-structures themselves, in that every θ-position at this level exhaustively identifies a chain; chains at S-structure and LF are mechanically given by D-structure information plus 'move α'. If, as we will argue, the representational characterization of chains is empirically superior, one might consider the opposite deduction: 'D-structures' are reduced to properties of chains read off from S-structures (and LFs), the independent mapping from D-structure to S-structure is dispensed with, and 'move α' is fully identified with the chain-formation algorithm.[5] In the remainder of our discussion we will not work out this possibility: we will keep the traditional organization of the theory, in spite of the intuitive appeal of the reductionist approach, concentrating on the basic aim of arguing for the representational characterization of chains. But it should be clear that, as soon as we look at chains as entities which are not parasitic on derivations, chain formation immediately becomes a serious competitor of 'move α': Why should there be two independent mappings relating S-structures and D-structures (in their role of 'pure' representations of θ-properties), giving the same results in the vast majority of cases? If our argument for the representational characterization of chains is successful, combined with simplicity considerations, it thus significantly increases the plausibility of the reductionist approach.

3 Anaphoric clitics and derived subjects

We will now consider some empirical consequences of the proposed formulation of θ-Theory and, in particular, of the formal definition of chain, showing that the system naturally solves descriptive problems which resisted explanatory accounts in previous frameworks.

Kayne (1975) noticed that passive is incompatible with reflexive–reciprocal cliticization in French. We illustrate the fact with Italian examples:

(8) a Gianni è stato affidato a *se stesso.*
       'Gianni was entrusted to himself.'
    b I nostri amici sono stati presentati *l'uno all'altro.*
       'Our friends have been introduced to each other.'
(9) a *Gianni *si* è stato affidato.
       'Gianni to-himself was entrusted.'
    b *I nostri amici *si* sono stati presentati.
       'Our friends to-each-other have been introduced.'

(8) shows that a stressed reflexive or reciprocal[6] is compatible with the passive construction; (9) shows that a clitic reflexive or reciprocal is not. That the problem does not involve cliticization per se is shown by the fact that (9) becomes grammatical if the clitic is nonanaphoric:

(10) a Gianni *gli* è stato affidato.
        'Gianni to-him was entrusted.'
     b I nostri amici *gli* sono stati presentati.
        'Our friends to-him were introduced.'

Why is (9) ungrammatical? Kayne suggested a solution in terms of extrinsic ordering: if reflexive cliticization is ordered before passive, and made sensitive to the presence of a subject co-indexed with the clitic, such structures as (9) will never arise. Of course this solution, perfectly acceptable within previous frameworks, is not available in the more restrictive GB Theory, which disallows arbitrary descriptive options such as stipulations of extrinsic ordering and contextual dependencies in the form of transformational rules. A different approach within a GB type system is proposed in Burzio (1982): reflexive–reciprocal clitics, base-generated in clitic position, are attributed the special property of requiring a 'local' antecedent in subject position not only as a consequence of the Binding Theory (hence not only at the levels where the latter applies), but at all syntactic levels, including D-structure. It then follows that reflexive clitics cannot be found in constructions with derived subjects, where their special property could not be fulfilled at D-structure.

Burzio's solution shares with Kayne's analysis the assumption that some special property of reflexive–reciprocal clitics, to be autonomously stipulated, is responsible for the noted effect; the stipulation of the idiosyncrasy is then removed from derivations and stated as a property of representations, in the spirit of current theoretical elaboration. Obviously, the ideal solution would be one in which the facts of (9) can be derived in full generality without requiring any special statement on the nature and properties of anaphoric clitics, neither on the rules nor on the representations involved. As a matter of fact, such an optimal solution is already provided by θ-Theory, and in particular by the definition of chain as formulated in (2). First of all, clitic structures are easily integrated within θ-Theory by assuming that clitics are arguments (on a par with nonclitic pronominal NPs) and clitic traces are nonarguments (on a par with NP traces; the parallelism between the two types of traces also seems to hold with respect to the Binding Theory, where both NP and cl-traces appear to count as anaphors). Hence, cl-trace chains closely correspond to NP-trace chains:

(11) a Gianni la$_i$ guarda e_i.
 'Gianni her sees e.'
 b Gianni si$_i$ guarda e_i.
 'Gianni himself sees e.'

The object θ-role of the verb *guardare* ('theme') is respectively assigned to the chains *(la, e)* and *(si, e)*. Consider now the structure of such examples as (9):

(12) Gianni$_i$ [$_{VP}$ si$_i$ è stato affidato e'_i e''_i].

where e' is the trace of the NP *Gianni* and e'' is the trace of the dative reflexive clitic (linear order between e' and e'' is irrelevant). This sentence is ruled out by the θ-Criterion at S-structure: the only chain structure which would fulfil the requirements of θ-Theory would be (*Gianni*, e'), (*si*, e''), in correspondence with the two θ-roles assigned to the direct and indirect objects in this structure; but such a chain structure cannot be produced by the chain-formation algorithm. An immediate consequence of definition (2), and in particular of the crucial use of the notion 'Local Binder', is the following:

(13) Chain formation cannot 'skip' intervening binders.

This excludes (*Gianni*, e') as a possible chain for (12), since it would skip the intervening binder *si* (and in fact also the intervening binder e''). As is easy to ascertain, any chain structure allowed by the definition violates the θ-Criterion, hence such structures as (12) are systematically excluded by θ-Theory, Q.E.D.[7]

The consequence just drawn on the incompatibility with anaphoric cliticization holds not only for passives, but for any other structure involving a derived subject: such a structure would have the form

(14) $NP_i \ldots [_\alpha si_i \ldots e_i \ldots]$

where e is the trace of NP. Formation of the appropriate chain structure would be inevitably blocked by the intervening binder si (and by the trace of si), hence no well-formed output would ever result. The prediction is correct: Burzio (1982) points out that reflexive–reciprocal cliticization is also incompatible with impersonal passive and ergative structures. Consider the following impersonal passives occurring with stressed reflexive–reciprocals:

(15)a Gianni$_i$ si$_{imp}$ affiderà e_i a se stesso$_i$.
 'Gianni si will entrust (= will be entrusted) to himself.'
 b I due bimbi$_i$ si$_{imp}$ affideranno e_i l'uno all'altro$_i$.
 'The two children si will be entrusted to each other.'

These sentences should not be confused, as the glosses indicate, with the homophonous strings in which si is a reflexive direct object, and the subject is a 'deep' subject (i.e., with the respective interpretations, 'Gianni will entrust himself to himself' and 'The two children will entrust themselves to each other'). A third-person reflexive–reciprocal clitic assumes the form ci when in contiguity with impersonal si, for example,

(16)a Quando Gianni si compra una macchina ...
 'When Gianni for-himself buys a car ...'
 b Quando ci si compra una macchina ...
 'When ci (somebody) for-himself buys a car ...'

Now, cliticization of the anaphors in (15) gives rise to ungrammaticality:

(17)a *Gianni$_i$ ci$_i$ si$_{imp}$ affiderà e'_i e''_i.
 b *I due bimbi$_i$ ci$_i$ si$_{imp}$ affideranno e'_i e''_i.

(These structures are acceptable in the irrelevant interpretation in which ci is a first-person plural pronoun: 'The two children will be entrusted to us.') The impossibility of (17) immediately follows on a par with the ordinary passive construction.

Burzio (1981), developing Perlmutter's (1978) Unaccusative Hypothesis, convincingly argues that the surface subjects of such verbs as *venire* (to come), *cadere* (to fall), and, in general, all verbs taking *essere* (to be) as aspectual auxiliary in Italian, have the status of derived subjects. That is, we have S-structures like the following:

(18) a I due nemici$_i$ spesso vengono e_i in mente l'uno all' altro.
'The two enemies often come to mind to each other.'
b Il ladro e il poliziotto$_i$ sono caduti e_i l'uno addosso all'altro.
'The thief and the policeman fell on each other.'

If the anaphor is cliticized, Burzio points out, the corresponding structures are ill-formed:

(19) a *?I due nemici$_i$ spesso si$_i$ vengono e'_i in mente e''_i.
'The two enemies often to-each-other come to mind.'
b *?Il ladro e il poliziotto$_i$ si$_i$ sono caduti e'_i addosso e''_i.
'The thief and the policeman on-each-other fell.'

The degree of ill-formedness determined by anaphoric cliticization in these structures ('ergative' structures, according to Burzio's terminology) is generally less strong than the one determined in passive, impersonal passive, and, as we will see, raising, and in certain cases it reduces to slight deviance. But even in the weakest cases the predicted contrasts hold, at least in terms of relative acceptability. Take for instance the class of 'psychological' predicates, and contrast the 'ergative' *piacere* ('to please') and the 'accusatives' *attrarre, disgustare, impressionare* ('to attract,' 'disgust,' 'impress'). The difference in status is highlighted by the auxiliary choice:

(20) a Il film è piaciuto a Maria.
'The movie *is* pleased to Maria = The movie pleased M.'
b Il film ha attratto/disgustato/impressionato Maria.
'The movie has attracted/disgusted/impressed Maria.'

An anaphoric (reciprocal) clitic designating the experiencer is fully acceptable with the accusative verbs, and deviant, even though only slightly, with the ergative:

(21) a ?I due si piacciono vicendevolmente.
'The two each-other please mutually.'
b I due si attraggono/disgustano/impressionano vicendevolmente.
'The two each-other attract/disgust/impress mutually.'

The variable and often reduced strength of the ill-formedness with ergatives is presumably to be attributed to the fact that the ergative status of a verb is, in part at least, an idiosyncratic property of the specific lexical item, which would allow for the marginal possibility of reanalysing an ergative structure as nonergative at S-structure (i.e., of disregarding the trace in the VP, for example, in (18)). This marginal possibility is not expected to exist when the derived status of the subject is not a consequence of a lexical idiosyncrasy, but follows from general properties of the construction, as in ordinary and impersonal passive, whence the much stronger and lexically invariable ill-formedness determined by anaphoric cliticization in these constructions. Whether this or some other independent factor is responsible for the reduced and lexically variable unacceptability with ergatives, we can subsume the deviance of (19), for example, under the general case (14), and trace it back to a violation of the θ-Criterion.[8]

Especially interesting is the case of raising structures. With verbs corresponding to the *seem* class in English, the 'experiencer' θ-role is optionally assigned to a NP introduced by the preposition *a*. When the experiencer is lexical (or a stressed pronoun or anaphor), its most natural position is clause-initial; otherwise, it is cliticized:[9]

(22) a A Piero, Gianni$_i$ non sembra [e_i fare il suo dovere].
'To Piero Gianni doesn't seem to do his duty.'
   b Gianni$_i$ non gli sembra [e_i fare il suo dovere].
'Gianni doesn't to-him seem to do his duty.'

The experiencer can be realized as a stressed reflexive or reciprocal. The resulting sentences undoubtedly are pragmatically rather difficult, but do not appear syntactically ill-formed:

(23) a Ormai, perfino a se stesso Gianni$_i$ sembra [e_i non fare il suo dovere].
'At this point, even to himself Gianni seems not to do his duty.'
   b L'uno all'altro, i due candidati$_i$ risultavano [e_i poter vincere].
'To each other, the two candidates appeared to be able to win.'

The corresponding sentences with a reflexive–reciprocal clitic are completely impossible:

(24) a *Gianni$_i$ si sembra [e_i non fare il suo dovere].
'Gianni to-himself seems not to do his duty.'
   b *I due candidati$_i$ si risultavano [e_i poter vincere].
'The two candidates to-each-other appeared to be able to win.'

The otherwise surprising impossibility of (24) follows again from θ-Theory: these sentences instanciate the abstract structure (14), and are excluded on a par with the corresponding passive, impersonal, and ergative structures: the intervention of *si* (and its trace, not indicated in (24)) blocks chain formation between the main and the embedded subject position, hence the structure is ruled out by the θ-module in the usual way.

As for the contrasting well-formedness of (23), it can be attributed either to the sentence-initial position of the co-indexed experiencer phrase (as such it would not interfere with chain formation), or to the fact that the reflexive or reciprocal in (23) is embedded within a PP, hence its c-domain does not extend beyond this node, and in particular does not include the embedded subject trace, thus becoming irrelevant for the process of chain formation. The second solution is supported by two facts. In the first place, if the experiencer phrase is placed in immediately postverbal position, we obtain a marginal sentence whose status exactly corresponds to i of footnote 9, not to (24):

(25) a *?Gianni$_i$ sembra perfino a se stesso [e_i non fare il suo dovere].
     'Gianni seems even to himself not to do his duty.'
   b *?I due candidati$_i$ risultavano l'uno all'altro [e_i poter vincere].
     'The two candidates appeared to each other to be able to win.'

Moreover, in English, sentences with an immediately postverbal experiencer are natural, and an anaphor is allowed in this position (from Chomsky 1982b: 19):

(26) They seem to each other [e to be happy].

The correct solution therefore seems to be that the object of *a/to* does not c-command elements outside the PP, and is thus uninfluential in the process of chain formation.[10]

Our approach predicts a sharp difference between raising and control structures: all things being equal, the latter should not be incompatible with reflexive–reciprocal cliticization. Compare the following:

(27) a NP$_i$ ... si$_i$ ... [[e]$_i$ ...].
    b NP$_i$ ... si$_i$ ... [PRO$_i$ ...].

While in (27)a, *si* interferes in chain formation, no problem for θ-Theory arises in (27)b since NP and PRO, autonomous arguments, must belong to independent chains. Indeed the following control sentences corresponding to (27)b are perfectly well-formed ((28)a is a case of dative control, (28)b is a case of subject control):

(28) a Gianni$_i$ si$_i$ impone [di PRO$_i$ fare il suo dovere].
     'Gianni himself compels to do his duty.'
   b I due concorrenti$_i$ si$_i$ sono promessi [di PRO$_i$ essere leali].
     'The two competitors to-each-other promised to be loyal.'

This sharp contrast between raising and control strongly supports the fundamental intuition behind the classical analysis of these constructions in generative grammar. Consider passive, raising, and control structures: the classical idea, since Rosenbaum (1967), was that the correct analysis of raising structures should group them with passive, not with control, in spite of superficial evidence to the contrary. The discriminating test provided by the incompatibility with anaphoric cliticization, under our assumptions, confirms the fundamental correctness of the traditional insight. In fact, a very simple explanatory account of the asymmetry is provided by the proposed analysis, which straightforwardly updates the classical approach, phrasing it in terms of chain formation and θ-Theory.

Notice that our account, making crucial reference to θ-Theory, does not exclude such structures as (27)a per se, but only as a consequence of a violation of the θ-Criterion. It then follows that if, for some reason, a concrete instance of (27)a does not violate the θ-Criterion, all things being equal, it should be well-formed. Such a case does, in fact, exist. Examples are provided by a small class of raising verbs in French which take an intrinsic reflexive clitic, for instance:

(29) Jean$_i$ s$_i$'avère [e_i être parti].
'Jean turns out to have left.'

In (29) *se* is not an argument and does not participate in the process of θ-role assignment: it is simply an element of the idiomatic verbal form *s'avérer*. Since it is an anaphor, it must be co-indexed with *Jean*, and cannot be 'skipped' in chain formation, but the resulting chain (*Jean, se, e*) gives rise to a well-formed result, since it contains exactly one argument, *Jean*. This conclusion converges with Kayne's (1984, Chapter 10) analysis of complex inversion in French, which allows chains containing chain-internal nonarguments in A' position.

The acceptability of (29) is to be contrasted with the ungrammaticality of the following:

(30) *Jean$_i$ se$_i$ semble [e_i être parti].

where *se* is an argument participating in θ-role assignment (it should receive the role 'experiencer'). There is no chain structure for this sentence which could fulfil the requirements of θ-Theory; (*Jean, e*) is not allowed by the definition of chain, and any other possibility is either irrelevant for, or violates, the θ-Criterion. The contrast between the formally identical (29) and (30) is thus uniquely due to the different status of *se* with respect to θ-Theory in the two examples.[11]

In closing this section, it should be noticed that the facts of (8)–(9), (15)–(17), (18)–(19), and (23)–(24) provide empirical support for the representational characterization of chains. If chains were 'memories' associated to NPs, faithfully recording applications of 'move α', nothing would prevent formation of well-formed chains for the ungrammatical examples of the above pairs (e.g., (*Gianni, e'$_i$*), (*si, e''$_i$*) for (9)a), and the proposed explanation of their deviance would be lost. In conclusion, in at least one class of clear cases in which the two conceptions of chain differ in empirical consequences, the representational view appears to be superior in that it provides a natural explanation of an otherwise mysterious phenomenon.

4 Small clauses

Once we have motivated our analysis for a well-established class of cases involving derived subjects, following the usual methodology we can utilize it as a diagnostic for more controversial cases. The issue we consider in this section is the small clausal analysis of certain verbal complements. Verbs of the *sembrare* class can occur in superficial environments consisting of a preverbal subject, a dative experiencer and a postverbal AP (or other predicative) complement:

(31) a Gianni mi sembra intelligente.
'Gianni to-me seems intelligent.'
  b Loro ci risultano in regola con le tasse.
'They to-us appear in good order with taxes.'

Reasonable assumptions on the uniformity and minimality of lexical information (there is only one verb *sembrare* involved in structures like (22) and (31)b) suggest that more structure is involved in (31) than the simple labelled bracketing of the phonetically realized material. In particular, it is tempting to analyse (31) in a fully parallel way with ordinary raising structures: the complements have a clausal structure whose empty subject position is bound at S-structure by the surface main subject:

(32) a $Gianni_i$ mi sembra $[e_i$ intelligente].
  b $Loro_i$ ci risultano $[e_i$ in regola con le tasse].

This conclusion can be made to follow from the Projection Principle: informally, since *sembrare* assigns the θ-role 'theme' to the clause *Gianni (essere) intelligente*, this clause must be categorically represented on all syntactic levels, including S-structure (cf. Chomsky 1981: 33).

If this structural hypothesis is correct, we would expect ungrammaticality of structures corresponding to (32) when the experiencer is a reflexive–reciprocal clitic. The prediction is borne out:

(33) a *$Gianni_i$ si_i sembra $[e_i$ intelligente].
'Gianni to-himself seems intelligent.'
  b *$Loro_i$ si_i risultano $[e_i$ in regola con le tasse].
'They to-each-other appear in good order with taxes.'

In (33) the main subject cannot become a member of a chain with its trace because of the intervening binder *si* (and its trace), and the structures are ruled out by the θ-Criterion. Notice that, as in the cases previously discussed, it is perfectly clear what these structures would mean, were they grammatical. For instance, (33)a would be equivalent to:

(34) Gianni$_i$ si$_i$ considera [e_i intelligente].
 'Gianni himself considers intelligent.'

The difference is that in (34) the main subject position is a θ-position, assigned the role 'experiencer', hence it need not (cannot) enter into a chain with other positions. In (33)a the main subject position is a θ̄-position (the role 'experiencer' being assigned to the dative), hence chain formation is necessary but impossible because of the intervening clitic, whence the ungrammaticality of the structure. The small clausal analysis of (31) thus receives significant support.

A potential problem for this analysis might arise from the following observation. Chomsky (1981) has suggested that a sentence like (35)a is to be treated as a raising construction, whose S-structure is (35)b:

(35)a John strikes Bill as intelligent.
 b John$_i$ strikes Bill [as e_i intelligent].

Here an anaphor seems to be possible in the direct object ('experiencer') position:

(36) They$_i$ strike each other$_i$ [as e_i intelligent].

However, under minimal assumptions, the structure should be excluded by θ-Theory since formation of the chain (they, e) should be prevented by the intervening binder *each other*. Why is (36) acceptable? One obvious possibility would be to reject a raising analysis of these structures. As a matter of fact, such an analysis involves a plain violation of so-called Burzio's generalization ('in a clause no θ-role is assigned to the subject iff no Case is assigned to the object' (see Burzio 1981 for detailed discussion)): *strike* would assign a Case to the object, but no θ-role to the subject. Therefore, if Burzio's generalization is valid and can be maintained to hold without exception, the raising analysis of (35) must be abandoned. In the second place, even if the raising analysis turns out to be tenable, there are reasons to believe that the object of *strike* does not c-command the following predicate. That is, the structure is:

(37) NP [$_{VP}$ [$_{VP}$ strike NP] as ...]

This is shown by the fact that a variable in the object position of *strike* can license a parasitic gap in the predicate, a possibility which is expected to exist only if the variable does not c-command the parasitic gap (example from Chomsky's MIT class lectures, fall 1981):

(38) Who$_i$ did the pamphlet [$_{VP}$ [$_{VP}$ strike e_i] as being insulting to e_i]?

Moreover, consider the following:

(39) a John strikes Bill as more intelligent than him.
  b John strikes everyone as more intelligent than him.

In (39)a, *him* can be understood as coreferential to *Bill*. In (39)b, if we link *him* to the quantifier, the sentence acquires a weak crossover flavour which is only expected if *everyone* does not c-command *him* (for reasons discussed in Koopman and Sportiche 1982). If there is no c-command between the object position of *strike* and the predicative complement, the potential problem raised by the acceptability of (36) disappears, even if we adopt a raising analysis for this construction.

We can now turn to predicative structures involving *essere* (to be) or other copulative verbs. Various recent analyses (Stowell 1978; Couquaux 1979; Burzio 1981) treat copulative verbs as raising predicates that take small clausal complements. In particular, this analysis enables Burzio to explain the fact that, in Italian, copulative verbs select *essere* 'to be' and not *avere* 'to have' as aspectual auxiliary; this case being subsumed under the general process of auxiliary assignment in Italian. In the remainder of this section, we use our analysis of chain construction to test the small-clause hypothesis with this class of verbs; but before coming to that a digression on clitic movement in copulative structures is necessary. A complement of the predicative adjective can be cliticized to the copulative verb, as in (40)b:

(40) a Gianni è affezionato a lui.
  'Gianni is affectionate to him.'
  b Gianni *gli*$_i$ è affezionato e_i.
  'Gianni to-him is affectionate.'
  c Gianni$_i$ gli$_j$ è [$_{SC}$ e_i affezionato e_j].

Given the small-clausal analysis, this fact calls for an explanation: the S-structure corresponding to (40)b would be as in (40)c. In the usual assumption that traces of clitics are anaphors, one would expect (40)c to be ill-formed, as a violation of the Binding Theory. However, the governing category of e_i appears to be the small clause, and e_i does not have an antecedent in it.[12] Before suggesting a solution, it is necessary to notice that this problem is not simply an artifact of the small-clause analysis for *essere*: that it exists in general is clearly shown in less controversial cases of small-clause structures, such as the complements of verbs like *rendere* 'to render', *ritenere* 'to believe', and so forth. As far as overt anaphors and pronouns are concerned, such small clauses clearly count as governing categories: only the subject of the small clause can be the antecedent of the anaphor, and an overt pronominal complement is not disjoint in reference with the main subject.

(41) I nostri amici$_i$ hanno reso [$_{SC}$ Maria$_j$ più affezionata $\begin{Bmatrix} \text{a stessa}_j.] \\ \text{*a se stessi}_i.] \\ \text{*l'uno all'altro}_i.] \\ \text{a loro}_i.] \end{Bmatrix}$

'Our friends rendered Maria more affectionate to $\begin{Bmatrix} \text{herself.'} \\ \text{themselves.'} \\ \text{each other.'} \\ \text{them.'} \end{Bmatrix}$

But a clitic can be extracted from the small clause and cliticized to the main verb, giving a marginally acceptable result:

(42) ?I nostri amici gli$_i$ hanno reso [$_{SC}$ Maria più affezionata e_i].
'Our friends to-him rendered Maria more affectionate.'

The question then is why the small clause counts as governing category for the overt anaphor or pronoun in (41), but not for the clitic trace in (42). It is immediately plausible that whatever answer is correct for (42) should be extendable to (40)c. I would like to suggest the following: the main verb and the embedded predicate in (42) and (40)c can undergo a process of reanalysis, creating the complex predicates *rendere affezionato* 'to render affectionate' and *essere affezionato* 'to be affectionate'. It is not necessary to think of this process as involving a radical restructuring. The superscripting notation of Rouveret and Vernaud (1980) seems to be adequate. We would then have

(43) ...cl$_i$ V' [$_{SC}$ ... A' e_i ...],

where the clitic trace is governed by the complex predicate V' ... A'. Since the governor of the clitic trace is fully specified only in the main clause, the governing category of the clitic is the main clause itself, where the trace is bound by the clitic, as required by the Binding Theory. Hence, the structure is grammatical. On the contrary, when the complement of the adjective is phonetically realized as an anaphor or a pronominal, no such extension of the governing category is allowed. The abstract structure is

(44) ...V' [$_{SC}$ ... A' [$_{PP}$ P NP]].

No matter whether reanalysis between V and A takes place, the governor of the NP remains the preposition *a* (that prepositions cannot become members of complex predicates through reanalysis in Romance is shown in Kayne 1984, Chapter 5). Hence the governing category of the NP is always the small clause, and the otherwise surprising asymmetry between (41) and (42) is explained.

The reanalysis hypothesis is indirectly supported by the following observation: extraction of the clitic from the small clause is marginal at a variable degree if the lexical subject of the small clause intervenes between the verb and the adjective, while it is fully acceptable if no phonetically realized material intervenes:

(45) a ??Gli$_i$ ritenevo [$_{SC}$ tua sorella affezionata e_i].
  '(I) to-him believed your sister affectionate.'
 b Gli$_i$ ritenevo [$_{SC}$ e_j affezionata e_i anche tua sorella].
  '(I) to-him believe affectionate also your sister.'
 c Le persone$_j$ che gli$_i$ ritenevo [$_{SC}$ e_j affezionate e_i].
  'The people that (I) to-him believed affectionate.'
 d Maria$_j$ gli$_i$ era ritenuta [$_{SC}$ e_j affezionata e_i].
  'Maria to-him was believed affectionate.'

In (45)b, the subject of the small clause is moved to post-adjectival position. In (45)c, the subject position is vacated by Wh-movement and in (45)d by NP movement. This state of affairs is simply accounted for if we assume that V ... A reanalysis requires string contiguity, or adjacency, of the elements involved, not an unusual requirement for this class of processes (reanalysis remains marginally possible if the contiguity requirement is not met).

In this way it is possible to reconcile the small-clause analysis of the complement of *essere* with the fact that a clitic can be extracted from the predicate and cliticized to the copulative verb. We are now able to apply our test for the small clause nature of the complement. In fact, it is known since Kayne (1975) that reflexive–reciprocal clitics cannot be extracted out of AP complements of copulative verbs:

(46) a Gianni è affezionato a se stesso.
  'Gianni is affectionate to himself.'
 b *Gianni si è affezionato.
  'Gianni to-himself is affectionate.'
(47) a Loro sono simili l'uno all'altro.
  'They are similar to each other.'
 b *Loro si sono simili.
  'They to-each-other are similar.'
(48) a Loro sono odiosi l'uno all'altro.
  'They are hateful to each other.'

b *Loro si sono odiosi.
   'They to-each-other are hateful.'

This property directly follows from θ-Theory, given the small-clause analysis, in the now-familiar way: the structure of the *b* examples is:

(49) NP$_i$ si$_i$ essere' [$_{SC}$ e_i A' e_i].

NP$_i$ cannot receive its θ-role through chain formation with its trace because of the intervening binder *si*.[13] Notice that, as in previously considered cases, no semantic incompatibility seems to be involved in (46)–(48): stative verbs like *amare, assomigliare* ('to love', 'to resemble'), semantically very close to the adjectives, are perfectly compatible with anaphoric cliticization, as is the construction *fare pena/simpatia/tenerezza a NP* (literally, 'to make pain/liking/tenderness to NP'), thematically identical to *essere A a NP* ('to be A to NP'):

(50) a Loro si assomigliano.
        'They each-other resemble.'
    b   Loro si fanno pena/tenerezza/simpatia.
        'They to-each-other make pain/tenderness/liking.'

This strongly suggests that a structural explanation is in order for (46)–(48). It is also possible to show that extraction from an AP is not problematic per se for an anaphoric clitic. In fact, it yields a well-formed result in structures in which it does not interfere with chain formation. Compare the following:

(51) a *Maria$_i$ si$_i$ è [$_{SC}$ e_i fedele e_i].
        'Maria to-herself is loyal.'
    b   La sola persona$_i$ che Gianni$_j$ si$_j$ ritiene [$_{SC}$ e_i ancora fedele e_j] è Maria.
        'The only person that Gianni to-himself believes still loyal is Maria.'
(52) a *Maria$_i$ si è [$_{SC}$ e_i insopportabile e_i].
        'Maria to-herself is unbearable.'
    b   Gianni$_j$ si$_j$ rende [$_{SC}$ e_i insopportabile e_j anche Maria$_i$].
        'Gianni to-himself renders unbearable also Maria.'

Extraction of the anaphoric clitic from the AP is allowed by reanalysis, and can give rise to acceptable sentences, as (51)b and (52)b show. Ungrammaticality arises when the configuration created does not allow formation of the appropriate chains, as in (51)a and (52)a. Of course, if the wrong configuration is created in structures corresponding to (51)b and (52)b – for example, by passivizing the main verb – cliticization of the anaphoric

(53) a Maria$_i$ è stata resa [$_{SC}$ e_i insopportabile anche a se stessa$_i$].
       'Maria was rendered unbearable even to herself.'
    b *Maria$_i$ si$_i$ è stata resa [$_{SC}$ e_i insopportabile e_i].
       'Maria to-herself was rendered unbearable.'

In conclusion, there is no intrinsic prohibition against extracting an anaphoric clitic from an AP. The fact that in most cases this operation gives rise to an ungrammatical structure follows from general properties of the theory: the formal definition of chain and the θ-Criterion. This observation provides additional support for the small-clause analysis of the complement of copulative verbs.

Along the same lines, it is possible to show that there is no intrinsic incompatibility between passive and anaphoric cliticization. Consider the following:

(54) ?Questa è la missione$_i$ che Piero$_j$ si$_j$ ritiene [$_{SC}$ e_i affidata e_j direttamente da Dio].
      'This is the mission that Piero to-himself believes entrusted directly by God.'

In this sentence a reflexive clitic has been extracted from the passive predicate of a small clause. The sentence is marginal, as is generally the case when a passive small clause is embedded under such verbs as *ritenere*, but it clearly contrasts in acceptability with our standard case:

(55) *Piero$_i$ si$_i$ è stato affidato e_i e_i direttamente da Dio.
      'Piero to-himself was entrusted directly by God.'

We must therefore conclude that there is no intrinsic incompatibility between passive and anaphoric cliticization and ill-formedness arises only when the resulting configuration does not fulfil some general principle of the theory (as in fact generally happens, but in very special cases like (54)).

5 Must antecedents asymmetrically c-command anaphors?

Consider the following descriptive statement: a direct object can be the antecedent of an anaphoric prepositional object, but not of an anaphoric clitic. This is illustrated by the following examples for reflexives and reciprocals respectively:

(56) a Affiderò Gianni$_i$ a se stesso$_i$.
        '(I) will entrust Gianni to himself.'
     b *Si$_i$ affiderò Gianni$_i$.
        '(I) to-himself will entrust Gianni.'

c *Se$_i$ lo$_j$ affiderò.
'(I) to-himself him will entrust.'
(57)a Tu presenterai i tuoi amici$_i$ l'uno all' altro$_i$.
'You will introduce your friends$_i$ to each other$_i$..'
b *Tu si$_i$ presenterai i tuoi amici$_i$.
'You to-each-other will introduce your friends.'
c *Tu se$_i$ li$_i$ presenterai.
'You to-each-other them will introduce.'

Kayne (1975) argued that the impossibility of (56)b and (57)b is to be related to the incompatibility between anaphoric clitics and derived subjects. In fact, his extrinsic ordering solution is a way of relating the two classes of facts. The hypothesis that a genuine generalization exists can be expressed in a rather different way in the analysis proposed here. We suggest two different theoretical interpretations of the descriptive statement above. The second, but not the first, agrees with Kayne's original treatment in claiming that the two classes of facts are theoretically related. We then discuss the rather delicate empirical evidence which in principle discriminates between the two interpretations.

Considering the ungrammatical examples of (56)–(57) from the viewpoint of the GB models in the early eighties, we notice immediately that their ill-formedness cannot be attributed to ordinary c-command requirements on antecedent–anaphor relations. Given usual assumptions in such models, the c-domain of the direct object extends to the whole VP, and includes both the postverbal indirect object position and the preverbal clitic position (NB: the following discussion disregards the possibility that the clitic may occupy a VP-external position in the inflectional system, as proposed in Chapter 4; under such an analysis a clitic is never c-commanded by a VP internal object, therefore some of the problems discussed here do not arise). Therefore the distinction between (56)a/(57)a and (56)b/(57)b cannot be made on these grounds. This is equally true if the direct object itself is a clitic pronoun ((56) and (57)). In previous work (Rizzi 1979) we proposed that the relevant difference is that in the *a* examples the direct object asymmetrically c-commands the anaphor, while c-command is symmetric in the *b* and *c* examples. Suppose that the structural configuration in which 'antecedent binding' holds is asymmetric c-command, not simple c-command as is usually assumed. If this modification is accepted, the contrasts in (56)–(57) follow at once; only in the *a* examples does the direct object qualify as an appropriate antecedent.

Assuming the empirical adequacy of our original proposal, the natural question to ask is whether the asymmetry requirement is an intrinsic property of antecedent binding, to be stipulated in the formal definition, or whether it follows from other properties of the system. It is easy to ascertain that the asymmetry requirement, to the extent to which it appears empirically valid, is a theorem of the Binding module of the GB Theory. The binding principle specifies binding requirements not only for anaphors but also for the two other fundamental types of nominals, pronominals and lexical elements:

(58) Binding Principle:
    (A) An anaphor is antecedent-bound[14] in its Governing Category.
    (B) A pronominal is antecedent-free in its Governing Category.
    (C) A lexical element is free.

The asymmetry requirement is an immediate consequence of the interplay of the three principles. If α is an anaphor (assigned a governing category), then there must be an antecedent β c-commanding α; in turn, β can be either an anaphor, a pronominal, or a lexical element. Let us put aside the first case for the time being. Now, if β is a pronominal, it must be free in its governing category (which cannot be lower than the governing category of α), hence β cannot be c-commanded by α. Otherwise a would qualify as its antecedent binder, in violation of principle B. If β is lexical, it must be free, hence it cannot be c-commanded by α, otherwise principle C would be violated. The asymmetry requirements thus follow for pronominal and lexical antecedents. Turning now to examples (56)–(57), we notice that in the *a* examples both binding requirements are fulfilled: the anaphors are bound and the antecedents are free. This is not the case in *b* and *c*: the anaphors are bound, but also the lexical or pronominal antecedents are bound (by the c-commanding anaphoric clitics), hence these structures are ruled out by principles C and B, respectively.[15] In conclusion, the binding module of GB offers a simple and elegant explanation of the contrasts in (56)–(57), in that the asymmetric c-command requirement on binding follows, for the relevant cases, from the interplay between the three binding principles: anaphors must be bound, but antecedents, in the general case, must be free.

The proposed analysis implicitly denies the existence of a genuine generalization underlying the fact that neither an object nor a derived subject can be the antecedent of an anaphoric clitic. The following two ungrammatical sentences

(59)a *Si$_i$ affiderò Gianni$_i$ e_i.
    '(I) to-himself will entrust Gianni.'
  b *Gianni$_i$ si$_i$ è stato affidato e_i e_i.
    'Gianni to-himself was entrusted.'

are ruled out by two independent theoretical entities, the Binding Principle and θ-Theory respectively.

Alternatively, one could consider the possibility of unifying the theoretical account of the two facts under θ-Theory, along the following lines.

Consider (59)a. Since *si* and *Gianni* c-command each other, given our definition of 'Local Binder' (see Section 2), both can count as local binders of the clitic trace. Assuming, as the definition implicitly does, that such an ambiguity is tolerated by the system, this allows formation of both the following chain structures for (59)a:

(60)a (*si, e*), (*Gianni*)
   b (*si*), (*e, Gianni*)

If *a* is chosen, the structure is well-formed with respect to θ-Theory. If *b* is chosen, the θ-Criterion is violated: the first chain is assigned no θ-role, the second is assigned both θ-roles of the direct and indirect object. Now, if we want to unify the treatment of (59)a,b under θ-Theory, we can simply revise our definition of local binder in such a way that (60)a is excluded as a possible chain structure for (59)a: if only (60)b meets the definition of chain for (59)a then this structure is uniquely ruled out by θ-Theory, on a par with (59)b. This result can be formally achieved in a number of ways; for instance, consider the full tree-structure of the VP in the relevant case:

(61)
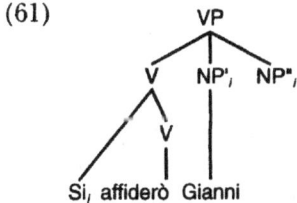

The path (in the sense of Kayne 1984, Chapter 7) connecting NP" and NP' is shorter than the one connecting NP" and *si*. If we define 'Local Binder' not in terms of c-command, but in terms of path (the local binder of α is the binder of α to which α can be connected through the shortest path), the chain formation algorithm will uniquely select (60)b as the chain structure for (59)a. This ungrammatical sentence will be excluded by the θ-Criterion, on a par with (59)b.

We thus have two possible approaches (in fact not mutually exclusive) for the ungrammaticality of (59)a: one in terms of the Binding Theory, which keeps (59)a and (59)b separate, and one in terms of θ-Theory, which covers both cases. Do these approaches differ on empirical grounds? They do differ in one case. Consider structure (61): if NP' is a lexical or pronominal noun phrase, both approaches correctly predict the ill-formedness of the structure. But if NP' itself is a (phonetically realized) anaphor, their predictions diverge: the 'Binding' approach predicts that, all things being equal, the structure should be acceptable, since principles B or C would become irrelevant. The 'Thematic' approach predicts unacceptability: irrespective of the intrinsic content of NP', this position would be uniquely identified as the local binder of the clitic trace, and this would give rise to the chain structure (*si*), (NP', *e*), ill-formed for the familiar reasons. Since the first approach is already given for free by the Binding Theory in its present form, and is the more 'liberal' one in the crucial empirical area, what is at issue is not really a choice between two alternatives, but rather the question of whether we need the extra effect of the revised definition of local binder.

The evidence is not entirely uncontroversial, but the general tendency clearly is that examples instantiating the relevant structure are at least marginally acceptable, given appropriate contextual conditions:

(62) a Dopo aver suscitato l'odio di tutti quelli che gli stavano attorno, Gianni ha finito per inimicarsi anche se stesso.
'After provoking the hatred of everyone who was around him, Gianni ended up pushing-against-himself even himself (lit. "making even himself an enemy of himself").'
  b ?Difficilmente un medico si prende in cura se stesso.
'It is difficult that a doctor on-himself (benefactive) takes-care-of himself.'
  c ?Nelle sue fantasticherie, talvolta Maria si immagina se stessa.
'In her daydreamings, sometimes Maria on-herself (benefactive) imagines herself.'

This state of affairs supports the 'Binding' approach. The marginal status of the data might cast doubts on the reliability of the evidence, but (62) clearly contrasts with the total, uncontroversial unacceptability of the corresponding examples in which the direct object position either is the (nonanaphoric) antecedent of the reflexive clitic, or is a trace in a passive structure:

(63) a *Si_i inimicherò $Gianni_i$.
'(I) against-himself will push Gianni.'
  b *Si_i prendo in cura $Gianni_i$.
'(I) on-himself take-care-of Gianni.'
  c *Si_i immagino $Gianni_i$.
'(I) on-himself imagine Gianni.'
(64) a *$Gianni_i$ si_i è stato inimicato e_i e_i.
'Gianni against-himself was pushed.'
  b *$Gianni_i$ si_i è stato preso in cura e_i e_i.
'Gianni on-himself was taken-care-of.'
  c *$Gianni_i$ si_i è stato immaginato e_i e_i.
'Gianni on-himself was imagined.'

The 'Thematic' approach to (59)a and (63), using the revised definition of 'Local Binder', would incorrectly predict an identical status for (62),

(63), and (64), which would all be assigned equally ill-formed chain structures, giving rise to a violation of the θ-Criterion.[16] Even if the marginality of (62) suggests some caution, the evidence thus favours the 'Binding' approach (59)a–(63), which predicts the acceptability of examples like (62). In conclusion, the 'asymmetric c-command requirement', which appears to hold in general in antecedent–anaphor relations, can be derived from the interplay of the Binding Principle, seems to provide the empirically correct account of the fact that a direct object cannot be the antecedent of an anaphoric clitic, a fact which is thus interpreted as theoretically independent from the incompatibility between anaphoric clitics and derived subjects.

6 Do traces require 'designated antecedents'?

In this section we consider a class of problems which the proposed formulation of θ-Theory straightforwardly solves. It is well-known that in contemporary French a clitic cannot be extracted from an embedded infinitive (apart from the causative construction):

(65)a Jean$_i$ veut [PRO$_i$ le$_j$ photographier e_j].
  'Jean wants to photograph him.'
 b *Jean$_i$ le$_j$ veut [PRO$_i$ photographier e_j].
  'Jean him wants to photograph.'

In the spirit of the classical analysis appealing to the Specified Subject Condition (Kayne 1975), we will attribute the ungrammaticality of (65)b to a violation of the Binding Principle: the clitic trace, an anaphor, is free in its governing category, the embedded clause. But this straightforward updating of the SSC solution has to deal with a very serious problem, pointed out by Richard Kayne: if the clitic is a reflexive, we find the same pattern as in (66):

(66)a Jean$_i$ veut [PRO$_i$ se$_i$ photographier e_i].
  'Jean wants to photograph himself.'
 b *Jean$_i$ se$_i$ veut [PRO$_i$ photographier e_i].
  'Jean himself wants to photograph.'

But (66)b cannot be excluded by the Binding Principle: due to their intrinsic nature, and the properties of the construction, the four nominals involved must bear the same index. Therefore, the clitic trace is not free in its governing category, being bound by PRO, and the requirement of the Binding Principle is thus fulfilled.

This fact could be interpreted as providing evidence that the locality requirement holding between a clitic and its trace is not to be characterized by the Binding Principle. There are a number of alternatives explored in the literature which might then receive support. Even if it does not seem implausible that the clitic–trace relation is ruled by a stricter requirement than the usual binding requirement for anaphors (Borer 1983), we would like to take here the conservative approach of keeping the classical analysis, which also appears to be the minimal analysis, and providing an independent solution for (66)b. As a matter of fact, this solution is already given by the θ-module. The only chain structure for (66)b which fulfils the θ-Criterion is

(67) (*Jean*), (PRO), (*se, e*).

But (67) cannot be formed from (66)b: the local binder of the clitic trace is PRO, hence the last chain of (67) is not allowed by the definition. Since, as is easy to verify, any other possible chain structure would violate the θ-Criterion, (66)b is ruled out by the θ-module.

Before coming to some consequences of the proposed analysis which have general theoretical import, it is worth noticing that this analysis has implications for the so-called 'Restructuring' problem. It is well known that sentences equivalent to (65)b and (66)b are grammatical in Italian and other Romance languages. In order to account for the apparent violation of SSC in such cases, we proposed, and gave independent motivation for, a restructuring rule which can optionally transform a biclausal structure into a simple clause with a complex 'verb' (Rizzi 1982, Chapter 1). Various precise formulations of this idea have subsequently been proposed in the literature. Our hypotheses on chain structures have nontrivial consequences on the choice of the appropriate formalism for restructuring. We focus here on one clear implication: there is evidence that restructuring and the kind of reanalysis which allows clitics to be extracted from small clauses are two distinct processes:

(68) a Loro$_i$ gli$_j$ erano ritenuti [e_i fedeli e_j].
    'They to-him were believed loyal.'
  b Loro$_i$ gli$_j$ dovevano [e_i parlare e_j].
    'They to-him had to speak.'

Example (68)a is a case of extraction from a small clause, for which we have proposed reanalysis following Rouveret and Vergnaud (1980). This process creates the complex predicate *ritenere fedele* which acts as the governor of the clitic trace; the clitic trace is thus assigned the main clause as its governing category, where it is bound by the clitic, as required. (68)b is a case of extraction from the infinitival complement of a restructuring verb, the raising verb *dovere* (no theoretical relevance should be attached to the brackets of the complement, which are simply specified for clarity of presentation). Now, an anaphoric (reciprocal) clitic is impossible in the first case, and acceptable in the second:

(69) a *Loro$_i$ si$_i$ erano ritenuti [e'_i fedeli e''_i].
   'They to-each-other were believed loyal.'
   b Loro$_i$ si$_i$ dovevano parlare.
   'They to-each-other had to speak.'

The ungrammaticality of (69)a is explained in the familiar way, by the impossibility of building the appropriate chains (*loro, e'*), (*si, e''*). But then (69)b cannot have a parallel structure (i.e., the one indicated by the brackets in (68)b), otherwise we would expect ungrammaticality. We must then exclude assimilation of restructuring with reanalysis in small clauses. The correct formalism for restructuring cannot be a simple annotation device (superscripting, or the like) which creates a 'complex predicate' while preserving the full configurational integrity of the reanalysed structure. A more radical device (as in our original proposal) must be adopted if we want to warrant empirical adequacy in the relevant cases. On the contrary, the minimal, 'annotational' view of reanalysis seems to be exactly what is needed for the case of extraction from small clauses.[17]

This observation has a significant theoretical consequence. Recent syntactic research has identified a number of processes apparently involving some sort of 'word formation' in the syntax, giving rise to the creation of complex 'lexical items' on certain levels of syntactic representation: 'complex verbs' in Romance and in the analysis of preposition stranding in English following Weinberg and Hornstein (1981); and complex 'adjectives' in the *easy to please* construction, according to the analysis of Chomsky (1981). Terms like 'restructuring' and 'reanalysis' are often used interchangeably in the literature, in the implicit assumption that such phenomena identify a homogeneous class. Our observation suggests that the class is not homogeneous: extraction of a clitic from an embedded clause in apparent violation of SSC can result from two independent types of processes of 'complex predicate' formation, which have different empirical consequences and seem to require rather different formal treatments.

We can now come back to our account of the ungrammaticality of (66)b. This case is a simple instance of a very general consequence of the proposed formulation of θ-Theory, which fills a systematic gap in the empirical domain of the Binding Principle. The assimilation of (NP and cl) traces to anaphoric elements in Chomsky (1981, Chapter 4) permitted an important simplification of the theory of movement rules: movement could be allowed to apply freely, and general conditions on antecedent–anaphor relations, independently necessary for overt anaphors, would reduce the massive overgeneration produced. This is clearly a desirable result. Still, a careful scrutiny of the relevant cases shows a peculiarity of antecedent–trace relations within the general class of antecedent–anaphor relations which could cast doubts on the proposed assimilation. While other anaphors do not put special requirements on the nature of their antecedents, a trace appears to require that its

150   Locality

antecedent be the moved phrase itself (or its trace): no other element can be the antecedent of a trace.

To illustrate, consider the following abstract S-structure: X and Y are A-positions (or, more precisely, positions relevant for principle A of the Binding Theory, which minimally include all A-positions and the clitic position):

(70) ...X_i... [$_\alpha$ ...Y_i... e_i...].

Suppose that the phrase X is moved directly from its base position e to a position outside α, the governing category of e. Suppose further that α contains a position Y, which happens to bear the same index as X and e. The structure is well-formed with respect to the Binding Theory since the anaphor e is bound in its governing category. Still, concrete instances of (71) are generally ill-formed, as (66)b shows (with one exception discussed below). θ-Theory fills in the gap. In principle, the following chain structures are possible for (70):

(71) a (X), (Y), (e).
    b (X, Y), (e).
    c (X), (Y, e).
    d (X, Y, e).

Supposing X to be an argument (the following remarks also apply if X is a non-argument, in connection with supplementary assumptions which I will not discuss here), from what has been assumed it follows that e is a θ-position and X is a $\bar{\theta}$-position, otherwise the θ-Criterion would be violated at D-structure (what follows holds as well if e is a $\bar{\theta}$-position which binds another trace in a θ-position, that is, if movement in (70) is not from a base position). The only option then concerns Y, which can be either a θ or a $\bar{\theta}$-position. If it is a θ-position, all the possible chain structures violate the $\bar{\theta}$-Criterion: in *a* there is a chain with an argument (X) which does not receive a θ-role, and a chain without an argument (e) which receives one; in *b* there is a chain without an argument which receives a θ-role (e); in *c* there is a chain with an argument which does not receive a θ-role (X), and the remaining chain receives two θ-roles; in *d* the chain receives two θ-roles. For Y in a θ-position, any chain structure associated to (70) is then ill-formed, whatever the intrinsic content of Y ((66)b instantiates the case with Y = PRO). If Y is a $\bar{\theta}$-position, chain structures *a*, *b*, and *c* are excluded as well by the θ-Criterion. As for *d*, it is allowed by θ-Theory if Y is a non-argument. In this case we would have one θ-role (assigned to position e) corresponding to a chain containing exactly one argument, as required by the θ-Criterion, in fact, this abstract case is instantiated by an acceptable structure:

(72) John$_i$ seems [e_i to have been fired e_i].

This is derived through direct movement of the NP *John* from its base position to the subject position of *seem*, plus accidental co-indexation of the empty category in subject position of the embedded sentence. θ-Theory permits only this instance of the abstract structure (70), and in fact it corresponds to a well-formed sentence.[18]

The proposed explanation of the ungrammaticality generally resulting from (70) has desirable theoretical consequences. In the lack of an alternative explanatory account, unacceptable sentences having the structure of (70) would suggest that traces do not simply require antecedents, but designate antecedents, that is, the moved phrases or their traces. But stipulating a bifurcation within the class of anaphors between those which require designated antecedents and those which do not would amount to reproducing the movement/non-movement distinction into the Binding Theory, thus virtually undermining a full assimilation of the output of movement to ordinary cases of antecedent–anaphor relations. But, as we have seen, no stipulation about designated antecedents is required: ungrammatical structures instantiating (70) are excluded by the θ-module, while the only cases allowed by the theory do, in fact, correspond to acceptable structures. The empirical problem raised by (70) is then solved, and the potential conceptual problem does not arise: the assimilation of traces to overt anaphors with respect to the Binding Theory can be maintained in full generality.

As a final remark, it can be noticed again that a derivational conception of chains would not permit the proposed account of the ungrammaticality of (68)b and, more generally, of (70). If chains were blind recordings of applications of 'move α', nothing would prevent formation of a chain including only X and its trace in (70), and the proposed explanation would be lost. This explanation, as well as all the main empirical results arrived at here, then argue for the representational conception of chains, and for the postulation of an autonomous chain formation algorithm dissociated from 'move α'.

Notes

1 Superscripts are simply used for notational convenience, in order to distinguish between the two traces, and do not have theoretical relevance in this context.

2 Chomsky (1981: 333) gives the following, more complex definition:
   $C = (a_1 \ldots a_n)$ is a chain iff:
   i a_1 is an NP;
   ii a_i locally A-BINDS a_{i+1}
   iii for $i > 1$, (a) a_i is a non-pronominal empty category, or
               (b) a_i is A-free;
   iv C is maximal, that is, not a proper subsequence of a chain meeting i–iii.

   Requirements i, iiia, and iv are self-evident: ii limits the notion 'Local Binding' to A-binders, that is, c-commanding argument positions co-indexed via superscripting or subscripting; iiib characterizes the case of an inverted subject co-indexed with the preverbal subject position. It seems to us that some of these requirements are likely to follow from other properties of the system (e.g., the maximality requirement), or are byproducts of the choice of specific technical devices (i.e., iiib), while the local binding requirement is the conceptual core of the notion. A possible reason for complicating our minimal definition is briefly discussed in footnote 18.

3 As a matter of fact, the verb *to seem* assigns a θ-role ('theme') to its complement clause. From now on we will disregard θ-roles assigned to clauses, which are irrelevant for our argument, and will focus on θ-role assignment to nominal expressions.

4 The case in which more than one chain structure can fulfil the θ-Criterion seems to arise only when an expletive is involved. For example, in

i   There arrived a man.

Given Burzio's (1981) hypothesis that the θ-position is the postverbal position, both the following chain structures would meet the requirement of the θ-Criterion:

ii   (There, a man)
iii (There), (a man)

This indeterminacy is in fact resolved by Chomsky's (1981) Visibility Hypothesis according to which a chain can be assigned a θ-role only if it has Case. This requirement is met by the chain in ii, but not in iii where the chain (a man) lacks Case, cannot receive a θ-role, and thus gives rise to a violation of the θ-Criterion.

5 The reductionist approach can be expressed in a slightly different, perhaps more perspicuous way. Chomsky (1981) suggests that the traditional derivational approach should be considered one possible concrete characterization of an abstract relation holding between levels of representation, a relation which can be more neutrally stated by saying that S-structures are formal objects factorizable into two components: D-structures and 'move α'. In the same vein, we could characterize the reductionist approach by saying that S-structures are factorizable into the two components, D-structures and chain formation. This possibility is straightforward for NP/cl movement; as for Wh-movement and, in general, for applications of 'move α' which do not give rise to chains in the original sense, we can have recourse to the extended notion of chain developed in slightly different ways by Aoun (1981), Cinque (1982b), Kayne (1984, Chapter 10). This approach leaves open the possibility that 'move α' applies in the syntax of Logical Form.

6 On the anaphoric status of the complex reciprocal construction *l'uno ... l'altro*, see Belletti (1982).

7 The proposed explanation assumes the so-called intrinsic characterization of null elements, according to which, for example, PRO and trace already differ in internal structure. Chomsky (1981, Chapter 6; 1982b) has proposed an alternative way of addressing the typology of null elements, the functional characterization, according to which there is only one abstract empty category, which is assigned to one of different types (PRO, trace, etc.) by an identification algorithm based on the properties of the local binder. In particular, if the local binder is in a θ-position, then the empty category is assigned to the type 'PRO'. This suggests an alternative approach to rule out (12). Given our definition of local binder. both the clitic and the clitic trace can be chosen as local binders of

the NP trace. Suppose that we revise our definition in such a way that e'' is uniquely chosen (this possibility is discussed in some detail in Section 5.2). Then (12) would be ruled out through the identification algorithm: the local binder of e' is e'', a θ-position, hence e' is PRO. Since this position is governed, the structure is ruled out by the general requirement that PRO must be ungoverned, ultimately a consequence of the Binding Conditions. The functional definition (and the Binding Theory) thus is a competitor of our account in terms of θ-Theory. The existence of this alternative (which, given supplementary assumptions holds for all the cases discussed here) clearly stems from the fact that the notion 'local binder' is crucially used both in the definition of chain and in the identification algorithm. This state of affairs underscores the theoretical tension existing between chain formation and the identification algorithm, suggesting that in a proper formulation of the theory reference to local binder should be made only once. Throughout this essay we couch our analysis in terms of θ-Theory in combination with the intrinsic approach to null elements (which we favour for reasons which cannot be adequately discussed in the present context). But it should be clear that our results can be simply translated in terms of the identification algorithm if the functional approach is chosen.

8 Burzio (1982) discusses another case of incompatibility with reflexive–reciprocal cliticization. In the causative *fare ... a* construction, the embedded object cannot be an anaphoric clitic:

i * Gianni si farà visitare a Mario.
    'Gianni himself will-make visit to M. = G. will make M. visit himself (G.).'

This state of affairs follows from Burzio's analysis since the corresponding D-structure would be

ii Gianni$_i$ farà [Mario$_j$ si visitare],

where the peculiar binding requirement of the anaphoric clitic (co-indexation with its subject) is not met. Of course, this account cannot be subsumed under our approach, since chain formation is simply irrelevant in this case. Our analysis thus forces the conclusion that i does not fall into a genuine generalization with (9), (17), and (19). That the requirement of a 'close antecedent' at D-structure is not the crucial (or sufficient) property involved here is independently suggested by the fact that structures corresponding to i with a stressed reflexive in embedded subject position are equally ill-formed. Example iii would have D-structure iv:

iii *Il medico si lascia visitare solo a se stesso.
iv Il medico$_i$ lascia [solo se stesso$_i$ si$_i$ visitare].
    'The doctor lets only himself visit himself.'

The D-structure requirement of the anaphoric clitic, according to Burzio's approach, would be fulfilled in iv, and still the sentence is unacceptable. An alternative analysis is possibly to be found along the lines indicated by Wehrli (1983) who suggests that i is to be treated on a par with the fact that a non-third-person pronominal clitic is impossible in these structures:

v *Gianni ti farà visitare a Mario.
    'Gianni will-make Mario visit you.'

According to Wehrli the right generalization encompassing i and v is to be stated in the form of a principle blocking the extraction of clitics which are not morphologically characterized as nondatives: the generalization thus includes reflexives, non-third-person pronouns (which have a single accusative–dative form) and third-person datives, and excludes third-person accusatives. Notice that the two classes also differ semantically in that the first requires (or highly prefers) animate antecedents, while the second does not. This might suggest a link with the animacy contraint often mentioned as a factor affecting the extractability of a clitic in Spanish (see Bordelois 1974).

9 If a nonclitic experiencer phrase is placed between the main verb and the complement the resulting structure is very marginal:

   i *?Gianni$_i$ sembra a Piero [e$_i$ non fare il suo dovere].
      'Gianni seems to Piero not to do his duty.'

The reason of the deviance of this structure is unclear, as is the position of the clitic trace in (22)b. We have thus decided to omit the specification of the clitic trace in the structural representations, since it is inessential for our argument.

10 Certain curious and poorly understood co-reference facts suggest that this conclusion is to be tempered. In the following sentence the object of *a* can be the antecedent of both a reflexive and a pronoun outside the PP at degrees of marginality which vary a lot from speaker to speaker:

   i Parlerò a Gianni$_i$ di sé$_i$/lui$_i$.
      'I will speak to Gianni about himself/him.'

This fact suggests that the PP node headed by *a* can be optionally disregarded, as a marked option, in computing the c-command relations. If it is not, the pronoun is possible; if it is, the reflexive is chosen. This possibility clearly is compatible with the text hypothesis. But the role of various types of PP nodes in defining c-domains, and the related question of co-reference relations between VP complements seems to interact with other factors (linear order, thematic hierarchies) in a complex way which has resisted explanation so far.

Notice incidentally that, given what has been proposed, the straightforward expectation would be that a language having stressed, nonprepositional experiencers in raising structures should not allow an anaphoric experiencer. The prediction seems to be borne out in Dutch, as Teun Hoekstra informs me:

   ii John lijht mij [*e* een aardige man te zijn].
       'John seems to me a nice man to be.'
   iii *Ik lijht [*e*. . .].
       'I seem to myself . . .'

But see the discussion of Section 4 on the *strike . . . as* construction for a factor which might interfere in the prediction.

11 The analysis of *s'avérer* can be extended to many cases of ergative verbs with an intrinsic reflexive clitic:

   i Il ramo si è rotto *e*.
      'The branch broke.'

We agree with Burzio (1981) in interpreting this reflexive as an idiomatic nonargument (in fact, an 'ergative marker') which does not affect the chain-formation process.

12 For the present discussion it is sufficient to adopt a simplified definition of 'governing category' like the following: α is the governing category of β iff α is the minimal NP or S which contains β and a governor of β. For a detailed discussion of this notion, see Chomsky (1981, Chapter 3).
13 As originally noticed by Kayne (1975), with different choices of adjectives the degree of deviance of the relevant structure can become weaker:

   i ??Loro si sono simpatici.
      'They to-each-other are nice.'
   ii ?Loro si sono vicini nelle circostanze difficili.
      'They to-each-other are close in the difficult circumstances.'

   To sum up the situation of the quality of the data, we find strong ill-formedness and no lexical variation with passive, impersonal passive, and raising predicates of the *seem* class (both with full infinitives and small clauses); we find an often weaker degree of deviance and lexical variation with ergatives and copulative predicates. We tentatively suggested a possible interpretation of the variability with ergatives. Extending this suggestion, it would seem that for some lexical choice of adjective, the biclausal structure can be marginally reanalysed as a simple sentence (i.e., instead of the discussed reanalysis process, we can marginally have the more radical restructuring mentioned in Section 6 below). We do not have a sufficiently refined analysis for an explanatory account of these acceptability hierarchies (if one is to be found at all), but it seems to us that the quality of the data strongly suggests that the basic fact to be explained is the general deviance of these structures, and the existence of marginal areas of variation is to be attributed to peripheral mechanisms.
14 Antecedent binding is generally understood as 'binding by an A-position'. But if the relation holding between a clitic and its trace is ruled by principle A, and hence is to be assimilated to antecedent binding, and if the clitic position is an A'-position, then the notion is to be refined. A characterization which would include both NP-trace and cl-trace relations, and exclude Wh-trace relations, as is required, could be in terms of clause-internal versus clause-peripheral position (the latter being defined by the context $[_{s}' \_\_\_ [_{s}')$: antecedent-binding is binding by a clause-internal position.
15 The complete structure of (57)b is:

   i *Tu si$_i$ presenterai i tuoi amici$_i$ e_i.

   We leave open here the question of whether the clitic itself, or the clitic trace (or both) is the element which counts as antecedent binder of *i tuoi amici*, determining the ill-formedness of the structure.
   It has recently been suggested that principle C can be dispensed with as an autonomous stipulation, its consequences being independently derivable (Chomsky 1982b). Of course any such reductionist approach must still somehow characterize the effects of Lasnik's (1976) non-coreference rule. In order to keep the above proposal in a system which does not stipulate principle C, we must therefore assume that whatever principle yields the result that lexical NPs cannot have antecedents, it will subsume such cases as (57)b.
16 Concerning (65)c, one might observe that *immaginarsi* could be considered an intrinsic reflexive (as is explicitly assumed by Kayne 1975 for the French equivalent *s'immaginer*), in which case one would not expect the ungrammaticality of (65)c, which should behave on a par with (30) and i of footnote 12, allowing chain formation (*Gianni, si, e*) (the second trace of (65)c would not be specified). Our approach thus seems to require an analysis of *immaginarsi* as

a nonintrinsic reflexive (at least, not in the same sense as *rompersi* and *s'avérer*). In fact, this seems to be justified on semantic grounds: the reflexive clitic has a rather definite 'benefactive' flavour in *immaginarsi*, while it does not seem to be amenable to any thematic interpretation in *rompersi* and *s'avérer*. Since no structure like (65)c seems to exist, we are left with the question of why a true intrinsic reflexive can be found with ergative and raising, but not with passive. The answer seems to be, along the lines of Burzio's (1981) discussion, that true intrinsic reflexives are 'markers of ergativity,' hence they can never occur in transitive structures. The nonexistence of passivizable intrinsic reflexive verbs would then reduce to the general incompatibility between ergativity and passivization.

17 Burzio's (1981) detailed study on restructuring proposes a full assimilation of the restructuring process with the causative rule VP preposing: this rule extracts the infinitival VP from the embedded clause rendering it transparent for further extractions. The structure of (68)b would be:

i   Loro$_i$ gli$_j$ dovevano [$_{VP_k}$ parlare e_j] [e_i VP$_k$].

This approach seems to make the wrong prediction on (69)b: the structure would be:

ii   Loro$_i$ si$_i$ dovevano [$_{VP_k}$ parlare e'] [e'' VP$_k$],

and the required chain (*loro, e''*) could not be formed because of the intervening binder *si*. The acceptable sentence would thus incorrectly be ruled out, hence our analysis appears to be incompatible with Burzio's treatment of restructuring.

As a matter of fact, the two approaches can be reconciled in a way which will be only sketched out here. Consider our standard case:

iii   *Gianni$_i$ si$_i$ è stato affidato e' e''.

So far we have attributed the 'intervention' effect to the reflexive clitic, but we have noticed that also the clitic trace 'intervenes' (in the relevant structural sense) between *Gianni* and e'. Suppose that we now push this observation to its extreme consequence, assuming that *only* the clitic trace determines the intervention effect, that is, this effect is somehow restricted to A-positions. This modification would render Burzio's structural hypothesis compatible with our analysis: the chain (loro, e'') could be formed in ii since the clitic, an A'-position, does not interfere, and the clitic trace e', an A-position, does not c-command e''. (69)a is still excluded since the clitic trace e'' cannot 'reach' the clitic because of the intervening A-binder e'. The contrast between (69)a and (69)b (with structure ii) would then reduce to the fact that e' c-commands e'' in (69)a, but not in ii, the position of the clitic becoming irrelevant.

Since the plausibility of this alternative depends on still unclear questions concerning the nature of the clitic–trace relation, we will leave the issue open. But even if Burzio's approach is adopted in conjunction with the suggested revision of the 'intervention effect', the point still remains that different formal devices must be used for (68)a and (68)b in order to reach empirical adequacy.

18 The fact that structures like (72) allow two distinct derivations via 'move α' (successive cyclic movement, or direct movement to the main subject position plus accidental co-indexation of the embedded subject) has been interpreted by Aoun in unpublished work as evidence for the reductionist approach men-

tioned in Section 2, under the methodological principle that the mapping between a given D-structure and the corresponding S-structure should be performed in a unique way.

The fact that the embedded subject position cannot be filled by an overt non-argument (expletive *there* or *it*) can be captured, at worst, by a stipulation in the definition of chain to the effect that intermediate nodes in the chain must be empty categories (see iii of Chomsky's definition quoted in footnote 2).

6 On the anaphor–agreement effect*

The following examples illustrate the well-known fact that a reflexive or reciprocal (henceforth an anaphor) must have its antecedent in the same simple clause. If the antecedent is in a higher clause, the structure is ill-formed:

(1) Bill thinks that *they* like *each other*.
(2) a **They* think that Bill likes *each other*.
    b **They* think that *each other* please Bill.

Does the ungrammaticality of (2)a and b represent a genuine linguistic generalization? Different versions of the Binding Theory (or of its antecedents) give different answers. For instance, the classical transformational approach (cf. Lees and Klima 1963 and subsequent work), a *Conditions* type framework and the standard approach to Binding within the Government Binding Theory (cf. Chomsky 1981) give a positive answer: there is a particular principle that is violated in both cases (respectively, the Clause Mate Condition, the Tensed S Condition, and Binding Principle A). On the other hand, the approaches to Binding in Chomsky (1980) and (1986a) give a negative answer, and claim that the two ill-formed examples violate two distinct conditions: (2)a violates the fundamental binding principle (the Specified Subject Condition, subsumed under Principle A), whereas (2)b violates a different condition (the Nominative Island Condition, subsumed under the Empty Category Principle).

In spite of the natural intuitive appeal of the first trend, English already offers rather straightforward empirical evidence favouring the second trend. If we slightly manipulate the structures in (2) by embedding the reciprocal within an NP, an asymmetry emerges: the structure in which the anaphor is embedded within the subject is notably more acceptable:

---

* This paper was presented at the annual meeting of the *Rivista di grammatica generativa*, Scuola Normale Superiore, Pisa, February 1986. Only minor revisions and bibliographical updatings have been introduced.

(3) a *They think that Bill likes *each other*'s pictures.
   b They think that *each other*'s pictures please Bill.

The literature on Binding of the last decade shows that it still is formally possible to give a uniform treatment of (2) and (3) through a unique principle, but this result requires a rather artificial definition of the opacity creating factor (the Accessible SUBJECT of Chomsky's *Lectures*). A more promising tack seems to be the one followed in Chomsky (1980; 1986a): (3) is the representative paradigm of the operation of the Binding Theory; things are blurred in (2) by the intervention of a disturbing factor which rules out (2)b.

This chapter adopts the latter approach, and tries to give a contribution to the identification of the disturbing factor involved in (2)b and similar examples. After a presentation of the theory of Chomsky (1986a) in Section 1, we will claim in Section 2 that there is a fundamental incompatibility between the property of being an anaphor and the property of being construed with agreement: the anaphor–agreement effect. The third section will deal with the peculiar binding properties of the subject position of subjunctive clauses in Romance, and the fourth section will be devoted to the theoretical interpretation of the anaphor–agreement effect.

1 An ECP based account

The fundamental empirical fact that all the versions of the theory of Binding have tried to capture is the near complementarity between anaphors and coreferential pronouns. In general, an anaphor is possible in environments in which a pronoun cannot be coreferential and, reciprocally, a pronoun cannot be coreferential in environments in which an anaphor is allowed to occur (the star in examples like (4)b refers to the impossibility of the coreferential interpretation):

(4) a Bill thinks that [they like each other].
   b *Bill thinks that [they like them].
(5) a *They think that [Bill likes each other].
   b They think that [Bill likes them].

Still, in some environments the complementarity disappears: the possessive position on an NP in English can host both an anaphor and a coreferential pronoun:

(6) a They like [their books].
   b [They like each other's books].

Conversely, the subject position of a subjunctive clause in Romance disallows both anaphors and coreferential pronominals: there is no way to express coreference between this position and the superordinate subject (the examples illustrate the effect in Italian; (7)b is fine if *lui* is not coreferential to *Gianni*):

(7)a *Gianni vuole che se stesso vinca.
   'Gianni wants that himself win.'
  b *Gianni vuole che (lui) vinca.
   'Gianni wants that he win.'

Let us postpone the discussion of the Romance case. The approach to Binding proposed in Chomsky (1986a) is specifically designed to account for the selective lack of complementarity illustrated in (6). We will now present a simplified version of this approach.

The general complementarity is captured by the fact that anaphors and pronominals have opposite binding requirements within the same local domain, their Governing Category (GC):[1]

(8) Binding Principles:
  A An anaphor must be bound in its GC.
  B A pronominal must be free in its GC.

So, in general, wherever an anaphor can survive (hence it can be bound), a pronoun must be free, non-coreferential. The partial lack of complementarity in such environments as (6) is accounted for through a proper definition of what counts as the Governing Category for a given element:

(8') Governing Category: Z is the Governing Category for X if Z is the minimal category with a subject containing X, a governor G for X, and where the binding requirements of X are satisfiable.

This system gives the correct result in the cases of (4), (5) and (6) (the governing categories are indicated by the brackets). In (4)a and (5)a, the GC of the anaphor is the lower clause, the minimal category with a subject containing the anaphor, a governor for the anaphor (the verb) and where the binding requirements of the anaphor are satisfiable in principle, under some indexation (the clause contains a position, the subject position, which can function as a binder for the anaphor in object position). In this system, assignment of the GC is done in part on the basis of the *virtual* binding properties (presence or absence of a position that could, under some indexation, function as a binder). Once this operation is performed, the *actual* binding properties are checked. The anaphor is in fact bound in its GC in (4)a, but not in (5)a, which is then ruled out by the Binding Principle. In (4)b and (5)b, the GC of the pronominal is again the embedded clause, the minimal category with a subject containing the pronominal, its governor and where the binding requirements of the pronominal can be fulfilled in principle. The actual binding properties are then checked: by Binding Principle B the pronominal must be free in its GC, as is the case in (5)b, but not in (4)b. Consider now (6)a–b. In (6)a the minimal category with a subject containing the anaphor and its governor is the NP *each other's parents*; still, the anaphor couldn't possibly have its binding requirements fulfilled within the NP: *qua* anaphor it should be bound, but there is no possible binder for it within the NP. So the binding properties of the anaphor are not satisfiable within the NP, the NP does not meet the definition of GC, and we have to move to the next higher category with a subject, the whole clause. Here the binding requirements of the anaphor are satisfiable, as there is a potential binder for it, the subject of the clause. The definition of GC is thus met. As the anaphor is in fact bound in its GC, the Binding Principle is satisfied. Consider now (6)b. If we try to compute the GC of the possessive pronominal, the first candidate is the NP *their books*, the smallest category with a subject (the pronominal itself) containing the pronominal and its governor (the noun). Moreover, the binding requirements of the pronominal are satisfiable within the NP: as pronominals must be free, this condition will always be trivially fulfilled in a structure in which there is no possible antecedent. So, the NP qualifies as the GC for the pronominal; as the pronominal is free in its GC, Binding Principle B is met, and the structure is well-formed even if the pronominal is bound outside its GC, as is the case in (6)b. The theory of Chomsky (1986a) thus achieves the result of accounting for the non-complementary distribution shown in (6) through a unique definition of GC for anaphors and pronominals, which correctly predicts the complementarity manifested in the other cases.[2]

This system also correctly accounts for the contrast between (3)a and b:

(3)a *They think that [Bill likes each other's pictures].
  b [They think that each other's pictures please Bill].

In (3)a the GC of the anaphor is the embedded clause, the anaphor is not bound in it, hence the structure is ill-formed. In (3)b the embedded clause does not qualify as a GC for the anaphor (there is no possible antecedent for it), therefore we must move to the main clause, which meets the definition of GC. The anaphor is in fact bound in the main clause, hence the structure is well-formed.

But this system appears to make the wrong prediction on paradigm (2):

(2)a *They think that [Bill likes each other].
  b *[They think that each other please Bill].

The ill-formedness of (2)a is accounted for, but (2)b is not: the embedded clause does not qualify as the GC for the anaphor because there is no possible binder for it. The main clause qualifies as the GC, and the anaphor is bound in it. So, the structure should be well-formed, contrary to fact.

Chomsky (1986a) is thus led to the conclusion that (2)b is not ruled out by the Binding Theory. He must then resort to an independent principle for this case. The proposal sketched out by Chomsky is the following. Suppose that anaphors move in the syntax of Logical Form to a position adjacent to (governed by) their antecedent; i.e., at LF sentence (9)a has a representation like (9)b, resembling the S-structure order of elements in the corresponding Romance examples:[3]

(9)a They saw each other.
  b They each other saw t.
  c Loro si videro t.

Under this assumption, the LF representation of (2)b would be the following:

(10) *They each other think that t please Bill.

This representation is ruled out by the Empty Category Principle, the principle that limits the possible occurrence of traces to properly governed positions.[4]

The impossibility of (2)a is thus traced back to the fact that an embedded subject is not extractable, neither by syntactic nor LF movement:

(11)a *Who do you think that t likes Bill?
   b *Mary seems that t likes Bill.
   c *Gianni la ritiene che t ami Piero.
     'Gianni her believes that likes Piero.'
   d *Je n'exige que personne soit arrêté.
     'I neg demand that nobody be arrested.'
   e *Personne [je n'exige que t soit arrêté].

(11)a is a case of Wh movement, b a case of NP movement (raising), c a case of clitic movement, d a case of LF movement of the negative quantifier, with LF representation in e (cf. Kayne 1984, Chapter 2 for discussion). According to Chomsky's proposal, the disturbing factor determining the asymmetry of paradigms (2)–(3) then is the ECP (cf. also an earlier proposal by Kayne 1984, Chapter 8 in terms of his Connectedness condition). This principle rules out (2)a, a structure which would otherwise be ruled in by the Binding Theory.

2 On the incompatibility between anaphors and agreement

In this section we will discuss cases somewhat analogous to (2)a, but such that neither the ECP nor the Binding Principle can draw the appropriate distinction to deal with them. The alternative we would like to explore originates from the observation that in (2)b, but not in (3)b or (6)b the anaphor is directly construed with verbal agreement. It could then be that there is an intrinsic incompatibility between the property of being an anaphor and the property of being construed with agreement, an incompatibility which could turn out to be more fundamental than current approaches would suggest.

The first case to be considered involves different classes of psychological verbs in Italian.

(12) a Loro amano lei.
        'They love her.'
     b A loro piace lei.
        'To them pleases her.'

The verb agrees with the preverbal experiencer in (12)a and with the postverbal theme in (12)b, which receives nominative Case. There are reasons to believe that the dative experiencer in (12)b can be in subject position: it has subject-like properties with respect to the theory of bounding, the theory of control, etc. (cf. Perlmutter 1983b; Belletti and Rizzi 1988). Now, the experiencer can bind an anaphoric theme in the first case, but not in the second:

(13) a Loro amano se stessi.
        'They love themselves.'
     b *A loro piacciono se stessi.
        'To them please themselves.'

An even more minimal pair is offered by the following cases:

(14) a A me importa solo di loro.
        'To me matters only of them.'
     b A me interessano solo loro.
        'To me matter only they.'

Importare takes a dative experiencer and a genitive theme, and *interessare* takes a dative experiencer and a nominative theme construed with agreement, like *piacere*. Again, the theme can be an anaphor in the first case, but not in the second:

(15) a A loro importa solo di se stessi.
        'To them matters only of themselves.'
     b *A loro interessano solo se stessi.
        'To them interest only themselves.'

The well-formedness of (15)a is important, in that it shows that the dative experiencer can function as the binder of an anaphor. What rules out

(13)b–(15)b? Not the Binding Principle, as there is a binder available in the same simple clause. ECP cannot be relevant either, as the postverbal position, lexically governed by the verb, is a possible extraction site:

(16) I libri che a Gianni sono piaciuti t di più ...
  'The books that to Gianni pleased most ...'

Of course, the property singling out (13)b–(15)b is that only in these examples is the anaphor construed with agreement. We thus have a case of anaphor-agreement effect not (immediately) reducible to the Binding Principle or to the ECP.

This is the clause-internal equivalent of a well-known case involving long-distance anaphors in Icelandic (Anderson 1982; Maling 1984). Icelandic allows an anaphor in object position of a subjunctive clause to be bound by a superordinate subject; this option does not exist if the anaphor is the nominative subject construed with agreement in the subjunctive clause (examples from Maling 1984):

(17)a Jón segir að Maria elski sig.
  'Jon says that Maria love+SUB SELF.'
  b *Jón segir að sig elski Maria.
  'Jon says that SELF love+SUB Maria.'

That the crucial discriminating factor is not the subject/non-subject status, but the presence or lack of construal with agreement is shown by the following: if the verb selects a quirky (non-nominative) case for the subject and the latter does not trigger agreement, then a long distance anaphor in subject position becomes possible:

(18) Hún sagdi að sig vantadi peninga.
  'She said that SELF+ACC lacked+SUB money.'

Moreover, verbs with a quirky subject and a nominative object construed with agreement do not allow the long distance anaphor to appear in object position; if the object is prepositional and not construed with agreement, the long distance anaphor can appear:

(19)a *Sigga telur að mér líki sig.
  'Sigga thinks that to me likes+SUB SELF+NOM.'
  b Sigga telur að mér líki vel við sig.
  'Sigga thinks that to me likes+SUB with SELF.'

Why are (17)a–(19)a ill-formed? An ECP based approach to (17)b would not generalize to (19)a, and would not seem to be able to distinguish (17)a and (18). Anderson and Maling both suggest that these structures may be simply excluded by assuming that the morphological paradigm of the long distance reflexive lacks a nominative form. But why should exactly the same gap exist in Italian (as well as in many other languages, no doubt)? Moreover, Italian provides clear evidence against the gap in the paradigm hypothesis: the same facts discussed before arise when first or second person reflexives are involved:

(20) a A voi importa solo di voi stessi.
        'To you+PLUR matters only of yourselves.'
     b *A voi interessate solo voi stessi.
        'To you+PLUR interest only yourselves.'

But first and second person stressed reflexives are formed by simply combining personal pronouns with the intensifier *stesso*. As nominative pronouns exist, there is no doubt that nominative reflexives of second and third person are morphologically possible, and the gap in the paradigm approach cannot be appealed to for these cases. The anaphor agreement effect thus seems to involve a deeper syntactic incompatibility than just the lack of a form in the Case paradigm.[5]

3 Disjoint reference in subjunctive clauses

A well-known property of subjunctive clauses in Romance is the fact that an overt or null pronominal subject cannot be coreferential to the immediately superordinate subjects:

(21) *Gianni$_i$ vuole che (lui$_i$) scriva un libro.
      'Gianni wants that he write a book.'

We will now sketch out an approach to this fact and show its relevance for the anaphor agreement effect. A natural analysis is the one proposed by Picallo (1985) and further elaborated by many other linguists:[6] if the governing category of the subject of a subjunctive clause extends to the main clause, the disjoint reference effect simply is a case of application of principle B of the Binding Theory. This approach is made plausible by the observation that the effect is limited to adjacent clauses: if the antecedent is not subjacent to the pronominal subject, coreference is possible:

(22) Gianni$_i$ spera che Maria voglia che (lui$_i$) scriva un libro.
      'Gianni hopes that Maria want that he write a book.'

This is exactly what is expected if the extension of the governing category of the subject solely involves the immediately superordinate clause. So, in (22) the GC on *lui* would be the intermediate clause *Maria voglia* ... , in which the pronoun would be free, as demanded by principle B. Nothing would exclude coreference with the main subject.

The technical question now arises of how this extension of governing category is to be achieved. Many current approaches try to relate the disjoint reference effect to the dependent, anaphoric nature of subjunctive. It is a fact that subjunctive subordinates manifest stricter 'sequence of tense' restrictions than indicative subordinates. For instance, in Standard Italian the sequence past–present is allowed with indicative, but not with subjunctive:

(23) a Gianni sapeva/diceva che io lavoravo/lavoro con voi.
        'Gianni knew/said that I worked/work with you.'
     b Gianni voleva/credeva che io lavorassi/*lavori con voi.
        'Gianni wanted/believed that I worked/work with you.'

The idea that subjunctive is an anaphoric tense is elaborated by Picallo (op. cit.), Raposo (1985b) and others. I will assume that this approach is basically correct. But why should the anaphoric nature of the tense determine an extension of the governing category of the subject? The approach to Binding of Chomsky (1986a) offers a simple solution. Suppose that we revise the definition of Governing Category given in (8') by adding the italicized part:

(24) Governing Category: Z is the governing category for X iff Z is the minimal category with a subject containing X, a governor G for X, and where the binding requirements of X *and G* are satisfiable.

That is, we are now demanding that not only the binding requirements of the element to which a GC is to be assigned, but also the binding requirements of its governor be satisfiable in principle in the domain under consideration. If this condition is not met, the domain in question does not qualify as a governing category. This modification is inconsequential in most cases: ordinary governors are lexical heads or referential tenses, entities which are assimilated to referential expressions as far as the theory of binding is concerned. As the binding requirement of a referential expression is that it must be free, this requirement is trivially satisfiable in any domain, hence the added requirement never affects the assignment of GC in such cases. Things change radically if the governor is anaphoric. To illustrate, consider the assignment of GC to the pronominal subject of an indicative and a subjunctive embedded clause:

(25) a Gianni dice che (lui) T+REF scriverà un libro.
        'Gianni says that he will write a book.'
     b Gianni vuole che (lui) T+ANAPH scriva un libro.
        'Gianni wants that he write a book.'

Recall that coreference is possible in a and excluded in b. In a, the GC of the pronominal subject is the embedded clause, the minimal category with a subject which contains the pronoun, its governor, the (Infl containing the) referential tense and where the binding requirements of the pronoun and of the referential tense are satisfiable (both must be free, and this requirement is obviously satisfiable in the embedded clause). On the contrary, the embedded clause does not qualify as the GC of the pronominal subject in (25)b, under definition (24): it is the minimal category with a subject containing the pronoun and its governor, the (Infl containing the) anaphoric subjunctive tense, but the binding requirements of the latter cannot be satisfied within the embedded clause: as an anaphoric tense, its binding requirements are only satisfiable in the next higher clause, which contains the required binder, a tense. We thus simply obtain the result that the GC of the pronominal subject in (25)a is the main clause, whence the disjoint reference effect.

Under these assumptions, the familiar problem arises, as Picallo pointed out. If the governing category of the subject is always extended to the next higher clause, an anaphoric subject should be permissible. This is not the case:

(26) *Gianni vuole che se stesso scriva un libro.
 'Gianni wants that himself write a book.'

We thus have a new instance of the anaphor-agreement effect.

4 On the theoretical status of the effect

Why should anaphors be intrinsically incompatible with agreement? Picallo (op. cit.) notices the problem raised by (26) and proposes the following: if Agreement is a kind of pronominal element, as is often assumed (cf. Chomsky 1981), and if it forms a chain with the element it is construed with, the construal of an anaphor with agreement could be barred by a clash in the specification of the two elements belonging to the same chain with respect to the features *anaphoric* and *pronominal*. If we try to implement Picallo's suggestion, we should be careful not to formulate the relevant consistency condition in too strict a manner, as the following chains must be ruled in:

(27) a *There* came *a man*.
 b Pourquoi *Jean* est-*il* parti?
 c Pourquoi *lui* est-*il* parti?
 d *John* was fired *t*.
 e *He* was fired *t*.
 f John expected *himself* to be fired *t*.

(27)a and b illustrate a chain involving a pronominal and an R-expression ((27)b is a case of Complex Inversion in French, on which see Kayne 1984, Chapter 10; Rizzi and Roberts 1989); the chain in c involves two pronominals, the ones in d, e, f involve, respectively, an R-expression and an anaphor, a pronominal and an anaphor, an anaphor and another anaphor (under the standard assumption that an NP trace is an anaphor). How could one bar the anaphor agreement configuration while allowing all these other combinations? One could proceed along the following lines. It is clear that R-expressions, pronominals and anaphors are ranked along a dimension of referential autonomy: R-expressions are always referentially autonomous, pronouns can be referentially autonomous, anaphors are never referentially autonomous. One could then imagine that the argument, the contentive element of a chain, must be the most referentially autonomous element in the chain (or, more precisely, there cannot be a non-argument in the chain which is higher in the referential autonomy hierarchy than the argument). If agreement is pronominal, this principle would suffice to rule out the anaphor agreement construal: in structures like (17)b, (26), etc. the anaphor, an argument, should be in chain with a non-argumental pronominal, the Agr specification, thus violating the proposed constraint. All the cases of (27) would still be ruled in, as in the relevant chains the argument never is lower than the non-argument with respect to the referential autonomy hierarchy. It is easy to verify that this approach covers all the cases that have been considered so far.

While the proposed condition on chains is not implausible and may have desirable empirical consequences in other domains, there is another, more sophisticated way of deriving the anaphor agreement effect that is worth exploring. If agreement has pronoun-like properties, anaphor–agreement configurations would manifest two elements having opposite binding requirements in a local construal: the anaphor should be bound, but the pronominal should be free; such contradictory requirements could not be simultaneously met in the same structure. So, the anaphor–agreement effect could have a theoretical status analogous to the PRO Theorem, barring the pronominal anaphor PRO from governed contexts. To implement this idea, we must first of all notice that the chain–internal binding relations must be irrelevant, i.e., the ill-formedness of (2)b, etc. cannot be due to the fact that the pronominal agreement is locally bound by the subject. No subject agreement construal would be possible if the local binding of the pronominal agreement by the subject sufficed to trigger a principle B violation. In fact, it is reasonable to assume that the binding principles solely concern genuine referential dependencies between different arguments. As a chain is a discontinuous manifestation of a single argument, and the only conceivable referential dependency between elements of the same chain is identity, it is natural to assume that the binding principles do not apply chain-internally (possibly with the exception of principle A), and only affect chain external relations. With this in mind, let us reconsider cases like the following:

(28) *A loro Agr piacciono se stessi.
 'To them please themselves.'

Here the anaphor must be bound, but the pronominal agreement must be free. So, there is no possible indexation of the structure that can simultaneously meet these contradictory requirements: if *loro* is coindexed with *se stessi*, the anaphor is bound, but also the pronominal agreement, necessarily coindexed with *se stessi*, is locally bound by *loro*, and principle B is violated; if *loro* and *se stessi* are contraindexed, principle B is met but principle A is violated. So, this case is straightforwardly ruled out by the Binding Principle.

A more complex case is the following:

(29) *They think that each other Agr will win.

To exclude (29), we must resort to our extension of Chomsky's binding theory motivated in Section 3, and interpret the assignment of the governing category (22) as an algorithm proceeding as follows: we first try the lowest maximal projection with a subject (Z) containing the element to be checked (X) and its governor (G) and we ask: if Z were the GC of X and G, would their binding requirements be virtually satisfiable? Or, more precisely, following Chomsky (1986a), is there a virtual indexation of the different elements which simultaneously satisfies the binding requirements of X and G with Z as their governing category? If the answer is yes, we assign Z as the GC of X and we check whether its binding requirements are actually satisfied. If the answer is no, we move to the next maximal projection with a subject and we repeat the procedure. If at some point a governing category is assigned to X, we proceed to check whether its binding requirements are actually satisfied. If no governing category is assigned to X and X is governed, the structure is ruled out: as Chomsky (1986a) notes, the Binding Theory must require that a governed element be assigned a GC, in order to rule out the following:

(30)a *Pictures of each other are here.
 b *Pictures of PRO are here.

In these structures there is no possible antecedent for *each other* or PRO, hence their binding conditions *qua* anaphors are not satisfiable, and no GC is assigned. If it was licit to leave a governed element without a GC, these structures could not be excluded as Binding Theory violations. So, the assignment of a GC to a governed element must be compulsory.

Under the algorithmic interpretation of the assignment of GC that we have sketched out, the situation is similar in (29): The lower clause does not qualify as a GC for the anaphor because its binding requirements are not satisfiable, there being no virtual antecedent; the higher clause does not qualify either: there is no virtual indexation simultaneously satisfying the contradictory binding requirements of the anaphor and of its (coindexed) pronominal governing Agr if the main clause is taken as their GC. So, no GC is assigned to the governed anaphor, and the structure is ruled out on a par with (30). The subjunctive case can be treated in the same manner: the presence of the anaphoric tense with the pronominal agreement within Infl does not affect things, and (26) can be excluded on a par with (30). On the other hand, the presence of the anaphoric tense within the complex governor of the subject remains crucial to account for the disjoint reference effect of (25)b, as before.[7]

The Icelandic case can be made to follow if we assume that the marked assignment of a larger governing category to long distance anaphors also follows the same procedure: a given domain Z qualifies as the GC of an element X only if there is a virtual indexation which satisfies the binding requirements of X and its governor G for Z = GC of X and G. Whatever device we choose to characterize the enlarged GC of long distance anaphors (cf., for instance, the discussion of Manzini and Wexler 1986), it is clear that neither the embedded clause nor the main clause will qualify as the GC of the anaphor in the ungrammatical examples: in the embedded clause of (17)b there is no virtual indexation satisfying the requirement of the anaphor, in the embedded clause of (19)a and in the main clause in all the cases, all indexations satisfying the requirement of the anaphor will violate the requirement of the pronominal, and vice-versa. If no GC can be assigned to the governed anaphor, the structure is ruled out as before.

5 Conclusion

Anaphors manifest a fundamental incompatibility with the local construal with agreement. This incompatibility is stronger than current accounts in terms of principle A or the ECP would lead one to expect. Analyses postulating a (semi)accidental gap in the morphological paradigm of the anaphor are conceptually and empirically too weak. We have proposed two possible interpretations of the effect (not necessarily incompatible), which both depend on the assumption that clausal agreement has a pronominal nature. The first attributes the effect to a well-formedness condition on chains which require the argument to be the most referentially autonomous element in the chain. The second, inspired by the PRO Theorem, looks at the anaphor agreement construal as a kind of discontinuous pronominal anaphor. This configuration is ruled out through a minor extension of the definition of governing category of Chomsky

(1986a), an extension independently motivated in part by the analysis of the surprising disjoint reference effects manifested by the subject position in subjunctive clauses.

Appendix

Comparative evidence brought to light in recent work bears on the issues addressed in this paper in important ways. Huang (1982) shows that the sentential paradigm and the NP paradigm are fully parallel in Mandarin Chinese. In object position, the anaphor *ziji* and the (coreferential) pronominal *ta* are in complementary distribution, as in English:

(31) a Zhangsan kanjian-le ziji.
        'Z. see+ASP SELF.'
     b *Zhangsan kanjian-le ta.
        'Z. see+ASP him.'
(32) a *Zhangsan shuo [ni kanjian-le ziji].
        'Z. said you see+ASP SELF.'
     b Zhangsan shuo [ni kanjian-le ta].
        'Z. said you see+ASP him.'

The specifier position of the NP allows both the anaphor and the coreferential pronoun:

(33) a Zhangsan kanjian-le [ziji de shu].
        'Z. see+ASP SELF's book.'
     b Zhangsan kanjian-le [ta de shu].
        'Z. see+ASP his book.'

Also the subject position of an embedded clause allows both the anaphor and the coreferential pronoun, in sharp contrast with English:

(34) a Zangsan shuo [ziji hui lai].
        'Z. said SELF will come.'
     b Zangsan shuo [ta hui lai].
        'Z. said he will come.'

In fact, the fully parallel behaviour of (33) and (34) is straightforwardly predicted by the approach to binding of Chomsky (1986a): in (33)a–(34)a, the lower clause or NP cannot qualify as the GC of the anaphor, as there is no possible binder for it, hence the GC is the main clause, in which the anaphor is properly bound. In (33)b–(34)b, the binding requirement of the pronominal (being free) is, of course, satisfiable within the lower clause or NP, which therefore qualifies as its GC. The pronoun is thus allowed to corefer to the main subject, outside its

GC. But why is the equivalent of (32)a excluded in English? We have proposed that this structure is not directly excluded by principle A of the binding theory, but by the interference of a disturbing factor, the anaphor–agreement effect (which is in turn amenable to deeper theoretical reasons, as we have seen). We therefore expect that the disturbing factor will not be found in Mandarin Chinese, which lacks the Agr specification completely. Due to the absence of agreement, the Chinese paradigm reflects the effect of the Binding Theory more transparently than English and other inflected languages.[8]

Notes

1. An element X is bound in a given domain iff there is another element Y in the same domain which c-commands X and is coindexed with X. Y c-commands X iff neither Y dominates X nor vice versa, and the first branching node dominating Y dominates X as well. An element is free in a given domain when there is no other element in the same domain which binds it.
2. A problem for this approach is raised by the fact that in (some) languages with a reflexive possessive the pronominal possessive is disjoint in reference. Danish is a case in point (examples adapted from Vikner 1985):

   i   Peter laeste sin artikel.
       'Peter read SELF's article.'
   ii *Peter laeste hans artikel.
       'Peter read his article.'

   On the other hand, in Italian the existence of the anaphoric possessive form *proprio* (Giorgi 1984) does not affect the possibility of a coreferential pronominal possessive:

   ii a Gianni ama la propria casa.
          'Gianni loves SELF's house.'
       b Gianni ama la sua casa.
          'Gianni loves his house.'

   We will leave this question open here. Cf. Burzio (1992) for important discussion on the subject.
3. The hypothesis of anaphor movement in LF was originally made by Belletti (1982) for the case of Romance non-clitic reciprocals, and by Lebeaux (1983) for various cases in English. See also Heim, Lasnik and May (1988).
4. According to the standard definition of Chomsky (1981), proper government is either government by a lexical category or government by an antecedent. Neither case of proper government is met in (10). Various more recent refinements of the ECP (e.g., Rizzi 1990a and references cited there) are compatible with this interpretation.
5. The same conclusion is reached, on the basis of different considerations, in Everaert (1988). This paper proposes a different approach to the whole problem, based on an extension of Kayne's Connectedness Condition, an approach that we will not attempt to assess here.
6. There is now an extensive literature on the topic. For different approaches, cf. Ruwet (1984), Suñer and Padilla-Rivera (1984), Jakubowicz (1985), Johnson (1985), Kempchinsky (1985, 1986), Raposo (1985b).

7 Whether Agr and T are base generated under the same node Infl or they are separate projections that are derivationally merged under head to head movement, as in many recent proposals, is immaterial in the present context.
8 Cf. Aoun (1985) and Chomsky (1986a) for different approaches to the difference between English and Chinese with respect to the binding properties of embedded subjects.

7 Argument/adjunct (a)symmetries

Introduction

Negation and negative operators block extraction of adjuncts, while they leave extraction of arguments unaffected (see Ross 1983 for the initial empirical observation):

(1)a How do(*n't) you think that John talked to Mary t?
   b Who do(n't) you think that John talked to t?

In previous work (Rizzi 1990a), I suggested that this asymmetry should receive a unified treatment with the familiar argument/adjunct asymmetries induced by Wh Islands under the ECP module:

(2)a *How do you wonder whether John talked to Mary t?
   b ?Who do you wonder whether John talked to t?

A unified analysis of locality on adjunct extraction was made possible by a relativization of the minimality principle on government, Relativized Minimality (RM). This principle also attempted to unify the locality effects on A' chains with other apparently quite different kinds of locality such as the Head Movement Constraint and the ban against Super-raising in A chains, illustrated in (3) and (4), respectively:

(3) *Have they could t left? (cf. Could they t have left?)
(4) *John seems that it is likely t to win.

A number of questions bearing on different aspects of the attempted unification have been raised in the recent literature. First of all, some authors have claimed that negative islands (and other 'weak' islands, in the sense of Cinque 1990) are best treated in semantic (Szabolcsi and Zwarts 1991) or pragmatic (Kroch 1989) terms; if this were correct, a unitary treatment with purely structural constraints such as the Head Movement Constraint would be out of question. Secondly, one outstanding problem for the attempted unification of locality in A and A' chains is that the former do not manifest any argument/adjunct asymmetry. In fact, A chains uniformly manifest the strong locality conditions that are characteristic of adjunct chains in the A' system, whatever the nature of the moved element: for instance, referential arguments and quasi-arguments of idiomatic expressions both exclude Super-raising with comparable force:[1]

(5)a *Advantage seems that it is likely to be taken t of John.
 b *John seems that it is likely to be taken advantage of t.

The central aim of this paper is to argue for the validity of the unified analysis of (1), (2) and (4) in strictly configurational terms. Two lines of argument will be pursued:

1 we will improve the RM mechanism responsible for the argument/adjunct asymmetries by sharpening its reference to Thematic Theory; this will permit a better understanding of the mentioned difference between the A and the A' system;
2 we will analyse an unexpected hybrid object: in some special constructions, A' chains don't exhibit any argument/adjunct asymmetry, and show a uniform requirement of strong locality, on a par with A chains. This unexpected behaviour will be shown to follow from the configurational approach to weak islands and the characterization of the argument/adjunct divide in terms of Theta Theory.

1 Relativized minimality

A uniform analysis of (1)a, (2)a, (3), (4) can be given through the assumption that the antecedents must be connected to their traces via a chain of antecedent government relations, and that the following minimality condition holds on government: a certain type of government relation is blocked by the intervention of a potential governor of the same type. More formally:

(6) Relativized Minimality: a government relation between X and Y is blocked if there is a Z such that:
 a Z is phrase-internal, non thematic.
 b Z is a position of the same type as X.
 c Z c-commands Y and does not c-command X.

(6)a is intended to exclude from the picture adjoined phrases and thematic argument positions which do not seem to give rise to minimality effects. Intervention effects are exclusively induced by heads and A and A' specifiers. (6)c expresses intervention in terms of c-command. (6)b expresses the relativization to the type of government. The theory specifies three kinds of positions that may be involved in government relations (antecedent government or head government): head positions and maximal projections in A or A' positions.[2]

Consider how (6) works for the different types of positions. If X is a head (hence we are checking head-government, or antecedent government in H° chains), potential interveners are heads; if X is an A' position (hence we are checking antecedent government in a Wh chain), potential interveners are A' specifiers (the only A' positions meeting the definition: adjoined positions are excluded by (6)a); if X is an A position (hence we are checking antecedent–government in NP-chains), potential interveners are A specifiers, subjects (complements and other thematic positions are again excluded by (6)a).

So, in (2)a, a crucial antecedent–government relation in the A' chain is blocked by the intervention of the lower Spec of C, hence the structure is ruled out. (1)a can be reduced to the same structural explanation if we assume that negative clauses involve an autonomous negative projection, NegP (Pollock 1989; Belletti 1990 and much subsequent work) whose Spec is always filled by a negative operator at the latest at LF.[3]

(7)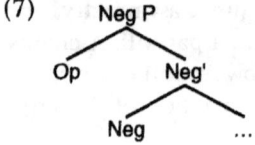

The specifier may be filled by a sentential negation operator, phonetically realized, as French *pas*, presumably English *not*, West Flemish *nie*, or phonetically null, as in Italian, Spanish, etc. Alternatively, it may be filled (at the latest at LF) by the movement of a negative quantifier. The negative head may be phonetically realized as French *ne*, Italian *non*, West Flemish *en-* (optionally), or null, as in English, German, etc. Such a uniform substructure will have an effect analogous to the effect of Wh CPs: the intervention of the A' specifier will block an antecedent government relation in A' chains. Negative islands and Wh islands can thus receive a uniform treatment under RM.

The head movement constraint and the ban against Super-raising also follow straightforwardly from (6): in (3) antecedent government of *t* from *have*, an H°, is blocked by the intervention of *could*, another H° ; in (4), antecedent government of *t* from *John*, an A position, is blocked by the intervention of *it*, an A specifier.

2 Arguments, adjuncts and Theta Theory

Why is it that argument extraction is not sensitive to the intervention of an A' specifier in (1)b, (2)b? In Rizzi (1990a, Chapter 3) I argued that argument variables are allowed to bear a referential index, which makes it possible for them to be connected long-distance with their operator through a binding relation, insensitive to RM.[4] In the case of adjunct variables the referential indexation is not available, hence the connection with the operator can only be established via a chain of government relations, sensitive to RM; whence the stricter locality on adjunct extraction.

The system then relies on a sharp enough definition of the conditions on the licensing of referential indices. In RM, I suggested that a referential index is licensed by an argumental theta role, a theta role corresponding to a participant in the event (Agent, Patient, Goal, etc. but not Quantity, Manner, etc.). We can then think of such an index as identifying the bearer of that role. Indices so anchored into thematic structures can connect elements at an unbounded distance.[5]

This approach properly captures the asymmetries observed in the A' system, but, as was repeatedly pointed out, it does not immediately capture locality in the A system. In particular, the explanation of the ban against Super-raising provided by RM is endangered by the indexation idea. Consider relevant cases such as (4), repeated here:

(4) *John seems that it is likely t to win.

The antecedent government relation between *John* and *t* is blocked by the intervention of the A specifier *it*, under RM; but why couldn't the relation be established via binding, given that a referential theta role is associated to the chain? To phrase the same problem in different terms, we should ask why it is the case that argument/adjunct asymmetries only arise for A' chains, while antecedent government is uniformly required in A chains. The answer provided in Rizzi (1990a) dealt with the problem by stipulating the observed distinction between A and A' chains, i.e., by stating that the former require antecedent government. On the other hand, Guglielmo Cinque (personal communication) observed that the special status of A-chains may be more interestingly derived from the fact that A-traces never are arguments for Theta Theory. A narrower characterization of the index licensing device can capitalize on this property.

I would like to slightly modify the RM approach by introducing a particular implementation of Cinque's suggestion. An initial approximation would be to restrict the possibility of referential indexation to the *argument*, rather than extending it to any member of a chain receiving an argumental Theta role. As NP-traces are non-arguments, they could not carry a referential index, therefore they should be connected to their antecedents via government, and would be subjected to the relevant subcase of RM. (4) and (5) would then be uniformly ruled out.

This still is too narrow a characterization for A' dependencies: in order to allow binding in the relevant A' chains, in addition to permitting a referential indexation on an argumental variable, we must permit the indexation of the operator, certainly a non-argument at SS and LF, as in (8)a:

(8)a Whom have you seen t?
  b You have seen whom?

But notice that in the corresponding DS (8)b, the operator is in a thematic position, hence it must count as an argument on this level, for the Theta Criterion to be fulfilled; so, one could assume that an element can carry a referential index only if it is an 'argument' on some level of representation, in the specific sense defined by Theta Theory:[6]

(9) X can carry a referential index only if it bears an argumental Theta role on some level of representation.

Consider A' chains of adjuncts:

(10) How did he speak t?

Here the A' chain contains no argument (no argumental or other Theta Role is assigned to it), hence neither the operator nor the variable can carry a referential index, binding is not available, the connection must be established via government; therefore, the relevant case of RM is operative and determines the strong locality effect that is manifested on this kind of relation, sensitive to Wh Islands, negative islands and other 'weak' islands.
  Consider now A chains:

(11) John was fired t.

In (11) *John* is the bearer of an argumental theta role, then it can legitimately carry an index. But the NP trace *t*, under current assumptions, is always a non-argument: at DS it does not exist, at SS it must pass the theta role on to the argument *John*; hence, under (9) the NP trace can't carry a referential index; as the connection with its antecedent cannot be established via binding, it must be established via government; therefore, under the relevant case of RM, the relation can never skip an intervening A specifier, and Super-raising cases such as (4) and (5) are banned in full generality.[7]
  In the remainder of this chapter, I would like to show that the lack of argument/adjunct asymmetries is not the exclusive property of A-chains. Some special cases of A' chains display the same behaviour, in that they uniformly require strict locality. This special behaviour can be shown to follow from our technical definition of the argument/adjunct divide, hence it provides further evidence for the proposed approach.

3 Partial Wh movement in German

A complex case of negative island strongly inviting a configurational analysis is offered by the partial Wh movement construction in colloquial German (van Riemsdijk 1983). I will follow here the thorough description and analysis of McDaniel (1989). In some varieties of German, a Wh element can be extracted from an embedded clause (as in (12)a), or moved to the Spec of C of the embedded clause and construed with an invariable scope marker (*was*) in the main Spec of C (as in (12)b). As (12) shows, the partial Wh movement strategy is blocked by an intervening negation, while full movement is not:

(12) a Mit wem glaubst du (nicht), dass Hans t gesprochen hat?
'With whom do(n't) you believe that Hans has spoken?'
b Was glaubst du (*nicht), mit wem Hans t gesprochen hat?
'WHAT do(n't) you believe with whom Hans has spoken?'
(= (12)a)

According to McDaniel's analysis, *was* is a kind of expletive in the A' system, connected to the contentive operator through an A' chain. I will assume that the construction of such a chain is enforced at S-structure by the necessity to satisfy the Wh Criterion on this level, as is required in German (see Chapter 9, footnote 8; cf. also McDaniel's 1989 principle (38)):

(13) Wh Criterion
A A Wh operator must be in a Spec/head relation with a X_{+Wh}.
B A X_{+Wh} must be in a Spec/head relation with a Wh operator.

The part of the Wh Criterion that is relevant here is principle A, which requires that a Wh operator be in the Spec of C of an interrogative clause (marked with the feature +Wh). The level of application of this principle may vary across languages, and it must be satisfied by S-structure in German (as in English, etc., but not in Chinese, Japanese, etc. where it must be satisfied only at LF): as a consequence of clause A of the Wh Criterion, a Wh element cannot be left in a 'wrong' Spec of C, e.g., the Spec of the −Wh C of a declarative clause. How can this constraint be reconciled with the very existence of partial Wh movement in German, which manifestly allows Wh Op's to stay in 'wrong' Spec's of C at S-structure? Suppose we interpret 'Wh operator' in (13) as meaning 'the head of the chain of the Wh operator'. Then, a Wh Op can be allowed to sit in a 'wrong' Spec of C provided that it is chain connected to an expletive operator (the head of its chain) in the appropriate Spec of C.[8] Therefore, the creation of a chain including the contentive and the expletive operator at S-structure is enforced by the Wh Criterion.

At S-structure, we thus have the following chain structures for (12)a and b:

(12')a (mit wem, t)
   b (was, mit wem, t)

The link (was, mit wem) of (12')b cannot be established through binding: the expletive operator *was* does not carry an argumental Theta role on any level of representation, hence it cannot bear a referential index under (9). So, the link must be established through government, and it fails when a negation intervenes under RM; therefore, the negated variant of (12)b is ruled out, ultimately as a violation of the Wh Criterion at S-structure. On the other hand, *mit wem* can carry a referential index in (12)a, the chain can be built via binding, therefore it is unaffected by the intervention of negation.

Notice that in partial Wh movement constructions the argument/adjunct asymmetry is wiped out: structures like (12)b with partial movement of an argument and an intervening negation are not better than the corresponding structures with partial movement of an adjunct:

(14)a Was hast du (*nicht) gesagt, wie sie geschlafen hat?
   'WHAT did you (not) say how she slept?'
   (= How did you (not) say that she slept?)
   b Was hast du (*nicht) gesagt, warum sie nicht kommt?
   'WHAT did you (not) say why she does not come?'
   (= Why did you (not) say that she does not come?)

This is expected under principle (9): the expletive operator can never have a referential index licensed under (9), regardless of whether the variable is an argument variable (a variable ranging over individuals) or not. We then expect this special type of A' dependency to uniformly require antecedent government, on a par with A dependencies.[9]

Dana McDaniel points out (personal communication) that Romani manifests a similar pattern: full Wh movement is (marginally) acceptable across an intervening negation, partial Wh movement is not:[10]

(15)a ?Kas na misline so o Demiri dikhl a t?
   'Whom don't you think that Demiri saw?'
   b *So na misline kas o Demiri dikhl a t?
   'WHAT don't you think whom Demiri saw?'

As is expected, a Wh operator patterns on a par with an intervening negation in blocking partial movement. The relevant contrasts are obscured in German by the particularly robust nature of the Wh island in this language, but they appear to be clearly detectable in Romani. McDaniel

(1989: 577) points out that overt Wh extraction from a Wh island gives rise to a marginally acceptable sentence in Romani (as in (16)a), whereas partial movement across a Wh island is ungrammatical (as in (16)b):

(16)a (?)Kas na jane sosqe o Demiri mislinol so marjum t?
     'Who don't you know why Demiri thinks that I hit?'
   b *So na jane sosqe o Demiri mislinol kas marjum t?
     'WHAT don't you know why Demiri thinks whom I hit?'

In (16)b, only the government connection is available to build a proper Wh chain, but antecedent government is blocked by the embedded Spec of C (*sosqe*) intervening between *so* and *kas* under RM. So, (16)b is ruled out, ultimately as a violation of the Wh Criterion. In (16)a the binding connection between *kas* and its trace is available under (9), therefore the structure is acceptable.

4 No Wh extraction from negative clefts

A clefted constituent can be negated or questioned, but not negated and questioned at the same time:

(17)a It is John that we should help.
   b It is not John that we should help.
   c Who is it ___ that we should help?
   d *Who is it not ___ that we should help?

This paradigm holds quite robustly across languages: the following small sample includes French, Italian, West Flemish, Modern Hebrew:

(18)a Ce (n') est (pas) Jean que nous devrions aider.
     'It is (not) Jean that we should help.'
   b Qui (*n') est-ce (*pas) que nous devrions aider?
     'Who is it (not) that we should help?'
(19)a (Non) è Gianni che dovremmo aiutare.
     'It (not) is Gianni that we should help.'
   b Chi (*non) è che dovremmo aiutare?
     'Who it (not) is that we should help?'
(20)a T is Valère (nie) dan-k doa gesien een.
     'It is V. (not) that-I there seen have.'
   b Wien is-t (*nie) dan-k doa gesien een?
     'Who is-it (not) that-I there seen have?'
(21)a ze (lo) haya xatul she-ra'ita.
     'It (not) was the cat that you saw.'
   b ma ze (*lo) haya she-ra'ita?
     'What it (not) was that you saw?'

There is nothing wrong with the interpretation of the starred variants of these sentences, were they grammatical they would have a perfectly sensible meaning: 'Which individual x is such that it isn't x that we should help?' So, there appears to be a structural ban against questioning negative clefts. Notice that here as well, the argument/adjunct asymmetry is wiped out, in spite of the fact that we are dealing with an A' dependency: extraction of *who* in cases like (17)d is completely impossible, about as bad as adjunct extraction in the same context:

(22)a It is not in this way that they should behave.
   b How is it (*not) that we should behave?

I would like to argue that this is another instance of negative island: the intervening negation blocks Wh movement. But if this is correct, why don't we find the familiar asymmetries? A natural answer is provided by the index licensing mechanism (9) in conjunction with the analysis of the cleft construction of Chomsky (1977a). According to this analysis, the focused element is base-generated in focus position and the cleft sentence is predicated of it. An empty operator binds the variable inside the cleft and is construed with the focused element, as in (23)a; the focused element can undergo Wh movement, as in (23)b:

(23)a It is John [Op that [we should help t]].
   b Who is it t' [Op that [we should help t]]?

We can think that there are two chains here, one including the variable and the null operator, the other including the clefted element and, if the latter is a variable, its operator; hence, in (23)a the two chains are (John), (Op, t), and in (23)b they are (Who, t'), (Op, t). We may wonder why such structures as (23) are well-formed in spite of the fact that no Theta role is assigned to the arguments *John, t'*. We will assume that elements base-generated in the focus position of clefts are exempted from the Theta criterion, and only submitted to the principle of Full Interpretation requiring them to be licensed; so, *John* is licensed in (23)a as the element of which the cleft sentence is predicated.[11]

The crucial property here is that the chain (Who, t') is not directly associated to a Theta role, and the variable t' does not admit a referential indexation under (9). Hence, the binding connection is excluded, only the government connection remains, but it is blocked by an intervening negation under RM. No argument/adjunct asymmetry arises here because the focused element never is an 'argument' in the relevant technical sense, as defined by Theta Theory.[12]

In this case too it is possible to draw a parallel between negative islands and Wh Islands, which also strongly disallow Wh extraction of a clefted element. A cleft can be rather naturally embedded in a declarative or interrogative clause in Italian and French. Wh extraction of the clefted element is somewhat marginal in the first case, but completely impossible in the second:

(24) a Credo che sia Gianni che dobbiamo contattare.
    'I believe that it is Gianni that we should contact.'
   b ?Chi credi che sia t che dobbiamo contattare?
    'Who do you believe that it is that we should contact?'
(25) a Mi domando se sia Gianni che dobbiamo contattare.
    'I wonder if it is Gianni that we should contact.'
   b *Chi ti domandi se sia t che dobbiamo contattare?
    'Who do you wonder if it is that we should contact?'
(26) a Tu crois que c'est Jean que je dois contacter.
    'You believe that it is Jean that I should contact.'
   b ?Qui tu crois que c'est ___ que je dois contacter?
    'Who do you believe that it is that I should contact?'
(27) a Tu te demandes si c'est Jean que je dois contacter.
    'You wonder if it is Jean that I should contact.'
   b *Qui tu te demandes si c'est ___ que je dois contacter?
    'Who do you wonder if it is that we should contact?'

Here too, no argument/adjunct asymmetry is found: examples like (25)b and (27)b are completely impossible, at the same level of inacceptability as adjunct extraction in the same context:

(28) a Credo che sia così che ci dobbiamo comportare.
    'I believe that it is like that that we should behave.'
   b ?Come credi che sia ___ che ci dobbiamo comportare?
    'How do you believe that it is that we should behave?'
(29) a Mi domando se sia così che ci dobbiamo comportare.
    'I wonder if it is like that that we should behave.'
   b *Come ti domandi se sia ___ che ci dobbiamo comportare?
    'How do you wonder if it is that I should behave?'

The parallel ill-formedness of (25)b and (29)b is expected, as in both cases a referential indexation is disallowed by (9), and the antecedent government connection is blocked by the intervening indirect question.

Moreover, as we now expect, negation is impossible in the path from the Wh element and its variable in the focus position of a cleft, no matter whether it is on the main verb or on the copula, while negation is possible in the path of the lower chain, between the variable and the empty operator:

(30) Chi (*non) hai detto che (*non) è t' Op che (non) dobbiamo contattare t?
    'Who did you (not) say that it is (not) that we should (not) contact?'

In (30) Op and t can carry a referential index under (9) (the chain bears an argumental Theta role, t is the argument at S-structure and Op is the argument at D-structure), therefore the connection is not affected by an intervening negation.[13,14]

As is to be expected, Wh movement from the focused position of clefts is not the only type of A' dependency giving rise to the observed locality effect. For instance, focalization in Italian (Cinque 1990, and Chapter 10), generally unaffected by an intervening negation (see (31)b)), can take place from the focal position of clefts (Smits 1989: 363), but not across a negation (see (32)b–d):

(31) a GIANNI dovete aiutare ___.
'Gianni you should help.'
b 'GIANNI non dovete aiutare ___.
'Gianni you should not help.'
(32) a E' Gianni che dovete aiutare.
'It is Gianni that you should help.'
b GIANNI è ___ che dovete aiutare.
'Gianni it is that you should help.'
c Non è Gianni che dovete aiutare.
'It is not Gianni that you should help.'
d *GIANNI non è ___ che dovete aiutare.
'Gianni it is not that you should help.'

The same explanation holds as in the case of Wh movement.

5 Conclusion

We have argued that the appropriate divide between elements sensitive and insensitive to weak islands is provided by Thematic Theory, and expressed in strictly configurational terms. We have chosen to express this divide in terms of the licensing of referential indices: indexed elements can enter into binding connections which are immune from weak islands. A referential indexation is only legitimate on elements that are arguments on some level of representation. This immediately explains why no long distance binding relation is ever possible in A chains: A-traces are never arguments, hence no referential indexation is legitimate.

We have discovered two cases of A' chains which also cancel argument/adjunct asymmetries and uniformly require strict locality, and have shown that their apparently hybrid properties are amenable to the same licensing principle. Partial Wh movement in German involves the construction of an A' chain headed by an expletive operator, which is never an argument, hence it is not allowed to carry a referential index; Wh extraction from the focused position of clefts, under Chomsky's (1977a) analysis of the cleft construction, involves the construction of an A' chain

Argument/adjunct (a)symmetries 185

which no (argumental) Theta Role is assigned to. Binding being barred, the only possible connection in these cases is provided by government, which obeys RM; whence the systematic sensitivity to negative and other weak islands.

Notes

1 See Rizzi (1990a: 78–80) on the fact that quasi-arguments of idiomatic expressions behave like adjuncts in A' chains.
2 The statement in (6) is simplified with respect to the formalization in Rizzi (1990a) in that the relativization of the blocking effect is stated directly in terms of types of positions, rather than through the notion of 'typical potential governor' of a certain kind.
  It has been proposed in the recent literature that the A/A' distinction may be relevant for head positions as well (Roberts 1991b). We will not explore the consequences of this refinement here.
3 The RM system is improved in two important respects here: Firstly, systematic reference to the NegP for all the cases of negative islands eliminates the *ad hoc* case by case search for a crucial A' specifier, as Frampton (1991) points out. Secondly, the necessary presence of the NegP with a filled A' specifier is enforced on principled grounds by the Negative Criterion (see Chapter 9, and Haegeman 1995).
4 Binding is defined in the familiar terms: c-command and sharing of referential index, with no further locality condition. It has been observed that the term 'referential index' may be misleading in this context (e.g., Frampton 1991); in fact, what is necessary for our purposes is to admit the existence of a quality of indices which permit non-local connections between elements (connections not subjected to RM), and that this quality of indices is licensed by configurational properties, having to do with Theta Theory; in the remainder we will keep the term referential index, but it should be stressed that nothing hinges on this particular terminological choice.
5 We may think that members of adjunct chains are not indexed at all, or that they carry weaker indices, not rooted into the thematic module, and which only survive under antecedent government. The first alternative obviously requires a definition of antecedent government which does not refer to coindexation.
6 On the mechanism allowing the same element to be an argument and a nonargument on different levels of representations, see Chapter 9, Section 4.
  'Only if' is used in (9) because other conditions having to do with the nature of the element enter into the licensing of a referential indexation. See Cinque (1990) for detailed discussion of such factors.
  Binding connections in relatives involving a base-generated resumptive pronoun (e.g., Shlonsky 1991), in which the operator is not an argument on any level of representation, can be established through the mechanism mentioned in footnote 10 for partial Wh movement in Romani relatives (the resumptive pronoun receives the index through (9), the null operator via predication from the head of the relative). On the other hand, if there are genuine cases of base generated resumptive strategies with questions, not just trace spell-out (Georgopoulos 1991 and much other recent work), (9) should be revised to allow a binding connection in such cases, possibly along the following lines:

i A referential index is legitimate on an element X only if:
  a X is in a chain with a referential argument, and
  b X is not lower than the referential argument.

186 *Locality*

i basically amounts to saying that a referential indexation for members of a chain is legitimate from the referential argument upwards, hence including base-generated operators, but not NP traces.

If we think of a chain as a sequence of positions connected through government or binding, there could arise a circularity here: chain is defined in part through binding, hence referential index, and the latter is licensed through i, which crucially refers to chain. To avoid the circularity, we could assume that referential indices are freely assigned to positions; this would allow free construction of chain links connected via binding (for instance, also in (10), (11), etc). The legitimacy of the referential indexation would then be checked at LF under i, which would rule out the improper cases. I will not pursue this approach here.

7 The same result holds for A chains involving expletives:

i There is a man in the garden.
ii *There seems that it is likely t to be a man in the garden.

If the expletive and the argument must form a chain already at S-structure (e.g., to ensure visibility of the argument), then ii is ruled out already on this level: as the expletive cannot carry an index under (9), the connection must be established via government, and it fails in ii. Moreover, if at LF the argument replaces the expletive (Chomsky 1986a), on this level of representation we obtain the following configurations (LF trace noted as t'):

iii A man is t' in the garden.
iv A man seems that it is likely t to be t' in the garden.

A binding connection is disallowed in the LF chain under (9), as the NP trace cannot bear an index, and a government connection is possible in iii and excluded in iv under RM.

8 If the language does not possess an expletive operator (e.g., English) the contentive operator itself must be in the appropriate scope position. On the mechanism allowing Wh *in situ*, see Chapter 9, Section 4.

9 If principle (9) must be revised along the lines of footnote 6, in order to keep the analysis of partial Wh movement we must follow Chomsky (1986a) and assume that chains created by movement must be distinguished at S-structure from CHAINS, purely representational connections established without movement. So, the chain structure of (12)b contains the CHAIN (was, mit wem) which does not license an indexation on *was* under i of footnote 6 because the CHAIN does not contain an argument. The rest of the analysis remains unchanged.

10 In Romani, the partial movement strategy is also available in relative clauses. Interestingly, McDaniel notices that in this case partial and full Wh movement do not contrast, and manifest the same acceptability level across an intervening negation:

i a ?Ake o chavo kas na mislinav so o Demiri dikhl a t.
   'Here's the boy whom I don't think that Demiri saw.'
 b ?Ake o chavo so na mislinav kas o Demiri dikhl a t.
   'Here's the boy WHAT I don't think whom Demiri saw.'

This asymmetry between relatives and questions can be understood as follows. The crucial difference is that in relatives both the head and the tail of the A' chain can be independently anchored to referential Theta roles. More precisely, in a relative like ib, the contentive Wh element *kas* and its trace are allowed to bear a referential index under (9). The expletive operator *so* is not allowed to carry a referential index as a primitive property; on the other hand the head of the relative has a referential index licensed under (9); we may assume that it can be transmitted from the head of the relative to the adjacent operator through predication; so, both the head and the tail of the A' chain end up bearing referential indices licensed by referential Theta roles, hence the binding connection is available, and the intervening negation is not influential. No such mechanism is available to assign an index to the head of the question chain in structures like (15)b, which therefore must resort to the antecedent government strategy, and manifests the expected sensitivity to the intervention of negation.

11 Therefore, in this account, the following is excluded by the principle of Full Interpretation, not by the Theta Criterion:

  i *It is John that Mary loves Bill.

12 See also Higginbotham's (1987) approach, in which the focused element of clefts is analysed as a predicate.

The West Flemish example looks problematic at this point. The focused NP precedes the negative marker *nie* in (19)a, so apparently it is scrambled out of the domain of negation, and still the further application of Wh movement in (19)b is impossible: how can negation still have a blocking effect in this case? Liliane Haegeman points out that the construction has the following three properties:

 1 The focused NP still is in the scope of negation in (19)a;
 2 Sentential adverbs which otherwise freely interpolate between a scrambled NP and negation don't naturally interpolate in this case:

     i T is verzekerst Valère nie da me gezien een.
        'It is probably Valère not that we seen have.'
     ii ???T is Valère verzekerst nie da me gezien een.
        'It is Valère probably not that we seen have.'

 3 If an NP is focused, the only possible order for negative clefts is NP *nie*, if a PP is focused, both orders *nie* PP and PP *nie* are possible:

     iii T is (nie) in Antwerpen (nie) dan'k goan weunen.
         'It is (not) in Antwerp (not) that-I live.'

This suggests that the NP is not moved out of the NegP in (20)a, rather it is adjoined to *nie* (this explains the fact that it is still interpreted in *nie*'s scope, and that an adverb cannot interpolate); moreover, this movement is compulsory for the NP in order to allow it to get Case (this explains the NP/PP asymmetry; see Haegeman (1991) on scrambling and Case assignment). As the focused element is not extracted from the domain of negation, in spite of the linear order, it comes as no surprise that further Wh movement will be sensitive to the negative island, as shown by (20)b.

13 Anthony Kroch (personal communication) points out that the acceptability of such examples as (16)d appears to improve if a modal is added:

  i Who couldn't it be that they helped?

188 *Locality*

But notice that there is another possible source for i, with the Wh element extracted not from the focus of the cleft but directly from the object position of the CP selected by the modal + copula:

ii It couldn't be that they helped John/who.

The hypothesis that i derives from ii is supported by the observation that the equivalent of i is ungrammatical if the element affected by Wh movement is the subject:

iii a *What couldn't it be that happened during the night?
    b What couldn't it be ___ that happened during the night.
    c What couldn't it be that ___ happened during the night.

iiia is excluded by our usual mechanism with representation iiib (as in 'It couldn't be this accident that happend during the night'), and by the *That-trace* effect with representation iiic (as in 'It couldn't be that this accident happened during the night').

14 Ken Safir (personal communication) points out that an operator can be connected to a resumptive pronoun in the focal position of a cleft across an intervening negation:

i This is the guy who it isn't him that we should help.

This raises the question of how a binding connection can be available here. We may think that pronouns, elements which are capable of freely picking a referent in the domain of discourse can freely bear a referential index (which may be passed on to the operator through the appropriate extension of footnote 6 (and/or of footnote 10)). If this is correct, then the domain of (9) should be restricted to elements which do not have the intrinsic capacity of picking a referent (variables, traces, operators, expletives . . .).

8 Direct perception, government and thematic sharing*

1 Peculiarities in categorial selection

Perception verbs often select unusual clausal complements. This tendency is remarkably consistent across the whole lexical class, and across languages. In this chapter I would like to discuss some ideas that may help us to understand this structural peculiarity, and tie it together with certain interpretive properties of perception verbs.

Let us start with a simple illustration of some unusual selectional properties. In Italian and French, perception verbs are the only verb class which selects clausal complements with overt accusative subjects:[1]

(1) a Vedo [Gianni tornare a casa].
'I see Gianni going home.'
b Je vois [Jean partir].
'I see Jean leaving.'

In English, the accusative plus infinitive construction is much more widespread than in Romance, as it is selected by epistemic and volition verbs among others (as in (2)a–b); still the infinitive selected by perception verbs has the peculiarity (shared with the complements of causative verbs) of lacking the infinitival marker *to*:

(2) a I expected [John to go home].
b I wanted [John to go home].
(3) I saw [John go home].

---

* This chapter was presented at the Workshop on the Logical Form of Perceptual Reports (Gargnano, September 8, 1990). I would like to thank Adriana Belletti, Robin Clark and the participants in the Gargnano workshop, in particular Andrea Bonomi, Guglielmo Cinque, Maria Teresa Guasti, Jim Higginbotham and Jaap Van Der Does for their helpful comments.

Another peculiar clausal construction which is quite usually selected by perception verbs involves an accusative subject plus a present participle; this is illustrated by the following examples in English, French, Catalan, Ancient Greek and Modern Hebrew, respectively (the third and fourth examples are taken from Noonan 1985):

(4) a I saw [John going home].
   b J'ai vu [Marie sortant du cinéma].
      'I saw Mary leaving the movie theatre.'
   c Vaig veure [la dona passant per la duana].
      'I have seen the woman going through the customs.'
   d Eîde [autòn paùonta].
      'He saw him stopping.'
   e dan ra'a ['et miriam raca].
      'Dan saw DEF Miriam running.'

Again, in some such cases this is the only instance of accusative plus participle construction in the grammar of the language.

So, it appears that the linguistic expression of perception enforces the selection of special, often unique clausal complements. This simple consideration seems to provide a *prima facie* strong case for a theory of the lexicon–syntax interface such that the categorial selection, the formal environment in which a given lexical item can occur, is determined in part by the semantic properties of that item, as in Grimshaw (1979), Pesetsky (1982), Chomsky (1986a).

That the semantics of perception plays a crucial role in categorial selection is strongly suggested by another observation: perception verbs display peculiar selectional properties only in one particular interpretation, i.e., when they express *direct perception*; in the other possible interpretation of *indirect perception* (realizing through possibly indirect clues that a given state of affairs holds), they pattern with other well-behaved complement taking verbs.

Let us illustrate this point through some of the clausal complements that the Italian verb *vedere* can take:

(5) a Ho visto che Gianni ha lavato la macchina.
      'I saw that Gianni washed the car.'
   b Quando ho visto [di [PRO essere in difficolta']], ...
      'When I saw to be in trouble ... (= When I saw that I was in trouble, ...).'
(6) a Ho visto [come [hai risolto il problema]].
      'I saw how you solved the problem.'
   b Non vedo [come [PRO risolvere il problema]].
      'I don't see how to solve the problem.'

(7) Ho visto [Gianni lavare la macchina].
'I saw Gianni wash the car.'

Vedere can take a tensed declarative (5)a and its infinitival control counterpart (5)b, a tensed indirect question and its infinitival counterpart (6)a–b, and the peculiar accusative with infinitive structure (7) (as well as other types of complements mentioned below). Now, there is an important interpretive difference separating (5)–(6) from (7). The latter expresses direct perception, in the sense that it would be false if I didn't actually see Gianni involved in a car-washing event. There is no such implication in (5)–(6). (5)a, for instance, could be true if I didn't witness any car-washing event, nor see Gianni, but realized in a more indirect way that Gianni washed the car (for instance, I inferred it from the fact that the floor of his garage was wet). Similarly, (6)a does not imply that I witnessed any problem-solving event, nor that I saw you, etc. So, the selectional properties of indirect perception *vedere* are analogous to those of familiar verbs of believing, saying, remembering, etc.; for instance *ricordare* (remember) takes types of complements that parallel (5) and (6):

(8)a Ricordo [che [hai risolto il problema]].
   'I remember that you solved the problem.'
  b Ricordo [di [PRO aver risolto il problema]].
   'I remember to have solved the problem (I remember that I solved the problem).'
  c Ricordo [come [hai risolto il problema]].
   'I remember how you solved the problem.'
  d (Non) ricordo [come [PRO risolvere il problema]].
   'I (don't) remember how to solve the problem.'

Let us now try to express in more precise syntactic terms the structural peculiarity of the complements of direct perception verbs. Is it possible to identify some uniform formal property across the different cases? An often repeated observation is that the complements of perception verbs tend to be reduced structures, formally more impoverished than ordinary clausal complements (see, for example, Higginbotham 1983; Clark 1988; Roberts 1988). Such notions can be perspicuously expressed in terms of current syntactic theory. The structure of the clause is seen as a successive embedding of structural layers, each one being the projection of a head, in the sense of X-bar Theory. For instance, the embedded clause in a sentence like *I think that John has left* will be analysed as a projection of the complementizer *that*, the CP, which takes as a complement the projection of the inflection (realized here as an auxiliary), the IP, which in turn takes the subject NP as its specifier and the verbal projection, the VP, as its complement (see Chomsky 1986b for discussion):

(9)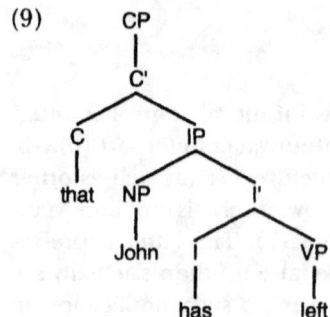

A clausal structure can then be said to be reduced or impoverished if one or more structural layers are missing.

Now, (7) can be said to be reduced with respect to (5)–(6) in a clear formal sense: (5) and (6) have a complementizer and its projection, the CP layer, overtly manifested by *che*, *di* and the Wh pronoun, respectively, while (7) lacks this layer. Also, as the other cases of accusative with infinitive or accusative with participle illustrated by (1)–(3)–(4) imply direct perception and lack Comp, we seem to have the embryo of a generalization: direct perception tends to require reduced clausal complements, in which (at least) the CP level is missing. Due to the lack of the intervening CP layer, the perception verb can directly govern the subject of the embedded clause, and, for instance, determine its accusative Case.

2 Pseudo-relatives and the relevance of government

If the equation 'peculiarity = clausal reduction = lack of the CP level (at least)' appears to be a valuable first approximation, there are various counterexamples. In particular, in Romance (and other languages) direct perception verbs typically select a construction which requires an important qualification of the reduction idea. This is the pseudo-relative construction (see Kayne 1975; Graffi 1980; Burzio 1986; Guasti 1988 and the references cited there), illustrated in the following example:

(10) Ho visto Gianni che usciva dal cinema.
 'I saw John leaving the cinema.'

In (10), the perception verb is followed by an NP followed by a clause introduced by the complementizer *che* (that), at first sight no different from an ordinary relative clause. But, as is discussed at length in the references quoted, (10) differs radically from a relative clause, both in formal and interpretive properties. First of all, the constituent NP+clause is interpreted clausally, e.g., can be resumed by the clausal pro-form *ciò (che)* (what) in the pseudo-cleft construction:

(11) Ciò che ho visto t è [Gianni che usciva dal cinema].
'What I saw is Gianni going out from the movie theatre.'

Second, the construction differs in many syntactic properties from ordinary relatives. To mention just one, we can observe that the NP of the pseudo-relative can solely correspond to the subject of the clause (see (12)a–b), while the NP heading a normal relative clause can correspond to the subject, object or any other appropriate syntactic position ((12)c–d):

(12) a Ho visto Gianni che ___ abbracciava Maria.
        'I saw Gianni hugging Maria.'
     b *Ho visto Gianni che Maria abbracciava ___.
        'I saw Gianni Maria hugging.'
     c Non conosco l'uomo che ___ abbracciava Maria.
        'I don't know the man that hugged Maria.'
     d Non conosco l'uomo che Maria abbracciava ___.
        'I don't know the man that Maria hugged.'

As is pointed out in the references quoted above, the pseudo-relative expresses direct perception: compare the following cases:

(13) a Vedo che Gianni lava la macchina.
        'I see that Gianni washes the car.'
     b Vedo Gianni che lava la macchina.
        'I see Gianni washing the car.'
     c Vedo Gianni lavare la macchina.
        'I see Gianni wash the car.'

The pseudo-relative (13)b patterns with the accusative with infinitive (13)c, and not with the tensed complement (13)a, in that it implies direct perception: (13)b, on a par with (13)c, would be false if I didn't see Gianni, nor witness any car-washing event. So, the pseudo-relative appears to violate the tentative generalization mentioned above: the clausal structure is not reduced, there is an overt complementizer, hence a CP, and still the construction necessarily expresses direct perception.

In order to properly emend the generalization, we must now make a specific hypothesis on the structure of the pseudo-relative, as well as of the accusative with infinitive construction. Following Guasti (1988), I will assume that the NP of the pseudo-relative is in the specifier of the CP;[2] as for the accusative with infinitive I assume, with Belletti (1990), that it involves a bare IP, and I adopt standard assumptions for the tensed declarative. The three sentences of (13) will then have the following representations:

(14) a Vedo [che [Gianni lava la macchina]].
   b Vedo [Gianni che [___ lava la macchina]].
   c Vedo [Gianni lavare la macchina].

Given these representations it is quite clear what b and c have in common as opposed to a: in b and c an argument of the embedded clause, the subject, is governed by the perception verb under any current definition of government (e.g., Chomsky 1986b; Rizzi 1990a, etc.), while in (14)a the perception verb is too far away to govern anything in the argument structure of the embedded clause; in particular, the intervening CP layer blocks government of the subject.[3] It then appears that the crucial common property is not the structural reduction *per se*, but rather the fact that a member of the argument structure of the embedded clause is directly governed by the perception verb. One device to obtain this result is indeed structural reduction, as in c, by stripping away the CP layer which blocks government; another device is to put a member of the embedded argument structure 'high enough', thus making it accessible to external government, as in the pseudo-relative (14)b.

3 Government and direct perception of arguments

That the government relation from the perception verb affects the direct perception interpretation can be easily shown. Let us concentrate on the implications that can be drawn from perceptual reports on whether or not an argument of the embedded clause is directly perceived. Clearly detectable subject/non-subject asymmetries exist in cases like (14)b–c, which appear to depend on government. Consider the following two sentences:

(15) a Ho visto Gianni richiamare i cani.
     'I saw Gianni call the dogs back.'
   b (?) Ho visto i cani venir richiamati da Gianni.
     'I saw the dogs be called back by Gianni.'

(15)a implies that I have seen Gianni, but not that I have seen the dogs: suppose that I have seen Gianni whistle into his ultrasound whistle that I know is used for dog retrieval; (15)a seems to me to naturally describe this state of affairs, even if I haven't seen any dog around. On the other hand, (15)b, slightly marginal as passives generally are in this environment, implies that I have seen the dogs, not that I have seen Gianni. For instance, it could naturally describe a state of affairs such that I have seen various dogs converge to a point of the forest where I know that Gianni hides, even if I haven't actually seen him. The same interpretive difference emerges quite clearly with the pseudo-relative:

(16) a Ho visto Gianni che richiamava i cani.
      (implies: I have seen Gianni, not necessarily the dogs)

b Ho visto i cani che venivano richiamati da Gianni.
    (implies: I have seen the dogs, not necessarily Gianni).

On the contrary, the two full clauses do not imply any direct visual perception of an embedded argument:

(17) a Ho visto che Gianni richiamava i cani.
    'I saw that Gianni called back the dogs.'
   b Ho visto che i cani venivano richiamati da Gianni.
    'I saw that the dogs were called back by Gianni.'

Both could describe a state of affairs in which my ultrasound detector informed me that Gianni's dog whistle was at work, even if I didn't directly see either Gianni or the dogs. The partial generalization which emerges is quite clear: when a perception verb takes a clausal complement, direct perception of some argument of the complement is implied only if this argument is governed by the verb. Various grammatical constraints give the result that only the grammatical S-structure subject of the complement may be governed by the higher verb. Notice that the directly perceived argument is not necessarily the D-structure subject, nor the argument that is thematically more prominent according to some hierarchy (Jackendoff 1972), as passive sentences like (15b) clearly show. If the embedded subject (in fact, *a fortiori* any embedded argument) is not governed by the higher verb, as in (17), no direct perception is implied.

The same point is illustrated by the following examples:

(18) Ieri a teatro ho visto Frank Sinatra dare un premio a Bob Hope, ma il tipo che mi stava davanti mi copriva parzialmente la visuale, così non ho potuto vedere Bob Hope / # Frank Sinatra
    'Yesterday at the theatre I saw Frank Sinatra give a prize to Bob Hope, but the guy seated in the next row covered in part my visual field, so I couldn't actually see Bob Hope / # Frank Sinatra.'

Claiming that I haven't actually seen the subject of the clausal complement sounds contradictory (we use the symbol # to indicate this), while claiming that I haven't seen the object does not. Again, the S-structure grammatical function of the two arguments seems to be relevant to determine the asymmetry, rather than some sort of intrinsic thematic prominence: if, with a different lexical choice for the verb, the subject is the goal of the prize-awarding action and the agent is VP-internal, the corresponding sentence implies that I have seen the goal:[4]

(19) ... ho visto Bob Hope ricevere un premio da Frank Sinatra, ... ma non sono riuscito a vedere Frank Sinatra / # Bob Hope.
    '... I saw Bob Hope receive a prize from Frank Sinatra, ... but I didn't manage to actually see Frank Sinatra / # Bob Hope.'

The relevance of government for direct perception is also clearly shown by a different case, pointed out by Andrea Bonomi. It arises in structures in which the subject of the infinitive is omitted, an option unavailable in English but possible in Romance: compare the following two cases:

(20) Ho visto Gianni/un uomo/qualcuno sparare al presidente.
 'I saw Gianni/a man/someone shoot at the president.'
(21) Ho visto sparare al presidente.
 'I saw someone shoot at the president.'

Both structures express direct perception of a shooting event, but only the former implies that I saw the shooter. Hence (21), but not (20), would naturally allow the following continuation:[5]

(22) ... ma non ho visto lo sparatore.
 '... but I didn't see the shooter.'

Why is it so? It has been argued that (21) involves a bare infinitival VP, without a structurally represented subject (Burzio 1986); if this is correct, the observed contrast conforms to our generalization: direct perception of the subject is implied in (20) but not in (21), in which the understood subject is not represented in the structure, hence *a fortiori* not governed by the perception verb.

It should be noticed that there is an obvious subclass of cases in which direct perception of the subject of the complement is not implied, even if government from the perception verb holds: this happens when the subject is an expletive, a non-referential pronoun (example (23)b from Higginbotham 1983)

(23)a I saw it raining.
 b I wouldn't like to see there be so many mistakes.

In order to integrate (23) we can simply amend the generalization by saying that direct perception is implied of the *referential* argument of the complement which is governed by the perception verb. Other putative counterexamples occasionally mentioned in the literature (e.g. Gee 1977: 474) seem to me much less convincing, and insufficient to undermine the robust trend illustrated by the previous examples (see also footnote 4).

The formal generalization that we have arrived at may look quite arbitrary, but it can easily be construed in an intuitively acceptable way. The government relation is a formal (slightly generalizing) characterization of the notion 'complement of a head'. So, when the subject of a clause is governed by a higher verb, it becomes, in this somewhat extended formal sense, a complement of that verb, and we may expect it to share at least some properties with ordinary complements. For instance, it shares with ordinary direct objects the assignment of accusative Case. As the direct perception of the nominal direct object of a perception verb is always implied (i.e., *I saw John in the room* implies that I had a direct perception of John, not just that I indirectly inferred his presence in the room), it is not too surprising that this property carries over to a governed subject of the embedded clause.

4 Thematic sharing

If we try to express this intuition in a more precise way, various formal and empirical problems arise. It is generally assumed that the semantic selection of a verb is expressed in part through a Thematic (or Theta) Grid, a list of the thematic (semantic) roles that the verb assigns. We can assume that the following Theta Grid is associated to a verb like *see*:

(24) <Experiencer _____ Theme>

That is, in a sentence like

(25) Maria ha visto Gianni
      'Maria saw Gianni'

the subject receives the role of experiencer, the individual submitted to the perceptual experience, and the object receives the role of theme, the individual or thing that is perceived. Here no problem arises for the two fundamental principles that ensure well-formedness in this domain, the Projection Principle, and the Theta Criterion (see Chomsky 1981), in that there is a one-to-one correspondence between theta roles and constituents, as the two principles require in complementary ways. Things are more complex if we look at the accusative with infinitive and at the pseudo-relative:

(26)a Maria ha visto Gianni richiamare i cani.
      'Maria saw Gianni calling back the dogs.'
    b Maria ha visto i cani venir richiamati da Gianni.
      'Maria saw the dogs being called back by Gianni.'
(27)a Maria ha visto Gianni che richiamava i cani.
      'Maria saw Gianni calling back the dogs.'
    b Maria ha visto i cani che venivano richiamati da Gianni.
      'Maria saw the dogs being called back by Gianni.'

Here, as we have seen, we must overtly express the fact that Maria has seen the grammatical subject of the complement and a certain dog-retrieving action, without necessarily seeing the object or other postverbal complements; so, it looks as if the subject *and* the infinitival predicate (or the pseudo-relative) both played the role of theme of the perception verb. The most straightforward way to express this state of affairs would be to say that in these cases the verb has two themes (say, one nominal and one clausal, in essence the proposal of Guasti 1988); this would predict, under standard versions of the Projection Principle, that two distinct constituents should follow the perception verb in these cases. This appears to be incorrect. For instance, the possibility (somewhat marginal for the infinitive) to form the following pseudo-clefts suggests that only one constituent is involved:

(28) a ?Ciò che ho visto è Gianni correre da sua madre.
      'What I saw is Gianni running to his mother.'
   b Ciò che ho visto è Gianni che correva da sua madre.
      'What I saw is Gianni running to his mother.'

Let us consider two other simple arguments for assuming a unique postverbal constituent in such cases, the first one quite familiar, the second one new. In English the NP in the accusative infinitive (or participle) construction can be an expletive, an option that is restricted to clausal subjects (Akmajian 1977; Gee 1977; Higginbotham 1983); this possibility then seems to require the clausal analysis indicated by the parentheses:

(29) I saw [it raining yesterday].

Second argument: infinitives which are not in a context of Case assignment in Italian are always introduced by a prepositional complementizer. This happens, for instance, in the case of complements of nouns or adjectives, and in all the cases of object control (or anyhow in all the cases in which the infinitive is in the position of a second object, with the case taken up by the first object):

(30) a La possibilità *(di) partire.
        'The possibility of to leave.'
    b Pronto *(a) partire.
        'Ready to leave.'
    c Hanno colto/beccato/sorpreso Gianni *(a) rubare le more.
        'They caught Gianni stealing blackberries.'

This generalization may have a natural explanation in terms of Case Theory (for discussion, see Acquaviva 1989). Now, if the NP and the infinitive were two independent constituents in the case of perception verbs, as in (31)b, we would have here a violation of this generalization. If the sequence forms a clause, as in (31)c, there is no violation: the infinitive here is in the immediate context of a case assigner, the main verb, hence the preposition is not needed:

(31) a Hanno visto Gianni rubare le more.
'They saw Gianni stealing blackberries.'
b Hanno visto [Gianni] [rubare le more].
c Hanno visto [Gianni rubare le more].

Even if the issue of the constituent structure is quite complex, and much more remains to be said, I would like to conclude on the basis of this evidence that there is only one postverbal constituent in these cases, which under standard assumptions on the Projection Principle leads us to discard the hypothesis that a direct perception verb assigns two VP-internal theta roles.

The other possibility that we are now led to explore is that there is only one theme (i.e., the same theta grid is (24) also corresponds to (26) and (27)), but both the clause and its subject can simultaneously fulfil this role. This is what I will call *thematic sharing*. This approach straightforwardly gives the right interpretation, but raises a problem for the Theta Criterion: how can the same role be simultaneously associated with two distinct elements, a configuration that violates the biuniqueness of roles and assignees which the Theta Criterion requires? So, it looks as if in these cases, whatever path we take, one biuniqueness requirement is violated, either the one enforced by the Projection Principle or the one enforced by the Theta Criterion. Here I would like to take the second path, showing that the problem with the Theta Criterion is relatively more benign.

Suppose that the association of theta roles to arguments involves coindexation of slots of the Theta Grid of a verb with arguments under government from the verb (i.e., an argument is theta marked by a verb iff it is governed by the verb and coindexed with a slot in its theta grid), as in Stowell (1981). Then, having the subject and the clause sharing the theme role would amount to having them both governed by the verb and coindexed with the theme slot in the verb's grid. We know that in the accusative with infinitive and in the pseudo-relative the embedded subject is governed by the verb, so the first condition is met. But how can the second be met, i.e., how can a clause and its subject share the same index?

In fact, there is a formal mechanism which, under standard assumptions, precisely ensures this result: specifier-head agreement, which minimally involves coindexation of the subject with the inflectional head of which it is the specifier. If this index percolates up to the maximal projection of the agreeing head, we have the intended configuration. Let us assume that the heads of IP and CP in the cases of accusative with infinitive and pseudo-relative contain an abstract agreement specification. We then have:

(32) a Maria ha visto [Gianni$_i$ AGR$_i$ richiamare i cani].
   $<E \_T_i>$
b Maria ha visto [Gianni$_i$ che+AGR$_i$ [___ richiamava i cani]].
   $<E \_T_i>$

These representations do not raise any problem for the Projection Principle: there is a unique internal theta role, and a unique complement constituent, the clause. They do not violate the Theta Criterion either, if the biuniqueness that this principle requires is seen as involving indices and slots in theta grids: in (32) there is a unique index per slot. Notice that Gianni ends up construed with two theta roles in (32): agent of *richiamare* and theme of *vedere*; this is not excluded under our interpretation of the Theta Criterion, and seems to correctly correspond to the interpretation of the sentences (for a discussion of other apparently admissible cases of double Theta marking see Chomsky 1986a).[6]

Apart from the interpretive property we have discussed, there is syntactic evidence that the embedded subject position is theta marked by the main verb in (32). In passive sentences in Italian the object can be moved to subject position, or remain *in situ*:

(33) a Hanno dato un premio al direttore.
    'They gave a prize to the director.'
  b Un premio è stato dato t al direttore.
    'A prize was given to the director.'
  c E' stato dato un premio al direttore.
    'Was given a prize to the director.'

On the contrary, the subject of a small clause can be moved, but not left *in situ* in passive:

(34) a Ritengo [alcune persone poco intelligenti].
    'I consider some people not very intelligent.'
  b Alcune persone sono ritenute [t poco intelligenti].
    'Some people are considered not very intelligent.'
  c *Sono ritenute [alcune persone poco intelligenti].
    'Are considered some people not very intelligent.'

Similarly with raising, NP movement appears to be obligatory:

(35) a Alcune persone sembrano[t essere entrate nell'appartamento].
    'Some people seem to have come into the apartment.'
  b *Sembrano [alcune persone essere entrate nell'appartamento].
    'Seem some people to have come into the apartment.'

These facts have been interpreted by Belletti (1988) in terms of her partitive Case approach. In a nutshell, her idea is that verbs deprived of their capacity to assign accusative Case, such as passive participles, retain the capacity to assign a special partitive Case (which, among other things can only occur on indefinite NPs). Partitive Case, contrary to accusative Case, is inherent, and as such it can only be assigned by a verb to one of its theta marked arguments. (33)c is fine, because the direct object can receive partitive from the theta marking verb, (34)c and (35)b are out because the embedded subject is governed but not theta marked by the main verb, hence partitive assignment is excluded.

Now, leaving the embedded subject *in situ* when a perception verb is passivized gives a distinctly more acceptable result with respect to Raising and epistemic small clauses:

(36) a Ho visto alcune persone entrare nell'appartamento.
      'I saw some people enter into the apartment.'
    b Alcune persone sono state viste entrare nell'appartamento.
      'Some people were seen enter(ing) into the apartment.'
    c Sono state viste alcune persone entrare nell'appartamento.
      'Were seen some people enter(ing) into the apartment.'

If (36)c is made possible by partitive Case assignment, we must conclude that the embedded subject is theta marked by the perception verb.

5 Propositional and individual themes

The interpretive mechanism that I have proposed involves the sharing of a theme theta role between a clause and its subject, and is made possible by two formal ingredients: government by the higher verb, and a certain coindexation pattern that arises through agreement. We should now ask why this peculiar thematic sharing only arises with perception verbs. A particularly interesting case is raised by epistemic and volitional predicates in English, which involve some kind of clausal reduction, and in which the two formal conditions for thematic sharing are arguably met; still, the interpretive phenomenon is not found. Consider the following pairs:

(37) a John believes your story.
    b John believes your story to be false.
(38) a John wants Mary.
    b John wants Mary to leave.

The main verb governs (assigns Case to) the embedded subject in the b examples (perhaps indirectly in (38)b), an abstract agreement relation within the infinitive presumably is possible, hence the formal conditions for thematic sharing would seem to be met. Still the meaning of the structures clearly indicates that there is no thematic sharing: the b examples do not imply at all the a examples, and the contents of the belief and of the desire simply are the propositions 'your story is false' and 'Mary should leave'. Moreover, our syntactic test for theta marking under Belletti's partitive hypothesis shows that an embedded subject governed by an epistemic verb is not theta marked (see (34)c). Why are things so different with perception verbs, i.e., why is it the case that (39)b implies (39)a?

(39) a John saw Mary.
  b John saw Mary leave/leaving.

I would like to suggest that the difference is due to the different nature of the theta role assigned to the clause in the two cases: this theta role is close enough to the theta role normally assigned to a nominal in the case of the perception verbs, but not in the case of epistemic or volition verbs; hence the thematic sharing is possible only in the first case. Following Higginbotham (1983), I will assume that the clause in (39)b denotes an event, an entity that is essentially assimilated to an individual, while the clause in (37)b and (38)b denotes a proposition. Now, given the rather fundamental nature of this distinction (see Zucchi 1990 for discussion), we may think that individual and propositional theta roles are distinct, and in particular, that we have an individual theme role and a propositional theme role. This suffices to account for the observed difference. In both (39)a and b, the perception verb assigns an individual theme role, i.e., we have the same theta grid:

(40) <Experiencer ___ Theme$_{ind}$>

The individual theme role is uniquely received by the nominal object in (39)a, and shared by the clause and its subject in (39)b. The two cases of (37) and (38), on the other hand, differ in the nature of the assigned theta role, which is individual in a and propositional in b:

(41) a <Experiencer ___ Theme$_{ind}$>
   b <Experiencer ___ Theme$_{prop}$>

So, no sharing is possible in b, as the propositional role that the clause receives is not appropriate for its nominal subject, which would require an individual role. Even if the formal ingredients for theta role sharing would seem to be met by certain epistemic and volitional structures such as (37)b and (38)b, the phenomenon cannot take place given the intrinsic nature of the roles involved. The difference ultimately reduces to the fact that epistemic verbs only assign propositional roles to their clausal complements, while perception verbs can assign event theme roles to clausal complements, a subcase of individual roles.[7]

Our analysis of thematic sharing in accusative with infinitive and in the pseudo-relative crucially involves the postulation of an abstract agreement on the highest clausal projection. We have seen how, by assuming this agreement, we can account for thematic sharing, but we have not said why direct perception verbs should require such an agreement specification to head their clausal complements. Let us conclude this section by noticing that the non-propositional nature of the theme role assigned by direct perception verbs may answer this question, and further highlight the functional role of this agreement specification. Individual theta roles are typically assigned to nominal expressions; if we turn this observation into a requirement of the canonical structural realization of an individual role (i.e., its bearer must be marked +N), then we may think of the agreement features, nominal features in nature, as a device to make the clause +N, hence a suitable recipient of an individual role.

In short: direct perception verbs assign individual theme roles to their complements; the canonical structural realization of an individual role is a category marked +N; so, a clause can be formally selected by a direct perception verb only if its head is marked +N. One device to fulfil this requirement (not the only one: see the last section) is that the head of the clause has nominal agreement features (either at the IP level, or at the CP level, as in the pseudo-relative); in this case, a peculiar indexing pattern is created which makes thematic sharing possible, and expresses the fact that the subject of the clause is directly perceived.

6 A syntactic reflex of abstract agreement

Does the postulated abstract agreement have any overt syntactic reflex? Actually, there may even be a morphological reflex: the pseudo-relative in French involves the complementizer *qui*, which has been argued elsewhere on independent grounds to be the form of the complementizer agreeing with its specifier (i.e., *qui* = *que* + *AGR*. For discussion, see Rizzi 1990a):

(42) J'ai vu Marie qui sortait du cinéma.
'I saw Marie leaving the movie theatre.'

A potentially interesting syntactic reflex has to do with Case Theory. There is one respect in which at least some clausal complements of perception verbs behave quite differently from other clausal complements in which the subject is governed by a higher verb. In Italian a pseudo-relative and, somewhat more marginally, an accusative with infinitive, can be separated from the verb, for instance in the pseudo-cleft construction:

(43)a Ciò che ho visto è Gianni che correva a casa.
'What I saw is Gianni running home.'
b ?Ciò che ho visto è Gianni correre a casa.
'What I saw is Gianni running home.'

Italian does not have accusative with infinitive complements with epistemic verbs to contrast with this case, but has non-verbal small clauses with epistemic verbs. In this case, pseudo-clefting the small clause gives a completely impossible result:

(44)a Ritengo [Gianni intelligente].
   'I consider Gianni intelligent.'
   b *Ciò che ritengo è Gianni intelligente.
   'What I consider is Gianni intelligent.'

Similarly, in French, pseudo-relative, participial and (again, more marginally) infinitival perception clauses allow pseudo-clefting, while epistemic small clauses do not:

(45)a Ce que j'ai vu c'est Marie qui sortait du cinéma.
   'What I saw is Marie leaving the movie theatre.'
   b Ce que j'ai vu c'est Marie sortant du cinéma.
   'What I saw is Marie leaving the movie theatre.'
   c ?Ce que j'ai vu c'est Marie sortir du cinéma.
   'What I saw is Marie leaving the movie theatre.'
   d *Ce que je crois c'est Marie heureuse.
   'What I believe is Marie happy.'

And in English, while complements of epistemic and volition verbs resist pseudo-clefting, at least the -ing complements of perception verbs allow this process:

(46)a *What I believe is John to be intelligent.
   b *What I want is Mary to leave.
   c *What I expect is Bill to go home.
   d What I saw is Lucy going home.

A natural account of the ill-formedness of (44)b, (45)d and (46)a–c is offered by Case Theory: there is no Case to be assigned to the lexical subject of the clefted clause, as it has been removed from the government domain of its Case assigner, the main verb. The plausibility of a Case-theoretic account is enhanced by the fact that (46)c becomes acceptable if an independent Case assigner, the complementizer *for*, is available for the subject in the clefted position:

(47) What I want is for Mary to leave.

Why is it that (43), (45)a–c and (46)d are essentially well-formed? Notice that some Case-transmission mechanism from the position of the variable must be assumed to account for the well-formedness of cases in which the clefted constituent is a NP:

(48) What I want t is this/two cars.

See Barss (1986) for an analysis of various similar 'connectivity' effects in the pseudo-cleft construction. The difference between (48) and (46)a–c is obviously that, in the former, the NP which needs Case is coindexed with the variable, hence case can be inherited from it (through the formation of the complex chain that Barss discusses) while in the latter there is no such coindexation, no extended chain formation, hence no inheritance is possible. Again, if the subject and the clause are coindexed in (46)d, etc., we will have the following indexing pattern:

(49) Ciò che ho visto t_i è [Gianni$_i$ che+AGR$_i$ ___ correva a casa].

The subject of the pseudo-relative Gianni is coindexed with the pseudo-relative, which in turn is coindexed with the variable; if Case, as the theta role, is essentially a property of the index, Case inheritance will be possible here.

7 Conclusion

We have suggested that different formal and interpretive peculiarities of perception verbs can be given a partially unified account within certain natural assumptions on the relationship between syntax and semantics. A major distinctive property of perception verbs, when they express direct perception, is that they select clausal complements designating events, special kinds of individuals. In terms of Theta Theory, they assign an individual theme role to the complement. If the canonical structural realization of individual roles is a nominal category, the clausal complement of perception verbs must be nominal, i.e., have a nominal head. A natural device to make a clausal head nominal is to assign it nominal agreement features. Such agreement features (at the I level in the accusative with infinitive, at the C level in the pseudo-relative) determine a peculiar indexing pattern, with the subject coindexed with the clause, which has formal and interpretive reflexes. The main formal reflex involves Case Theory: the complement will allow pseudo-clefting, contrary to other clausal complements in which the embedded subject receives Case from the main verb. The interpretive reflex is thematic sharing: the theme of the perception verb is simultaneously the clause and its subject, both theta marked by the verb. This accounts, among other things, for the subject/non-subject asymmetries which have been detected.

Appendix: speculations on the naked infinitives

The naked infinitive in English differs from the -ing construction and the accusative plus infinitive in Romance in that it resists pseudo-clefting:

(50) *What I saw t was John run.

This has led Akmajian to conclude that the NP and the naked VP do not form a constituent here; but this conclusion appears to be incorrect on the basis of the evidence mentioned before.[8]

A more promising line of argument is suggested by the observation that the naked infinitive construction differs from the -ing construction and the Romance equivalent in a number of other respects: the subject of the -ing construction can be moved by Wh movement, passive and is reasonably natural under Heavy NP Shift:[9]

(51) a I saw John running.
　　 b John was seen t running.
　　 c Who did you see t running?
　　 d I saw t running – the student whom you just mentioned.
(52) a Ho visto Gianni correre a casa.
　　 b Gianni è stato visto t correre a casa.
　　 c Chi hai visto t correre a casa?
　　 d Ho visto t correre a casa – lo studente di cui mi hai parlato.

On the other hand, the naked infinitive allows Wh movement of the subject, but not passivization nor a natural application of Heavy NP Shift:

(53) a I saw John run.
　　 b *John was seen t run.
　　 c Who did you see t run?
　　 d *?I saw t run – the student whom you just mentioned.

In this respect, the behaviour of the naked infinitive strikingly resembles the behaviour of tensed clauses, which also allow Wh movement of the subject, but not NP movement nor Heavy NP Shift:

(54) a I believe [[John was here]].
　　 b *John was believed [[t was here]].
　　 c Who did you believe [t [t was here]]?
　　 d *I believe [[t was here]] the student whom you just mentioned.

The ill-formedness of (54)b–d is generally attributed to the Empty Category Principle. This principle requires traces to be properly governed, a condition that is not met in b and d, in which the intervening CP layer blocks government from the higher verb. The condition is met in c, in which the Wh element passing through the Spec of Comp ensures proper government of the subject trace (perhaps in the indirect way argued for in Rizzi 1990a).

Taking this parallel seriously would then lead us to adopt Kayne's (1984, Chapter 2) proposal that naked infinitives involve more structure than meets the eye, and in particular that the equivalent of a CP level is to be postulated on top of the infinitival structure:

(55) I saw [[John run]].

The accusative Case would then be transmitted from the perception verb to the head of the clause C, and then assigned to the subject.[10] This structure would make (53)b–d immediately explicable in terms of the ECP, as the perception verb would be too far away to properly govern the subject trace; (53)c would be on a par with (54)c, with the subject trace licensed by the movement through Comp. We would then continue to postulate a reduced IP structure for the -ing construction and the Romance accusative with infinitive, with the perception verb directly governing the subject trace and satisfying the ECP in (51)b–d and (52)b–d.[11]

I will not discuss here the many ramifications of this analysis. Let me just mention the fact that if syntactic evidence forces us to adopt some version of this approach, the basic generalization that we have tried to capture is in danger: the naked infinitive clearly involves direct perception, and still no direct government inside the lower clause from the higher verb would be permitted. Now, if we look across languages, we find that Universal Grammar appears to offer at least another device for the linguistic expression of direct perception, more minimal than clausal reduction and the upgrading of the subject to a verb governed position. This is illustrated by the following Russian case: according to Noonan (1985), direct perception of a state of affairs can be expressed in Russian by an indicative tensed clause which only differs from an ordinary sentential complement in that it is headed by the special complementizer *kak*:

(56) Ja videl [kak [Boris citaet knigu]].
    'I saw COMP Boris read the book.'

If the ordinary complementizer *cto* is selected, the sentence is well-formed, but it does not express direct perception, as the corresponding English case, 'I saw that Boris read the book'. For instance, if the embedded clause involves a predicate that cannot be 'immediately perceived' in a natural way, the structure with *cto* is fine and the one with *kak* is deviant (thanks to Tali Siloni for providing these examples):

(57)a Ja vizu [cto [on durak]].
    'I see that he (is) stupid.'
  b *Ja vizu [kak [on durak]].

It then appears that direct perception can also be expressed by the simple selection of a special CP level. We may again speculate that the special complementizer expresses the nominal feature +N, required to make the clause compatible with the event theta role characteristic of direct perception.[12]

It may then be the case that the naked infinitives, under some version of Kayne's analysis, will turn out to be structurally closer to the Russian (and German) tensed construction than to the Romance and Germanic cases involving genuine clausal reduction.

Notes

1 The Case is morphologically manifested when the subject is cliticized (*Je le vois partir*, 'I him see leave'). The causative verb *laisser* (let) shares this property with perception verbs in French (*Je laisserai Jean partir*, 'I will let Jean leave'). The corresponding structure is marginal in Italian. We will generally gloss the Romance accusative with infinitive construction (as well as the pseudo-relative construction of Section 2) by using the accusative -ing construction in English. See footnote 12.
2 Cinque (1995, Chapter 8) shows that different kinds of pseudo-relatives should be distinguished. Our considerations apply (at least) to the kind instantiating a CP constituent.
3 We may think of government as a local relation between a head and a phrase in its immediate environment. The locality may be thought of as determined by a minimality principle, which blocks government across a potential governor (see the references quoted in the text). So, the perception verb does not govern the embedded subject in (14)a due to the intervention of the potential governor *che*. There is no such intervening element in (14)b–c, hence the verb governs *Gianni* in these cases.
4 Things are somewhat more complicated if other perception verbs are taken into account, but the same basic generalization seems to me to hold in many clear cases:

i a Ho sentito Gianni fare una telefonata a Piero.
    'I heard Gianni make a phone call to Piero.'
  b Ho sentito Piero ricevere una telefonata da Gianni.
    'I heard Piero receive a phone call from Gianni.'

The first is natural while the second is distinctly odd in a situation in which I have only heard Gianni's voice. The same asymmetries arise, perhaps even more sharply, with the corresponding pseudo-relatives. Jim Higginbotham points out that the systematic nature of these asymmetries was noticed in Fiengo (1974).
5 In fact, if I saw on TV the famous sequence of the Dallas assassination, I could accurately describe my perceptual experience by saying (21), not by saying (20), even in the variant with *qualcuno* (someone).
6 If the embedded subject is technically Theta marked by the perception verb, one may wonder what excludes a structure in which it would not be theta marked clause internally. Such structures are of course totally impossible:

i a *Maria ha visto Gianni nevicare.
    'Maria saw Gianni snowing,'
  b *Maria ha visto Gianni che Piero richiamava i cani.
    'Maria saw Gianni that Piero was calling back the dogs.'

In other words, why is it that ia is impossible in the interpretation in which Maria simultaneously saw Gianni and a certain snowing event, and ib is impossible in the interpretation in which Maria simultaneously saw Gianni and a certain dog-retrieving event in which Gianni was not involved? A reasonable answer is that i is still excluded as a Theta Criterion violation at D-structure.

when the network of agreement relations has not been established which would ensure the peculiar sharing of theta roles that we have assumed (we must also make the usual assumption that accidental coindexing does not suffice). Hence, at D structure either the clause or the subject is theta marked, but not both, and this violates the Theta Criterion.
7 Of course, the indexing pattern of (32), etc. should not be interpreted as meaning that the subject is coreferential to the clause. In order to avoid this we have to assume that events are close enough to individuals to allow thematic sharing, but different enough to exclude that coindexation between expressions designating individuals and events may be interpreted as expressing coreference. This is still compatible with the assumption that the main dividing line is between propositions and individuals/events.
8 Notice also that not only does the subject of the naked infinitive resist NP movement, but also the predicate resists VP preposing:

i * . . . and go home I saw him t.

This property is completely unexpected under a non-clausal analysis. See Roberts (1988) for an account that presupposes the clausal analysis.
9 Non-verbal small clauses selected by perception verbs in English tend to pattern with -ing complements, in that they can be (at least marginally) pseudo-clefted, in sharp contrast with epistemic small clauses:

i ?What I saw was John nude.
ii *What I consider is John intelligent.

Moreover the NP can undergo NP movement and Heavy NP Shift, in addition to Wh movement:

iii John was seen t nude.
iv Who did you see t nude?
v   I saw t nude – the student whom you just mentioned.

The contrast i–ii follows from the fact that the peculiar indexing pattern permitting thematic sharing and Case transmission is possible in i but not in ii for the reasons discussed in Section 5.
10 The evidence presented in Belletti (1990) to show that no inflectional projection is present in the naked infinitive construction can be reconciled with Kayne's analysis under the assumption that in (55) CP immediately dominates a bare VP with a subject, a VP small clause in the sense of Koopman and Sportiche (1991). If this is correct, the naked infinitive would simultaneously involve more and less structure than the corresponding construction in Romance: more because it would involve a CP level, less because it would not involve any IP-type level.
11 Essentially the same analysis of naked infinitives is proposed in Lightfoot (1991: 92).

There is also an interpretive property with respect to which the Romance accusative with infinitive construction (as well as the pseudo-relative) patterns with the -ing form in English, rather than with the naked infinitive. As Jim Higginbotham points out, the action denoted by the naked infinitive is necessarily complete, while this is not the case with the -ing construction:

i   I saw Mary cross the street.
ii I saw Mary crossing the street.

Example i implies that I saw Mary reach the other side of the street, while ii does not. Now, it seems to me that both the Romance constructions lack the 'complete action' implication:

iii Ho visto Maria attraversare la strada.
iv Ho visto Maria che attraversava la strada.

Both sentences (the judgement being sharper for the pseudo-relative) could be used if I didn't actually see Maria reach the opposite side of the street.

12 This is not implausible as the special complementizer *kak* is homophonous to the Wh form meaning *how*, clearly a nominal element. Falkenberg (1990) points out that German can use an analogous device to express direct perception:

i Paul sah Fritz kommen.
  'Paul saw Fritz coming.'
ii Paul sah, wie Fritz kam.
  'Paul saw how Fritz came.'
iii Paul sah, dass Fritz kam.
  'Paul saw that Fritz came.'

The first structure is accusative with infinitive, the second involves a special complementizer homophonous with the Wh word for *how*, and the third is a *that* clause. The first and the second, but not the third, imply direct perception.

If naked infinitives, as well as the Russian and German construction, manifest the subject–object asymmetries discussed in Section 3, we would have to assume that the nominal complementizer is coindexed with the subject of the clause. (50) may still be excluded if Case transmission in the extended chain can provide an NP with Case, but not activate a Case assigner (the nominal C in (55)).

Part III
Cartography

9 Residual verb second and the Wh Criterion

Some natural languages do not allow the subject to intervene between the Wh element and the inflected verb in main questions. This constraint is illustrated by English and Italian:

(1)a *What Mary has said?
   b *Che cosa Maria ha detto?

The two languages apparently use different strategies to avoid the forbidden sequence: English preposes the inflected Aux, Italian (like Spanish, Catalan, Romanian, etc.) uses zero realization or postposing of the subject:

(2) What has Mary said?
(3)a Che cosa ha detto?
     'What has said?'
   b Che cosa ha detto Maria?
     'What has said Maria?'

Two questions arise:

1 What excludes the forbidden sequence?
2 Are the English and Romance salvaging strategies as different as they look?

Focusing initially on the first question and on the English case, we assume that the required adjacency between Wh and I is to be expressed in terms of Chomsky's (1986b) approach to the structure of clauses: in main questions, I to C movement must apply, and create a Spec-head configuration involving the Wh element and the inflected verb. Subject–auxiliary inversion can thus be reduced to a special case of Verb Second (as in den Besten 1983), in turn a particular instance of head to head movement. I will call 'residual V-2' such construction-specific manifestations of I to C movement in a language (like English and the modern Romance languages except Raetho-Romance) which does not generalize the V-2 order to main declarative clauses.

Question 1 can then be restated as: what triggers residual V-2? I would like to propose that the application of I to C movement in this and other similar cases is enforced in order to satisfy the Wh Criterion, a general well-formedness condition on Wh structures, which is also ultimately responsible for the SS distribution and LF interpretation of Wh operators. Sections 1 and 4 introduce and refine the Wh Criterion. Sections 2 and 3 show how the application of Subject Aux inversion in English is enforced by the Wh Criterion. Section 5 extends the analysis to inversion with negative operators. Section 6 deals with Subject Clitic Inversion in French along similar lines. In Sections 7 and 8 we go back to question 2, and provide an analysis of inversion in Romance interrogatives partially in terms of the Wh Criterion.

1 The Wh Criterion

In English, the Spec of Comp of an interrogative clause must be filled by a Wh element at S-structure, hence the *in situ* strategy is excluded:

(4) *I wonder [[you saw who]].

Wh *in situ* is possible in multiple questions, but the Wh element must stay in an argument position; if it is moved to an A' position which is not the appropriate scope position, as the embedded Spec of C in (5)b, the structure is excluded:

(5)a Who believes [[Mary went where]]?
  b *Who believes [where [Mary went t].

Following standard practice, we will assume that the complementizer of a question is marked by the feature +Wh. We can then state the following principle:

(6) The Wh Criterion:
  A A Wh operator must be in a Spec-head configuration with X_{+Wh}.
  B An X_{+Wh} must be in a Spec-head configuration with a Wh operator.

Example (6) is the updated version of the principle first proposed in May (1985), made compatible with the theory of Comp of Chomsky (1986b). Here I develop the analysis sketched out in Rizzi (1990b).

As the feature +Wh on a clausal head (most typically a C) designates the fact that the projection of that head (CP) is a question, the Wh Criterion simply expresses the fact that at the appropriate level of representation, interrogative operators must be in the Spec of CPs which are interpreted as questions and, reciprocally, CPs interpreted as questions must have interrogative operators as specifiers. The Wh Criterion thus requires configurations of the following shape:

(7)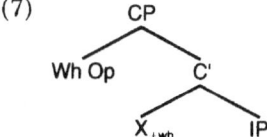

As a general well-formedness principle on the scope of Wh operators, (6) can be taken as a criterial condition applying universally at LF. So, in languages lacking syntactic Wh movement, such as Chinese and Japanese, question operators must be moved in the syntax of LF to satisfy the Wh Criterion at this level, thus giving rise to ECP and other locality effects that have been much discussed since Huang (1982).

On the other hand, it can be argued that the Wh Criterion applies earlier in other languages. For instance, the impossibility of (4) and (5)b can be naturally accounted for through the assumption that in English the Wh Criterion must be fulfilled at S-structure. Example (4) violates clause B if the criterion: the verb *wonder* selects an embedded question, hence a CP whose C is marked +Wh; this C is not in a Spec-head relation with a Wh operator at S-structure, in violation of B. As for (5)b, it contains a Wh operator that is not in a Spec-head configuration with a +Wh head (*believe* selects a declarative, hence a CP whose head is not wh), and therefore it violates clause A of the Criterion. In Section 4, we will come back to the fact that if the Wh element remains in an argument position, as in (5)a, it does not determine a violation of the Wh Criterion at S-structure.

2 Subject-Aux inversion in English

We can now show that the Wh Criterion provides a simple account of the fundamental paradigm of Subject-Aux inversion in English.

We assume that this process involves structure-preserving movement of I to C.¹ To simplify matters, let us concentrate on cases of Wh movement of the direct object, and see how it interacts with I to C movement. We have to deal with the following eight representations, depending on whether Wh movement has taken place or not, whether I to C movement has taken place or not, and whether the interrogative is independent or embedded:

(8)a *[[Mary has seen who]].
   b *[Who [Mary has seen t]].
   c *[has [Mary t seen who]].

    d [Who has [Mary t seen t]].
(9)a *I wonder [[Mary has seen who]].
   b I wonder [who [Mary has seen t]].
   c *I wonder [has [Mary t seen who]].
   d *I wonder [who has [Mary t seen t]].

Only two of the possible combinations are well-formed. Let us consider the embedded paradigm first. The verb *wonder* selects an indirect question, hence an embedded C marked wh. The D-structure representation then is

(10) I wonder [C$_{+wh}$ [Mary has seen who]].

If nothing happens, the corresponding S-structure is ruled out by clause B of the Wh Criterion, as a Wh clausal head is not in the required configuration with a Wh operator at S-structure; this accounts for (9)a. In (9)b, Wh movement has applied, the required Spec-head configuration has been created and the Wh Criterion is satisfied. (9)d is excluded by whatever principle accounts for the root character of I to C movement: Rizzi and Roberts (1989) argue that a restrictive enough formulation of the Projection Principle rules out such cases; alternatively, one may think that the specification Wh fills the embedded C, and makes it unavailable as a landing site for I to C movement (as any other filled C).[2]

Example (9)c is ruled out at the same time by clause B of the Wh Criterion and by whatever principle rules out embedded I to C movement.

Let us now consider the main clause paradigm (8). The first question to ask is how the Wh specification can occur in main clauses. I will assume that this, as well any other substantive feature specification cannot occur 'for free' in a structure, and must be licensed somehow. The occurrence of Wh in an embedded Comp is determined by a standard licensing device, lexical selection. What about main questions? Of course, the theory of licensing cannot be too demanding: there must be at least a position in a structure whose properties and specifications are independently licensed, i.e., a point which the chain of licensings can be anchored to, and start from. It is natural to assume that such a position can be the main inflection (or one of the main inflectional heads, if some version of the Split Infl hypothesis is adopted, as in Pollock 1989), i.e., the head that also contains the independent tense specification of the whole sentence. I would like to propose that among the other autonomously licensed specifications, the main inflection can also be specified as wh.

That a verbal inflection can carry such a specification is strongly suggested by the fact that, in some natural languages, the verb manifests a special morphology in interrogatives (see Clements 1984 for Kikuyu; Chung 1982 for Chamorro; Georgopoulos 1985, 1991 for Palauan; Haïk,

Koopman and Sportiche 1985 for Moore; Tuller 1985 for Hausa; Haïk 1990 for a comparative analysis of these cases; see also Kayne 1984 and Roberts 1993a on interrogative *-ti* in colloquial French). If we make the assumption that I can carry wh, the functional role of Subject-Aux inversion becomes clear: this instance of residual I to C movement moves the Wh specification high enough to allow satisfaction of the Wh Criterion. Let us see how this system works. If the main I is specified wh, the common D structure of the different cases of (8) is the following:

(11) [C [Mary has$_{+wh}$ seen who]]?

If nothing happens, the representation (8)a is ruled out by clause B of the Wh Criterion at S-structure (no Wh operator in the Spec of inflection); (8)b and c are ruled out for the same reason. (8)d is well-formed: I carrying Wh is moved to C, the Wh operator is moved to its Spec, and the configuration required by the Wh Criterion is met:

(12) [Who has$_{+wh}$ [Mary t seen t]]?

We thus obtain the result that obligatory Subject-Aux inversion in interrogatives is enforced by the same principle which is responsible for the distributional and interpretive properties of Wh operators.[3]

3 Wh movement of the subject

If the application of *do* support is a reliable cue that I to C movement has applied, we must conclude from the following examples that I to C movement cannot apply when a subject is moved (irrelevantly, (13)a is possible with emphatic *do* in I):

(13)a *[Who does [t t love Mary]]?
    b [Who C [t loves Mary]]?

Actually, two distinct problems arise here:

1 Why is I to C movement incompatible with subject movement?
2 Why is I to C movement allowed not to apply in (13)b without violating the Wh Criterion?

Starting from the first question, three additional cases suggest that I to C movement creates a configuration in English which does not license a subject trace:

1 Heavy NP Shift of the subject is impossible in interrogatives (as well as in declaratives. For discussion, see Rizzi 1990a):

(14) a Have they left?
　　b *Have t left – all the people who you invited?

2   Embedded V-2 may be triggered by a preposed negative element (see below and Chapter 10 for discussion); in that case, object extraction has the flavour of a Wh Island violation, while subject extraction across the preposed I is distinctly worse:

(15) a I think that never did he help her.
　　b ??The woman who I think that never did he help t.
　　c *The man who I think that never did t help her.

3   McCloskey (1992) points out that, in Hiberno-English, I to C can take place in embedded questions, and familiar subject–object asymmetries arise in cases of extraction:

(16) a You asked them would they marry him.
　　b ??Which one did you ask them would they marry t?
　　c *Which one did you ask them would t marry him?

Examples are adapted from McCloskey, op. cit. (73); we leave open here the question of why this instance of I to C is not root.

In Rizzi (1990a) it is argued that (13)a and (14)b are ruled out as violations of the proper head government requirement of ECP. Suppose this is stated as follows:

(17)　t must be head-governed by X° within X' (the immediate projection of X).

If the derived structure of I to C movement in English (and more generally in residual cases of V2) is the following, as argued in Rizzi and Roberts (1989):

(18)
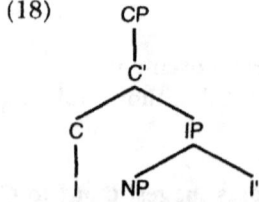

then a trace in subject position is not allowed to occur: it is not governed by C (inert for government in non-V2 languages), and it is governed by I, but not within its immediate projection I'. Hence, the proper head government requirement (17) is violated. This account of (13)a–(14)b can be immediately extended to cover (16)c and (17)c (the latter extension is explicitly envisaged by McCloskey (op. cit.)).

It remains to be determined why the structure not involving I to C movement is well-formed, and does not violate the Wh Criterion. A possible approach would be to assume that the subject does not move at all, hence the representation is simply the following, rather than (13)b:

(19) [[who Infl$_{+Wh}$ loves Mary]].

The subject simply remains in the Spec of Infl endowed with the Wh feature, and the Wh Criterion is satisfied within IP in this case. Some technical problems are raised by this minimal solution:

a   If Infl is associated to the lexical verb through affix hopping in English (Chomsky 1957, 1991), and this process involves the whole content of the node, then the feature Wh would also be lowered into the VP, hence it could not be in a Spec-head configuration with the subject at S-structure.
b   The Spec of IP should be allowed to count as an A' position in this case.
c   There is no obvious position for the variable in (19) (even assuming the 'subject within VP' hypothesis, an empty category in VP internal (or adjoined) position would not receive Case).

These technical problems (and, more forcefully, the empirical argument concerning similar French cases discussed in Friedemann 1990) suggest that representation (13)b is to be favoured (problems b and c do not arise, and problem a is not worse). But why is the Wh Criterion not violated?

I would like to propose that the Wh Criterion must be interpreted as requiring that the *chain* of the relevant head position has the feature +Wh, not necessarily the position itself. Can we build the proper chain in (13)a? I and the inflection containing +Wh, lowered to V, are coindexed and already form a chain. If the subject locally moved to the Spec of C triggers agreement in C (Rizzi 1990a), we obtain the following indexing pattern:

(20) [Who$_i$ C$_i$ [t$_i$ I$_i$ love-s$_{+Wh, i}$ Mary]]?

Within the standard assumption that agreement is minimally expressed by coindexation, the subject trace is coindexed with Infl as well as with *who*; the latter is coindexed with C, hence, by transitivity, C is coindexed with I. Assuming that two coindexed positions in a local binding relation can always be put together into a single chain (provided that no independent well-formedness condition is violated: see Chapter 5), C forms a chain with I and with the lower inflection containing +Wh. Hence, the Wh Criterion is met at S-structure.

We must now show that this extension does not overgenerate. Why is the chain option restricted to the local movement of the subject? Consider the pattern of indexation that arises when any other element is moved to Comp, e.g., the direct object:

(21) Who C [Mary I loves t].

In this case, the Wh operator must be contraindexed with the subject because of strong cross-over (if they were coindexed, the variable would also be coindexed with the subject, and principle C would be violated). Hence, by transitivity, C is contraindexed with I and no chain can be formed. As C cannot be endowed with the +Wh feature through chain formation in this case, the only available device to fulfil the Wh Criterion is I to C movement. We then derive the conclusion that Subject-Aux inversion applies obligatorily in all the cases in which the moved element is not the local subject.

4 Functional definition of Wh operators

Wh *in situ* is impossible in English in single questions; in multiple questions it is possible provided that one Wh operator has been moved to Comp:

(22) a *You gave what to whom?
   b What did you give t to whom?

This may suggest, at first sight, that the two clauses of the Wh Criterion apply asymmetrically in English: B must be fulfilled at S-structure, but A can be delayed until LF. According to this approach, (22)a is excluded because clause B is violated at S-structure, as the +Wh feature in I is not supported by a Wh operator in its Spec. On the other hand, a Wh operator can be left *in situ* in (22)b if clause A can be delayed until LF, as clause B is fulfilled in the now familiar way (I to C movement and Wh movement of one of the two operators). This corresponds, in essence, to the interpretation of May (1985).

I would like to consider a different possibility here. Some empirical reasons have already been mentioned to assume that both clauses of the Wh Criterion apply at S-structure in English (we will come back to them in a moment). But, if this is so, why is Wh *in situ* at all possible?

I believe the solution is provided by a refinement of the notion 'Wh operator'. The needed refinement is independently justified to solve a paradox that Wh constructions raise for Theta Theory. Consider the following two fairly uncontroversial statements:

(23) i The Theta-Criterion applies at DS, SS, LF.
  ii Variables are arguments.

Consider also DS (24)a and its SS (24)b, as well as the multiple question (25) at SS:

(24) a Mary saw whom?
  b Who did Mary see t?
(25) Who t saw whom?

By (23)i, the verb *see* assigns a theta role to its object at DS, hence *who*, the assignee, must be an argument in (24)a. By (23)i, the verb assigns a theta role at SS, and by (23)ii, this role is received by the variable in (24)b; hence *who* must be a non-argument here, otherwise there would be an argument too many. Therefore, the same element functions as an argument and as a non-argument at different levels. The same paradox arises in (25) with two distinct occurrences of the same element at the same level, SS: here the subject theta role is assigned to the variable, therefore *who* must be a non-argument; on the other hand, *whom* is the only possible recipient of the object theta role, hence it must be an argument.

This paradox was noticed in Chomsky (1981: 115), and is also discussed in Cinque (1986); I will assume an adapted version of the approach proposed in these references, cutting some corners (for relevant discussion, see Brody 1990b). Suppose that the notion Wh operator is defined in part in functional terms, in the following manner:[4]

(26) Wh operator = a Wh phrase in an A' position.

A Wh phrase as such is an argument, unless it is an operator according to (26). So, in (24)a, *whom* is in an A position, hence it does not qualify as an operator, it is an argument and receives the object theta role; in (24)b it is in an A' position, it qualifies as an operator. It is not an argument, hence the object theta role can be assigned to the variable. Similarly, in (25), *who* qualifies as an operator, and the subject role can be assigned to the variable, while *whom* is an argument, and receives the object role. The paradox is thus resolved.[5]

We can now go back to the basic paradigm of Wh *in situ*. The well-formedness of (22)b is now compatible with the assumption that the Wh Criterion applies entirely at SS in English: the Wh element *in situ* is in an A position, therefore it does not qualify as an operator under the functional definition (26), hence clause A of the Wh Criterion does not apply to it and no violation is produced at SS. Clause A applies to the Wh operator in Spec of C, and it is satisfied in the familiar manner.

In addition to the conceptual advantage of allowing a uniform application of both clauses of the Wh Criterion, a system involving the Wh

Criterion at SS and the functional definition (26) has the interesting empirical consequence of deriving a generalization observed by Aoun, Hornstein and Sportiche (1981). These authors pointed out that Wh movement in English seems to behave as follows: it can move an element from the position of the variable to the appropriate scope position in the syntax or (in multiple questions) in LF, but this movement must take place entirely in one component. In other words, in multiple questions, a Wh element can be left *in situ* in an argument position at S structure, as in (27)a, and undergo LF movement from there to its scope position at LF, but it cannot be moved to an intermediate A' position in the syntax, as in (27)b, to continue its movement to its scope position in LF (see also Georgopoulos (1991) for discussion):

(27) a Who thinks [C [Mary saw whom]]?
 b *Who thinks [whom C [Mary saw t]]?

This generalization is explained by the Wh Criterion applying at SS and the independently needed functional definition of Wh operators (26): in (27)a, at S-structure *whom* does not qualify as an operator because it is not in an A' position, hence clause A of the Wh Criterion is not violated. It must then be moved in the syntax of LF when (26) is superseded by the general requirement mentioned in footnote 5. In (27)b, on the other hand, *whom* is in an A' position at SS, it qualifies as an operator according to (26), but then the structure is ruled out at SS by clause A of the Wh Criterion: a Wh Operator is not in the required configuration with a +Wh head (the corresponding C is −Wh, given the selectional properties of *think*).

There are other instances of the same descriptive generalization which are now subsumed by the Wh Criterion applying at SS.

1 Lasnik and Saito (1984, 1992) point out that an embedded topicalized constituent cannot be a Wh element involved in a multiple question:

(28) a Who believes that John, Mary likes t?
 b *Who believes that whom, Mary likes t?

In (28)b, *whom* is in an A' position, hence it qualifies as a Wh operator, and the structure is ruled out as a violation of clause A of the Wh Criterion at SS.[6]

2 In French certain quantificational specifiers of the direct object can be extracted and moved to a VP initial position (an A' specifier position according to the analysis of Rizzi 1990a; whether movement or simple construal is the relation involved in (29)b is not crucial here):

(29) a Il a lu beaucoup de livres.
   'He has read a lot of books.'
  b Il a beaucoup lu [t de livres].
   'He has a lot read of books.'

Obenauer (1976) noticed that when the NP specifier is interrogative (*combien*), it can be extracted (as (30)) or left *in situ* within the NP (as in (31)a), but not left *in situ* in the VP initial position (as in (31)b):

(30) Combien a-t-il lu [t de livres]?
   'How many did he read of books?'
(31) a Il a lu combien de livres?
   'He read how many books?'
  b *Il a combien lu de livres?
   'He has how many read of books?'

We will come back in Section 6 to the general possibility of leaving a Wh element *in situ* in main interrogatives in French. The impossibility of (31)b can be attributed to the Wh Criterion applying at SS, plus the functional definition (26): *combien* in (31)b qualifies as a Wh operator, as it is a Wh element in an A' position; it is not in a Spec-head relation with a +Wh head, hence it violates clause A of the Wh Criterion at SS.[7]

3 It has been noticed that a direct object can be scrambled in presubject position in German, but a Wh element *in situ* does not allow this process:

(32) a Warum hat Peter dieses / welches Buch gekauft?
   'Why has Peter this / which book bought?'
  b Warum hat dieses /*?welches Buch Peter gekauft?
   'Why has this / which book Peter bought?'

Examples are taken from Grewendorf and Sternefeld (1990). If the scrambled position is an A' position, this restriction follows from the Wh Criterion: the Wh element qualifies as a Wh operator, hence clause A of the criterion is violated at SS (thanks to Guglielmo Cinque and Sten Vikner for pointing out this consequence of our analysis). Notice that this restriction follows from the fact that the Wh Criterion applies at SS in German; we predict that a scrambling language in which the Wh Criterion applies at LF only should not disallow scrambling of a Wh element. This prediction appears to be borne out in Japanese (Saito 1985).

Before leaving this topic, we must introduce a refinement of our functional definition of Wh operator. Different considerations suggest that the A/A' distinction is too rough:

1   A Wh element *in situ* is possible in heavy NP shifted position, presumably an A' position (e.g., a shifted NP licenses a parasitic gap, see Chomsky 1982 for discussion; the following example is due to R. Kayne):

(33) Which of the students borrowed t from you which of the theses?

2   In French certain adverbials (for instance manner adverbials) can be left *in situ*:

(34) Il a parlé comment?
      'He spoke how?'

Presumably the positions involved in (33) and (34) are A', and still the *in situ* strategy is possible. The natural refinement that immediately comes to mind is that the functional definition of operator refers to a more articulated notion of scope position:

(26') Wh operator = a Wh phrase in a scope position.

By scope position we mean a left-peripheral A' position (either a Spec or an adjoined position). This excludes right-peripheral positions and the base-generated position of VP adverbials.[8,9]

5 Negative Inversion and the Negative Criterion

When a negative constituent is preposed in English, I to C movement applies obligatorily:

(35)a I would do that in no case.
     b *In no case I would do that.
     c In no case would I do that.

It seems quite natural to try to relate this case to the obligatory application of I to C in questions. The relation between questions and negatives in this context is strengthened by the observation that negation patterns with the Wh operators in the selection of a special inflection in the languages discussed in Haïk (1990) (see Section 1). Moreover, question and negative operators pattern alike in blocking adjunct extraction (for relevant discussion, see Rizzi 1990a, Chapter 1). In the system of the latter reference, such a blocking effect is due to the fact that these operators differ from other operators in that they fill an A' specifier position at LF. I would now like to state this scope requirement as resulting from the fact that such affective operators must fulfil at the appropriate level of representation an appropriate generalization of the Wh Criterion: informally, affective operators must be in a Spec-head configuration with a head marked with the relevant affective feature. The negative counterpart of (7), the 'Negative Criterion' would then involve the following configuration:[10]

(36)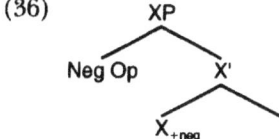

How is a clausal head endowed with the feature +neg? Following Pollock (1989), I will assume that negative sentences involve an independent clausal projection, the Negative Phrase. Following Belletti (1990) I will assume that it is an intermediate projection between the Agr Phrase and the Tense Phrase:

(37)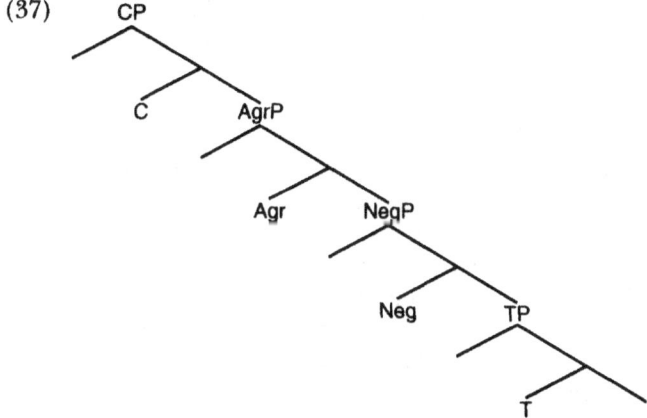

I will also assume, as is natural, that the feature +neg is licensed in the head position of the NegP, and that an inflected verbal element can be associated with this feature when it passes through Neg under head to head movement, as proposed in Moritz (1989).

We can now understand the pattern in (35) if we assume that the negative counterpart of (clause A of) the Wh Criterion applies at SS in English. In (35)a, the negative element is not in a scope position, hence the (negative counterpart of) functional definition (26') does not apply, and at SS there is no negative operator to worry about. In (35)b, the negative element is in a scope position, hence it qualifies as a negative operator; but then clause A of the Criterion is violated at SS, as C is not endowed with the +neg feature. I to C movement can salvage the structure in (35)c by moving the +neg feature to C. The triggering force of I to C movement then is, in essence, the same as in the interrogative case.[11]

Putting together some previous observations, we can notice that an important asymmetry arises between questions and negatives in embedded contexts: the former disallow I to C movement in standard English, while negative preposing in embedded clauses requires it:

(38) a I wonder when (*did) he helped her.
     b I think that never *(did) he help her.

We have already discussed possible accounts of (38)a. As for (38)b, Rizzi and Roberts (1989) have proposed that this is a case of CP recursion, with the higher C filled by *that* and the lower C hosting I to C movement (see Chapter 11 for various refinements). The contrast ultimately reduces to the fact that in English verbs select for interrogative clauses, but not for negative clauses. Embedded interrogatives then sharply differ from main interrogatives, in which no selection is involved, while embedded negatives (in cases of negative preposing) must resort to the same device as main negatives, a marked option made possible by CP recursion.

6 Subject clitic inversion in French

A pronominal subject and the inflected verb invert in French interrogatives, a process which has also been analysed as a special instance of residual V-2 (e.g., Rizzi and Roberts 1989 and references cited there). If we compare the English and French paradigm in main clauses, the salient emerging fact is that French allows more options. Restricting again our attention to the movement of the object and of the inflected verb, we find that three of the four possible combinations are well-formed in French, while only one is possible in English (see (8)):

(39) a [[Elle a rencontré qui]]?
        'She has met who?'
     b [Qui [elle a rencontré t]]?
        'Who she has met?'
     c *[a-t- [elle t rencontré qui]]?
        'Has she met who?'
     d [Qui a-t- [elle t rencontré t]]?
        'Who has she met?'

That is, in addition to the simultaneous movement of the object and the inflected verb ((39)d), the simple movement of the object ((39)b) and the full *in situ* strategy ((39)a) are also possible, the combination of I to C movement and Wh *in situ* ((39)c) being the only excluded option. The first approach that comes to mind to express such a less restrictive system would be to assume that the Wh Criterion does not apply at SS in French, hence the creation of the required Spec head configuration could be delayed until LF. But this approach is clearly inadequate in view of the fact that the embedded paradigm is as restrictive as the English equivalent: only the structure resulting from the simple movement of the object is well-formed:

(40) a *Je ne sais pas [[elle a rencontré qui]].
 'I don't know he has met who.'
 b Je ne sais pas [qui [elle a rencontré t]].
 'I don't know who she has met.'
 c *Je ne sais pas [a-t- [elle t rencontré qui]].
 'I don't know has she met who.'
 d *Je ne sais pas [qui a-t- [elle t rencontré t]].
 'I don't know who has she met.'

In order to deal with this paradigm, we are lead to assume that the Wh Criterion must be satisfied at SS in French: the embedded C is specified +Wh because of lexical selection, hence (40)a and c are ruled out as violations of clause B of the Wh Criterion at SS; whatever principle excludes embedded applications of I to C (in some languages) will rule out (40)d (and redundantly (40)c).

This leaves open the question of the extra options that are allowed in the main paradigm (39), in particular the option of Wh *in situ*. Notice that the latter instantiates a kind of LF root phenomenon: in French, Wh *in situ* in single questions (i.e., LF Wh movement) is restricted to unembedded clauses (in the sense that a Wh *in situ* is always construed with the main C; of course the Wh element can be located in an embedded clause). If the root non-root asymmetry is ultimately to be understood as a consequence of the Projection Principle, it would be desirable to link our LF root phenomenon to the same principle.

I would like to propose that the two additional well-formed structures of the main paradigm in French are made possible by an extra option concerning the licensing of the +Wh feature on the head of a clausal constituent. We have assumed that lexical selection and free licensing in the main Infl are the only available devices in English. Suppose that French disposes, as an extra option, of the following agreement process:

(41) Wh Op X → Wh Op X_{+Wh}.

That is to say, we assume that a Wh operator can endow a clausal head of the Wh feature under agreement. Of course, the very configuration required by the Wh Criterion is an agreement configuration with respect to the feature Wh (as pointed out in a different context by Kuroda 1988); but we are now distinguishing agreement as a static configuration, in which a Spec and a head are each independently endowed with a given feature, from the kind of dynamic agreement illustrated in (41), in which the specifier is able to endow the head with the relevant feature specification. If the satisfaction of the Wh Criterion always involves static agreement, we are now claiming that the special extra option that French has is dynamic agreement, as stated in (41). We will assume that dynamic agreement can freely apply in the syntax or in the syntax of LF in French.

Let us first consider (39)a. At DS no clausal head has the Wh feature, hence at SS the Wh Criterion is not violated: clause B does not apply because there is no Wh head, clause A does not apply because the Wh element does not qualify as a Wh operator under the functional definition (26'). In the syntax of LF the Wh element can be moved to the Spec of C, from where it can endow C with the feature Wh under dynamic agreement (41); then, at LF the structure satisfies the Wh Criterion. The corresponding derivation is not available in English, due to the lack of dynamic agreement: so, if the feature Wh is not specified at DS under Infl, the language has no device to introduce it later on, and the structure corresponding to (39)a will inevitably violate clause A of the Wh Criterion at LF.

Consider now (39)b. At DS no clausal head has the feature +Wh. Wh movement applies in the syntax, then C can be endowed with the feature +Wh through dynamic agreement. At SS (and at LF) the Wh Criterion is satisfied. The same configuration does not arise in English due to the lack of dynamic agreement. The two extra options of French (39)a and b are thus reduced to a unique additional device that this grammatical system has – dynamic agreement – and illustrate applications of this device in the two components of LF and syntax proper, respectively.[12]

Example (39)d is analysed exactly as in English: I is independently endowed with the Wh feature, and I to C movement permits satisfaction of the Wh Criterion at SS (and at LF). As for (39)c, in the variant in which I is endowed with the Wh feature at DS, it is excluded by the Wh Criterion at SS; in the variant in which I is not intrinsically endowed with the Wh feature, it is presumably excluded by whatever principle excludes I to C movement in non-Wh constructions, e.g., in declaratives, in a non V-2 language like French (possibly a version of Chomsky's 1991 economy principle).

Why is it that dynamic agreement does not increase the grammatical options in embedded contexts (see (40))? In particular, as (40)a is ill-formed, we must rule out the following derivation: at DS the embedded C is not specified wh, hence the Wh Criterion is not violated at SS; at LF Wh movement applies and C is endowed with Wh through dynamic agreement, hence the Wh Criterion is fulfilled at LF. How is this derivational path excluded? The answer is provided by the Projection Principle: the specification of the embedded C is determined by the lexical selectional property of the main verb; if the value −Wh is selected at DS by the verb *savoir* ('to know'), then this specification cannot be changed at subsequent levels under the Projection Principle. Therefore dynamic agreement is irrelevant in embedded contexts, and the root nature of Wh *in situ* (LF Wh movement), is successfully traced back to the Projection Principle.

Lasnik and Saito (1992) point out that Japanese manifests a somewhat similar root/non-root asymmetry. The interrogative particle *ka* (glossed as +Wh) is obligatory in embedded questions and optional in main questions:

(42) Mary-ga [John-ga nani-o katta *(ka)] siritagatte iru (koto).
      Mary   John   what   bought +Wh want-to-know   fact.
      'The fact that Mary wants to know what John bought.'
(43) John-ga doko-ni ikimasita (ka).
      John   where   went   +Wh.
      'Where did John go?'

Examples are taken from Lasnik and Saito, op. cit., Chapter 1, (24)–(25). In our terms, a C endowed with the Wh feature at S-structure is pronounced *ka* in Japanese (that *ka* is a manifestation of C is very plausible, given the fact that it follows the inflectional elements in a rigidly head-final language). We may assume that Japanese is like French in that it also allows a C to be endowed with the Wh feature via dynamic agreement at LF. This gives the variant without *ka* of (43): C is empty at SS; at LF, Wh movement applies, C receives the feature Wh via dynamic agreement, and the Wh Criterion is satisfied at LF. In embedded contexts, the presence or absence of Wh is a matter of lexical selection, hence the dynamic agreement option has no effect, and only the variant of (42) with *ka* is well-formed, under the Projection Principle.

If Japanese and French share dynamic agreement, they differ (among other things) in that the Wh Criterion applies only at LF in Japanese, hence the Wh element can remain *in situ* also in embedded questions, as well as in main questions with and without *ka*. The same root/non-root asymmetry, ultimately determined by the Projection Principle, thus has quite different manifestations in the two languages.

7 I to C movement in Italian interrogatives

In Italian, as in English, the sequence Wh element – subject – inflected verb is excluded in main interrogatives:

(44) a *Chi Maria ama?
         'Who Maria loves?'
     b *Che cosa il direttore ha detto?
         'What the director has said?'

These structures become possible if the subject is in postverbal position, as in (45)a, or is null, as in (45)b:

(45) a Chi ama Maria?
         'Who loves Maria?' = 'who does Maria love?'

b Che cosa ha detto?
  'What has said?'

The observational constraint is that the Wh element must be left-adjacent to the inflected verb. It appears to be desirable to trace back the impossibility of (44) to the same theoretical explanation that we introduced for the obligatoriness of Subject–Aux inversion in English, hence assume that the linear adjacency of the Wh operator and the inflected verbal element manifested by (45) actually results from the movement of the latter to C. A straightforward extension of the analysis of English would run as follows: suppose that Wh is licensed in main clauses under I, as in English. Then (44) violates the Wh Criterion at SS. If the inflected verb moves to C, the Wh Criterion is met, as in (45).

The plausibility of this hypothesis and the parallel with the English case is reinforced by the observation that I to C movement applies in Italian in hypothetical clauses, another environment in which it can apply in English. It was observed in Rizzi (1982), Chapter 3, that the hypothetical complementizer *se* (if) can be dropped only with a postverbal or null subject:

(46)a *(Se) Gianni fosse arrivato, tutti sarebbero stati contenti.
     '(If) Gianni had arrived, everybody would have been happy.'
   b (Se) fosse arrivato Gianni, tutti sarebbero stati contenti.
     '(If) had arrived Gianni, everybody would have been happy.'
   c (Se) fosse arrivato in tempo, Gianni sarebbe stato contento.
     '(If) had arrived in time, Gianni would have been happy.'

In the reference quoted, this is analysed via an *ad hoc* rule optionally deleting *se* when string-adjacent to the inflected verb (hence inapplicable when the subject intervenes, as in (46)a). A more interesting and natural analysis would simply assume that *se* can be replaced by the inflected verb under I to C movement, as in the English (and French) counterpart of this construction. In (46)a, I to C movement has not applied, as the position of the subject shows, hence *se* cannot disappear.

So, the I to C approach offers a promising unified analysis of different cases in English and Italian. Still, this unification raises several questions. There are some crucial properties with respect to which the Italian case differs from the English case. If the observational adjacency requirement manifested by (45) is a consequence of I to C movement, one would expect the subject to be allowed to appear immediately after the auxiliary, as in the corresponding English case. This is incorrect, the subject can only appear after the past participle:

(47)a *Che cosa ha il direttore detto?
      'What has the director said?'

b Che cosa ha detto il direttore?
'What has said the director?'

Why is (47)a excluded? One possible approach would be to claim that the sequence aux + past participle forms a unique constituent of level X which is moved to C as a whole. This is quite implausible, though, in view of the fact that adverbs and floated quantifiers can intervene between the auxiliary and the past participle (see also the detailed evidence against an incorporation analysis of the past participle within the auxiliary in Belletti 1990). A more promising analysis is offered by the account given in Rizzi and Roberts (1989) of the corresponding French case, which can be straightforwardly extended (for relevant discussion, see also Roberts 1993a). Consider the following contrast:

(48)a Où est-elle allée?
'Where is she gone?'
b *Où est Marie allée?
'Where is Marie gone?'

Rizzi and Roberts (op. cit.) propose that I to C movement in French destroys the context of nominative Case assignment (limited to the Spec-head configuration with Agr), hence (48)b is ruled out as a violation of the Case Filter. (48)a is well-formed because the clitic pronoun incorporates into the inflected verb in C, thus exploiting a different visibility option which does not rely on Case assignment (as in Baker 1988; Everett 1986). So, (47)a can be excluded in the same manner: if Agr in Italian only assigns nominative in the Spec Head configuration, I to C movement destroys the required configuration, and an overt subject cannot survive in the Spec/I position. No equivalent of (48)a is possible, as Italian lacks subject clitics. As for the possibility of (47)b, we must now assume that an independent assigner of nominative Case is available for a postverbal subject. Assuming a split-infl analysis of the clausal structure in the manner of Pollock(1989) with the relative order of projections of Belletti (1990), we can assume that T (or, possibly, a lower inflectional head: see appendix) is able to assign nominative under government. According to this approach Italian has two distinct positions for nominative assignment: the Spec of Agr and the lower subject position which is governed by the first inflectional head. That the two contexts must be dissociated is clearly shown by Romanian: in infinitival clauses lacking Agr an overt preverbal subject is excluded, while a postverbal subject is possible:

(49)a *Am plecat fără cineva a mă auzi.
'I have left without anyone hearing me.'
b Am plecat fără a mă auzi cineva.
'I have left without hearing me anyone.'

Motapanyane (1989, 1991) interprets this as showing that the tense specification of infinitives retains its Case assigning capacity in Romanian.[13] The facts of (47) can thus be made compatible with the hypothesis that I to C movement occurs in Italian interrogatives.

8 Inversion in embedded interrogatives

In English, I to C movement shows a clear asymmetry between main and embedded interrogatives. In Italian things are more complex. The embedded questions corresponding to (44) are quite marginal in the indicative, and acceptable, if still somewhat marked, in the subjunctive (also the indicative complements are fully acceptable if the subject is null or inverted, as in (51)a):

(50)a ??Tutti si domandano che cosa il direttore ha detto.
  'Everybody wonders what the director has said.'
 b Tutti si domandano che cosa il direttore abbia detto.
  'Everybody wonders what the director have said.'
(51)a Tutti si domandano che cosa ha detto (il direttore).
  'Everybody wonders what has said (the director).'
 b Tutti si domandano che cosa abbia detto (il direttore).
  'Everybody wonders what have said (the director).'

So, given the logic of the approach, indirect questions in the indicative mood also seem to involve I to C movement, even if the requirement is less strict than in main questions. Such a weakening of the root/embedded asymmetry awaits an explanation.

Things are even more sharply different from English in other Romance languages, in which the root/embedded distinction tends to disappear altogether. This is the case, for instance, in Spanish: according to Contreras (1989) the subject cannot intervene between the Wh element and the inflected verb neither in main nor in embedded questions:

(52)a *Qué Maria compró?
  'What Maria bought?'
 b *No sé qué Maria compró.
  'I don't know what Maria bought.'

Motapanyane (personal communication) observes the same fact in Romanian:

(53)a *Unde Ion s'a dus?
  'Where Ion has gone?'
 b Unde s'a dus Ion?
  'Where has gone Ion?'
(54)a *Nu ne-a spus unde Ion s'a dus.
  'They didn't tell us where Ion has gone.'

b Nu ne-a spus unde s'a dus Ion.
   'They didn't tell us where has gone Ion.'

A similar lack of contrast between main and embedded questions appears to hold in Catalan (J. Solà, personal communication).

Let us start with such extreme cases. Given the logic of our approach, one seems to be led to the conclusion that in these languages the functional head bearing the Wh feature uniformly is the tensed I, also in embedded contexts. We may speculate that the rich tensed I of these Null Subject Languages, the strong gravity centre of the clause, attracts specifications that may be more 'scattered' in languages with a weaker Infl, including the specification wh.

This idea seems to raise a technical problem involving the proper selection mechanism. If a verb like the Romance equivalent of *wonder*, etc. selects a Wh complement, this specification should be borne by the immediately subjacent head C, governed by the selector, while I would be too deeply embedded to bear a selected specification. But notice that the problem is not worse than the one raised by selection of subjunctive, which is also determined by the higher verb, and is morphologically manifested by the lower Infl. Two technical solutions come to mind: the selection could proceed stepwise, in that the main verb could select a C which in turn is a selector of a subjunctive I (Kempchinsky 1986); or it could be that a higher verb can directly select inflectional properties bypassing the complementizer under some kind of relativization of the minimality principle (for example, a variety of the one argued for in Baker and Hale 1990). Whatever solution turns out to be acceptable for the subjunctive case, it should be immediately extendable to wh.[14]

I will then assume that the Wh feature is expressed on the embedded Infl in (52), (54), etc. Therefore, examples like (52)b and (54)a are excluded by the Wh Criterion, on a par with the corresponding main clauses. As for the well-formed examples (54)b, etc., we could assume that I to C movement applies, thus satisfying the Wh Criterion. If C does not contain the feature Wh in these Romance languages, no recoverability violation is produced (see footnote 2).[15]

What about the Italian case? The subjunctive inflection is somewhat weaker than the indicative inflection, in that it contains systematic syncretisms, and does not license referential null subjects in one case (2nd person singular of the present). So, pursuing our physical metaphor, it is conceivable that it will exert a weaker gravitational attraction on other feature specifications, allowing them to appear more 'scattered' in the structure; in particular, Wh will be allowed to appear in an embedded C. Hence embedded I to C movement would not be required in subjunctive complements. As for the fact that even embedded indicative complements appear to be somewhat more acceptable in Italian (more precisely, there is a main/embedded asymmetry in relative acceptability that seems to be less detectable in the other Null Subject Romance languages), this may be due to the influence of the subjunctive option. Italian, contrary to other Romance languages, normally allows subjunctive Wh complements. Perhaps, a Wh indicative complementizer is marginally permitted on analogy with the subjunctive option. No such analogy may arise in languages like Spanish, which disallow the subjunctive option.[16]

Appendix: nominative assignment to postverbal subjects

McCloskey (1991) argues that nominative assignment under government requires adjacency between the assigner and the assignee; therefore, nothing can intervene between the inflected verb and the subject in a VSO language such as Irish. In this respect, nominative assignment under government tendentially patterns with the other instances of Case assignment under government, while nominative assignment under agreement does not manifest an adjacency requirement. McCloskey's hypothesis is confirmed by the fact that adjacency is required between C and the subject in West Flemish (see Haegeman 1992, who explicitly argues that C is the nominative assigner in that language), and between Aux and the subject in the Aux to Comp construction in Italian (as pointed out by Belletti 1990).[17] Consider also the adjacency requirement on genitive assignment under government in the Semitic languages (Siloni 1996).

McCloskey's hypothesis and our current assumption on Case assignment to postverbal subjects can now account for the somewhat variable adjacency requirement that appears to hold between the verb and the postverbal (non-dislocated) subject in Italian (Calabrese 1985):

(55)a ?Ha risolto il problema Gianni.
　　　'Has solved the problem Gianni.'
　　b ?Ha vinto la corsa Gianni.
　　　'Has won the race Gianni.'
　　c ??Ha parlato con Maria Gianni.
　　　'Has spoken with Maria Gianni.'

These examples become fully acceptable if the object does not linearly intervene between the verb and the subject, i.e., if it is cliticized:

(56)a Lo ha risolto Gianni.
　　　'It has solved Gianni.'
　　b L'ha vinta Gianni.
　　　'It has won Gianni.'
　　c Le ha parlato Gianni.
　　　'To+her has spoken Gianni.'

This contrast follows if nominative assignment under government requires adjacency.

A qualification is required by the fact that certain adverbs and quantifiers can intervene: the examples in (57) are fully acceptable, and (58)b clearly contrasts with (58)a:

(57) a Non parla più nessuno.
  'Not speaks anymore anyone.'
 b Vince sempre Gianni.
  'Wins always Gianni.'
(58) a Ha fatto tutto Gianni.
  'Has done everything Gianni.'
 b ??Ha fatto questo Gianni.
  'Has done this Gianni.'

Other adverbs cannot (naturally) intervene with a normal intonational contour:

(59) a ??Ha telefonato ieri Gianni.
  'Has telephoned yesterday Gianni.'
 b ??Ti contatterà domani Gianni.
  'You will contact tomorrow Gianni.'

The natural distinction between the adverbs and quantifiers of (57), (58)a and the adverbs or arguments of (58)b, (59) is that the latter must be VP internal (or final), while the former can fill a higher position to the left of the VP. This is clearly shown, for instance, by the fact that only the former can naturally precede the adverb *bene* (well), presumably left-adjoined to the VP:

(60) a Gianni non parla più bene.
  'Gianni does not speak anymore well.'
 b Gianni gioca sempre bene.
  'Gianni plays always well.'
 c Gianni ha fatto tutto bene.
  'Gianni has done everything well.'
(61) a *Gianni ha fatto questo bene.
  'Gianni has done this well.'
 b *Gianni ha parlato ieri bene.
  'Gianni has spoken yesterday well.'
 c *Gianni giocherà domani bene.
  'Gianni will play tomorrow well.'

Notice also that *bene* itself cannot naturally intervene between the verb and a postverbal subject:

(62) a ?Ha giocato bene Gianni.
'Has played well Gianni.'
b ??Ha fatto tutto bene Gianni.
'Has done everything well Gianni.'

So, the adverbial elements of (60) can be in the specifier position (or adjoined to the projection) of an inflectional head which the verb moves through (see also the typology of positions arrived at in Belletti 1990):

(63) ... V+I (tutto) t_1 (bene) t_V (Obj) (ieri) (Subj).

It then appears that postverbal subjects must be linearly adjacent to the first inflectional head above the VP (indicated by t_1 in (63), presumably to be identified with T in simple tenses, and with the participial morphology in complex tenses), which can thus be identified as the nominative Case assigner under government.[18]

Notes

1 This analysis, made possible by Chomsky's (1986b) approach to the structure of clauses, has a clear explanatory advantage over previous transformational analyses (of this and other V-2 type phenomena) in that, under natural assumptions on X-bar theory and structure preservation, it immediately explains

   1   Why exactly two positions are involved (not one or three);
   2   Why they are one head and one maximal projection (not two heads, or two maximal projections);
   3   Why they are in that order.

   Empirical evidence that the auxiliary actually moves to C is provided by the fact that the preposed auxiliary cannot co-occur with *if* in hypothetical clauses **If had he said that* ... (nor in yes–no indirect questions in Hiberno-English, which otherwise allows Subject–Aux inversion: see McCloskey 1992 and example (16) below).

2 In German, embedded V-2 is possible in the declarative complement of some verbs, but never in embedded questions:

   i   Ich weiss nicht was er gekauft hat.
       'I don't know what he bought has.'
   ii *Ich weiss nicht was hat er gekauft.
       'I don't know what has he bought.'

   This may be accounted for by assuming that Wh fills the C position of the question, thus making it unavailable for I to C movement. Notice that in main questions I to C movement is possible, and obligatory, as in English. See Tomaselli (1989), Vikner (1990, 1995) and references cited there and, for relevant diachronic evidence, Tomaselli (1990).

3 Relatives and exclamatives, two constructions involving Wh elements, share with (embedded) questions the fact that Wh movement is obligatory. They

differ from main questions in English and French in that they do not trigger I to C movement, a property that is particularly relevant in main exclamatives:

i a How smart is he?
   b 'How smart he is!'
ii a Combien a-t-il mangé?
     'How much has he eaten?'
   b Combien il a mangé!
     'What a lot he has eaten!'

As all these operators belong to the Wh class, in order to capture the different cases, a refinement of the +−Wh feature system is needed (e.g., questions are +Wh +Q, relatives and exclamatives are +Wh −Q, etc.: see Rizzi 1990a, Section 2.9, for discussion). I will assume that relatives and exclamatives are also in the scope of the appropriate extension of the Wh Criterion, which accounts for the obligatoriness of Wh movement, and that the different properties of these constructions are related to the different licensing conditions of the relevant features.

4 A Wh phrase is a phrase containing a Wh element; this definition should be refined by referring to the subclass of interrogative Wh elements (e.g., in Italian *chi, quale,* but not *cui, il quale,* etc.; see Cinque 1982a), with different subcases of the Wh Criterion referring to different subclasses of operators: see footnote 2. Moreover, not every phrase containing a Wh element qualifies as an operator, there are restrictions generally referred to as Pied-piping conventions (Ross 1967). We will omit these two refinements here.

5 It is also necessary to assume that the functional definition (26) holds at DS and SS, but not at LF, where it is superseded by a stronger principle according to which all elements endowed with intrinsic quantificational force are operators at this level, and must be moved to an appropriate scope position. See May (1985) for a proposal along these lines. We need such a principle to enforce general LF movement (hence capture ECP effects) of Wh elements *in situ*. This principle is perhaps to be restricted to non discourse-linked Wh phrases, along the lines of Pesetsky (1987).

6 If topicalization involves adjunction to IP, as proposed by Baltin (1982), Lasnik and Saito (1984, 1992), or base-generation in an independent Top node (Chomsky 1977a; Cinque 1990), this case is independent from (27); if topicalization involves movement to the Spec of C (with CP recursion in case of embedded topicalization), (27) and (28) reduce to the same case. But see Chapter 10 for relevant discussion.

7 The Wh Criterion is not violated in (31)a because, given the usual pied-piping conventions, the Wh element there can be the entire direct object, which is in an A position, hence it does not count as a Wh operator at SS.

8 McDaniel (1989) analyses an interrogative construction in German and Romani which involves a Wh element in a lower Comp connected to the appropriate Comp position through a chain of dummy scope markers (a kind of A' expletives according to McDaniel). This case can be integrated if the Wh Criterion is interpreted as applying on the head of the A' chain of the Wh operator. See Chapter 7 for relevant discussion. We leave open here the many problems raised by some of the Slavic cases discussed in Rudin (1988).

9 The Wh Criterion has an empirical coverage very close to Lasnik and Saito's (1992) system of filters and conditions, expressed in the traditional theory of Comp involving only one position, i.e., [Comp S]. A quick comparison between the two systems may be helpful. Lasnik and Saito introduce the following filters (we keep their numbering):

i(13) A +Wh Comp must have a +Wh head (SS).
(14) A −Wh Comp must not have a +Wh head (SS).
(35) All Whs must be in a +Wh Comp at LF.
(53) *[...Head$_i$...]$_j$, where i ≠ j.

Example i(13) closely resembles clause B of the criterion, and rules out such cases as (9)a (the Comp selected by a verb like *wonder* is +Wh; the element moved to the unique Comp position becomes the head of Comp in Lasnik and Saito's system); i(14) rules out such cases as (27)b, it is then the closest correspondent to the independently needed functional definition (26) in our system; notice that i(14) does not extend to (28)b (under the IP-adjunction analysis), (31)b and (32)b. Example i(35) corresponds to clause A of the Wh Criterion. Finally, (53) is introduced by Lasnik and Saito to account for Baker's (1970) influential observation that the following example ii is ambiguous between LF's iii a and b, but it does not allow the interpretation corresponding to LF iii c:

ii Who remembers where we bought what?
iii a Who remembers where+what we bought t t'?
    b Who+what remembers where we bought t t'?
    c *Who+where remembers what we bought t t'?

Example c would be derivable, in principle, via LF movement of *where* to the main Comp, and subsequent movement of *what* to the embedded Comp. As the moved element becomes the head of Comp in Lasnik and Saito's system, and the index percolates from a head to its projection, the change of head of the embedded Comp in the LF derivation of c would create the ill-formed configuration i(53).

We can immediately translate their approach to this example within our system (avoiding assumptions incompatible with the restrictive approach to X' Theory and structure preservation of Chomsky 1986a) through the reasonable assumption that agreement specifications cannot be changed in the course of the derivation. So, if the embedded C agrees with *where* at SS, it cannot agree with another element at LF, which excludes the derivation of iii c. This assumption is the equivalent of filter i(53). It should also be noticed that the derivation of iii c violates Strict Cyclicity in the syntax of LF.

10 See Haegeman and Zanuttini (1991) for detailed discussion of this extension in the context of their analysis of negative concord in Romance and Germanic varieties.
11 If the feature +neg is specified in the SS representation of (35)a, we must deal with the fact that clause B of the Negative Criterion is not violated at SS. One possible approach would be to say that this clause only applies at LF. Alternatively, one could assume that the feature +neg is not present in the SS representation, and that it can be specified on a clausal head at LF through the 'dynamic agreement', the mechanism introduced in Section 6 to deal with the possibility of Wh *in situ* in French.
12 The application of dynamic agreement in the syntax and at LF can be dissociated in a grammatical system. Spanish appears to allow Wh *in situ* in single questions (Torrego 1984: 103), but disallows the equivalent of (36)b with an overt subject (Contreras 1989): in terms of the proposed system, it has dynamic agreement applying at LF, but not in the syntax. The reciprocal case is represented by Brazilian Portuguese, which allows the equivalent of (36)b but excludes Wh *in situ* in non echo-questions (C. Figuiredo, C. Quicoli, personal communication) (Modern Hebrew patterns alike: Shlonsky 1988; Siloni, personal communication).

13 A reflex of this dissociation is found in Italian in the peculiar infinitival construction illustrated below, roughly paraphrased as an hypothetical clause, which allows a postverbal lexical subject, but not a preverbal subject:

   i Per averne parlato anche Gianni, vuol proprio dire che la cosa è di dominio pubblico.
      'If even Gianni spoke of it, this really means that the thing is generally known.'
   ii *Per anche Gianni averne parlato,...

Example ii violates the Case filter, while for i we must assume, following Motapanyane (1989), that the infinitival tense (or, possibly, a lower inflectional head) assigns nominative. We leave open the question of why the option is limited to this peculiar construction in Italian. Notice also that in all infinitives pronominal intensifiers in postverbal position (roughly equivalent to the stressed reflexives in English: I myself, etc.), when construed with the subject, have the nominative form:

   iii Ho deciso di parlare anch'io di questa storia.
       'I decided to speak I too of this story.'

14 A clear case of dissociation between C and the feature Wh in both main and embedded contexts is provided by Hungarian, in which Wh is always associated to the functional head, distinct from C, whose specifier is the focus: see Puskas (1992); see also Kiss (1990) and Maracz (1990).
15 Alternatively, it could be that I to C does not apply, and the target of Wh movement is the Spec of I position. We will not explore this alternative here.
16 In Italian there is an additional clear asymmetry between *perché* (why) and the other Wh elements (argumental or not), in that the former does not require adjacency to the inflected verb. This is true in both main and embedded contexts with indicative:

   i a *Dove Gianni è andato?
         'Where Gianni is gone?'
      b *Come Gianni ha parlato?
         'How Gianni has spoken?'
      c Perché Gianni è partito?
         'Why Gianni is left?'
   ii a ??Mi domando dove Gianni è andato.
         'I wonder where Gianni is gone.'
      b ??Mi domando come Gianni ha parlato.
         'I wonder how Gianni has spoken.'
      c Mi domando perché Gianni è partito.
         'I wonder why Gianni is left.'

Similar asymmetries are found in Spanish (Contreras 1989) and Catalan (Solà, personal communication), while no asymmetry is apparently manifested in Romanian (Motapanyane, personal communication). In English *why* does not manifest any comparable asymmetry with respect to the other Wh elements, in that it obligatorily triggers Subject–Aux inversion in main interrogatives.

Perhaps *perché* can be (but does not have to be) analysed as a C, possibly an option connected to its morphological analysis (per + che) which relates it to the complementizer. It could then be analysed on a par with *se* (if, whether), which manifests +Wh on C, and hence does not require I to C movement (an empty interrogative operator in the Spec of C should be assumed in both cases). It should be noticed that in different varieties of Veneto, a northern Italian dialect, a form of *perché*, on a par with *se*, is incompatible with an overt C (which generally co-occurs with Wh elements in its Spec in that dialect), as Poletto (1993) points out. Notice also that in Romanian *why* is expressed by a two-word phrase (*de ce*), and is not morphologically related to the complementizer, which may account for its different behaviour. In Italian, *per che ragione* ('for what reason') also does not trigger I to C movement, but this may be related to the fact that the obligatoriness of I to C in interrogatives is generally weakened when a discourse-linked Wh is involved, for unclear reasons.

17 In gerunds and, more marginally, in some infinitive and subjunctive complements, the order Aux Subject past participle is possible in Italian:

i Avendo Gianni deciso di partire, ...
   'Having Gianni decided to leave, ...'

This construction is analysed in Rizzi (1982), Chapter 3, as involving movement of the auxiliary to C, hence as an instance of I to C movement, in current terms. To account for the well-formedness of i as opposed to (3)a, we could then assume that the gerundival (more marginally the infinitival and the subjunctive) inflection is able to assign nominative under government. See Roberts (1993a) for a refinement of this approach. Belletti (1990) has noticed that an adverb like *probabilmente* (probably) can be inserted in i after the subject, but not between the auxiliary and the subject.

18 Why is it that a trace of the lowest inflectional head suffices to assign nominative under government, while a trace of the highest inflectional head (Agr) does not suffice to assign nominative under agreement in (47)a? Following the proposal in Rizzi and Roberts (1989), I will assume that the moved inflectional head continues to govern the postverbal subject in (63) under Baker's (1988) Government Transparency Corollary, a principle that has no equivalent for agreement relations. So, a governing head, if moved, continues to govern its domain, but an agreeing head, if moved, ceases to be in an agreement configuration with its original Spec, hence nominative Case cannot be assigned in (47)a.

10 The fine structure of the left periphery

Introduction[1]

Under current assumptions, the structural representation of a clause consists of three kinds of structural layers, each layer an instantiation of the X-bar schema:

1 The lexical layer, headed by the verb, the structural layer in which theta assignment takes place;
2 The inflectional layer, headed by functional heads corresponding to concrete or abstract morphological specifications on the verb, and responsible for the licensing of argumental features such as Case and agreement;
3 The complementizer layer, typically headed by a free functional morpheme, and hosting topics and various operator-like elements such as interrogative and relative pronouns, focalized elements, etc.

In the mid-eighties, each layer was identified with a single X-bar projection (VP, IP, CP), but this assumption quickly turned out to be too simplistic. Under the impact of Pollock's (1989) influential analysis of verb movement, IP dissolved into a series of functional projections, each corresponding to a single feature specification overtly or abstractly expressed on the verbal system (Agr, T, Asp, ...). Kayne's (1984) binary branching hypothesis naturally led to the postulation of multiple VP layers for multi-argument verbs, e.g., along the lines of Larson (1988) and much related work.

Various proposals in the recent literature indicate that the complementizer layer should share the same fate: much more than a single X-bar schema seems to constitute the left (pre-IP) periphery of the clause.[2]

In this article, I would like to explore some aspects of the fine structure of the left periphery. The first part (Sections 1–5) is devoted to the identification of the basic configurational structure. Four kinds of elements typically occurring in the left periphery will be taken into account: interrogative and relative pronouns, topics and focalized elements. Studying the interactions between these elements, we will be led to postulate an articulated array of X-bar projections which will be assumed to constitute the complementizer system. The second part (Sections 6–11) concerns a number of adjacency and anti-adjacency effects involving elements of the C system and different kinds of fillers of the subject position (overt DP, PRO, trace) which are amenable to an explanation in terms of the assumed structure of the C system. The core of the empirical material to be discussed is drawn from Italian, French and English, with occasional comparative extensions to other Romance and Germanic languages.

A preliminary word on the theoretical framework adopted in this work is necessary. An idea borrowed from the system presented in Chomsky (1993) will play a crucial role: syntactic movement (or, more neutrally, the formation of non-trivial chains in syntax) is 'last resort' in the precise sense that it must be triggered by the satisfaction of certain quasi-morphological requirements of heads. As I will be concerned with the A' system, I will phrase such requirements in the style of the Criteria (Chapter 9, Haegeman 1995b and much related work), rather than as feature checking, the main reason for this choice being that such features have an interpretive import (Wh, Neg, Top, Foc, ...): they determine the interpretation of the category bearing them and of its immediate constituents (e.g., see Section 2), function as scope markers for phrases with the relevant quantificational force in a local configuration, etc., so that their role cannot simply be to trigger movement and disappear from representations. Independently from the particular style of presentation, the 'last resort' intuition provides the conceptual justification for postulating a rich and articulated structure to host the different kinds of phrases moved to the left periphery: no free preposing and adjunction to IP is permissible, all kinds of movements to the left periphery must be motivated by the satisfaction of some criterion, hence by the presence of a head entering into the required Spec-head configuration with the preposed phrase. So, the 'last resort' guideline will be critical for drawing the map of the left periphery; the presence and action of the system of heads involved will be independently detected by the various adjacency and anti-adjacency effects that we will focus on in the second part. A restrictive theory of adjunction (following Kayne 1994 and related work) is also instrumental for this endeavour.

On the other hand, in the following discussion I will continue to assume that Relativized Minimality (RM) is a representational principle, and that one of the core structural relations allowed by UG is head government, as in Rizzi (1990a) and contra Chomsky (1993). As for the second point, head government continues to be needed, as far as I can see, for optimally simple accounts of various familiar subject–object asymmetries of the *that*-t kind, as well as for many cases in which a head enters into some kind of 'action at a distance' with the specifier of its complement (for Case assignment/checking or the licensing of different kinds of ec's). A number of examples of this sort are analysed in what follows; I will adopt approaches based on head government and will occasionally allude to properties of possible alternatives not referring to head government, even though no systematic comparison will be attempted.

As for the representational view of RM, it is not the goal of the present article to argue for this theoretical option, and I intend to address the issue in independent work (see also Manzini 1992, 1995; Brody 1995 for relevant discussion). It should be clear though that there is a significant (even though not a necessary) connection between the two conservative assumptions I am making. One consequence of the representational view of RM is that head government comes for free as the local environment within which a head can 'act at a distance' upon a maximal projection. The action at a distance between a head and a maximal projection and the different kinds of chains obey the same fundamental locality principle under the representational view of RM, a unification that is missed if locality on chains is expressed derivationally.

1 The Force–Finiteness system

One important question to be asked at the outset of a study on the complementizer system is: what is the role of the complementizer in the clausal structure?

We can think of the complementizer system as the interface between a propositional content (expressed by the IP) and the superordinate structure (a higher clause or, possibly, the articulation of discourse, if we consider a root clause). As such, we expect the C system to express at least two kinds of information, one facing the outside and the other facing the inside.

Consider first the information looking at the higher structure. Complementizers express the fact that a sentence is a question, a declarative, an exclamative, a relative, a comparative, an adverbial of a certain kind, etc., and can be selected as such by a higher selector. This information is sometimes called the clausal type (Cheng 1991), or the specification of Force (Chomsky 1995). Here we will adopt the latter terminology. Force is expressed sometimes by overt morphological encoding on the head (special C morphology for declaratives, questions, relatives, etc.), sometimes by simply providing the structure to host an operator of the required kind, sometimes by both means (this is the rare case, presumably due to an economy of representation type principle favouring overt expression of a certain substantive specification on the head or on the specifier, but not simultaneously on both: see Cheng 1991; Sportiche 1996).

The second kind of information expressed by the C system faces the inside, the content of the IP embedded under it. It is a traditional observation that the choice of the complementizer reflects certain properties of the verbal system of the clause, an observation formalized, for example, by 'agreement' rules between C and I, responsible for the co-occurrence of *that* and a tensed verb, of *for* and an infinitive in English (Chomsky and Lasnik 1977), etc. A straightforward manner to account for these dependencies would be to assume that C contains a tense specification which matches the one expressed on the lower inflectional system (an idea which goes back at least to den Besten 1977). On the other hand, the 'temporal' properties encoded by C are very rudimentary. For instance, in Italian the form *che* co-occurs with present, past and future indicative, with present and past subjunctive and present and past conditional, thus distinguishing these forms from infinitival, gerundival and participial clauses, a situation which is quite general in Romance and Germanic. So it appears that, at least in these language families, C expresses a distinction related to tense but more rudimentary than tense and other inflectional specifications on the verbal system: finiteness.

I will assume here that the finiteness distinction is a valid linguistic one, even though its morphological realization can vary somewhat from language to language. Languages tend to split verbal paradigms into two classes of forms. Finite forms can manifest mood distinctions (indicative, subjunctive, conditional and/or other distinctions of the realis/irrealis type), manifest tense and subject (person) agreement and co-occur with overt nominative subjects. Non-finite forms do not manifest mood distinctions, in the core case they do not express person agreement, and do not co-occur with nominative subjects. They have a more rudimentary system of tense distinctions (e.g., in many languages non-finite forms do not have a morphological present/future distinction, can express past only through the periphrastic form aux + past participle, etc.). The first class of forms co-occurs with complementizers of the *that* kind, the second does not. Various dissociations from these core clusters are apparently tolerated,[3] but a split along these lines is robustly attested cross-linguistically.

Following much recent work (e.g., Holmberg and Platzack 1988), I will then assume that the C system expresses a specification of finiteness, which in turn selects an IP system with the familiar characteristics of finiteness: mood distinctions, subject agreement licensing nominative Case, overt tense distinctions (these specifications being subjected to some cross-linguistic variation, as we have seen).

Again, we should think of finiteness as the core IP-related characteristics that the complementizer system expresses; languages can vary in the extent to which additional IP information is replicated in the complementizer system: some languages replicate mood distinctions (special subjunctive complementizers in Polish, etc.), some replicate subject agreement (different Germanic varieties; Bayer 1984; Haegeman 1992; Shlonsky 1994), some seem to express genuine tense distinctions (Irish, Cottell 1994), negation (Latin, Celtic), etc.[4]

How does the CP system relate to the rest of the clausal structure? Recent proposals consider the IP system an extension of the V system: the different inflectional heads are V-related in that they attract the verb (overtly or covertly) to check its morphological specification (Chomsky 1993), so that the whole IP system can be seen as an extension of the verbal projection (an 'extended projection', in the sense of Grimshaw 1991). Should the CP system be considered an analogous extension of the IP system, hence ultimately of the VP? I believe there is a substantial difference between the two cases. Whatever 'inflectional' properties C reflects, they are not encoded in the form of verbal morphology, in the general case: they are expressed on free functional morphemes (*that, que,* etc.) which, if anything, look nominal more than verb-like, as they often resemble demonstrative pronouns, Wh elements, certain kinds of nouns ('fact', and so on), etc. So, I will continue to assume that the C system is fundamentally distinct from the I system, the latter but not the former being V-related in the general case.[5,6]

2 The topic–focus system

If the Force–Finiteness system expresses the selectional relations between a C system and the immediately higher and lower structural systems, the C system can have other functions which are by and large independent from selectional constraints.

A traditional articulation of the clause that typically involves the left periphery is the articulation in topic and comment, as expressed by the English construction referred to as Topicalization:

(1) Your book, you should give t to Paul (not to Bill).

The topic is a preposed element characteristically set off from the rest of the clause by 'comma intonation' and normally expressing old information, somehow available and salient in previous dicourse; the comment is a kind of complex predicate, an open sentence predicated of the topic and introducing new information.

Formally similar but interpretively very different is the focus–presupposition articulation:

(2) YOUR BOOK you should give t to Paul (not mine)

Here the preposed element, bearing focal stress, introduces new information, whereas the open sentence expresses contextually given information, knowledge that the speaker presupposes to be shared with the hearer (see below for further refinements). If the interpretive relation of the preposed element to the open sentence is very different, virtually the opposite in the two cases, the form of the two articulations appears to be constant in English (even though significant differences emerge at a more refined analysis: see Culicover's 1992 discussion, based in part on Gundel's 1974 analysis, and, on focus, Rochemont and Culicover 1990).

Other languages sharply distinguish the form of the two articulations as well. We will briefly analyse here two Italian constructions which illustrate the point. In Italian, and more generally in Romance, the topic–comment articulation is typically expressed by the construction that Cinque (1990) has called Clitic Left Dislocation (CLLD), involving a resumptive clitic coreferential to the topic (this construction differs from left dislocation in languages which do not possess clitic forms in a number of respects, so that the English gloss, involving a non-clitic resumptive pronoun, is somewhat misleading: see Cinque 1990: 57–60 for relevant discussion; see also Cecchetto 1994; Iatridou 1991):

(3) Il tuo libro, lo ho letto.
    'Your book, I have read it.'

The focus–presupposition articulation can be expressed in Italian by preposing the focal element (focalization) and assigning it special focal stress:

(4) IL TUO LIBRO ho letto (, non il suo).
    'Your book I read (, not his).'

In Italian this structural option is restricted to contrastive focus, i.e., (4) presupposes that you believe that I have read something different from your book, and corrects this belief. It could not be felicitously uttered as conveying non-contrastive new information, i.e., as an answer to the question, 'What did you read?'. Other languages use the clause initial focus position for non-contrastive focus as well (Hungarian: Horvath 1985; Kiss 1987; Brody 1990a, 1995b; Puskas 1992, 1996 and references quoted there; Albanian: Turano 1995; Greek: Tsimpli 1994). Some other languages (e.g., French) do not seem to use a structural focus position, at least in the overt syntax (Spanish seems to have a focus construction similar to the Italian one: Laka 1990).

I will assume here that these two articulations are expressed by the usual building block of syntactic representations: the X-bar schema (whether the schema is a primitive, or can be derived from more elementary principles (Kayne 1994; Chomsky 1995) is irrelevant for our purposes). That is, topic–comment has the following structure:

(5)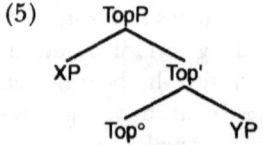

XP = topic
YP = comment

A Top° head, a functional head belonging to the complementizer system, projects its own X-bar schema with the following functional interpretation: its specifier is the topic, its complement is the comment. Top° defines a kind of 'higher predication', a predication within the Comp system; its function is thus analogous to the function of AgrS within the IP system, which also configurationally connects a subject and a predicate. The most basic difference between higher and lower predication is that the former involves a specifier which is an A' position.

Analogously, a Foc° head takes the focus as its specifier and the presupposition as its complement:

(6)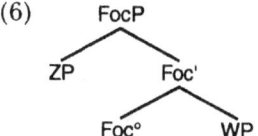

ZP = focus
WP = presupposition

Here, too, Italian seems to possess a lower focalization, involving focal stress (possibly contrastive, but not necessarily so) on an element *in situ* (see Antinucci and Cinque 1977; Calabrese 1982; Cinque 1993; Belletti and Shlonsky 1995):

(7) Ho letto IL TUO LIBRO (, non il suo).
    'I read YOUR BOOK, not his.'

But it is conceivable that at LF (7) will have a representation involving (6) if the focal element must be moved to a peripheral position, as Chomsky's (1976) classical analysis of Weak Crossover implies.

While Top° and Foc° are phonetically null in Italian, they may be pronounced in other languages. For instance, Aboh (1997) argues that the focus particle *wè* in Gungbe should be analysed as Foc°, an analysis immediately plausible for many other cases of such markers found across languages (we will not analyse here other constructions involving focalization such as clefts and inverse copular sentences; see Moro 1997).

As for the topic or focus interpretations of the specifiers in (6) and (7), we will assume that a constituent endowed with topic or focus features must end up in a Spec/head configuration with Top or Foc, respectively; in other words, there are Topic and Focus Criteria, reminiscent of the Wh and Neg Criteria (Chapter 9, Haegeman 1995b). Focus and topic movement are then brought into line to the view that movement (or, in more neutral terms, the construction of non-trivial chains) is 'last resort', and must be triggered by the satisfaction of a criterion (or feature checking, in

Chomsky's 1993 terminology). In fact, under such a restrictive theory we expect that no kind of (syntactic) movement to the left periphery may involve free, optional adjunction to IP (LF movement may still involve IP adjunction if it is triggered by the necessity of properly interpreting certain expressions, as in May 1985); we will see later on that there are strong empirical reasons against this rather usual analysis of different kinds of preposing, and in favour of a uniform X-bar analysis involving (5) and (6).

How is the topic–focus system integrated into the force–finiteness system? We think of the latter as the essential part of the C system, so we assume it to be present in all non-truncated clausal structures (that is, except in ECM and other 'S' deletion' contexts). On the other hand, it is reasonable to assume that the topic–focus system is present in a structure only if 'needed', i.e., when a constituent bears topic or focus features to be sanctioned by a Spec-head criterion. If the topic–focus field is activated, it will inevitably be 'sandwiched' in between force and finiteness, as these two specifications must terminate the C system upward and downward, in order to meet the different selectional requirements and properly insert the C system in the structure. So, we should have:

(8) ... Force ... (Topic) ... (Focus) ... Fin IP

We will see later on that this positional property of the topic–focus system is instrumental for the explanation of several adjacency and anti-adjacency effects. For the time being we can simply observe two straightforward empirical reflexes of the theory of C that is taking shape.

In Italian, and more generally in Romance, prepositional elements introducing infinitives such as *di* in (9)b are generally considered the non-finite counterparts of the finite complementizer *che* of (9)a (for relevant evidence, see Rizzi 1982; Kayne 1984); still *che* always precedes and *di* always follows a left-dislocated phrase (examples like (11)b are slightly marked if compared to the corresponding cases of CLLD with finite embedded sentences, but the contrast with (11)a is very sharp):

(9)a Credo che loro apprezzerebbero molto il tuo libro.
  'I believe that they would appreciate your book very much.'
 b Credo di apprezzare molto il tuo libro.
  'I believe "of" to appreciate your book very much.'
(10)a Credo che il tuo libro, loro lo apprezzerebbero molto.
  'I believe that your book, they would appreciate it a lot.'
 b *Credo, il tuo libro, che loro lo apprezzerebbero molto.
  'I believe, your book, that they would appreciate it a lot.'
(11)a *Credo di il tuo libro, apprezzarlo molto.
  'I believe "of" your book to appreciate it a lot.'
 b Credo, il tuo libro, di apprezzarlo molto.
  'I believe, your book, "of" to appreciate it a lot.'

This distribution is hardly consistent with a theory assuming a unique C position, while it can be immediately expressed within the current articulated theory of C by assuming that *che* manifests the force position, while *di* manifests the finiteness position, hence they show up on opposite sides of the topic. We will come back to this peculiar distribution in Section 5.[7]

A similar type of argument is provided by the distribution of different kinds of operators hosted by the C-system. In Italian, relative operators must precede topics, while question operators must follow topics in main questions and can follow or (slightly marginally) precede them in embedded questions:[8]

(12) a Un uomo a cui, il premio Nobel, lo daranno senz'altro.
'A man to whom, the Nobel Prize, they will give it undoubtedly.'
 b *Un uomo, il premio Nobel, a cui lo daranno senz'altro.
'A man, the Nobel Prize, to whom they will give it undoubtedly.'
(13) a *A chi, il premio Nobel, lo daranno?
'To whom, the Nobel prize, will they give it?'
 b Il premio Nobel, a chi lo daranno?
'The Nobel Prize, to whom will they give it?'
(14) a Mi domando, il premio Nobel, a chi lo potrebbero dare.
'I wonder, the Nobel Prize, to whom they could give it.'
 b ?Mi domando a chi, il premio Nobel, lo potrebbero dare.
'I wonder to whom, the Nobel Prize, they could give it.'

This distribution suggests that relative operators occupy the highest specifier position, the Spec of Force, while question operators can occupy a lower position within the topic/focus field (the ordering in (13)a being blocked by the fact that I to C movement is compulsory in main questions, for reasons discussed in Chapter 9. See below for more detailed discussion of these positional properties. The crucial point here is again that a theory involving a unique C head and projection does not seem equipped to deal with such simple distributional constraints.

3 On some differences between topic and focus

Topic and focus constructions are similar in several respects as A' constructions involving the left periphery of the clause, and their structural similarities are further stressed by the assumption that the same configurational schema is involved. Nevertheless, they differ in a number of respects, which highlight a fundamentally different nature. A detailed analysis of these two constructions is beyond the scope of this article. Drawing on Cinque's (1990) analysis, we will concentrate on five salient differences, which are directly relevant for our main topic.[9]

1 Resumptive clitic. A topic can involve a resumptive clitic within the comment. If the topicalized constituent is the direct object, the clitic is

obligatory. On the other hand, a focalized constituent is inconsistent with a resumptive clitic (Cinque 1990: 63):

(15)a Il tuo libro, lo ho comprato.
  'Your book, I bought it.'
   b *Il tuo libro, ho comprato t.
  'Your book, I bought.'
(16)a *IL TUO LIBRO lo ho comprato (non il suo).
  'YOUR BOOK I bought it (not his).'
   b IL TUO LIBRO ho comprato t (non il suo).
  'YOUR BOOK I bought (not his).'

2 Weak Crossover. A topic never gives rise to any Weak crossover effect. Such effects are detectable with focus, even if the judgement is somewhat difficult (Culicover 1992 has observed an analogous distinction between topic and focus in English):

(17) Gianni, sua madre lo ha sempre apprezzato.
  'Gianni, his mother always appeciated him.'
(18) ??GIANNI sua madre ha sempre apprezzato t (non Piero).
  'GIANNI his mother always appreciated, not Piero.'

3 Bare quantificational elements. Quantificational elements (no-one, all, etc.) which are not associated to a lexical restriction within the DP cannot be topics in CLLD constructions, while they easily allow focalization (Rizzi 1986 and Chapter 3; on the special behaviour of *qualcosa, qualcuno* (something, someone) see Cinque 1990: 74ff.):

(19)a *Nessuno, lo ho visto.
  'No-one, I saw him.'
   b *Tutto, lo ho fatto.
  'Everything, I did it.'
(20)a NESSUNO ho visto t.
  'NO-ONE I saw.'
   b TUTTO ho fatto t.
  'Everything I did.'

4 Uniqueness. A clause can contain as many topics as are consistent with its (topicalizable) arguments and adjuncts. On the contrary, there is a unique structural focus position and focalization of two elements as in (22) is excluded (Benincà 1988: 144):

(21) Il libro, a Gianni, domani, glielo darò senz'altro.
  'The book, to John, tomorrow, I'll give it to him for sure.'
(22) *A GIANNI IL LIBRO darò (non a Piero, l'articolo).
  'TO JOHN THE BOOK I'll give, not to Piero, the article.'

A focus and one or more topics can be combined in the same structure. In that case, the focal constituent can be both preceded and followed by topics:

(23) A Gianni, QUESTO, domani, gli dovrete dire.
 'To Gianni, THIS, tomorrow, you should tell him.'

5 Compatibility with Wh. A Wh operator in main questions is compatible with a Topic in a fixed order (Top Wh), whereas it is incompatible with a Focus:

(24)a A Gianni, che cosa gli hai detto?
 'To Gianni, what did you tell him?'
 b *Che cosa, a Gianni, gli hai detto?
 'What, to Gianni, did you tell him?'
(25)a *A GIANNI che cosa hai detto (, non a Piero)?
 'TO GIANNI what did you tell (, not to Piero)?'
 b *Che cosa A GIANNI hai detto (, non a Piero)?
 'What TO GIANNI did you tell (, not to Piero)?'

On the other hand, both Top and Foc are compatible with a preceding relative operator (see (12)a and (44) below).

The next section is devoted to showing that, in terms of a slight updating of Cinque's (1990) approach, the first three differences can be traced back to one basic distinction: focus is quantificational, topic is not. In Section 5 we will tentatively suggest that the fourth difference is also directly linked to an interpretive distinction between the two constructions, and then we will address the fifth difference in the context of an articulated theory of the C system.

4 Focus is quantificational, topic is not

Let us concentrate on the first three differences. Starting from the second property, we follow Lasnik and Stowell (1991) and assume that WCO is a distinctive characteristic of A' relations involving genuine quantification. So, A' dependencies must be split into those involving a quantifier which binds a variable and those that involve non-quantificational A' binding, binding of a null epithet or a null constant (*nc*, as in Chapter 11). The two cases are illustrated by questions and appositive relatives:

(26)a ?*Who does his mother really like t (=vbl)?
 b John, who his mother really likes t (=nc) ...

Chomsky (1986a) had proposed that the principle of Full Interpretation requires that variables be strongly bound, where strong binding means either assignment of a range or assignment of a value from an antecedent.

We can rephrase Lasnik and Stowell's (1991) proposal as distinguishing these two cases more sharply: A' dependencies, all sensitive to Strong Crossover (principle C), split into variable binding by a quantificational operator (assigning a range to the variable, as in (26)a) and binding of a null constant by an anaphoric operator (whose role is to connect the null constant to an antecedent, as in (26)b). The former, but not the latter, is sensitive to Weak Crossover.

Assuming WCO to be a diagnostic, the contrast in (17)–(18) leads us to conclude that focus involves quantificational A' binding while topic does not, as the interpretation of the two constructions suggests.

If focus is quantificational and topic is not, the first difference also follows: the focalized element in (16) must bind a syntactic variable (a non-pronominal empty Xmax category in an A-position). This happens in (16)b, but not in (16)a, in which potential bindees are the clitic and its trace, neither of which qualifies as a syntactic variable: the clitic is an overt pronominal head, its trace is an X° trace (if clitic movement involves an initial step qua Xmax to Spec AgrO, the initial trace is a DP-trace and the one in Spec/AgrO is an X° trace, neither of which qualifies as a variable). So, the structure is ruled out by the component of the principle of Full Interpretation which requires that quantifiers bind variables (Cinque 1990: 180, footnote 10).

Under classical assumptions on the typology of empty categories, (15)b is ruled out in a symmetric way: the topicalized element is not quantificational, as the lack of WCO shows. Therefore, the empty category in object position has no legitimate status: it cannot be a variable, as there is no quantifier to bind it, nor can it fulfil the conditions of any other type of *ec* (PRO, pro or DP-trace). (15)a is fine, as the *ec* in object position has the legitimate status of a clitic trace (Cinque 1990: 71–72).[10]

If we accept Lasnik and Stowell's split within A' dependencies, the argument excluding (15)b should be sharpened. We must exclude the possibility that the *ec* in (15)b be a null constant, A' bound (hence identified) by the topic phrase. Consider some typical cases of A' chains not giving rise to WCO:

(27) a John is easy [Op to please t].
 b John has Mary [Op to talk to t].
 c John is too stubborn [Op to talk to t].
 d John, who I just met t.
 e Gianni, Op che ho appena incontrato t.
  'Gianni, that I just met.'
 f Op habe ich schon t gesehen.
  '(it) have I already seen.'

Examples (27)a–c are familiar English constructions involving null operators; examples (27)d–e are appositive relatives in English and Italian, involving an overt and a null operator, respectively; (27)f instantiates the discourse bound null operator construction of colloquial German and many other languages. Suppose then that the licensing of null constants is not freely available, but is restricted to a designated kind of A' binder, the anaphoric operator (an element inherently characterized as an operator but different from quantificational operators in that it does not assign a range to its bindee; rather, the anaphoric operator seeks for an antecedent, to which it connects its bindee). Anaphoric operators are typically but not necessarily null. For instance, as we have just seen, relative pronouns involved in appositive relatives are anaphoric operators in general; still, they may – or must – be overt, depending on language specific conditions:

(28) A null constant is licensed by an anaphoric operator.

So, (15)b continues to be excluded: it involves no genuine quantification, hence no licit variable, and no anaphoric operator, hence no licit null constant, under principle (28).

Why is the English gloss of (15)b well formed? Again, I will basically follow Cinque's (1990) updating of Chomsky's (1977a) analysis of English topicalization and assume that it involves a null operator identified by the topic:

(29) Your book, [OP [I bought t]].

The null operator (a non-quantificational anaphoric operator) licenses the null constant under principle (28). The null constant status of the trace is further confirmed by Lasnik and Stowell's diagnostic, the lack of WCO effects:

(30) John$_i$, his$_i$ mother really likes t$_i$.

So, I am assuming that the parameter differentiating English and Romance topic–comment structures resides in the non-availability of the null anaphoric operator in Romance topic–comment. Null operators and clitics are functionally equivalent here in that they establish the connection between the topic and the open position in the comment; Romance has the second device freely available while English, which lacks clitics in general, reverts to the first device.[11]

Languages may choose whether the anaphoric operator in a given construction is overt or null; we have already seen that appositive relative operators are null in Italian and overt in English (this may in turn be the consequence of a more abstract structural difference, see Cinque 1982a and the recent discussion of the issue in Bianchi 1995). Analogously, other Germanic languages differ from English in allowing the overt realization (as a so-called D-pronoun) of the anaphoric operator involved in topic–comment structures:[12]

(31) Den Hans, den kenne ich t seit langem.
'The Hans, whom I have known for a long time.'

Let us now turn to the fact that the resumptive clitic becomes optional if the topic is a pronominalizable PP (as in (32)) and it is, of course, absent if the PP cannot be pronominalized as the benefactive in (33):

(32) A Gianni, Maria (gli) ha parlato recentemente.
'To Gianni, Maria spoke to him recently.'
(33) Per Gianni, Maria lavora da molto tempo.
'For Gianni, Maria has worked for a long time.'

Later on I will provide evidence suggesting that the clitic is not really optional in (32) and the two cases instantiate two distinct constructions. The question still remains why the PP topic can directly license an empty category in these cases. Here again, we can follow Cinque and assume that the classification of null elements into anaphors, pronominals and variables determined by the feature system $+-a, +-p$ is a unique characteristic of DPs in A-position; it does not extend to PPs, either because they are not DPs, or they do not constitute A-positions. In fact, we do not have anaphoric or pronominal PPs; cases of clitic PPs such as *ne* and *ci* in Italian, for which pronominal status is often assumed, have been shown to behave like non-pronominal (and, of course, non-anaphoric) elements with respect to the binding principles (Belletti 1994).

So, the *ec* left in the VP in (32)-(33) must be chain connected to an antecedent in order to fulfil the identification requirement of the ECP, exactly as any other trace (see, for example, Rizzi 1990a, and Chapter 11 for discussion), but no further requirement is put on the nature of the antecedent, and the non-quantificational topic can fulfil this role.[13]

Consider now the third difference, the fact that quantified expressions cannot be topics, as in (19), whereas they can be focus, as in (20). These quantified expressions must bind a variable at LF, but they can't in (19): neither the clitic nor the clitic trace qualify and, if the quantified expressions are further moved by QR leaving a trace in topic position, this trace does not qualify as a variable because it is an A' position. On the other hand, a well-formed variable is available at S-structure and at LF in (20), so these structures are fine. This is, in essence, the analysis in Rizzi (1986).

Things are complicated somewhat if we observe that CLLD of quantified expressions is significantly improved, sometimes to full acceptability, if the quantified expression includes a lexical restriction:

(34)a ?Nessuno dei tuoi libri, lo conosco veramente bene.
  'None of your books, I know it really well.'
 b ?Ciascun (ogni) membro della commissione, lo devi contattare personalmente.

'Each member of the committee, you should contact him personally.'
c Tutti i tuoi libri, li ho rimessi a posto.
  'All your books, I put them back.'
d Molti libri, li ho buttati via.
  'Many books, I threw them away.'

Why is (34) different from (19)? I will assume that QR can further extract the quantifier from the DP, yielding such LFs as

(35) Molti [ec libri] Top°, [li ho buttati via].

Here the structure is fine: the quantifier binds the variable within the Spec of Top°, which in turn is connected to the pronoun. No principle is violated here. On the other hand, the same structure involving a bare quantifier is ill-formed, as before:

(36) *Molto ec Top°, [lo ho capito].
      'Much, I understood it.'

If the bare quantifier does not move at LF, it will have no variable to bind, thus violating Full Interpretation. If it moves yelding (36), the structure will be ill formed: the *ec* is not in an A (or functional) position, hence it does not qualify as a variable and FI is violated again.[14]

5 Some incompatibilities and ordering constraints

The fourth difference between topic and focus is that there can be an indefinite number of topics but only one structural focus position per clause in Italian (see (22)). At first sight, this would seem to support more diverging structural analyses for the two articulations than we have proposed. An idea that immediately comes to mind would be to exploit the X-bar schema for focus, thus deriving the uniqueness of focus from the general uniqueness of specifiers under binary branching X-bar theory, and assume an adjunction analysis for topic, under usual assumptions on the reiterability of adjunction (but see Kayne 1994 for a more restrictive view on adjunction). So, consider the following possible permutations of topic and focus:

(37)a Credo che a Gianni, QUESTO, domani, gli dovremmo dire.
            C   Top   Foc   Top   IP
      'I believe that to Gianni, THIS, tomorrow we should say.'
    b Credo che domani, QUESTO, a Gianni, gli dovremmo dire.
            C   Top   Foc   Top   IP
    c Credo che domani, a Gianni, QUESTO gli dovremmo dire.
            C   Top   Top   Foc   IP

d Credo che a Gianni, domani, QUESTO gli dovremmo dire.
   C   Top   Top   Foc   IP

e Credo che QUESTO, a Gianni, domani, gli dovremmo dire.
   C   Foc   Top   Top   IP

f Credo che QUESTO, domani, a Gianni, gli dovremmo dire.
   C   Foc   Top   Top   IP

In between the phonetically realized complementizer *che* and the IP, we can have a sequence of topics followed by a focus, followed by another sequence of topics:

(38)   ... C° (Top*) (Foc) (Top*) ...

One could then assume that a unique focal head can project its X-bar schema (FocP) in between C and IP and that topics can be freely adjoined to IP (or, in the terms of the structure proposed in Section 2, to FinP immediately above IP) and FocP.

In spite of its appeal, I will not adopt this analysis. There is empirical evidence in favour of the more symmetric theory of topic and focus presented in Section 2. In short, the intervention of topics induces certain locality effects which are best treated under the assumption that a whole X-bar projection is involved, rather than a simple adjunction structure. This argument is developed in the following sections. For the moment, let us just concentrate on the observed asymmetry: if both topic and focus involve an X-bar schema, the obvious way to express the asymmetry is to assume that the Top Phrase is recursive, while the Foc Phrase is not. But why should it be so? A simple inspection of the interpretive properties of the two constructions may provide an adequate answer.

Let us go back to the proposed interpretation of the projection of Foc, reproduced here for convenience:

(39)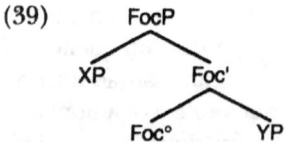

The specifier is the focal element, while the complement of Foc is the presupposition, the given information. Consider now a recursion of FocP, that is, the option of realizing YP itself as a FocP.

(40)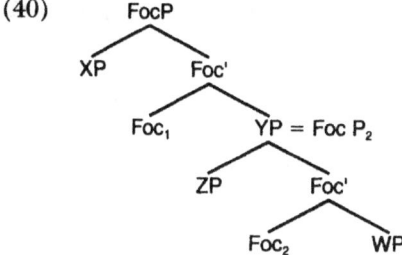

Such a structure would contain a focus position ZP, the specifier of the lower focal head, Foc_2. But this would be inconsistent with the proposed interpretation: YP is the presupposition of the higher focal head Foc_1, and as such it can only specify given information. So, recursion of FocP is banned by the interpretive clash that would arise. No such interpretive problem arises in the case of a recursion of Top: nothing excludes that a comment (the complement of the topic head) may be articulated in turn as a topic–comment structure, so that the topic phrases can undergo free recursion. If this speculative proposal is correct, we can continue to assume a structurally uniform analysis for Top and Foc, and derive the observed difference with respect to recursion from an interpretive peculiarity of Foc.[15]

Based on the arguments of the preceding sections, I have proposed the following articulated structure for the complementizer system.

(41)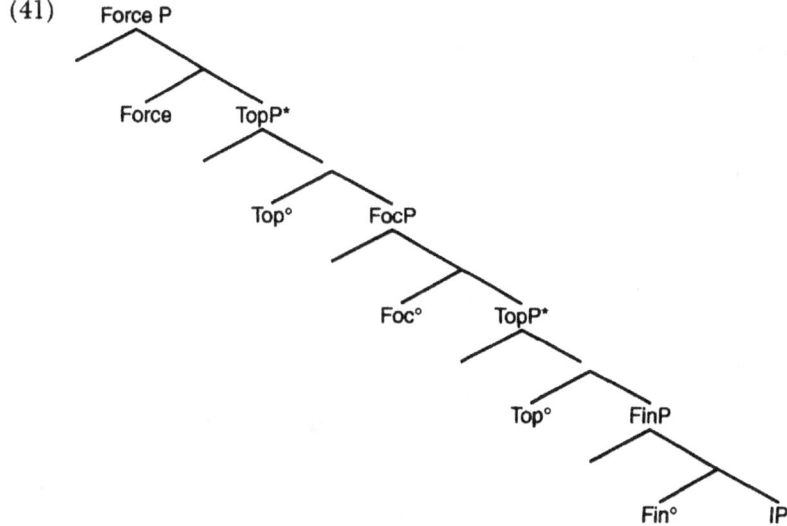

This structure can now be immediately used to account for a number of ordering constraints involving elements of the C system.

We have already seen that relatives sharply contrast with main questions in Italian in that relative and question operators must respectively precede and follow a topic:

(42) a Un uomo a cui, il premio Nobel, lo daranno senz'altro.
'A man to whom, the Nobel Prize, they will give it undoubtedly.'
   b *Un uomo, il premio Nobel, a cui lo daranno senz'altro.
'A man, the Nobel Prize, to whom they will give it undoubtedly.'
(43) a *A chi, il premio Nobel, lo daranno?
'To whom, the Nobel prize, will they give it?
   b Il premio Nobel, a chi lo daranno?
'The Nobel prize, to whom will they give it?'

On the basis of (41) we are immediately led to conclude that relative operators occupy the specifier of Force, the one position which cannot be preceded by topics, while question operators occupy a lower position.[16]

Things get more precise as soon as we observe that relative pronouns are compatible with a focalized constituent in a fixed order, while question operators in main questions are not, regardless of the ordering (the contrast between (44) and (45) was referred to as the fifth difference between Top and Foc in Section 3):

(44) a Ecco un uomo a cui IL PREMIO NOBEL dovrebbero dare (non il premio X).
'Here is a man to whom THE NOBEL PRIZE they should give (not prize X).'
   b *Ecco un uomo IL PREMIO NOBEL a cui dovrebbero dare (non il premio X).
'Here is a man THE NOBEL PRIZE to whom they should give (not prize X).'
(45) a *A chi IL PREMIO NOBEL dovrebbero dare?
'To whom THE NOBEL PRIZE should they give?'
   b *IL PREMIO NOBEL a chi dovrebbero dare?
'THE NOBEL PRIZE to whom should they give?'

If the relative pronoun is in the Spec of Force in (41), it is expected to be compatible with a lower focus, as in (44)a. As for the incompatibility of the question operator and a focalized constituent illustrated by (45), the possibility that immediately comes to mind is that the question operator sits in the Spec of Foc in main questions, hence focalized constituents and question operators compete for the same position and cannot co-occur. An apparent problem for this analysis is raised by the fact that there seems to be a positional asymmetry between question operators and focus: a focalized constituent can be followed by a topic, but a main question operator cannot:

The fine structure of the left periphery 259

(46) (Domani,) QUESTO (a Gianni,) gli dovreste dire.
 '(Tomorrow,) THIS (to Gianni,) we should say.'
(47) (Domani,) che cosa (*a Gianni,) gli dovremmo dire?
 '(Tomorrow,) what (to Gianni,) we should say?'

At first sight, this asymmetry seems to suggest that question operators do not move as far as Foc in (41) and fill a lower position, one that cannot be followed by a Top, such as the Spec of Fin in (41). But if this were correct, question operators would not be competing with focalized constituents for the same position; so, why should the incompatibility shown by (45) arise?

In fact, there are good reasons to think that the asymmetry in (46)–(47) is not due to a positional difference but follows from an independent factor: even a normal preverbal subject cannot intervene between the question operator and the verb, while it can intervene between a focalized constituent and the verb:

(48) QUESTO Gianni ti dira' (, non quello che pensavi).
 'THIS Gianni will say to you (, not what you thought).'
(49) *Che cosa Gianni ti dira'?
 'What Gianni will say to you?'

In Chapter 9 the impossibility of (49) is derived from the Wh Criterion: a Wh operator and a head endowed with the Wh feature must be in a Spec/head configuration at S-structure (or before Spell-out, if one opts for a formalization of things following Chomsky 1993; for a reformulation of the Criterion approach within the guidelines of Chomsky 1993, see Friedemann 1995; see also Guasti 1996). If the Wh feature is generated under T in main questions, I to C movement must apply to bring the feature to the C system, where the Criterion is satisfied. In (49) I to C has not applied, as the word order shows, hence the Criterion is violated. This analysis can now be immediately transposed to the more articulated C structure of (41). The question operator ends up in the Spec of Foc in main questions, where it competes with a focalized constituent, whence the incompatibility of (45). If that position is filled by a Wh element, the inflected verb, carrying the feature Wh, must move all the way up to Foc° to permit satisfaction of the Wh Criterion. Both (47) and (49) (when the lower Top is present) are excluded as violations of the Wh Criterion: in (49) the inflected verb has not moved out of the IP, as the intervening subject shows; in (47) it may have moved to FinP but not further, as the intervening Top shows. In neither case is the required Spec/head configuration created, so that the structures are ruled out by the Wh Criterion (I cannot move past the lower Top either, yelding the order Wh V+I Top IP, as Top blocks I movement: see Section 6 below).

In contrast with interrogative structures, I to C movement is not triggered by focalization in Italian: if there is a Focus Criterion (as I am assuming here), the focus feature is inherently possessed by the Foc° head and no movement of an inflectional head is required.[17]

So, when the Spec/Foc of (41) is filled by a non-Wh focal element, both a preverbal subject and one or more topics can occur. In this way, the apparent asymmetry between questions and focus of (47) can be reconciled with the natural hypothesis that they occupy the same position in main questions.[18]

6 Adjacency effects on Case

In this section we will discuss the following descriptive generalization: whenever the Case properties of the subject depend on an element of the complementizer system, no preposed phrase of any sort can intervene between this element and the subject.

In order to explain this generalization, we must first extend our analysis of topic–comment structures from simple argumental topicalization to all sorts of cases of preposing, adverb preposing in particular (*Yesterday, John came back*, etc.).

A rather common analysis of adverb preposing in English assumes adjunction of the preposed element to IP (or S); sometimes this analysis is assumed for argumental topicalization as well: Baltin (1982); Rochemont (1989); Lasnik and Saito (1992). The approach we have adopted for argumental topicalization is, in essence, an updating of Chomsky (1977a); Cinque (1990): the topicalized element is in the Spec of a Top head, with a null anaphoric operator in the immediately lower Spec to ensure connection with the open position in the sentence. Now, it is not plausible that adverb preposing may involve the anaphoric null operator, which appears to be restricted to argumental material; apart from that, the analysis of argumental topicalization can be extended. So, we can hold constant the assumption that adverb preposing involves a TopP, but we must assume that the adverb itself moves from its base position to the TopP, without the mediation of Op (alternatively, if the 'preposed' adverb is a sentential adverb, it could be base-generated in the Top system: cf. Longobardi 1980; Cinque 1990; Rizzi 1990a). We will see later on that there are reasons to assume that the adverb is adjoined to the TopP, rather than moving to its Spec, but this refinement is unnecessary at the moment.

A straightforward conceptual motivation for the involvement of TopP in adverb preposing, and against the simple adjunction to IP is offered again by Chomsky's (1993) approach to movement (/formation of non-trivial chains): if movement is a last resort operation, and (at least syntactic) movement is always triggered by the satisfaction of some (concrete or abstract) morphological requirement, there can be no free adjunction to IP (or to any other category) in the overt syntax. Adverb preposing, on a par with argumental topicalization, must be triggered by the satisfaction of a Topic Criterion; this naturally leads, under usual assumptions, to the postulation of a Top head and phrase also for simple adverb preposing.

An immediate empirical counterpart of this conceptual argument has to do with the selectivity of the landing site of preposing. The preposed element must land in an IP-peripheral position; but if the process involved simple adjunction to IP, what would prevent movement to other potential adjunction sites, i.e., in between the modal and the VP, a position which can host various kinds of adverbials (and, under May's 1985 analysis, is a possible landing site of QR), but not a topicalized constituent, as in (50)b? And what would prevent adjunction to the whole CP, as in (50)c?

(50)a Around Christmas, John will come home.
 b *John will, around Christmas, come home.
 c *I think, around Christmas, that John will come home.

Standard accounts of (50)b involve the assumption that adjunction cannot apply to arguments (Chomsky 1986b; McCloskey 1992), while the problem raised by (50)b is hardly even mentioned (but see McCloskey 1992: 2). Both problems disappear at once under the criterial approach to Adverb preposing: movement is to an IP-peripheral position because the TopP is a component of the C system; it cannot be external to the Force marker *that* because the higher verb selects the specification of Force, not the TopP. Verbs select for declaratives or questions, not for clauses with or without topic (or focus).[19]

If preposed phrases of all kinds (not just topicalized arguments) always detect a TopP projection in the C system, many adjacency effects discussed in the literature are amenable to a straightforward explanation. Consider first the fact that a preposed adverb can intervene between a tensed complementizer and the subject, but not between *for* and the subject in English:

(51)a ... that John will leave tomorrow.
 b ... that, tomorrow, John will leave.
(52)a ... for John to leave tomorrow.
 b *... for, tomorrow, John to leave.

Case theory provides a natural explanation in conjunction with our assumptions on preposing of the adverbial phrases. In order to be able to determine Case on the subject, *for* must be in a sufficiently local configuration with it, hence it must be in the lowest head of the C system, finiteness. Therefore, there is no room for a TopP in between *for* and the IP (see structure (41)), hence the order in (52)b cannot arise. If we were to assume that *for* could be generated under a higher head of the C system, the occurrence of a lower TopP would give rise to the following structure:

(53) [for [tomorrow Top° ... [John ...

in which *for* would be too far away from *John* to determine its Case, under Relativized Minimality (that UG must allow for the possibility of a prepositional complementizer higher than Fin is shown below).[20]

The same explanation can extend to the adjacency constraint between absolutive *with* and the subject of the small clause:

(54)a With John unavailable at the weekend, ...
   b *With, in the weekend, John unavailable, ...

(cf. '...that, in the weekend, John is unavailable'). If the small clause has no C system (see footnote 3), then there cannot be any TopP to host the preposed phrase. Even if the TopP could be present, it would disrupt the local relation between *with* and *John* which is necessary for Case assignment.

That case is crucial for determining the ill-formedness of (52)b (and (54)b) is suggested by the contrast with (51)b, in which the overt complementizer *that* is not involved in Case assignment to the subject (which is determined by the T-Agr complex), hence it can occur in a higher head of the C system, Force, compatible with a lower TopP.

The contrast between (51) and (52) is not minimal, though, as we are comparing a finite and a non-finite structure. A more minimal pair with (52) would be provided by a construction with the following characteristics: an infinitival complement involving a lexical subject and a prepositional complementizer, but with the Case of the subject not determined by the preposition. The relevant construction exists in West Flemish (Liliane Haegeman, personal communication; see Haegeman 1986 for discussion.):

(55) Mee (?gisteren) zie nie te kommen, ...
   'With yesterday she not to come, ...'

These infinitives introduced by *mee* (with) have the lexical subject marked with nominative Case, which is presumably determined by abstract Agr, not by the prepositional complementizer (which would be expected to govern accusative or oblique). So, under the Case approach it comes as no surprise that adverb interpolation is possible (if somewhat marginal): the prepositional complementizer is not involved in Case assignment to the subject, so it can occur on a higher head of the C system, and it is consistent with the occurrence of a lower TopP. The contrast between English and West Flemish then strongly suggests that the adjacency effect observed in (52)b should be closely tied to the Case properties, rather than to some general distinction between finite and non-finite clauses.

Even more straightforward evidence for the role of Case is provided by Brazilian Portuguese. The infinitive introduced by preposition *pra* (for) has its subject marked nominative or, in colloquial registers, oblique; in the former case, but not in the latter, an adverb can interpolate (Cristina Figueiredo-Silva, Lucienne Rasetti, personal communication; see Figueiredo-Silva 1994 for further discussion):

(56) a Ela me deu o livro pra (amanhã) eu ler.
       'She gave me the book for tomorrow I to read.'
    b Ela me deu o livro pra (*amanhã) mim ler.
       'She gave me the book for tomorrow me to read.'

While in (56)a nominative Case is determined by Agr in the infinitival structure, oblique Case is plausibly determined by the preposition *pra* in (56)b. So, under a Case approach, it is expected that adverb interpolation will be excluded in (56)b and possible in (56)a.

If nominative Case is assigned by the auxiliary in C in the Italian Aux-to-Comp construction (Rizzi 1982), the fact that an adverb cannot intervene is amenable to the same explanation:

(57) a Essendo egli improvvisamente tornato a casa, ...
       'Having he suddenly come back home, ...'
    b *Essendo improvvisamente egli tornato a casa, ...
       'Having suddenly he come back home, ...'

(cf. '... poiché improvvisamente egli è tornato a casa' = Because suddenly he has come back home).[21]

This case is apparently akin to the well-known fact that in Aux inversion structures in English nothing can intervene between the inflection moved to C and the overt subject, even though the role of Case is not obvious here (but see Rizzi and Roberts 1989):

(58) a ... that yesterday John came.
    b *Did yesterday John come?

If I to C movement involves movement to Fin, then there is no intervening TopP to host the preposed adverb in between I and the subject, under structure (41). On the other hand, in some cases it is plausible that I moves to a higher head of the C system, for example in conditionals:

(59) a If (yesterday) John had done that, ...
    b Had (*yesterday) John done that, ...

Here the preposed auxiliary alternates with *if*, which can precede a preposed adverb and hence must be higher than Fin. If the auxiliary actually replaces *if*, as is plausible here, then at least this instance of I to C may be able to move higher than Fin.

So, what rules out the following representation?

(60) Had [yesterday Top° [John I° done that]] ...

We are led to assume that Top° in English is not a suitable host for I movement, so that (60) is excluded by the Head Movement Constraint (the ECP under RM): I cannot move to Top° by assumption, and the higher head of the C° system normally filled by *if* is too far away for the required antecedent government relation to hold.[22]

7 Adjacency effects on PRO

An apparently different kind of adjacency effect exists in control structures between a head of the C system and PRO in subject position. As was briefly discussed in Section 2, in Italian, *di* is often considered the infinitival counterpart of the finite complementizer *che*, but the distribution of topics is the opposite in the two cases, because topic must follow *che*:

(61) a *Penso, a Gianni, che gli dovrei parlare.
        'I think, to Gianni, that I should speak to him.'
    b Penso che, a Gianni, gli dovrei parlare.
        'I think that, to Gianni, I should speak to him.'

On the other hand, a topic is strongly disallowed in between the prepositional complementizer *di* and the infinitival IP, while it can precede *di*:

(62) a Penso, a Gianni, di dovergli parlare.
        'I think, to Gianni, "of" to have to speak to him.'
    b *Penso di, a Gianni, dovergli parlare.
        'I think "of", to Gianni, to have to speak to him.'

The contrast (61)a–(62)a clearly shows that *che* and *di* do not occupy the same position: at S-structure, *che* occupies the highest position of the C system, the Force head, preceding the topic string, while *di* occupies a lower position, presumably the finiteness head. Why should it be so? And, in particular, why should *di* be forced to occur on the lowest head of the C system?

It is a remarkable fact that control infinitives pattern with infinitival (and finite) clauses in which the case of the lexical subject is determined by some element of the C system in that they both require adjacency between this element and the subject position:

(63) *C° [XP Top° ... [PRO ...

The traditional approach to the distribution of PRO in terms of the PRO Theorem does not seem to be well equipped to capture this constraint: it is not clear why the intervening TopP should determine a violation of the PRO Theorem (particularly in cases of CLLD, in which, as the subject/object asymmetries discussed in Section 8 show, Top° clearly does not have the capacity to govern a lower Spec position). The null Case approach to PRO of Chomsky and Lasnik (1991) looks more promising in this respect, if properly adapted.

The null Case approach captures the distribution of PRO by stipulating that PRO requires a null Case, sanctioned by the minimal inflection, the inflection of infinitives; its occurrence is then restricted to the subject position of non-finite clauses.

As such, the null Case approach has nothing to say on the descriptive constraint (63).

On the other hand, as Watanabe (1993) has observed, this variant of the null Case approach has the weakness of not expressing one of the fundamental distributional constraints on PRO, which is the fact that it cannot occur in non-finite structures not protected by a CP layer:

(64) a *It seems [PRO to be happy].
     b *John believes [PRO to be happy].
     c *John considers [PRO happy].

These predicates select IP complements or small clauses in the non-finite paradigm. The non-occurrence of PRO here immediately follows from the PRO theorem (PRO is governed by the higher predicate), but not from the null Case approach: why should these non-finite inflections not license the null Case? In order to deal with this problem, Watanabe stipulates that null Case cheching in AgrS creates a new feature [+F] which in turn must be checked by movement of AgrS to the C system. But this follow up operation and the feature involved have no independent status or justification, apart from the fact of expressing a dependency between C° and PRO in a system which disallows head government.

As we are admitting head government for other reasons (cf. Introduction), we can directly rephrase the null Case approach in a way consistent with Watanabe's observation by stipulating the following principle:[23]

(65) Null Case is sanctioned by [-fin] under government.

So, the different cases of (64) can be excluded, under (65), because of the lack of the C system (implying the lack of the required -fin specification). The adjacency effects summarized in (63) can now be treated on a par with the adjacency effects in cases in which the lexical subject has its Case sanctioned by a non-finite complementizer ((52)b, (54)b, (56)b, etc.). The similarity of the adjacency effects in the two cases thus seems to lend straightforward support to the null Case approach to PRO (with the proposed revision).

8 Adjacency effects on traces

If topicalized elements involve an independent X-bar projection in the C system, we expect that the presence of a topicalized element will interfere with subject extraction, under standard assumptions on the licensing of traces. In fact, we find two opposite, almost contradictory, kinds of interactions: some preposed elements block subject extraction; other preposed elements alleviate *that*-trace violations and make subject extraction possible. We shall call these two effects adjacency and anti-adjacency effects on traces, respectively. Let us concentrate on the former in this section.

First of all, intervening CLLD phrases induce subject–object asymmetries in French:

(66) a ?Je ne sais pas à qui, ton livre, je pourrais le donner t.
'I don't know to whom, your book, I could give it t.'
b *?Je ne sais pas qui, ton livre, t pourrait l'acheter.
'I don't know who, your book, t could buy it.'
(67) a ?Un homme à qui, ton livre, je pourrais le donner t.
'A man to whom, your book, I could give it t.'
b *? Un homme qui, ton livre, t pourrait l'acheter.
'A man who, your book, t could buy it.'

A verbal complement can be moved across a topic with slightly marginal results in questions and relatives; movement of a subject across a topic determines a clear decrease of acceptability. These asymmetries are obviously reminiscent of the familiar subject–complement extraction asymmetries (*that*-trace effects, which produce somewhat sharper contrasts; on this, see below):

(68) a A qui crois-tu que Marie va parler t?
'To whom do you believe that Marie is going to speak t?'
b *Qui crois-tu que t va parler à Marie?
'Who do you believe that t is going to speak to Marie?'

Comparative evidence supports the hypothesis that (66)–(67) are parallel to (68). Italian, a language which does not show subject–complement asymmetries of the kind illustrated in (68) (ultimately as a function of the positive fixation of the Null Subject Parameter, see Rizzi 1982, Chapter 4; 1990a: 62–65 for discussion), also allows subject and complement extraction across a topic at the same level of acceptability:

(69) a Un uomo a cui, il tuo libro, lo potremmo dare.
'A man to whom, your book, we could give it.'
b Un uomo che, il tuo libro, lo potrebbe comprare.
'A man who, your book, could buy it.'

As for English, a language which typically shows *that*-trace effects, Lasnik and Saito (1992) observe that topicalization also determines detectable asymmetries, in spite of the fact that even complement extraction across a topic is quite degraded:

(70) a ??The man to whom [that book [I gave t t]].
 b *The man who [that book [t gave t to me]].

(adapted from Lasnik and Saito 1992)

Some cases of complement extraction across a topic are more natural (Baltin 1982); this produces sharper asymmetries (on the effect of stress on the acceptability of such cases, see below):

(71) a ?A man to whom [liberty [we should never grant t t]].
 b *A man who [liberty [t should never grant t to us]].

Let us first consider the French paradigm. In Rizzi (1990a, Chapter 2) the following analysis of standard subject–complement asymmetries is proposed: the ECP requires that traces must be properly head-governed (governed by a head within its immediate projection); a trace in complement position is properly head governed (by the verb), but a trace in subject position normally is not, as C is inert for government; so, (68)b is excluded as an ECP violation. Movement of the subject may be well formed in cases like (72):

(72) Je ne sais pas [qui C° [t pourrait l'acheter]].
 'I don't know who could buy it.'

Here the analysis, expressed within a traditional theory of C, assumed that the Wh element in the Spec of C could trigger abstract agreement on C (sometimes with audible morphological effects) which turned C into a proper head-governor for the trace in subject position. Under the current assumptions on a structured C system, it must be the case that finiteness, the lowest C head interfacing the IP system and structurally adjacent to the subject, can be endowed with Agr features to ensure well-formedness of the subject trace. If the Wh elements end up in a Spec higher than Spec/Fin in (72), there must be a higher head endowed with Agr features to license the subject trace in Spec/Fin; a more precise characterization of the possible occurrence of Agr features on a given head is proposed in Section 11. Consider now the structural representation of such examples as (66)b, etc. under the X-bar analysis of topics (C here is whatever head of the complementizer system has the Wh element in its Spec in indirect questions):

(73) Je ne sais pas [qui C° [ton livre Top° ... [t pourrait ...]]].

Here, even if C is turned into a governor via agreement, it is too far away to license the subject trace, due to the intervening head Top°, a standard case of Relativized Minimality effect. If Fin, lower than Top, is endowed with Agr features, things do not change: the trace in subject position t would be well-formed, but the subject should move through the Spec of Fin to license the Agr features on this head, and the trace in the Spec of Fin, t', would now be the offending trace:

(74) Je ne sais pas [qui C° [ton livre Top° [t' Fin+Agr [t pourrait...]]]].

Example (66)b with representation (74) is close enough to (68)b to make it possible to appeal to the same structural explanation for both cases of subject/non-subject asymmetries; on the other hand, it is different enough to leave room for an account of the different strength of the effect with respect to ordinary *that*-trace effects. Assuming uniform strength for all ECP violations, the somewhat weaker deviance of (66)b could be due to the possibility of resorting to a deviant device of a different kind to avoid the ECP violation. For instance, if t' is omitted from representation (74), no ECP violation would arise, and the source of the deviance would be the fact that Agr in Fin is not locally licensed by its specifier (alternatively, it could be that the structure resorts to an unlicensed occurrence of the null operator Op, a null element which does not fall under the ECP, to support the Agr features in Fin; or that the structure makes an improper use of the 'bypassing' device to be introduced in Section 11). None of these (deviant) devices is available for the subject position, so that (68)b can only produce a straight ECP violation.

If we had assumed that topics in the CLLD construction are adjoined to IP, such contrasts as (66)a–b would be unexpected. One could deal with them through the stipulation that adjunction creates a barrier for government (Lasnik and Saito 1992). Since, under the X-bar analysis of the topic–comment articulation, the result follows straightforwardly from core principles of locality, I take these asymmetries to provide evidence for the X-bar analysis.

The same analysis accounts for the ill-formedness of English examples such as (70)b and (71)b (modulo the independent differences between Romance CLLD and English topicalization). Under the null operator analysis of English topicalization, the complete representation of (71)b would be, for the relevant part:

(75) A man [who C° [liberty Top° [Op [t should never grant to us]]]].

Suppose that the null Op sits in the Spec of the Fin head. Then, no Agr features can occur in Fin to satisfy the ECP on t: among other things, such features would have to agree with Op, hence disagree with t, and we continue to assume that Agr features have their governing capacity restricted to elements coindexed with them. If Agr features were specified on some higher head of the C system (say, under Force), they would be too far away from t to have any beneficial effect, under RM (see the following sections for additional discussion of this case). Again, an analysis of English topicalization based on simple IP-adjunction would not offer an equally principled analysis of the asymmetries.

Moreover, a generalized adjunction analysis is not selective enough to lead one to expect the following asymmetry. Adverb preposing contrasts sharply with argument topicalization in that it does not affect subject extraction:

(76) a *I wonder who, this book, would buy around Christmas.
  b I wonder who, around Christmas, would buy this book.

In the face of this contrast, and restricting one's attention to adjacency effects on traces, one could be tempted to assume that adverb preposing differs from argumental topicalization in that it does involve simple adjunction to IP, a structure which is transparent to government relations, so that the well-formedness of the subject trace is not affected:

(77) I wonder who C+Agr [around Christmas [t would buy this book]].

On the other hand, this analysis is inconsistent with the conceptual argument for assuming the involvement of a TopP also with adverb preposing, and the supporting empirical evidence provided by the adjacency effects on Case, with respect to which argument topicalization and adverb preposing pattern alike. We are then left with the question of why adverb preposing involves a structure which triggers adjacency effects on Case but is transparent for adjacency effects on traces. This point is addressed in the next section in the context of the anti-adjacency effects.

In order to conclude the survey on the adjacency effects on traces, I will now take a brief look at some such effects involving traces in A-chains. We have seen in (69) that Italian differs from French in that CLLD does not induce subject–object asymmetries in A'-chains, a fact that is amenable to other similar contrasts between the two languages as a consequence of the different fixation of the Null Subject Parameter. But adjacency effects are detectable in Italian if we look at A-chains. Here the relevant contrast is between raising and control: control infinitives are compatible with CLLD (with the dislocated element preceding the infinitival complementizer, as we have seen), while raising infinitives are not. Compare, in particular, the different behaviour of the control and raising use of *sembrare* (seem):

(78) a Gianni pensa, il tuo libro, di PRO conoscerlo bene.
    'Gianni thinks, you book, of to+know it well.'

b Mi sembra, il tuo libro, di PRO conoscerlo bene.
   'It seems to me, your book, of to+know it well.'
c *?Gianni sembra, il tuo libro, t conoscerlo bene.
   'Gianni seems, your book, to know it well.'

If raising infinitives must involve a bare IP in order to allow the subject trace to be properly governed by the main V, there is no room for a TopP to occur in such structures; on the other hand, control infinitives can (and must) involve a CP system, so that they are compatible with a TopP.[24]

A more subtle case of incompatibility with a dislocated phrase is provided by the special Romance construction involving Wh extraction of the subject from the infinitival complement of an epistemic verb, a complement which does not allow an overt subject *in situ* (Rizzi 1982, 1990a; Kayne 1984):

(79) Un uomo che ritengo (*a Gianni,) potergli parlare.
      'A man whom I believe (to Gianni) to be able to talk to him.'

Here a C structure (say, minimally, a -Fin head) is needed to ensure, on the one hand, the fact that the subject trace satisfies the ECP, and, on the other hand, the Case-licensing of the chain of the subject by the higher verb:

(80) Un uomo che ritengo [t' -Fin [t potergli parlare]].

But then, if a TopP occurs, it will make t' inaccessible to V for case licensing and satisfaction of the ECP, so that the structure will be ill-formed. Again, no such effect is found with the control structure, normally possible with epistemic verbs in Italian:

(81) Ritengo, a Gianni, di potergli parlare.
      'I believe, to Gianni, to be able to speak to him.'

Here, no special relation must be established between the main V and (the chain of) PRO, hence a TopP can occur in the C system.

9 Anti-adjacency effects

In the previous sections, the intervening head of the TopP was detected through a negative effect, the blocking of a locality relation that was required to hold between a higher head and a lower subject position. Interesting complementary evidence for the postulation of such a head is the positive effect to be discussed here: in a nutshell, in some cases an otherwise ill-formed occurrence of a subject trace is made possible by the presence and action of an intervening Top layer (in an indirect way, as we shall see in a moment).

Consider a typical *that*-t effect, as in (82)a below. In this context, argument topicalization and adverb preposing differ sharply. If embedded argument topicalization applies (with comma intonation and the pragmatics of topic–comment), as in (82)b, the effect is not alleviated (but if the preposed element bears focal stress, the acceptability improves; see below on this effect):

(82) a *A man who I think that t knows this book very well.
 b *A man who I think that, this book, t knows t very well.

On the other hand, Bresnan (1977: 194) observed that an adverb interpolating between *that* and the subject trace renders the structure clearly more acceptable (thanks to Kinsuke Hasegawa for bringing Bresnan's observation to my attention in the context of his comment paper to Rizzi 1993, Tokyo, November 1992); these facts have been analysed independently in Culicover (1992, 1993) and Fukui (1993). Consider the following examples from Bresnan's article:

(83) a *An amendment which they say that t will be law next year.
 b An amendment which they say that, next year, t will be law.
(84) a *Which doctor did you tell me that t had had a heart attack during an operation?
 b Which doctor did you tell me that, during an operation, t had had a heart attack?

Bresnan considers such examples 'mildly awkward'. Culicover appears to consider them fully grammatical. In any event, there seems to be a consensus that a clear contrast exists between the two cases.

We will call this improvement effect an 'anti-adjacency effect', in that it arises when an intervening adverb or adverbial PP makes the subject trace non-adjacent to *that*. That the adverb must be higher than the subject trace is shown by the fact that a lower (IP internal) adverb does not give rise to the effect, Hasegawa (personal communication) points out:

(85) *Who did she say that t hardly speaks to her?

And the effect is selective enough to distinguish between argument topicalization (82)b and adverb preposing ((83)b, etc.).

Here I will develop an analysis along the lines of the approach proposed by Culicover (1992) (but rejected in Culicover 1993 for reasons that we will come back to) and, more directly, of the independent proposal sketched out in Rizzi (1993, footnote 6) in response to Hasegawa's point. As a first approximation, we can think that the preposed adverb or PP has the effect of licensing a head of the C system (in an indirect way, as we shall see in a moment) which in turn licenses the subject trace, thus alleviating the ECP violation.

(86) ... that ... next year ... X° [t will be law

Various questions arise at this point: What is X°? Why is its presence contingent on the preposed adverbial? Why does it license the subject trace?

As for the first and third questions, we clearly want to unify this case as much as possible with other successful cases of subject extraction. If in such cases subject extraction is made possible by an agreeing Fin specification, this should be the device involved in (86) as well. But why should an agreeing Fin be allowed to co-occur with *that* just in case an adverb has been preposed?

So far we have not taken a position as to the question of whether force and finiteness must be specified on distinct heads of the complementizer system or whether they can be specified syncretically, on a single head. We have only observed that these two specifications must be structurally adjacent, respectively, to the lower IP and the higher VP structure in order to meet selectional constraints. Suppose that the force–finiteness system can be expressed by a single item drawn from the functional lexicon. In English, for embedded finite declaratives we have the alternation *that/0*, I will continue to assume that the latter, but not the former, is consistent with Agr:

(87) That = +decl, +fin
      0 = +decl, +fin, (+Agr)

The analysis of the simple cases of subject extraction then proceeds as in Rizzi (1990a). If the form *that* is selected, the trace in subject position remains non-properly governed and ECP is violated. If *0* is selected, it is turned into a governor by the Agr specification (which, in turn, is sanctioned by the passage of the subject through its specifier, where it leaves t'), and it properly governs the subject trace t (in turn, t' is properly governed by the higher verb):

(88) a *Who do you think [t' that [t will win the prize]]?
     b Who do you think [t' *0* [t will win the prize]]?

Suppose now that the topic–focus field is activated in the C system. Then, the force–finiteness system cannot be realized on a single C head anymore because either one or the other specification would not be adjacent to its selecting or selected domain. The force–finiteness system must then split into two heads which sandwich the topic–focus field. So, in examples like the following, the force specification, which interfaces the C system (and the whole clause) with its selector (the higher V) must be manifested by *that* above the topic:

(89) a I think that next year John will win the prize.
     b Bill said that your book, he really liked.

The finiteness specification, which interfaces the C system with the IP, must be manifested by a zero C head (Fin) under the topic. So, we should revise (87) in the following way:

(90) That = +decl, (+fin)
     0 = (+decl), +fin, (+Agr)

That expresses declarative force and may optionally express finiteness; *0* expresses finiteness, and may optionally express declarative force (as well as agreement). In simple cases, in which the force–finiteness system can be expressed on a single head, *that* and *0* are functionally equivalent and alternate (there are further restrictions on the occurrence of *0* that we will come back to in Section 11); in complex cases in which force and finiteness must split because the topic–focus system is activated, the higher head, expressing pure force, must be realized as *that* and the lower head, expressing pure finiteness, must be realized as *0*:

(91) ... [that [next year Top° [*0* [John will win the prize]].

As expected under this analysis, the two specifications do not alternate in the 'splitting' case: the lower specification cannot be realized as *that* and, more importantly, the higher specification cannot be realized as *0* (Rochemont 1989; Nakajima 1993; Grimshaw 1997):

(92) I think *(that) next year, (*that) John will win the prize.

We are now in a position to explain the anti-adjacency effect. When the topic–focus field is activated by a preposed adverbial, force and finiteness must split, and we get a representation like (91). If the subject is extracted, as the lower *0* expressing Fin can be associated with Agr, we get (93)a; t is properly governed by Fin with the Agr specification, but what about t', whose presence in the Spec of Fin is needed to license the Agr specification? I will assume here that Fin can move head to head to the next available head, here Top, yielding representation (93)b, and from that position it can properly govern t', thus satisfying the ECP (the trace of Fin° +Agr, italicized in (93)b, licenses t).[25]

(93)a ... that [next year Top° [t' Fin° +Agr [t will be law]]].
    b ... that [next year [Fin° +Agr [Top°]] [t' *Fin° +Agr* [t will be law]]].

According to this analysis, whether or not the moved subject ultimately passes through the Spec of *that* is immaterial for the anti-adjacency effect, as the critical actions (licensing of Agr in Fin and of the two traces of the subject) take place under *that* in these complex structures. This predicts that we should find anti-adjacency effects also in indirect questions (abstracting away from the independent subjacency effects), in which the Spec of Force, filled by the Wh operator, would not be available for movement of the subject. In fact, Culicover (1993) detects an anti-adjacency effect in such cases as well (his example (20)b is adapted here):

(94) It is this person that you might well wonder whether for all intents and purposes dislikes you.

Here the structure would be:

(95) ... whether [for all intents ... Top° [t' Fin+Agr [t ...

and the analysis would proceed exactly as in the case of the declarative (Fin° endowed with Agr moves to Top°, from where it can license t'; its trace licenses t).

We should now make sure that the analysis is selective enough to account for the difference between adverb preposing and argument topicalization. Remember that the latter in English must involve a null operator, which we have assumed to be sitting in the Spec of Fin. So, a relevant representation with subject extraction across a topicalized phrase would be:

(96) ... that [this book Top° [Op Fin° [t knows ...

Here the Fin head is not available to salvage t (if it hosted Agr features, they should agree with Op in its Spec, hence they would disagree with t, and t could not be licensed).[26]

The question which remains to be answered is: why is this technique contingent on the presence of the preposed adverbial? That is, why couldn't one always violate the *that*-t constraint by separating force and finiteness, hence have a lower agreeing *0* finiteness head licensing the subject trace and co-occurring with a higher *that* (with t' licensed by head movement of Fin°+Agr to *that*)?

(97) Who do you think [that [t' Fin°+Agr [t will win the prize]]]?

This representation must be barred, otherwise we would have free violations of *that*-t. So, the descriptive generalization appears to be that we can have the split between Force and Finiteness (and the consequent salvaging of the subject trace) only if the split is forced by the activation of the topic–focus field. This state of affairs has an obvious 'last resort' flavour, and as such is reminiscent of much discussed economy constraints (Chomsky 1991, 1993, 1995, etc.). I will assume the following economy principle to constrain the structure-building process:

(98) Avoid structure.

This is much in the line of analogous proposals by Crisma (1992), Safir (1992), Grimshaw (1993), Speas (1994), Giorgi and Pianesi (1994), and other recent work (the principle has no exact equivalent in Chomsky's system, but is akin to his Economy of Representations).

The effect of principle (98) in the case at issue is intuitively clear: as the grammar of English has the option of expressing force and finiteness in a single head, this option wins over the option of selecting two separate heads (which would imply two X-bar projections); the latter becomes permissible only if the former is not available because of the activation of the topic–focus field, which forces the split (otherwise, selectional constraints would be violated). This happens in (93) and (94), but not in (97), which is barred by principle (98). So, (98) is operative up to the satisfaction of selectional constraints, as is obvious: a principle of structural parsimony cannot win over the fundamental structure building principles. On the other hand, the ECP is weaker than (98): a structural layer cannot be added to a representation just to salvage an ECP violation.[27]

This is rather straightforward intuitively, but the question arises as to how (98) may work formally. Let us assume the basic idea of Chomsky's (1995) approach: economy is computed by comparing derivations within a given reference set, and selecting the simplest. The question then reduces to how the reference set is defined. Chomsky's proposal is that it is fixed on the basis of the numeration, the set of items picked from the lexicon to act as heads in the syntactic representation to be formed. But this definition does not help in our case: (97) and (88) would have different numerations (the latter with a syncretic Force-Fin head, the former with two separate heads for force and finiteness, a permissible option in English, as the well-formedness of (93) shows), so there could not be any blocking effect of (88) over (97) if the reference set is defined on the basis of the numeration.

On the other hand, it may be desirable to consider less strict definitions of the reference set. Consider, for instance, the basic distributional constraint on *do* support: *do* can occur only when it is needed (Grimshaw 1993). It is natural to try to express this constraint in terms of an economy principle like (98) (Rizzi 1995), but this is not possible if the reference set is restricted by the numeration: structures with and without *do* would always have distinct numerations. The same problem may be raised, for example, by the distributional constraints on certain kinds of expletives (in German, Icelandic, etc.), which are limited to positions in which they are needed to satisfy the V-2 constraint. So our case seems to belong to a larger family of cases having this structure: functional element X can occur only if it is needed to satisfy some structure-building principle. It is natural to try to explain these constraints through principle (98), but this requires a less strict definition of the reference set. A simple modification which achieves the desired result here is that we define the reference set exclusively on the basis of the *lexical* elements of the numeration: functional elements do not define the reference set, rather their occurrence is limited by principle (98) (this is very similar to the approach, expressed within Optimality Theory, by Grimshaw 1997).[28]

10 Anti-adjacency effects with negative preposing

Culicover (1993) discusses a problem for his own (1992) analysis of what we have called the anti-adjacency effect: the effect is triggered by preposed negative elements as well:

(99) Leslie is the person who I said that at no time would run for any public office.

Even though in such cases the linear order cannot show whether I to C has applied or not, the negative element has clausal scope here (with licensing of a phrase-external polarity item), a state of affairs in which inversion is normally required:

(100)a At no time would Leslie run for any public office.
 b *At no time Leslie would run for any public office.

Culicover concludes that inversion must have applied in (99) as well, so that the representation must be:

(101) ... that at no time would [t I run ...

On the other hand, it is well-known that, in other contexts in English, I to C does not license a subject trace. For instance, Hiberno English embedded interrogatives, which allow I to C movement, strongly disallow subject extraction, as McCloskey (1992) points out (see also Henry 1995):

(102)a I wonder would she do that?
 b *Who do you wonder would t do that?

So, Culicover's conclusion is that cases like (99) raise an intractable paradox: on the one hand we observe the anti-adjacency effect, with the preposed negative element able to license an otherwise ill-formed subject trace; on the other hand the preposing should have triggered I to C movement, a context which, in general, precludes the occurrence of a subject trace. This problem leads Culicover to abandon his own analysis of anti-adjacency, and the whole underlying approach to the licensing of subject traces.

I would like to show that the above facts can be integrated into the analysis of anti-adjacency developed in Section 9, which shares the background and many elements with Culicover's original analysis; in fact the phenomenon provides important (if intricate) evidence for that family of approaches.

The key empirical observation is provided by Culicover himself (op. cit., footnote 4): if we take a structure like (99) but involving no modal or auxiliary, the variant with (unstressed) *do* is deviant and the variant without is fine:

(103) a ??Leslie is the person who I said that only in that election did run for public office.
b Leslie is the person who I said that only in that election ran for public office.

If subject extraction does not apply, the judgement is reversed, with *do* insertion and inversion obligatorily applying:

(104) a I think that only in that election did Leslie run for public office.
b *I think that only in that election Leslie ran for public office.

If we take, as seems reasonable, the ill-formedness of the structure with *do* and, even more clearly, the well-formedness of the structure without *do* as evidence that inversion has not applied in (103), we reach a rather surprising conclusion: inversion with a preposed negative element must apply except in cases where the subject has been extracted, as in (103) (and, by analogy, (99)). Why should this be so?

In fact, there is another familiar case in which I to C movement, otherwise obligatory, does not apply in connection with movement of the subject. This happens with main questions on the subject:

(105) a Who did you see t?
b *Who you saw t?
(106) a *Who did see you?
b Who saw you?

I will reproduce here the basic elements of the analysis presented in Chapter 9: I to C movement is compulsory in (105) in order to carry the Wh feature, generated under T, to C, as is required to fulfil the Wh Criterion at S-structure (or before Spell-out); in fact, if I to C does not apply, as in (105)b, the structure is ill-formed. On the other hand, I to C movement cannot apply in the case of a subject question (106)a because the subject trace does not satisfy the ECP in that environment (see the discussion of (102)b above); nevertheless, the Wh Criterion is satisfied: as the subject has been moved from its base position in the VP to the Spec of C through the Specs of T and AgrS, we obtain the following representation:

(107) [Who C° [t AgrS° [t T°$_{+Wh}$ [t V° ...]]]]

C, AgrS and T have specifiers belonging to the same chain, so that, assuming Spec-head coindexation, they share the same index. As they are in the appropriate local relation (no other head intervenes), they can form a representational chain which possesses the Wh feature (still sitting under T); if we define the Wh Criterion on chains (a Wh operator must be in a Spec/head configuration with a head whose chain possesses the Wh feature), we achieve the desired result: I to C is not required to fulfil the Wh Criterion just in case the questioned element is the subject. This device is not available in (105)b: the specifiers of C and AgrS (and T) are contraindexed, so that the heads are contraindexed, too, and no representational chain connecting C to T can be built. The only option to satisfy the Wh Criterion with non-subject main questions then is to move I (T) to C, as in (105)a.

Going back to negative preposing, I will assume that I to C movement in this case is triggered by the Negative Criterion (Chapter 9; Haegeman and Zanuttini 1991; Haegeman 1995b): the Neg feature, which I assume to be generated under T on a par with the Wh feature, must be brought up to the C system if a negative element is preposed in order to create the required Spec/head configuration. So, for instance, (104)a is fine and (104)b is ruled out as a violation of the Neg Criterion because the Neg feature has not reached the C system. Consider now the representation associated to (103)b (and (99)). I will assume for concreteness that the preposed negative element is moved to a Foc phrase, but labels don't matter much here. Assuming the technique adopted for ordinary antiadjacency effects, we would have the subject passing through Spec/fin (leaving trace t'''), from which it can license agreement features in Fin, which in turn license the subject trace t'' in Spec/AgrS; Fin° then moves to Foc°, from where it licenses t''':

(108) ... [only in that election Foc° [t''' Fin°+Agr [t'' AgrS° [t' T°$_{+neg}$ [t ran ...]]]]]

Remember that the Neg feature is under T. Now, T is coindexed with the subject trace in its Spec t' and both AgrS and Fin are coindexed with other traces of the subject chain, t'' and t'''. So, exactly as in the case of a subject question, there is a representational chain connecting Fin, AgrS and T through the transitivity of indexation. As Fin further moves to Foc°, we end up with a representational chain connecting Foc° (to Fin to AgrS) to T, the head endowed with the negative feature. Hence, the Neg Criterion can be fulfilled without I to C movement, in parallel with the satisfaction of the Wh Criterion with subject questions. If the subject had not been extracted, the option of the representational chain would not arise:

(109) ... [only in that election Foc° [Fin° [Bill AgrS° [t' T°$_{+neg}$ [t ran
        ...]]]]]

Here Agr in Fin cannot be activated, as it would not be supported by a specifier, hence there is no way to build a representational chain connecting Foc° to the negative feature, so that the only option to satisfy the Neg Criterion is to apply I to C movement. In conclusion, the system deals with Culicover's observation that anti-adjacency effects are determined by negative preposing without raising any paradox. At the same time, it offers an explanation for the surprising observation that I to C movement, generally obligatory with negative preposing, does not apply when the subject is extracted; it does so by drawing a close parallel with the other major gap in the application of I to C movement: main questions on the subject.

11 Some differences between English and French

French does not show anti-adjacency effects of the English kind. Remember that in cases of successful subject extraction in French the agreeing complementizer is not *0*, but the overt form *qui*; if the agreeing form does not occur and C is in the unmarked form *que*, an ECP violation is produced, as in (110)a:

(110)a *Voici l'homme que je crois t que t pourra nous aider l'année prochaine.
        'Here is the man who I believe that will be able to help us next year.'
     b Voici l'homme que je crois qui t pourra nous aider l'année prochaine.
        'Here is the man who I think "qui" will be able to help us next year.'

The paradigm remains essentially unchanged if an adverbial interpolates between C and the subject trace; the ECP violation is not alleviated and the agreeing form of C must occur:

(111)a *Voici l'homme que je crois que, l'année prochaine, t pourra nous aider.
        'Here is the man who I believe that, next year, will be able to help us.'
     b Voici l'homme que je crois qui, l'année prochaine, t pourra nous aider.
        'Here is the man who I think "qui", next year, will be able to help us.'

Some speakers do not find any improvement in (111)a in comparison to (110)a; other speakers find a very slight improvement (say ?* vs *) which does not seem comparable to the robust effect found in English, which appears to hold systematically across speakers. We will come back to this nuance in a moment after giving an analysis of the core comparative fact, the essential lack of anti-adjacency in French. Consider the structure of (110)a–b under our analysis, assuming maximal uniformity with what was proposed for English:

(112) ... je crois [que [l'année prochaine Top° [t' Fin° [t...]]]]

Assume that Fin can also be endowed with Agr features in French, an option which is presumably what permits simple subject questions such as *Quel garçon t est venu?* (Which boy came?). Then, the offending trace could not be t, and should be t' here. Remember that t' is licensed in the English equivalent (93), under the proposed analysis, by the option of having Fin jump by head movement to Top, from where it can properly govern t'. We are then led to locate the difference between the two languages in this device: if Fin cannot jump to Top in French, t' would remain in violation of the ECP, and the lack of anti-adjacency effects would be expected. But why should this instance of head to head movement be permissible in English and barred in French? I would like to speculate that this subtle contrast is related to a more conspicuous difference between the two grammatical systems.[29]

English has null complementizers for subordinate declarative clauses, whereas French does not.

(113) a I think (that) John will come.
b Je crois *(que) Jean viendra.

The zero finite complementizer of English has the characteristic distribution of traces, as Kayne (1984, Chapter 3) and Stowell (1981) have pointed out; it is possible in clauses that are internal arguments, but not in subject or preposed clauses:

(114) a I didn't expect [*0* [John could come]].
b *[*0* [John will come]] is likely.
c *[*0* [John could come]], I didn't expect.

A natural way to express this distribution is to assume that a trace is actually involved. Pesetsky (1995: 8) proposes that the null finite complementizer is affixal, and incorporates onto the higher V. The observed distribution then follows from the ECP. Our analysis of subject extraction in cases like *Who do you think came?* remains unchanged, except that it is now *the trace* of the agreeing Fin which properly governs the subject trace. In anti-adjacency configurations, things continue to work essentially in the same way, with the affixal (and agreeing) Fin moving to the next higher head, except that here the target is not the higher V, but another head of the C system, Top (or perhaps Foc in cases like (103)b, and possibly the cases mentioned in the last paragraph of footnote 26).

In the corresponding French structure (111)a, as French complementizers are not affixal, the agreeing Fin head cannot jump further, and t' continues to violate the ECP. So, if our speculation is on the right track here, the English–French contrast (102)–(112) may be reduced to the more conspicuous and familiar contrast (113)a–b.

We still have to account for the well-formedness of (111)b in French: if the higher C element is in the agreeing form *qui*, subject extraction is fine across a preposed adverbial. This is not expected on the basis of what we have been assuming so far. The structure would be:

(115) ... t" qui [l'année prochaine Top° [t' Fin°+Agr [t pourra ...]]]

Here t is properly governed by Fin, but t' violates the ECP: Fin cannot jump to Top, Top itself is unable to license t' (otherwise (111)a would be well-formed too), and the agreeing form *qui* is too far away from t' to have a beneficial effect on it, under RM.

In short, paradigm (111) shows that adverb preposing is transparent to subject extraction in French, which is not affected either positively or negatively, and this transparency is not fully expressed by our analysis. In order to account for the well-formedness of (111)b within our frame of assumptions there are two basic possibilities. Either structure (115) is made more impoverished, to the effect that t' becomes close enough to *qui* to be licensed by it;[30] or the structure is made richer than (115), and there is a device which allows the subject chain to bypass the Top layer without damage, and to benefit from the presence of *qui*. As the second possibility seems to involve a less radical departure from assumptions that we have adopted so far, I will pursue it here.

Let us then focus on the second possibility. How can the subject chain successfully bypass the TopP in (111)b? Clearly, Top should have the quality of licensing t' here, but in such a way that the higher agreeing C *qui* should continue to be relevant for the global well-formedness of the chain. So, we can try to use the same method, and ascribe to Top the same governing device that we attributed to Fin: Agr. This gives us the opportunity of rethinking the distribution of Agr in somewhat more general terms.

What makes an abstract (sometimes concrete) Agr specification available to the C system and, more generally, to any structural system? Following Shlonsky (1997), I will assume that Agr specifications are available to heads containing certain substantive specifications: tense (AgrS), aspect (Agr of Past Participle), perhaps V (AgrO), and so on. In the C system, a natural substantive specification that Agr can occur with is finiteness. So, the AgrFin technique to allow subject extraction is just a particular case of the general distributional property of Agr.

Going back to (115), suppose that the null Top head is also among the substantive heads (with finiteness, tense, aspect, etc.) which can combine in a similar way with an Agr specification. At first sight, this does not seem to help for our problem: in general, Agr is able to govern an element it agrees with, but an Agr specification in Top would not be in an agreement configuration with any member of the chain of t' (if anything, it could agree with the topicalized adverb, not what we need here). On the other hand more structure may be involved in this case. A fairly standard assumption on the structure of the IP system is that, when a substantive head X is endowed with Agr features, an independent Agr projection can crop up on top of it:

(116)

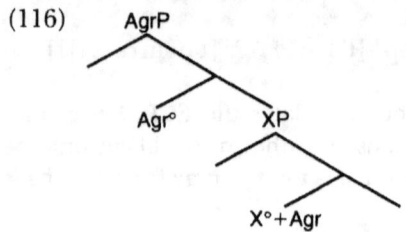

This extra projection has the function, among others, of making a specifier available for checking the Agr features with a phrase in the required local configuration. For instance, in Romance past participle agreement, the aspectual head hosting the participial morphology (with its Spec possibly filled by an aspectual adverbial) is assumed to license an Agr projection where agreement is checked with the object (with clitics and in other constructions preposing the object). Suppose this possibility exists for the C system as well.[31]

The structure of (111)b could then be:

(117) ... t''' qui [t'' Agr° [l'année prochaine Top°+Agr [t' Fin+Agr [t pourra ...]]]]

Here t' is licensed by the Agr features in Top, these features in turn are licensed in a configuration like (116) by the passage of the subject through the Spec of the Agr(Top) projection; t'' is licensed in turn by agreeing *qui*, etc. In this way, the Top phrase is successfully bypassed and the crucial effect of *qui* made compatible with our analysis of adverb preposing. Example (111)a remains excluded because we still have an offending trace, t'', in the equivalent of (117) with the non-agreeing form *que*.

We should now make sure that the proposed device does not overgenerate. In particular, we do not want to lose the important fact that CLLD blocks subject extraction in French (see Section 8): how can this fact be reconciled with the device that we have just introduced to allow the subject chain to bypass a TopP with adverb preposing? Clearly, adverb preposing and CLLD differ in that the latter but not the former blocks extraction of the subject; so, there must be at least one structural property distinguishing the two cases, and making the 'bypassing' device unavailable with CLLD.

A further facet of the problem is added by an observation due to Christopher Laenzlinger. In Section 4 we have discussed the fact that the resumptive clitic, obligatory when the dislocated element is the direct object, becomes optional when the dislocated element is a PP:

(118) Au Pape, personne n'oserait (lui) parler ainsi.
'To the Pope, nobody would dare to talk to him like that.'

Now, Laenzlinger has observed that the two cases pattern differently with respect to the licensing of a subject trace:

(119)a ?*Je me demande qui, au Pape, t oserait lui parler ainsi.
'I wonder who, to the Pope, would dare to talk to him like that.'
  b ?Je me demande qui, au Pape, t oserait parler ainsi.
'I wonder who, to the Pope, would dare to talk like that.'

Movement of the subject across a preposed PP is slightly marginal, but the presence of the resumptive clitic makes the structure detectably more degraded. The contrast in (119) immediately invites the conclusion that it is not appropriate to analyse these structures as involving an optional clitic; rather, we should postulate two distinct structural representations: simple PP preposing, which does not affect subject extraction (except a weak subjacency-like effect), and CLLD of the PP, which does. The first construction is the only device available to create a topic–comment configuration with a non-cliticizable PP (an adverbial PP, for instance), and it is not available with the object DP for the reason discussed in Section 4. Cliticizable PPs allow both devices, CLLD and simple preposing, and this gives rise to the apparent optionality of the clitic. In sum, argumental PP preposing in French patterns by and large with adverb preposing in not blocking subject extraction, and contrasts with CLLD (but see footnote 32).

How can we express this contrast? The structural difference between Spec and adjoined position suggests itself again: we continue to assume that the Topic in CLLD is in the Spec of a TopP, a structural layer that interferes with subject extraction in the way that we have discussed. It could be that the preposed PP is adjoined, hence in a configuration transparent to government relations. On the other hand, we do not want to lose the conceptual and empirical arguments which have lead us to postulate a TopP for every kind of preposing involving a Topic-comment interpretation. But we can use the Specifier/Adjunct distinction in a more subtle manner.

Suppose that the Top projection may optionally have a specifier (I assume this option to be the general case, unless special principles hold such as the extended clause of the EPP for AgrS). If Spec is not projected, the topicalized element is adjoined to TopP; I will assume that the adjunction configuration is adequate to satisfy the Top Criterion (Chomsky 1993 explicitly assumes that the adjoined position is a part of the checking environment of a head). So, a topic XP can be in one of the two following configurations, both sufficient to satisfy the Top Criterion:

(120)

(121)

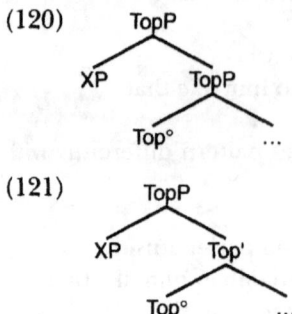

The analysis to be proposed will have the following form: simple preposing may involve structure (120), a configuration which can be bypassed by the subject chain. On the other hand, CLLD must involve configuration (121), which blocks the subject chain by determining an ECP violation on the subject trace.

Let us consider how this idea can be implemented. As for configuration (120), we continue to assume that it can be bypassed by the subject chain in the way suggested for (117): Top° may be endowed with Agr features, hence license a higher AgrP through whose specifier the subject can be moved.

(122)

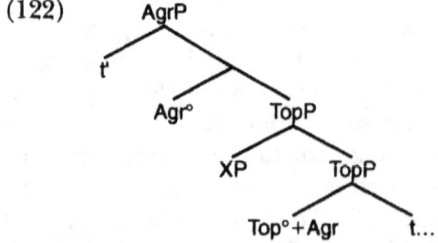

Now, suppose that this option is not available in case the topic phrase occupies the Spec of TopP, as in (121). A natural motivation for this may be that if an agreeing head has a specifier, it can't refrain from agreeing with it (see Chomsky 1995 for relevant discussion expressed in slightly different terms); so, in the equivalent of (122) but containing substructure (121) instead of (120):

(123)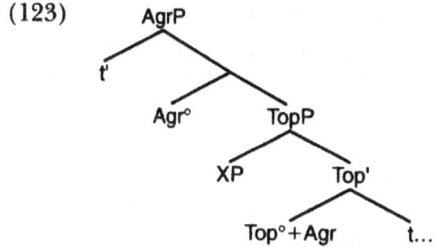

The presence of Agr features on Top could not have any beneficial effects on the subject trace, as the Agr specification would be taken up by the topic XP. On the other hand, if the agreeing head does not have a Spec, as in (122), the Agr features on Top are not taken up by XP and can be related to a licensing specifier (t') through the mediation of the independent Agr projection, thus bypassing the adjoined topic XP; the Agr features in Top° can then be construed with t' in (122), hence fulfilling the proper government requirement on t.

Then, in order to account for Laenzlinger's contrast, we have to make the assumption that CLLD must necessarily involve configuration (121), while (120) is restricted to simple preposing. Again, there seems to be a natural motivation for this. Simple preposing plausibly involves a single chain, from the position in which the PP is selected to the position in which it satisfies the Top Criterion (possibly through a number of intermediate steps). CLLD, on the other hand, appears to involve two arguments, the topic phrase and the clitic pronoun, hence two chains; as only one theta role is available for them, the construction must then involve some kind of chain composition (Chomsky 1986b) forming a single composed chain at LF. In other cases of chain composition (the *easy to please* construction for instance, or the case discussed in Chapter 3), both chains entering the composition operation must meet certain conditions, must be independently licensed in some sense. Suppose that a minimal licensing requirement is that each chain must be selected, must have one member in a selection configuration (specifier or complement) with a selecting head. So, the dislocated phrase must be in configuration (121), in the Spec of Top, in order to be available for composition with the clitic chain. But so, the dislocated phrase is incompatible with an agreement specification which could license a subject trace, hence CLLD, contrary to simple PP preposing, always blocks subject extraction.[32]

12 Conclusions

1 The complementizer system minimally consists of a specification of force, accessible to higher selection, and a specification of finiteness, selecting a finite (or non-finite) IP.

2   It may also consist of a topic and a focus field, expressing the topic-comment and focus-presupposition articulations, respectively. Within 'movement as last resort' guidelines, there is no free optional preposing and IP adjunction: all instances of preposing to the left periphery must be triggered by the satisfaction of a Criterion. Topic-comment and focus-presupposition articulations involve two instances of the larger family of A' Criteria. These guidelines naturally lead one to assume special Top and Foc heads and projections for topic and focus constructions.

3   In English topic-comment structures, the topic sits in the Spec of TopP and is locally construed with a null operator mediating the topic and the comment; in Romance, topic-comment is typically expressed by the CLLD construction. A number of properties differentiating topic and focus (compatibility with a resumptive clitic, sensitivity to WCO, . . .) follow from the assumption that only the latter involves genuine quantification, the former involving a non-quantificational A' dependency.

4   The global articulation of the topic-focus field in Italian involves a FocP surrounded by recursive TopPs, this configuration being in turn sandwiched in between the Force–Finiteness system, as in tree (41). The non-recursiveness of FocP may be a consequence of its own interpretive characteristics. Different types of elements fill different positions in (41). Straightforward distributional evidence suggests that relative pronouns are in the Spec of Force, while interrogative pronouns in main questions compete with focused phrases for the Spec of Focus. Complementizers such as *that*, *que*, etc. are in Force° (when the topic–focus field is activated), while prepositional complementizers in Romance are in Fin°.

5   In non-finite structures in which the Case properties of the subject are determined by an element of the C system, this element must be under Fin; if it was on a different head (and a lower head of the C system was activated), the required local configuration (head government) would not hold, under Relativized Minimality. So, many well-known adjacency effects are immediately explainable. The adjacency effect between a prepositional complementizer and PRO in Romance is amenable to the same explanation under a slight revision of the null Case approach to PRO.

6   Extraction across French CLLD gives rise to subject–object asymmetries, as is expected under the X-bar analysis of Top: in this construction, at least one trace member of the chain of the extracted subject inevitably violates the head government requirement of the ECP under Relativized Minimality, hence subject extraction is blocked.

7   Argumental topicalization in English also blocks subject extraction, as is expected. On the other hand, adverb preposing gives rise to an

apparently opposite effect: a *that*-t violation is alleviated by the intervention of a preposed adverbial (an anti-adjacency effect). Under our interpretation, the preposed adverbial licenses enough C structure to ensure the survival of the subject trace. More precisely, force and finiteness, normally expressed as a syncretic head, must split when the topic field is activated by a preposed adverbial. The lower Fin, endowed with Agr features, properly governs the subject trace, as in all successful cases of subject extraction. In the absence of the preposed adverbial, a principle of structural economy enforces the choice of a minimal C structure with the syncretic force–finiteness head, which gives rise to an ECP violation if the subject is extracted across *that*. The fact that negative preposing gives rise to anti-adjacency effects, as well as the surprising fact that I to C movement with negative preposing ceases to be obligatory exactly when the subject is extracted, receive a unitary analysis under the proposed framework.

8 The lack of anti-adjacency effects in French is related to the lack of affixal complementizers in this language. The fact that (the structure associated to) a preposed adverbial is nevertheless transparent to subject extraction is interpreted by sharpening the assumptions on the possible occurrence of Agr features: they can be associated to every substantive head, and an independent AgrP can be projected; this makes it possible for the subject chain to 'bypass' the TopP associated to the preposed adverbial. The apparently optional occurrence of the clitic in certain cases of CLLD is shown to determine the blocking of subject extraction, thus suggesting that two distinct constructions with different structural properties are signalled by the presence or absence of the clitic.

Notes

1 Preliminary versions of this paper were presented in class lectures at the University of Geneva (1993–94, 1994–95), at the 3ème Cycle Romand on Syntax and Pragmatics, Neuchâtel, January 1994, and in talks at the University of Florence, June 1994, April 1995 and at DIPSCO, Istituto San Raffaele, Milan, February 1995. This research is part of the FNRS project 11-33542.93. Thanks are due to Adriana Belletti, Guglielmo Cinque, Brent de Chenes, Grant Goodall, Maria Teresa Guasti, Liliane Haegeman, Ur Shlonsky and Michal Starke for helpful comments.

2 One class of attempts to integrate into the CP system more material than a single X-bar schema can contain involves the assumption that CP may undergo a limited recursion (Rizzi and Roberts 1989; McCloskey 1992; this volume, Chapter 9); other attempts directly involve the postulation of heads of the C system distinct from the lexical complementizers (Culicover's Polarity head 1992; Shlonsky's agreement in C 1994 (a development of Cardinaletti and Roberts' 1991 and Roberts' 1993a idea of AgrS recursion), as well as much recent literature on focus (see below)). See also Nakajima's (1993) explicit reference to a Split-C hypothesis. Work on V-2 languages has also envisaged the possibility of a structured C-system (e.g., Muller and Sternefeld 1993). Rein-

hart's (1981) earlier proposal for a multiple C structure was motivated by bounding theoretic considerations.

3 As for agreement, certain paradigms do not manifest any overt morphological form of subject agreement (English past and future, English subjunctive, the normal verbal paradigms in Mainland Scandinavian) and still co-occur with *that* type complementizers; conversely, inflected infinitives in Portuguese possess morphological marking for subject person agreement, and still do not co-occur with *that* type complementizers. As for tense, Latin infinitives express the present/past (and periphrastic future) distinction, and still we do not want to consider such forms finite (no nominative Case assigned to subjects, etc.). In spite of these and many other cases of dissociation, the generalization still holds that finite forms are more richly specified for features of the Tense-Person Agreement-Mood complex (the latter presumably being a unique characteristic of finiteness). See also George and Kornfilt (1981) for an earlier discussion of this notion.

4 If a finite verbal form must be selected by a C system bearing the feature [+fin], we account for the fact that direct selection of IP from a higher verb is limited to non-finite verbal forms. This is shown by the absence of exceptional Case marking with finite structures, as well as by the impossibility of Heavy NP Shift (under the analysis of Rizzi 1990a: 34–35):

i   a *I believe [him is smart].
    b *I believe [t is smart] every student who ...
cf.
ii a I believe [him to be smart].
    b T believe [t to be smart] every student who ...

ECM-like constructions appear to be possible with subjunctive complements in languages with missing or highly restricted non-finite verbal forms: see Guasti (1993), Turano (1993) on the Albanian causative construction, Rivero (1991) on Romanian. Perhaps V can directly select IPs with the minimal specification of finiteness that the language allows, which is subjunctive in languages basically lacking infinitives.

One should also observe that indirect questions can be finite or infinitival clauses, but not small clauses:

iii a John does not know of what he can be proud.
    b John does not know of what to be proud.
    c *John does not know of what proud.

Presumably, if the C system always starts from +-fin, it must select an IP on which the feature can be defined; as finiteness is a verbal feature, non-verbal small clauses cannot have a C system, hence they offer no structural slot in which a Wh element could be hosted, so that small clause questions are predicted not to exist. Another consequence of the lack of C system for small clauses is that there are no control argumental small clauses (*John wants PRO rich), if PRO is licensed by -fin, as is argued in Section 7 (the ill-formedness of iii could then also fall under this larger class of cases). Control small clauses appear to be possible in adverbial position in such expressions as *while PRO at home, if PRO in doubt*, etc., in which presumably the adverbial subordinator is different enough from the ordinary clausal C system to be consistent with a propositional content not specifiable for finiteness, and still capable of licensing PRO. The C-like particles introducing certain small clauses analysed in Starke (1994) could perhaps be treated as subordinators (in the sense of footnote 6) rather than as markers of -fin.

5 Things may be different in full V-2 languages, in which the inflected verb typically moves to C in certain tensed clauses; presumably in such cases one particular choice of +fin attracts the finite verb to have its finiteness feature checked by the tense specification on V. Even this case differs from verb movement to an inflectional head, though, in that V movement is not sanctioned by any special affix on the verb.

6 As for the assumption that the force head closes off the C system upwards, it should be noticed that operators do not always fill the highest Spec of the C system. For example, interrogative operators are placed in a lower Spec position in Italian, see Section 5. I will also continue to assume that in such cases the highest head of the C system expresses Force, as is required if selection takes place in a strictly local configuration; the actual position of the operator is determined by the relevant A' Criterion (on which see the next section), and may or may not coincide with the Spec/Force. An alternative is suggested by Bhatt and Yoon's (1991) distinction between type markers (our force heads) and simple subordinators, heads which make a clause available for (categorial) selection independently of its force. If this proposal is combined with ours, a tripartite system would result (subordinator, force, finiteness). This possible refinement will not be developed here.

7 Additional straightforward evidence for an articulated C system is provided by the existence, in some languages, of strings of complementizers occurring in a fixed order, e.g., the Danish case discussed in Vikner (1991).

8 Example (13)a becomes more acceptable if the Wh element is stressed; in that case, the structure receives a kind of echo interpretation (to express surprise or disbelief in reaction to somebody else's statement, for example). The contrast (12)–(13) was already noticed and discussed by Cinque (1979: 113–114), who argued on this basis for a different position of relative and interrogative pronouns (thanks to Guglielmo Cinque for drawing my attention to this reference); see also Grosu (1975) for an early discussion of the topic.

9 It should be noted here that my terminology is slightly different from Cinque's: he follows the traditional terminology in using the term 'topicalization' to refer to the English constructions (1) and (2); he then extends this term to cover the Italian construction (4). I try to avoid the term topicalization, and refer to (1) and (3) as topic (comment) structures and to (2) and (4) as focus (presupposition) structures.

10 The possibility of a topic–comment structures of the following kind in French:

   i Les gâteaux, j'adore.
      'The cakes, I love.'

   is presumably related to the capacity that a restricted class of verbs (*aimer, adorer, connaître,* ...) has of licensing *pro* in object position with a referential interpretation, a capacity shared by certain French prepositions (see Zribi-Hertz 1984 for discussion). With most verbs, the French paradigm is like the Italian one, with the clitic obligatorily present:

   ii Les gâteaux, je *(les) ai mangés à midi.
      'The cakes, I ate (them) at lunch.'

11 As for the focus construction in English (as in (2)), it could have the same syntax as the topic construction and involve a null operator, sitting in the Spec of the complement of Foc° (much as a cleft construction); on the other hand, the mediation of the null operator is not needed in this case under our assumptions, as the focal element should be able to directly bind a variable in

(2), on a par with the Italian equivalent (16)b. So, *a priori* we would expect a possible structural difference between Top and Foc in English as well. In fact, Culicover (1992) observes that Top induces subjacency-like effects (on which see also Rochemont 1989, Lasnik and Saito 1992 and references quoted there), while Foc does not (at least, not to the same extent), a contrast which suggests the existence of a structural difference between the two constructions. See also footnote 26 for the different behaviour of the two constructions with respect to anti-adjacency.

12 See Koster (1978: 199ff) for an analysis of this construction in Germanic. As for the possibility of non-focal topicalization in V-2 Germanic, we should either follow the reference quoted (see also Cardinaletti 1984) and assume that a null operator identified by a topic is always involved in such cases, or assume that V-2 endows the specifier of the head attracting the inflected verb of the capacity to license a null constant.

13 Of course, we want to be able to admit that the preposing of a PP can determine a genuine operator variable structure in some cases, e.g., in questions like *To whom did you talk?*, or a genuine null constant interpretation, e.g., in appositive relatives like *A man to whom I talked*, but here we could invoke a reconstruction process as in Chomsky (1993) and maintain that variable and null constant interpretation are restricted to DPs.

14 Moreover, the entire Spec of Top is moved out in (36), but this does not seem to be a well-formed option: in general, A' criteria cannot be satisfied 'in passing', that is, a Wh element cannot satisfy the Wh Criterion in an embedded C and then be moved to the main C system.

15 Other functional categories like T, Asp, D, Agr, do not admit free recursion, under economy of representations, because one specification is sufficient, hence maximal (but on limited Agr recursion in clitic constructions see Chapters 3 and 4). This does not apply to Top or Foc though, as there can be no constituents involved.

The proposed analysis of the impossibility of FocP recursion also correctly predicts that a FocP can be activated in a main clause i, in an embedded clause ii, but not in both simultaneously, iii:

i A GIANNI ho detto t che dovremmo leggere il tuo libro.
   'TO GIANNI I said that we should read your book.'
ii Ho detto a Gianni che IL TUO LIBRO dovremmo leggere.
    'I said to Gianni that YOUR BOOK we should read.'
iii *A GIANNI ho detto che IL TUO LIBRO dovremmo leggere.
    'TO GIANNI I said that YOUR BOOK we should read.'

Example iii is excluded because the embedded clause is part of the presupposition of the main Foc, hence it cannot contain a Foc position. Predictably, Topic–comment structures of the CLLD kind are possible in main and embedded clauses simultaneously:

iv A Gianni, gli ho detto che il tuo libro, lo dovremmo leggere.
    'To Gianni, I said to him that your book, we should read it.'

16 This is only a first approximation: on the position of relative operators, see the detailed discussion of Bianchi (1995), conducted within the guidelines of Kayne (1994) and based in part on a previous version of the present article, an analysis which I will not be able to discuss here.

17 The location of the Foc feature may vary across languages, as many languages (e.g., Hungarian) require I to C movement with left-peripheral focalization. In

this case, the lower Top position of (41) is not activated (its presence would block I to Foc movement), exactly as in main questions in Italian. Perhaps a reflex of this UG option is found in the fact that some speakers of Italian find the activation of the lower TopP (e.g., in (37)b) marginal if compared to the activation of the higher TopP (as in (37)d). For such speakers, the Foc feature may preferentially be located in the inflectional system, whence the preferred application of I to C with focus. Alternatively, these speakers may be (more) sensitive to a weak subjacency-like effect induced by the lower TopP on the movement of the focal element: cf. the marginality detected by speakers of French in examples like (66)a.

18 As we have already seen (example (14), repeated here) a topic preceding the Wh element is fully acceptable, and a topic following the Wh element is marginal in embedded questions:

i a Mi domando, il premio Nobel, a chi lo potrebbero dare.
'I wonder, the Nobel Prize, to whom they could give it.'
b ?Mi domando a chi, il premio Nobel, lo potrebbero dare.
'I wonder to whom, the Nobel Prize, they could give it.'

The marginal acceptability of the latter is not surprising, as the obligatoriness of I to C movement is weakened in embedded questions (see Chapter 9). The fact that the Wh element is marginally compatible with an embedded focalized element in embedded questions, in clear contrast with main questions, may suggest that the Wh element can sit in an independent position distinct from Spec/Foc in embedded questions.

ii a ?Mi domando A GIANNI che cosa abbiano detto (, non a Piero).
'I wonder TO GIANNI what they said (, not to Piero).'
b *A GIANNI che cosa hanno detto (, non a Piero)?
'TO GIANNI what did they say (, not to Piero)?'

The properties of this position, as well as of the other special positions filled by certain Wh elements (*perché* (why) and Wh with lexical restriction: Chapter 9, footnote 16; exclamative Wh elements: Benincà 1995) or of the other kinds of C elements in different Romance varieties discussed in Poletto 1993, Bianchi 1995 and references cited there, could lead to further extensions of the maximal structure of C along lines that will not be investigated here.

19 McCloskey (1992: 15) points out that 'external' preposing of a whole adverbial clause is marginally possible in some cases:

i ?He promised, when he got home, that he would cook dinner for the children.

Here one could assume, with McCloskey, that this case involves genuine CP recursion, as is particularly plausible for cases in which *that* occurs twice (McCloskey 1992, footnote 12):

ii She maintained that when they arrived that they should be welcomed.

I will leave open here the question of why this option seems to be restricted to full adverbial clauses.

20 If Case Theory does not appeal to the notion of head government, as in the system of Chomsky (1993), some other notion of locality will be needed to express the fact that the intervening X-bar structure in (53) disrupts the

required Case configuration. For instance, in a move feature analysis following Chomsky (1995), one could assume that the Case features on *John* cannot reach *for* at LF because of the intervention of Top.

It should be noticed that the environment for a potential violation of Case theory of the kind illustrated in (53) may simply not arise here: in fact, preposing of an element to a position external to *for* does not seem to give rise to an acceptable structure either (*I would very much prefer, this book, for you to read immediately*), so one seems to be lead to conclude that *for* always expresses force and finiteness syncretically (in the sense of Section 9), and therefore no topic–focus field can be activated with this choice of C. In this respect, *for* is different from the infinitival complementizer *di* in Italian, which is compatible with an external topic (see Section 7).

21 The impossibility of (57)b is sharper than in the corresponding structure with a lexical subject NP presumably because *egli*, as a weak pronoun (Cardinaletti and Starke 1994), strongly disallows being left in a position lower than the highest subject position.

22 Actually, a weaker assumption is sufficient: Top does not allow I to move through it to Force, i.e., there is no Top to Force movement (direct movement of I to Force being barred by RM in (60)).

It should be noticed that, even in main questions like (58)b, it is not obvious that I to C movement stops at Fin: if it is the case in general that the Wh element sits in the Spec of focus in main questions (see Section 5), then the auxiliary should reach Foc° in order to satisfy the Wh Criterion, a position that may be followed by a TopP if structure (41) is transposed to English. So, the HMC analysis seems to be needed to exclude (58)b on a par with (59)b.

23 This analysis can be straightforwardly expressed within Chomsky's (1995) move features approach, which comes very close to reintroducing the head government relation in Case Theory. Alternatively, if one assumes that C systems can be normally endowed with concrete or abstract Agr features (Rizzi 1990a; Haegeman 1992; Shlonsky 1994, etc.) one could think that it is the nonfinite Agr in the C system which licenses PRO in a Spec-head configuration.

24 Speakers of French are reluctant to accept CLLD with infinitives. Nevertheless, a detectable contrast exists between control and raising (C. Laenzlinger, personal communication):

i ??Je pense, ton livre, pouvoir le comprendre.
'I think, your book, to be able to understand it.'
ii *Marie semble, ton livre, pouvoir le comprendre.
'Marie seems, your book, to be able to understand it.'

25 This way of satisfying the ECP on t' by moving the head agreeing with it to the next higher head position seems to be in contrast with the fact that, in an analogous configuration, I to C movement does not license a subject trace (Rizzi 1990a: 40; Chapter 9, and the following section). Still, we can express the difference between the two cases by observing that, with I to C, a governing head (I) moves to a head of a different categorial type (C), whereas in the structure derived from (93), a head of the C system (Fin) moves to another head of the C system (Top) from where it can properly govern t', if we intend proper government as government within a projection of the same categorial type (slightly modifying Rizzi 1990a: 32). In order to express this distinction we must now crucially appeal to the assumption (see Section 1) that the I and the C systems are distinct.

Postulating head movement of Fin° solves the technical problem raised by Culicover (1993) on the status of the trace licensing agreement in C. The assumed head movement is not simply a 'local' technical solution, as it crucially contributes to the explanation of the difference between English and French with respect to the anti-adjacency effect (Section 11).

The assumption that Fin can move to Top is not inconsistent with the assumption that an intervening Top blocks (further) movement of a lower head to Force (Section 6): Top may be able to host a lower head without being itself movable to a higher head position (see footnote 22).

26 Here it becomes crucial to assume that Op goes to Fin; this hypothesis is supported by the fact that, if argument topicalization and adverb preposing take place in the same structure, the preferred order is with the topicalized argument internal (i is more acceptable than ii):

i Around Christmas, this book, you should buy.
ii This book, around Christmas, you should buy.

This order is expected if Op goes to Spec of Fin, and if only argument topicalization, not adverbial PP preposing, involves the null operator. On the other hand, ii is not totally excluded; moreover, if the argumental topic and the preposed adverbial appear in that order, there seems to be a detectable anti-adjacency effect (even though the judgement is difficult):

iii This is the man who I think that, this book, around Christmas, should buy.

All this then suggests the following interpretation: the null Op involved in argumental topicalization normally goes to Spec/fin; this explains the preferred order of i over ii and the lack of anti-adjacency effects with argumental topicalization (as per the discussion in the text); but Op can survive in a higher position as a marked possibility if the Top position immediately higher than Fin is taken up, as is shown by the marginal possibility of the order in ii. In this case, if the subject is extracted an anti-adjacency effect is expected, and indeed it seems to exist in structures like iii (with all the caveats justified by the complexity of this kind of judgement).

The idea that the null operator is responsible for the lack of anti-adjacency effects with argumental topicalization in English has one additional interesting consequence. Ian Roberts (personal communication) observes that structures like (96), excluded with the topic intonation on the preposed object, improve if the preposed object bears focal stress. Culicover (1993, footnote 1), observes the same improvement effect of focal stress with preposed argumental PPs. The existence of anti-adjacency effects with English focalization is expected, under our analysis, if focalization, contrary to (English) topicalization, does not involve a null operator, as suggested in footnote 11 (if no null operator is involved in the equivalent of (96), Fin can be endowed with Agr features licensed by the passage of the subject in its Spec, and capable of licensing the subject trace, etc.). So, there are two significant, if subtle, differences between English topicalization and focalization with respect to subjacency (see footnote 11) and anti-adjacency effects which may both be related to the absence of a null operator in the second construction. See also de Chenes (1995) for discussion of other factors alleviating *that*-t violations.

27 I remain agnostic here as to the question of whether the theory should contain an explicit statement of relative strength, or this selective interaction just follows intrinsically from the fact that selectional constraints are directly invoked in the structure building process, where (98) is operative, while ECP applies on representations that are already formed.

28 The proposed analysis assumes that force and finiteness can be expressed in a single head, and that this option is enforced by economy unless the activation

of the topic–focus field makes it non-viable. Alternatively, one could consider the possibility that the force–finiteness is 'agglutinative' as many other syntactic subsystems seem to be, hence it always involves two distinct heads:

i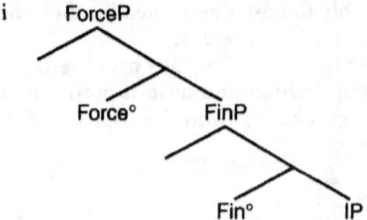

The analysis can then be rephrased in the following form: in i the representation can involve a single item from the functional lexicon (*that* or *0*), generated under Fin and moved to Force to check the force features. If the Top-Foc field is activated (assuming that Fin° would not be allowed to move through the heads of the Top-Foc field all the way up to Force), two distinct items from the functional lexicon are needed (*that* for force and *0* for finiteness), a possibility which gives rise to the anti-adjacency effects in the way we have discussed. This possibility is not freely available due to Economy, whence the lack of free *that*-t violations.

29 The slight improvement that some speakers find in (111)a, compared to (110)a, could be related to the possibility of not leaving a trace in the Spec of an agreeing Fin. Then there would be no ECP violation, at the price of leaving in the structure a non-licensed occurrence of Agr features, a violation which may be felt by these speakers as slightly less severe than an ECP violation.

30 For example, it could be that adverb preposing, contrary to our assumptions so far, does not necessarily involve an independent TopP: one could consider the possibility that Fin itself can be endowed with Top features, and a preposed adverbial can satisfy the Top Criterion by adjoining to the FinP. If this alternative is adopted, the analysis of anti-adjacency would become less straightforward than in Section 9: it should express the fact that a syncretic force + fin head cannot bear the required Top features, so that the split is required when a preposed adverb is to be integrated, with the consequence of determining anti-adjacency effects in English along the lines indicated in Section 9. See footnote 32 below for potential empirical support for the alternative proposed in this footnote.

31 We do not take a position here on whether the double structure (116) is compulsory whenever a substantive head is endowed with Agr features, or it is simply an option, which is taken just in case an extra specifier is needed to license the Agr features. In the latter case, everything that has been said so far can be left unchanged; in the former, all the structures involving Agr features associated to a substantive head should involve the extra Agr layer, with no significant additional modification of the analysis.

32 Adverbial PP preposing in French still differs from argument PP preposing in a subtle way: the latter, but not the former, determines a weak subjacency-like effect (see (119)b) when something is extracted; this suggests that the two cases should not be fully assimilated. One possibility is to restrict the adjunction analysis proposed in the text (adjunction to the TopP) to argumental PP preposing, and go back to the proposal of footnote 30 for adverbial PP preposing (direct adjunction to a FinP endowed with Top features); so, both adverbial and argumental preposed PPs can be bypassed by the subject chain (as, in both cases, the preposed element can sit in an adjoined position, to FinP and

TopP, respectively), but only the latter involves an autonomous TopP, which may be deemed responsible for the weak subjacency effect. CLLD cannot be bypassed by the subject chain for the reason discussed in the text, and determines a weak subjacency effect on non-subject extraction (cf. (66)a, etc.) because a TopP is involved.

The tripartite system of Romance (CLLD, argument PP preposing, adjunct PP preposing) appears to reduce, in English, to the bifurcation between argument topicalization (of both DPs and PPs) and adverbial PP preposing, the first blocking subject chains and determining subjacency-like effects on non-subject extraction, the second not blocking subject chains (in fact, determining anti-adjacency effects) nor determining subjacency-like effects for non-subject extraction. For the first case, we continue to assume the null operator construction, which is inconsistent with the 'bypassing' device, as we have seen. For the second, we may also adopt the proposal of footnote 30. What appears to be missing in English is the option of adjoining a preposed argumental PP to TopP, an option apparently blocked by the generalized availability of the null operator structure for all cases of argumental topicalization in this language.

Part IV
Acquisition

11 Early null subjects and root null subjects*

1 Introduction

Around the age of two, children freely drop subjects, irrespective of whether or not the target language is a Null Subject Language. For instance, the phenomenon is typically found in the acquisition of English and French:

(1) a ___ want more.
    b ___ find Giorgie.
    c ___ is broken. (Hyams 1986)
(2) a ___ boit café.
    b ___ fait un autre.
    c ___ est tombé. (Pierce 1989)

Much recent work on the acquisition of English provides robust evidence for a selective drop of subjects: by and large, learners freely drop subjects, not obligatory objects (Valian 1991; Wang et al. 1991; Hyams and Wexler 1993). So, the early null subject is not trivially amenable to some global strategy of structural reduction.

Hyams (1986) interpreted this state of affairs in terms of the Null Subject Parameter (Rizzi 1982; Jaeggli and Safir 1989; Chapter 2, this volume): the initial setting is the null subject value. Learners of English, French, etc. have to reset the parameter on the basis of experience, and this is normally done a few months after the second birthday. I would like to retain of Hyams' seminal approach the idea that the early null subject

---

* Versions of this paper at different stages of elaboration were presented at the GLOW Workshop *The Development of Government and Inflection* (Leiden, March 28, 1991), at the symposium *Syntactic Theory and First Language Acquisition: Cross Linguistic Perspectives* (Cornell, April 25, 1992), at the Certificat de spécialisation of the University of Geneva and at the Language Acquisition Seminar of SISSA, Trieste. I am grateful to the audiences of these events and to Adriana Belletti, Guglielmo Cinque, Marc-Ariel Friedemann, Teresa Guasti, Liliane Haegeman and an anonymous reviewer for helpful comments and suggestions.

stage manifests a genuine grammatical option and cannot be reduced to extragrammatical factors (see Hyams and Wexler 1993 for a detailed discussion of this issue). On the other hand, a number of structural properties of the early null subjects are emerging which suggest that this phenomenon is quite different from the drop of subjects in an adult grammatical system like Italian.

In the first part of this chapter, I would like to discuss some such properties and identify the major configurational constraint: by and large, the early null subject is possible in the first position of the structure, that is, in the specifier of the root. I will then suggest that such a configurational constraint is not specific to transitional systems in acquisition: instances of root null subjects can be found in adult grammatical systems, hence they represent a genuine option of Universal Grammar. Various questions are raised by the existence of root null subjects in acquisition, in special registers, and in normal adult languages: what is the status of the null element involved? How is it licensed and identified? How does it differ from a discourse-bound null operator (Huang 1984)? Why is this option lost in the course of the acquisition of English and many other languages? I will try to provide a partial answer to these questions by developing an analysis of root null subjects based on the typology of null elements proposed in Lasnik and Stowell (1991).

2 Some structural properties of early null subjects

Valian (1991: 39) points out that null subjects occur very rarely after a preposed Wh element in her corpus (natural production from 21 learners of English ranging from 1;10 to 2;8): only 9 null subjects out of 552 Wh questions in which the Wh element is not a subject; i.e., (3)b does not occur as a regular variant of (3)a:

(3)a Where daddy go?
   b Where go?

This is a significant and surprising finding, especially in view of the fact that a null subject in this environment is perfectly acceptable in a Null subject language (e.g., in Italian: *Dove va?* 'Where (he) goes?'; *Cosa fai?* 'What (you) do?', etc.).

As Valian's observation is quite isolated in the acquisition literature, I tried to find confirmation elsewhere. A preliminary check of the standard Brown (1973) corpora, available through CHILDES (see MacWhinney and Snow 1985) confirms the observed tendency (thanks to Rick Kazman for technical help). In the whole of Eve's corpus (20 recordings from 1;6 to 2;4) I counted 12 null subjects out of 191 Wh questions with a non-subject Wh element. Roeper (1991), addressing the issue, lists a number of examples with null subjects following a Wh element from the Adam corpus. Such cases indeed exist, but they are quite limited: if we look at the first 10 files of the Adam corpus, in which null subjects in declaratives are well over 50% (57% according to Bloom 1990; see also Hyams and Wexler 1993), we find 21 cases of null subjects out of 158 questions with non-subject Wh elements. The proportion of null subjects in this environment thus drops to a percentage (13%) close to the one of null objects in the same corpus (8% according to Bloom 1990) (but see Rizzi 1998 for an important refinement based on Roeper and Rohrbacher (1994)).[1]

Another relevant element is provided by the apparent existence of Wh questions without movement in early English. The Adam corpus presents quite a few cases of Wh *in situ*:

(4)a They are for who? (Adam 25)
   b It's a what? (Adam 26)
   c He may do what to me? (Adam 33)

The majority of these cases (22 out of 34) involve a null subject; here is a sample:

(5)a see what bear? (Adam 03)
   b and do what? (Adam 25)
   c use dat for what? (Adam 25)
   d have what? (Adam 31)
   e doing what? (Adam 35)
   f cutting what? (Adam 35)
   g close what? (Adam 36)
   h fighting what? (Adam 36)
   i sing what song? (Adam 38)

The existence of a consistent *in situ* strategy in early English is, of course, far from being established by this small sample of examples (but see Radford 1990 and Whitman, Lee and Lust 1991 for supporting evidence and discussion). If confirmed, it would raise various interesting questions, as Wh *in situ* is not a property of the target language (apart from echo-questions): why does it arise? How and when is it delearned? Let me put these questions aside for the moment.[2]

Let us simply note the high proportion of null subjects with *in situ* questions, which suggests that early null subjects are not affected by the status of the sentence as a question, but by the preposing of the Wh element.

Another crucial property of the early null subject is that it is limited to main clauses. Roeper and Weissenborn (1990) point out that no cases of null subjects are produced by the learner of English in the first finite subordinate clauses. This observation is confirmed by Valian (1991) who found no case of null subject out of the 123 examples of tensed subordinate clauses of her corpus. One could observe that this state of affairs may not be very significant for the analysis of the structural properties of early null subjects: after all it could be that the child starts producing finite subordinate clauses after the end of the null subject stage. But this interpretation is strongly disfavoured by the fact that we also find occasional cases in which a pronominal subject is dropped in the main clause and not in the embedded clause in the same utterance, or anyhow in immediate succession, for example:

(6)a ___ went in the basement # that what we do # after supper.   (Eve 19)
  b ___ know what I maked.   (Adam 31)

Again, this observation invites a systematic verification; if confirmed on a larger scale, it strongly supports the hypothesis of a structural incompatibility between early null subjects and embedding, rather than a simple succession of acquisition stages.[3]

As in the previous case, this is quite different from what we find in a null subject language of the Italian type, in which a zero subject pronoun is equally possible in main and embedded subject position:[4]

(7) ___ so che cosa ___ hai detto.
  '(I) know what (you) said.'

In conclusion, the early null subjects produced by learners of English appear to obey a strong distributional constraint: their natural environment is the first position of the structure, they tend not to appear after a preposed element and they do not appear in embedded clauses, two properties which are quite different from what we find in adult null subject languages.

What happens in the acquisition of Italian? Does the Italian learner around the age of two produce null subjects with the structural properties of early English? Or does she already conform to the properties of adult Italian? Even small production samples strongly suggest an early convergence to the properties of adult Italian: we typically find examples like the following, with a null subject following a preposed Wh element (examples taken from the Martina corpus, see Cipriani et al. 1992, available on CHILDES (thanks to T. Guasti for technical help)):

(8)a Ov'è?   (1;8)
      'Where is?'
  b Cos'è?   (1;10)
      'What is?'
  c Che voi?   (2;3)
      'What (you) want?'
  d Pecché piangi?   (2;3)
      'Why (you) cry?'

e Quetto cosa fa? (2;5)
   'This what does?'

In the Martina corpus (13 recordings roughly each month from 1;7 to 2;7), we find that, out of 35 questions with a non-subject Wh element, 20 have a null pronominal subject.

Even though the database is limited, the indication is quite clear: early null subjects in the acquisition of Italian are not restricted to the first position; in this respect, the early system is just like adult Italian. The emerging picture thus seems to support the hypothesis of an early fixation of the Null Subject Parameter: around the age of two, learners of English and Italian have already converged to the values of the parameter expressed by the adult languages. The early null subject manifested in the acquisition of English is a different phenomenon, structurally characterized by the fact that it is limited to the initial position, the specifier of the root.[5]

The next question I want to ask is whether such a root null subject is a special property of transitional systems in acquisition, or it is actually found in some adult grammatical systems, i.e., it corresponds to a genuine option of Universal Grammar.

3 Subject drop in diaries

The closest analogue to the observed properties of the Early Null Subject is found in certain abbreviated varieties of English and other languages. Haegeman (1990) notices the following cluster of properties in the register of diaries:

1 Subjects can be freely dropped even if the standard register of the language does not allow this, for example, in English and French; dropped subjects are not necessarily first person, as the French example shows:

(9) A very sensible day yesterday. ___ saw no-one. ___ took the bus to Southwark Bridge.
    ___ walked along Thames Street . . .
                          (Virginia Woolf, *Diary*, Vol. 5, 1936–41, pp. 203–4)
(10)a ___ m'accompagne au Mercure, puis à la gare . . .
       (he) takes me to Mercure, then to the station . . .
    b ___ s'est donné souvent l'illusion de l'amour . . .
       (he) often gave himself the illusion of love . . .
    c ___ me demande si . . . je lui eus montré les notes . . .
       (I) ask myself if . . . I would have shown him the notes.
       (Paul Léautaud, *Le Fléau*, Journal Particulier, 1917–1930, pp. 60–70)

Notice that the second and third line of the French example also show that a structurally represented null subject must be postulated, otherwise the anaphoric clitic would not be bound.

2   The subject can't be dropped after a preposed element:

(11)a ___ was so stupid!
    b *How stupid ___ was!

3   Main subjects can be dropped, embedded subjects can't (see also the third line of (10)):

(12)a ___ can't find the letter that I need.
    b *I can't find the letter that ___ need.

4   Subjects can be dropped, objects can't:

(13)a ___ saw her at the party.
    b *She saw ___ at the party.

So, on the basis of Haegeman's (1990) description, subject drop in diaries appears to be ruled by the same structural constraints which characterize early null subjects. Haegeman notices that the root character of subject drop suggests a topic drop type analysis, involving a discourse bound null operator in the matrix Spec of C binding a variable in subject position. Under such an analysis, the null operator would be in competition with an overt preposed operator, whence the ungrammaticality of (11)b, etc. But she also notices that under a topic drop analysis the subject–object asymmetry (13) is unexpected: why couldn't the null operator bind a variable in object position? Of course, the same difficulty arises for an unqualified topic drop analysis of the early null subject. On the other hand, the structural conditions on root null subjects and topic drop seem close enough to invite a detailed comparison.

4 Topic drop

In colloquial German (as well as in most V-2 Germanic varieties), it is possible to drop a main clause subject in the Spec of C in a V-2 configuration ((14)a). The option disappears in clause internal position, that is, when the Spec of C is filled by a preposed element, as in (14)b, and in embedded clauses, no matter whether V-2 ((14)c) or not ((14)d):

(14)a (Ich) habe es gestern gekauft.
        '(I) have it yesterday bought.'
     b Wann hat *(er) angerufen?
        'When has he telephoned?'

c Hans glaubt *(ich) habe es gestern gekauft.
 'Hans believes I have it yesterday bought.'
d Hans glaubt dass *(ich) es gestern gekauft habe.
 'Hans believes that I it yesterday bought have.'

We thus seem to find the same structural restrictions operative on the early null subject. Still, the dropping of arguments extends to preposed objects in colloquial German:

(15) (Das) habe ich gestern gekauft.
 'This have I yesterday bought.'

This apparent subject–object symmetry led researchers to analyse the construction as involving topic drop (Ross 1982), or, in current terms, movement of a discourse-bound null operator to the Spec of the root CP (Huang 1984), from where it could bind a variable in subject or object position. Under this analysis, (14)a and (15) would have the following parallel representations:

(16)a [OP habe [t es gestern gekauft]]
 b [OP habe [ich t gestern gekauft]]

If this analysis was correct, the analogy with our early null subjects would be partial at best. But Cardinaletti (1990) has pointed out that there remains an important asymmetry between subject and object drop: subject drop can involve pronouns with any person specification, provided that the dropped element is sufficiently salient in the context, whereas object drop is restricted to third person. For instance, a second person object pronoun can't be dropped even in the most favourable case of contextual saliency, question–answer pairs:

(17)a Hast du mich gesehen?
 'Have you me seen?'
 b Dich habe ich nicht gesehen.
 'You have I not seen.'
 c *___ habe ich nicht gesehen.
 '(You) have I not seen.'

If, in general, operators are intrinsically marked for third person (as is the case for interrogative operators, see below) the limitations on the object case follow from the structural analysis (16)b; but then, Cardinaletti concludes, subject drop should not involve a null operator, and representation (16)a should be revised. If (14) and (15) are to be dissociated as in Cardinaletti's proposal, then it becomes more plausible to partially assimilate the former case to the early English system.[6]

If the root null subject does not involve a discourse bound null operator, we are then left with the questions: what is its status with respect to the typology of null elements? How can we express its minimal differences with respect to the null operator constructions? None of the currently assumed *ec*s seems to have the right intersection of formal and interpretive properties.

5 Null constants

A recent proposal by Lasnik and Stowell (1991), henceforth L&S, offers a new option which is worth exploring. In the context of a general discussion of the scope of Weak Crossover (WCO) effects, they observe that certain null operator constructions (and also some A' dependencies involving overt operators, such as appositive relatives) differ significantly at the interpretive level from ordinary operator variable constructions, such as questions:

(18) a John wonders who to please t.
     b John is easy OP to please t.

The former involves quantification ranging over a possibly non-singleton set, in the latter the null element never ranges over a non-singleton set; rather, it has its reference fixed to that of the antecedent. This interpretive difference correlates to the sensitivity to the WCO effect: while both kinds of A' binding manifest sensitivity to Strong Crossover (SCO):

(19) a *Who$_i$ did you get him$_i$ to talk to t$_i$?
     b *John$_i$ is easy for us OP$_i$ to get him$_i$ to talk to t$_i$.

Only the former manifests WCO effects:

(20) a *Who$_i$ did you get his$_i$ mother to talk to t$_i$?
     b John$_i$ is easy for us OP$_i$ to get his$_i$ mother to talk to t$_i$.

L&S introduce a split between the two types of A' bound traces in accordance with the semantic intuition. Only the trace bound by a genuine quantifier is a variable; the trace bound by the non-quantificational empty operator is not. Instead, it is a non-variable R-expression to be assimilated to a null epithet or, more generally, to a null definite description. In order to properly distinguish it from the variable, we will call this new type of null element 'the null constant' (*nc*, terminological suggestion due to Cornelia Hamann). L&S then claim that WCO is a property of variables, hence null operator constructions, not involving variables, are exempted from it. On the other hand, both kinds of A' bound traces are R-expressions: as Principle C is a property of all R-expressions, the homogeneous behaviour w.r.t. SCO is accounted for.

How is the new type of *ec* to be characterized? As a straightforward alternative to L&S's functional definition, let me simply propose that the feature ±v(ariable) combines with the familiar features ±a, ±p, thus giving rise to 8 cases:

(21) 1 +a+p+v = *
     2 +a+p−v = PRO
     3 +a−p+v = *
     4 +a−p−v = NP−t
     5 −a+p+v = pro(res)
     6 −a+p−v = pro
     7 −a−p+v = vbl
     8 −a−p−v = nc

Of these, 1 and 3 are presumably excluded by the inherent incompatibility of +a (requiring A-binding) and +v (requiring A'-binding): a single element cannot simultaneously belong to the A and A' system.[7]

The remaining six combinations are all attested. Combination 2, 4, 6 and 7 are the familiar types; 5 is pro used as a resumptive pronoun (e.g., as in Rizzi 1982, Chapter 2; Georgopoulos 1991); and 8 is the null constant, a non-variable R-expression.

We are now left with the question: what forces A' binding of the null constant by a null operator? That is, as overt epithets and other definite descriptions can freely occur and directly pick up their referent in discourse, why can't the null variant do the same?

(22) I tried to visit John last week, but I was unable to persuade the guy / *ec to see me.

L&S's answer is: the null definite description, as all null elements, must satisfy an identification requirement which is fulfilled by the null operator. We can make this suggestion precise by assuming that the specific identification requirement on *nc* is the same one that holds for variables and other types of traces, i.e., the identification component of the ECP (in the sense of Rizzi 1990a), which holds for all non-pronominal empty categories:

(23) ECP (Identification): *ec* [−p] must be chain-connected to an antecedent,

where the antecedent can be an A or A' (or, irrelevantly here, X°) position, depending on the kind of chain.[8]

In sum, an *ec* [−a, −p] can be [±v]. If it is [+v] it is a variable and must satisfy (23) by being chain connected to a genuine quantifier (for example, a question operator), assigning it a range. If it is [−v] it is a null constant, it must still be chain connected to an A' element to satisfy (23) (it could not be A-bound, as it is an R-expression), but by a non-quantificational A' element, typically a null operator (see also Chapter 10). The other combinations (a variable bound by a non-quantificational operator, a null constant bound by a quantificational operator) are excluded by the appropriate version of the Bijection Principle, the principle barring vacuous quantification, or whatever principle requires quantifiers to bind variables and variables to be bound by quantifiers (Koopman and Sportiche 1982; Chomsky 1986a). Moreover, as the null constant is an R-expression, chain-connection to an element in A-position is barred by Principle C. A non-quantificational operator thus remains as the only possible identifier of the null constant.[9]

6 Discourse-identified null elements revisited

L&S's proposal directly refers to cases of sentence-bound null operator constructions (*easy to please*, parasitic gaps, etc.), but can be immediately extended to the empty elements bound by discourse, identified null operators. In fact, if we apply L&S's diagnostic criterion for null constants, the *ec* bound by a discourse-identified null operator in German falls into this class: it is sensitive to SCO, but not to WCO:

(24) a *Den Hans$_i$ hat er$_i$ t$_i$ gesehen.
       'Hans has he seen.'
     b *Op$_i$ hat er$_i$ t$_i$ gesehen.
(25) a Den Hans$_i$ hat [sein$_i$ Vater] t$_i$ gesehen.
       'Hans has his father seen.'
     b OP$_i$ hat [sein$_i$ Vater] t$_i$ gesehen.

We can now go back to Cardinaletti's (1990) asymmetry between the local subject case and all the other cases. In all the other cases, such as the object case, the null constant (*nc*) is bound by a null OP, which as such has intrinsic features of third person singular.

(26) [OP hat [er schon *nc* gesehen]] (ihn, es, *mich, *dich, ...)

What about the local subject case? If the representation of (27) was (28), it would be hard to distinguish the two cases:

(27) ___ habe es schon gesehen.
(28) [OP habe [*nc* es schon gesehen]]

One could not, for instance, simply claim that (27) can have a first person interpretation because the inflection endows OP with such features: if I had this capacity, what could exclude the possibility of non-third-person question operators in the appropriate contexts?[10]

(29) *Chi (di voi) sapete la risposta?
'Who (among you) know+3pl the answer?'

But there is a possible alternative representation for (27). It has been repeatedly noticed that the Spec of C position in V-2 languages can behave as an A position when the local subject is moved to it (with the trace in spec IP behaving like an NP-t: Holmberg 1986; Taraldsen 1986; Rizzi 1991). Suppose then that (27) allows a representation with the null constant in the Spec of C, binding an NP-t in the Spec of IP, and involving no null OP at all:

(30) [nc habe [t es schon gesehen]]

As the intrinsic limitation to third person is specific to operators, there is no reason to expect it in (30). Still (30) should violate the identification requirement of the ECP, as the null constant lacks a clause-internal identifier. Can (30) be made consistent with the ECP? A natural possibility is offered by an extension of an idea proposed by Chomsky (1986a) in the context of the theory of binding. According to Chomsky's proposal, the governing category of an element is the minimal domain with certain characteristics in which the binding requirements of the element are satisfiable in principle (see also Chapter 6 for discussion). Suppose that we extend and adapt this idea to the ECP by adding the following specification to (23):

(31) ... if it can.

So, an empty element must be identified in the way indicated by (23) if it can, that is, if there is a potential identifier, a c-commanding maximal projection (possibly, a c-commanding $X°$ for an empty head). This has the effect of exempting from the identification requirement the specifier of the root, the highest position of the structure, the position that c-commands everything and is not c-commanded by anything. The specifier of the root then is the only position in which an empty element can fail to have a clause internal identification, and is available for discourse identification. Under this interpretation of (23), an unbound null constant can survive in the Spec of the root in structures like (30), and receive its referential value in discourse.[11]

7 Cross-linguistic variation and developmental sequence

It is now natural to extend the proposed null constant analysis to all the observed cases of root null subjects, including the early null subject. But why is the option lost in adult standard English and French, for instance? The basic idea that I would like to develop to deal with both the cross-linguistic variation and the observed developmental sequence is that the possibility of a root null subject can arise when the Spec of the root is an A-position, and is lost in the varieties in which the Spec of the root is an A' position, not a suitable host for the null constant. Underlying this approach is the idea that the feature system ±a, ±p, (and ±v) defines empty elements in A-position: null elements belonging to the A' system are not classified by this feature system, so the null constant (on a par with the variable, PRO, the NP-t, etc.) simply cannot be defined in an A' position.

Let us start from a natural assumption on the nature of the root category. Following Stowell (1981), Radford (1988) and many others, I will assume that the following principle holds:

(32) Root = CP

This principle amounts to saying that we normally speak through propositions, not fragments of propositions: in the unmarked case, the root category is the canonical structural realization of the proposition, the CP.

Let us first consider the case of the Spec of C in a V-2 language such as German. I'll adopt the following definition of A-positions:

(33) A-positions: Theta positions and specifiers construed with Agr.
               (see Rizzi 1991 for discussion of the different cases)

Under this definition, the Spec of C in a V-2 language is an A position when the local subject is moved into it, as in:

(34) [Ich habe [t es schon gesehen INFL]]

The subject is construed with the Agr specification of the highest inflectional head; if the latter is moved to C and the local subject is moved to the Spec of C in V-2, the Spec-Agr configuration is reconstituted at the CP level, hence the Spec of C is an A-position under (33). The Spec of C can therefore host our null constant, and structure (30) is well formed. If the language also possesses the discourse linked null operator, as is the case in colloquial German, the null constant will also be possible in other structural positions, such as the object as in (26), provided that it is bound by the discourse-identified null operator in the main Spec of C, with the interpretive properties that we have discussed in the previous section.

In English, French and other non-V-2 languages the structure of the root is:

(35)
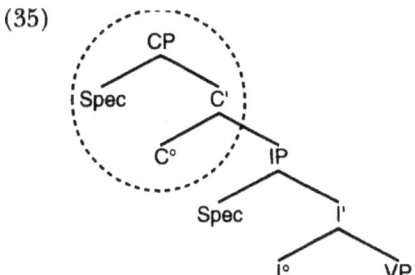

If the language possesses the discourse-identified null operator, a null constant in spec IP (or in any other position) will be possible, being bound by the null operator in the Spec of C (this may be the case of European Portuguese, according to Raposo 1986a). If the language does not have the discourse-identified null operator (as is the case in English or French) the null constant is not permissible in this configuration: the Spec of C is not a possible host because it is an A' position, the Spec of I is not a possible host because it is not the Spec of the root (but see Section 9); there is a higher position which can be a potential antecedent, the Spec of C, hence an unbound null constant in the Spec of IP is ruled out under (23).

Why is the root null subject option available in early English? Given the picture I have proposed, the most natural element to hold responsible for the developmental sequence is principle (32). Suppose that this principle is not operative initially, i.e., the encircled part can be omitted in (35) (can be omitted, but does not have to be omitted: in fact, much recent work on the early manifestation of V-2, strongly suggests that the possibility of starting from CP is available from very early on, e.g., Boser, Lust, Santelmann and Whitman 1991; Poeppel and Wexler 1991). If the CP layer is omitted, then the Spec of IP, an A specifier of the root, becomes a suitable host for the null constant, and the root null subject is allowed. No other position is available for the null constant: if the CP layer is present in (35), for instance in a question with Wh movement, the Spec of IP ceases to be the Spec of the root and an unbound null constant in this position is excluded by (23); similarly an unbound null constant in object position (or any other position) is excluded in, for example:

(36) *I met *nc*

because there are higher positions acting as potential identifiers (the subject position in (36)) hence (23) is enforced. As early English (like adult English) does not possess the discourse-identified null operator, the null constant is not permissible in any position other than the main subject position (when the CP layer is omitted), whence the observed subject–object asymmetry. As soon as principle (32) becomes operative (perhaps an event triggered by an inner maturational schedule, in the sense of Borer and Wexler 1987) the conditions for the root null constant cease to be met, and the early null subject disappears. Example (32) may remain a weak principle, though, susceptible to being 'turned off' on abbreviated registers and, perhaps, under special contextual conditions (possibly question–answer pairs, etc.).

8 Speculations on developmental correlations

If principle (32) is not operative initially, then root categories different from CPs are adequate starting points for early linguistic expressions. We have shown how the possibility of root null subjects follows from this property: if the CP layer can be omitted, then the structural conditions for the null constant in subject position are met. Do we expect other properties to correlate with root null subjects under this analysis? An immediate consequence of our proposal is that, if CP is not the compulsory starting point in early grammars, we would expect children to use a much wider variety of root categories, i.e., simple NPs, PPs, APs, (non-finite) VPs, different kinds of uninflected small clauses, etc. Arguing for such a scenario goes beyond the limits of the present chapter; I will just note in passing that the very high proportion of nominal or otherwise non-verbal utterances in children's production around the second birthday, as well as its sharp decline a few months later, is what the proposed approach leads us to expect. For instance, the proportion of utterances containing verbs in the production corpus of Valian's (1991) first group of English learners (age range 1;10–2;2) is only .27, a proportion that rises dramatically over .70 in her third and fourth group (age ranges 2;3–2;6 and 2;6–2;8, respectively; the author has excluded imperative sentences from this calculation). In our terms, as soon as (32) becomes operative, the option of using (non-verbal) fragments of CPs as complete utterances ceases to be generally available, and is confined to whatever special discourse contexts allow it in the adult grammar. See also Radford's (1990) comprehensive discussion of the early stages, particularly in connection with the early use of root small clauses.[12]

A less obvious property that may be related to early null subjects is the apparent *in situ* stage that was hinted at in the first section. Remember what the problem is: if learners of English go through a stage in which both syntactic Wh movement and Wh *in situ* are possible, how do they 'delearn' the *in situ* option, thus moving from a superset system to a subset system? Following a suggestion due to Michal Starke, we could think that the real option that the child has is not between choosing syntactic or LF Wh movement, but rather between choosing CP or a different category as the root: if CP is taken, then syntactic movement is obligatory as in the adult English grammar; if a different category is selected, then Wh movement cannot take place, there being no appropriate host, so Wh *in situ* is the only option (presumably with QR applying at LF to the Wh element as a salvaging strategy to create the necessary operator-variable structure). Under this interpretation, when principle (32) becomes operative in English, then the (parametrized) principle requiring obligatory movement in this language applies in full force, and Wh *in situ* is ruled out.[13]

Should one expect other co-occurrence relations between the root null subject and other properties of the early grammar? One could speculate that the delay in the operativity of (32) is related to the general parsimony of functional elements that the child's initial production manifests. Much recent work has shown that it is too radical to assume that the child's linguistic representations are purely lexical around the age of two: functional heads must be postulated in the child's grammar to account both for morphological analysis, the very presence of functional elements, and various word order phenomena (for instance, see Deprez and Pierce 1993 on French; Wexler and Poeppel 1993 and much other work on the acquisition of V-2 in German; Guasti 1992 on Italian, etc.). Still, a residue of the idea that initial syntactic representations are purely lexical (Lebeaux 1988; Guilfoyle and Noonan 1991; Platzack 1990; Radford 1990) seems to remain valid: the child's production around the age of two manifests a liberty of omission of functional heads that is not found in the target languages (see also Kazman 1990), for example:

1   Determinerless NPs appear to freely alternate with full DPs in the early stages of languages in which the determiner is obligatory, such as French (examples from Pierce 1989; see Friedemann 1992 and Radford 1990, who relate this property to the freer distribution of nominals in the early stages):

(37) a Pas pousser chaise papa.
        'Not push the chair papa.'
     b Fini café Madeleine.
        'Finished coffee Madeleine.'

2   The use of main clause participial sentences involves (at least) the omission of the functional head auxiliary (Bottari et al. 1992):

(38) a Fatto Diana.   (Diana, 1;11)
        'Done Diana.   (= Diana has done it)'
     b Che fatto la bimba?   (Diana, 2;0)
        'What done the little girl?   (= What has the little girl done?)'

3   The use of main clause infinitives found in many languages may involve the omission of tense (and/or of Agr), see Chapter 12;

Friedemann 1992; Guasti 1992; Wexler 1994 and references cited there for recent discussion (examples from Pierce 1989):

(39)a Monsieur conduire.
  'Man (to) drive.'
 b Tracteur casser maison.
  'Tractor break house.'

Some fundamental questions remain open in these cases, in particular the question of whether the (partial) lack of phonetically realized functional elements in production is to be expressed as blocking of spell-out for otherwise present categories, or it manifests the radical absence of the category. It is conceivable that different answers will be appropriate for different kinds of missing functional elements. If at least some cases of missing phonetic realization are to be analysed as involving radical absence of the category, then the non-operativity of (32) could be viewed as a special case of the overall parsimony of functional elements in the early grammar.[14]

9 Root expletive subjects

As is well-known, learners of English drop non-referential subjects as well as referential subjects:

(40) yes, ___ is toys in there.   (from Hyams 1986)

Can the null constant analysis be extended to cover this case? Notice first of all that some adult languages clearly extend the root null subject option to non-referential elements, e.g., Swedish (examples due to C. Platzack):

(41)a (Det) verkar som om ...
  'It seems as if ...'
 b (Det) telefonerades mycket igaar.
  'It was telephoned a lot yesterday.'

These appear to be genuine cases of root null subjects in that the zero variant of the expletive is only possible in initial position: when the Spec of C is filled by a different element in a V-2 construction, the expletive cannot be dropped:

(42) Igaar telefonerades *(det) mycket.
  'Yesterday was telephoned it a lot.'

So, UG apparently allows the null constant to be an expletive. If the unmarked case for an expletive is to be null, then it is natural that the child will take the null constant option for the expletive.[15]

Early null subjects and root null subjects 315

Some natural languages allow root null subjects only with the non-referential interpretation. This is the case of colloquial French, and may be true of some colloquial registers of English, even though the latter are less easy to tease apart from other registers in which referential subjects can also be dropped:

(43) a ___ semble/paraît/s'avère que Marie est malade.
   b ___ seems/appears/turns out that Mary is sick.
(44) a *___ dit/sait/pense que Marie est malade.
   b *___ says/knows/thinks that Mary is sick.

We find the root null subject properties again: if a Wh element is preposed, or if the structure is embedded, the expletive cannot be dropped.

(45) a Pourquoi semble *(t-il) que ...
   b Why does *(it) seem that ...
(46) a Jean dit que *(il) semble que ...
   b John says that *(it) seems that ...

Why is it that colloquial French and English retain the option of root null subjects but restricted to certain types of expletives (here we gloss over the fact that not all types of expletives can be naturally dropped in the relevant context)? The hypothesis that these systems also possess a structural device to suspend the application of (32) (say, on a par with the abbreviated registers) would require an independent parametrization of the referential interpretation (diary French would take the option of discourse-identified referential interpretation, colloquial French would not), not a very appealing possibility for many reasons.

A somewhat more interesting possibility is the following. Suppose that specifiers are optional in general, unless required by some special principle such as the EPP. Suppose then that the Spec of the root C can be missing, e.g. (35) can have the following shape:

(47)

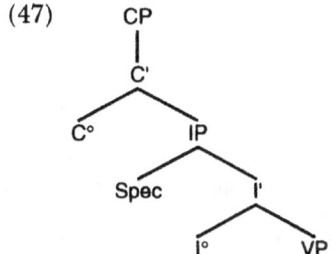

If this is correct, then an unbound null constant in the Spec of IP becomes possible again under (23), as there is no c-commanding maximal projection which may act as its antecedent. So, the non-referential *nc* is possible here, while it remains excluded from embedded contexts such as (46), or main contexts in which the Spec of C is present, such as (45). But this now leaves us without our structural explanation for the impossibility of the referential *nc*.

We can observe that, over and above the constraints discussed so far, there are strong restrictions on discourse identification, illustrated by the fact that a discourse-linked null operator in German must be in the root Spec of C: if it sits in an embedded Spec of C (even in a V-2 structure), the sentence is excluded:

(48) OP habe ich t schon gesehen.
 '(This) have I already seen.'
(49) *Hans glaubt OP habe ich t schon gesehen.
 'Hans believes that (this) have I already seen.'

It appears that discourse identification of an empty category is restricted to the root, cannot look more deeply inside the structure apart from the immediate domain of the root.

An intuitively plausible way to express this constraint is to generalize the idea we borrowed from Chomsky's binding theory and state it also as a constraint on discourse identification (while keeping it as a relaxing condition on principles of sentence grammar such as the ECP):

(50) A null element can be discourse-identified only if it is not c-commanded sentence-internally by a potential identifier.

So, the null constant in Spec IP in (47) is formally licit (if no Spec of C is selected, (23) is vacuous), but it cannot be discourse identified because it is c-commanded by C, a potential identifier (typically, heads function as identifiers at least for one type of null element, *pro*, see Chapter 2). As is always the case for formally licit but unidentified null elements (cf. much current literature on *pro*), this instance of the null constant can only function as a non-argumental expletive.

Notes

1 We leave the question open of determining the nature of the latter kind of omission. See also Hamann (1992), who found cases of non-root (middle-field) null subjects in special contexts at a later stage of the acquisition of German. Nevertheless, the general trend in the acquisition of V-2 languages seems to involve null subjects located in the Spec of the root (see, in particular, De Haan and Truijman 1988 on Dutch; on early null subjects in German see Meisel 1990; Clahsen 1991; Weissenborn 1992 and references cited there). It remains to be determined whether French early null subjects manifest similar occurrence restrictions (see Pierce 1989 and Friedemann 1992 for relevant discussion; preliminary results from Crisma 1992 seem to strongly support an extension of our analysis to early French).

2 The delearning problem arises because the child apparently shifts from a system allowing both syntactic movement and *in situ* (like, say, French in main clauses) to a system requiring syntactic movement, apparently a move from a superset system to a subset system. Of course, the problem arises only if a substantive number of the *in situ* examples are genuine questions. If they turned out to be analysable as echo questions in the general case, there would be no delearning problem (even though a different question would presumably arise: why are there so many echo questions in early English?). We will go back to this issue in the concluding remarks.

3 It also rules out for this case the possibility that the child may be interchangeably using two grammars for some time (one with null subjects and no subordination and the other with subordination and no null subjects) a possibility suggested in a somewhat different context by A. Kroch.

4 If anything, a zero pronominal subject is even favoured in embedded environments under coreference with the main subject, and compulsory when the embedded clause is adverbial. In the following, the zero pronoun must be selected to express coreference with the main subject:

   i Gianni canta quando (lui) è contento.
      'Gianni sings when (he) is happy.'

5 Another observation of Valian's (1991) is potentially relevant in this context. She notes that early null subjects in Italian are about twice as frequent as early null subjects in English, given comparable age groups. Even if relative frequencies, as such, do not immediately bear on the hypothesis of a structural difference (no direct frequency predictions are made by a structural hypothesis), if anything, the observed difference goes in the direction expected under a structural analysis of the sort advocated in the text: the null subject of Italian is possible in a larger set of structural environments, hence, all other things being equal, we would expect it to be more frequent than the early null subject in English.

   Do Italian learners possess the root null subject option, on top of the early positive setting of the Null Subject Parameter? I know of no empirical reason to exclude or confirm this possibility. On the other hand, if the suggestion of footnote 15 is correct, the availability of a *pro* subject may block the root null subject option in Early Italian. I will leave this question open.

6 Another reason for dissociating the dropping of local subjects in the specifier of the root from cases of topic drop comes from Swedish: in this langage, the dropping of the local subject can involve an expletive i, an element which cannot be topicalized, e.g., from the subject position of an embedded clause ii, whether or not it is dropped. Genuine cases of topic drop are restricted to referential elements, which can be topicalized iii:

   i   a (Det) verkar som om ...
          '(It) seems as if ...'
       b (Det) telefonerades mycket igaar.
          '(It) was telephoned a lot yesterday.'
   ii a *(Det) vet jag [t verkar som om ...]
          '(It) know I seems as if ...'
       b *(Det) visste jag [t telefonerades ...]
          '(It) knew I was telephoned ...'
   iii   (Det) visste jag [t skulle haenda].
          '(It) knew I should happen.'

Cases of root null subjects in adult languages are occasionally reported in the literature (see Kenstowicz 1989: 264 on Levantine Arabic and Somali; Solà 1992 on Corsican). The question of whether such cases are amenable to an analysis along the lines proposed in the text will be left open here.

7   This conclusion is also supported by the fact that languages using resumptive elements (overt variables) always use pronouns, never anaphors: the feature +v can mix with +p, but not with +a. Guglielmo Cinque and Robin Clark have pointed out that PROs giving rise to so-called PRO gate effects, i.e., alleviating Weak Crossover violations in examples like *Who did PRO visiting his relatives annoy t?* (Higginbotham 1980), may be analysable as cases of +v PRO. If this is correct, then the incompatibility of +v with +a should be restricted to the pure anaphor, i.e., the case of +a which is assigned a governing category.

8   See Rizzi (1990). In the terms of that system, the chain-connection can be established via antecedent government or via binding, depending on the availability of referential indices; see also Chapter 7. Guglielmo Cinque suggests that our null constant may be assimilated to a variable bearing a referential index in the sense of Rizzi (1990a) as sharpened by Cinque (1990), as opposed to a variable unable to bear such an index, hence available for antecedent government connections only. If this reduction is correct, the ±v feature is simply a descriptive label for an independently needed distinction (at least as far as [−a, −p] null elements are concerned).

9   A consequence of this system is worth noticing. It has been occasionally observed that, while the other three canonical types of *ec*s can (must) be the heads of A-chains, the purely anaphoric *ec* [+a, −p] can't, it can only be an A-trace, a non-head of chain; in other words, natural languages do not seem to allow null variants of overt anaphors, which typically head their own chains (while typically allowing null R-expressions and null pronominals that head their A-chains, on a par with their overt counterparts).

i   John saw himself / *ec*

See, for example, Brody (1985) for discussion. This gap follows from the proposed system, in fact from the interplay of the identification part of the ECP and the feature specification of the null elements: a [+a, −p] *ec*, *qua* [−p] is in the scope of (23), hence it must be chain connected to an antecedent; *qua* [+a] it must be locally bound by an A-antecedent; if the A and A' systems don't mix (see previous discussion), it follows that the *ec* must be chain connected to an A-antecedent, hence it is never the head of an A-chain, QED. This conclusion does not hold for other types of *ec*: [+a, +p], [−a, +p] are not in the scope of (23), hence chain formation with a higher element is not enforced; [−a, −p] is in the scope of (23), must be chain connected to an antecedent, but this antecedent can be an A' position, as the *ec* is [−a] (in fact the antecedent that the *ec* is chain connected to must be an A' position, due to principle C).

10 Overt and null operators can inherit features different from third person, but only from a binding antecedent, not from Agr:

i   Voi, OP che t sapete la risposta...
    'You, who know+3pl the answer...'
ii You are easy OP to please.

11 Example (30) also violates the formal licensing part of the ECP, proper head government (Rizzi 1990a). If, following Moro (1993), we restrict the proper head government requirement to the case in which a head intervenes between a null element and its identifier, the requirement will not apply to (30).

Note that our interpretation of (23) also provides an explanation of the fact that embedded C°s are generally overt, while main C°s can (must) be null (assuming roots to be CPs in the general case, see below): the head of the root lacks a potential identifier (a c-commanding head), hence it can be left empty. Consider also the possibility of dropping semantically empty fillers of I (*do, have, be*) in questions, but not in declaratives (Schmerling 1973; Akmajian, Demers and Harnish 1984):

  i (Are) you going to lunch?
  ii (Have) you ever been to Chicago?
  iii (Does) she like her new house?

I to C movement raises the Aux to the root head, where it can be null under our interpretation of (23). (The possibility of dropping a second person pronoun in this environment may involve incorporation of the pronoun into the null auxiliary, and/or be akin to the null subject of imperatives.)

12 Diaries and other special 'abbreviated' registers allowing root null subjects could now be characterized as retaining the non-operativity of (32). We would then expect, among other things, that on these registers discourse or textual units do not have to be full propositions, can be fragments of propositions. A quick perusal of Haegeman's corpus supports this hypothesis. In diaries, we typically find chunks of propositions corresponding to maximal projections different from CP, e.g.

  i Après-midi à discuter, puis agréable.
    'Afternoon to discuss, then pleasant.'   (P. Léautaud, op. cit.)

13 Notice that this approach requires that the principle in question, the Wh Criterion of Chapter 9, should also be interpreted as 'obligatory if satisfiable in principle'. For the sake of the argument, I have assumed that (4)–(5) are genuine questions. If a generalized echo question analysis is tenable, then the delearning problem does not arise.

14 All other things being equal, we could then expect root null subjects to disappear concomitantly with the loss of main clause infinitives, etc., even though one cannot *a priori* exclude the possibility that different principles enforcing the presence of different types of functional elements do not emerge simultaneously, but follow a maturational schedule.

15 Some languages allowing null constants (and null OPs) do not seem to like non-referential null constants, e.g., standard Dutch:

  i a (Hij) praatte erover.
      'He talked there-about.'
    b *?(Het) regent.
      'It is raining.'
    c *(Er) werd lang gedanst.
      'It was long danced.'

This may be an irreducible property of the language, to be learned through indirect negative evidence, or may be related to the fact that Dutch, contrary to Swedish, allows some cases of expletive *pro*: it could be that natural languages do not like to have two different types of null elements functioning as expletives (Icelandic may be problematic for this conjecture, see Sigurdsson 1989).

12 Some notes on linguistic theory and language development
The case of root infinitives*

Introduction

The study of language development in the last few years is marked by in-depth collaborations of theoretical linguists and developmental psycholinguists. In this chapter I would like to briefly discuss some major motives for this interdisciplinary venture from the viewpoint of the linguist (Section 1); then I will examine in detail a concrete example illustrating the approach and the disciplinary payoff which can be expected. The case that the paper focuses on is the following: around the age of two, language learners typically produce main clause declaratives with the verbs in the infinitival form, an option that is not found in the target languages. I shall argue that root infinitives are truncated structures (Section 3); they arise as a consequence of the option of 'stripping off' external clausal layers, an option which is characteristic of early grammars, while being banned from adult systems under normal circumstances. The same option is also arguably responsible of other properties of the early systems, such as the Early Null Subject (see Chapter 11). A number of structural properties of root infinitives, as well as their cross-linguistic distribution, will be shown to be amenable to the truncation analysis in conjunction with plausible auxiliary hypotheses (Sections 2–4).

1 Background

Why should a theoretical linguist be interested in the study of language development? The general answer to this question is straightforward: it is reasonable to hope that the study of language development will broaden the empirical basis of linguistic theory. If we try to be a little more analytical, three major points of interest can be identified:

---

* This paper was prepared for the Workshop 'Comparative Acquisition Studies', which took place at SISSA, Trieste, July 1993, in the framework of the *Trieste Encounters in Cognitive Sciences*. I am indebted to the participants in this event for helpful comments and discussion. Special thanks are due to Adriana Belletti, Harald Clahsen, Marc-Ariel Friedemann, Teresa Guasti, Liliane Haegeman, Cornelia Hamann, David Pesetsky, Amy Pierce, Andrew Radford, Tali Siloni, Michal Starke and Ken Wexler for commenting on the first draft of the paper.

1   Early operativeness of UG principles. Take the proposal that a given linguistic principle belongs to Universal Grammar (UG), based on standard linguistic arguments (poverty of stimulus, universality); then the hypothesis may be reinforced by the discovery that that principle is fully operative as soon as the child is able to manipulate structures of the relevant complexity. Results of this sort have been achieved, for instance, by Crain and Nakayama (1987) and Otsu (1981) for structure dependence and subjacency, respectively (see Crain 1992 for a detailed review of this research trend).

2   Explanatory capacity of UG mechanisms for development. The classical example here is Hyams' (1986) hypothesis that the theory of parameters (supplemented by assumptions on the initial values) could provide a direct explanation for certain developmental properties, such as the apparently universal Early Null Subject stage.

3   Development as the source of new empirical evidence for UG models. This is, in a sense, the natural counterpart of 2. The study of development could provide types of empirical evidence not available (or hardly accessible) in the study of the adult linguistic systems. Consider, for instance, the straightforward evidence provided by early production on the VP-internal position of the subject in English and French (Pierce 1989, 1992; Friedemann 1992).

Let me concentrate on the latter point of interest. The more or less radical novelty and impact of the developmental evidence very much depends on the role that UG turns out to have in constraining the early phases. The spectrum of the conceivable hypotheses on this issue is defined by two extreme positions:

i   No UG role: the early system is fundamentally different from the adult system (say, it is semantically based, rather than structurally based);
ii Full Adult UG: early systems are full fledged possible natural languages, they differ from target systems only as a function of parameter fixation; in some cases a parameter may be preset on some initial value and then reset on the basis of experience (alternatively, it may be the case that initially both values of a parameter are entertained, then one is selected on the basis of experience). In addition, there may be performance filters (e.g., working memory limitations) which may affect early production by triggering systematic omissions of certain classes of elements which are nevertheless present in the mental representations, etc.

If i is correct, then the study of development is essentially uninteresting for the theoretical linguist: the initial systems may be interesting objects of inquiry on their own, but the study of such objects does not interact with the study of adult systems. If ii is correct, then the study of development is interesting for the linguist in essentially the same sense in which the discovery of a new language or language family would be: we would dispose of some new concrete instantiations of the same object of inquiry, the class of UG-constrained systems, on which theoretical proposals could be tested; a quantitative enrichment of the available empirical evidence would then ensue.

As for the empirical adequacy of the two extreme positions, the first has been steadily losing plausibility: there is mounting evidence that the early systems are cast in the same mould as the adult systems; not only are they tightly constrained by UG principles, but also the fixation of some basic parameters (word order, verb movement, etc.) appears to take place very early on, as the correct value often is consistently manifested by the earliest syntactically relevant production (the so-called 'two-word stage'). The current debate on the UG role has then focused on a much more narrow range, opposing position ii to a very close variant of it:

ii' A slightly underspecified UG constrains the early systems, where underspecification does not just mean that some parameters are not fixed initially; rather it means that some principles or properties are not operative initially, but are triggered, or mature later in the mind (Borer and Wexler 1987).

There is now a very lively debate opposing ii and ii'; whatever position eventually prevails, the very nature of the focused range will inevitably strengthen the links between development and theoretical linguistics. It is perhaps not inappropriate for the linguist to notice that, if ii maximizes the relevance of linguistic theory for development, ii' may render the study of development of an even greater linguistic significance. The reason is that, given the tight deductive structure of the system, some very local underspecifications or deviations in the structure of UG may determine pervasive effects on the manifested language capacity. Then, under ii', development may be expected to provide more radical variations on the theme of UG constrained systems than those provided by the attested natural languages, thus enriching in a qualitative manner the empirical evidence available on the nature of language design.

I will not undertake here a detailed comparison between ii and ii'. Suffice it to say that, if position ii' is correct, then early systems should not only instantiate structures attested somewhere else in actual or potential natural languages, but also structures that no adult natural language will exhibit. In what follows, I would like to concentrate on a potential candidate for such a case.

2 Properties of root infinitives

Much recent work on acquisition has focused on the fact that, around the age of two, learners of different languages typically produce main clause declaratives with verbs in the infinitival form. I will base my presentation on the seminal work by K. Wexler on the topic (see Wexler 1994 and references cited there). The target languages in question (English, French, German, Swedish, ...) disallow this option; actually, it may well be the case that no adult language allows a root declarative with an infinitival verb. So, this is a case of a common property of the early systems that is not shared by adult systems, and which may even be banned by Universal Grammar.

The recent extensive literature on the topic convincingly argues that this isn't just a morphological problem (i.e., stemming from the fact that the child may not have learned the finite and non-finite morphology, so that he could be using finite and non-finite forms interchangeably): the child is well aware of the syntactic consequences of the morphological choice with respect to the placement of negation, V-2 type phenomena and the like (see Déprez and Pierce 1993 and references cited there). So, from the beginning of their linguistic production until about the middle of their third year of life, children typically produce declaratives with infinitival verbs (examples from Wexler 1994):

(1) a Voir l'auto papa.   (French)
        'See the car daddy.'
    b Thorstn das hab'n.   (German)
        'T. this have.'
    c Pappa schoenen wassen.   (Dutch)
        'Daddy shoes wash.'
    d Der ikke vaere.   (Danish)
        'It not be.'

What is remarkable about this phenomenon is that adult languages don't seem to allow infinitives as main clause declaratives, e.g., the examples in (1) are ungrammatical in the respective target languages. It is not the case that main clause infinitives are banned in general. Natural languages allow them in some special constructions, cf. the following cases in Italian:

(2) a Che cosa dire in questi casi?   (Question)
        'What to say in these cases?'
    b Io fare questo? Mai!   (Counterfactual)
        'Me to do that? Never!'
    c Partire immediatamente!   (Jussive)
        'Leave immediately!'
    d *Giocare al pallone.   (Declarative)
        'To play football.'

e Penso di giocare al pallone.   (Embedded Declarative)
  'I think to play football = I think I'll play football.'

What seems to be excluded is a root infinitival declarative: that is, if I see somebody playing football, I could not describe the scene by uttering (2)d. Why do we find such a selective distribution in adult languages? A natural idea is that clauses have a tense variable which must be fixed somehow (see Pollock 1989 and references cited there). In finite clauses, the overt finite morphology fixes the value of the tense variable; in embedded infinitives like (2)e, the tense variable is bound by the main clause tense value; main clause infinitives like (2d) are then excluded because their tense variable would remain unbound, ultimately a violation of Full Interpretation at LF. What about such special constructions as (2)a–c? It is arguable that they differ from declaratives in that they involve some kind of operator, as is overtly the case for questions and not implausible for the other cases. One possible line of thought could then be that the operators involved may unselectively bind the tense variable (in the sense of Heim 1982 and Pesetsky 1987). We may think of this option as a marked option that adult languages may adopt or not (e.g., English does not seem to naturally allow root infinitival questions). Whether or not this approach to the exceptional constructions is tenable, the fact remains that main clause declarative infinitives appear to be banned from adult languages.

Why are they allowed in the early stages? If it is the case that adult systems disallow this option, then we seem to have a significant challenge for approach ii. If we revert to approach ii', in the spirit of the underspecification idea we do not want to assume some extra licensing mechanism operative in the early systems to license the tense variable. The extra option should rather stem from the initial *lack* of some specification operative in later stages. Conforming to these guidelines, Wexler (1994) has proposed that children at the relevant age are not sensitive to tense values; on the basis of this hypothesis he proposes slightly different technical accounts of the optional infinitive stage based on the approaches to verbal morphology in Chomsky (1991, 1993). We could straightforwardly combine Wexler's proposal with our previous considerations and just say that, if children are not sensitive to tense values, there is no substantive tense variable to speak of at this stage of development (even though there may be the structural position for tense); whence no need for a binder and the free option of root infinitives.

Still, it would be desirable to explore tighter links between the root infinitives and other properties that seem to follow an analogous developmental pattern, e.g., the so-called Early Null Subject option, which also disappears around the middle of the third year of life in the acquisition of non Null Subject Languages (see Pierce 1989: 38 on the positive correlation between null subjects and utterances with non-finite tense in the acquisition of French).

Moreover, in the very recent literature some other properties of the root infinitives have emerged which, if confirmed, should be integrated. One important property is that root infinitives are found in declaratives, but not in Wh questions. This has been observed for French by Crisma (1992). For example, in the first period of the Philippe corpus (recordings from 2;1 to 2;2, corpus collected by Suppes, Smith and Leveillé 1973, available on CHILDES, see MacWhinney and Snow 1985) she found 117 main declaratives with a non-finite V out of a total of 491, but no non-finite Wh question out of a total of 35. In fact, none of the over 200 Wh questions of the Philippe corpus is non-finite. The same observation was independently made by Weissenborn (1994) for German: non-finite questions of the following sort are not attested in the early stages:

(3) (*)Was Hans essen?
    'What Hans eat?'

Based on this observation, Crisma and Weissenborn independently reach the conclusion that main clause infinitives are not full CPs, but truncated structures, possibly bare infinitival VPs; this conclusion is also arrived at on different grounds by Friedemann (1992).

The other important observation, due to Guasti (1992) is that main clause infinitives are very rare in the acquisition of Italian. Out of the three corpora of early production that she studied, one (Martina, recordings from 1;8 to 2;7) has root infinitives at less than 5% of the total of root clauses, the other two have only two (Diana, 1;10–2;6) and three (Guglielmo, 2;2–2;7) occurrences of root infinitives, respectively. The extreme rarity of the phenomenon is also confirmed by Cipriani et al. (1992), and by an inspection of the production corpus being collected in Parma (Giuseppe Cossu, personal communication). See also Wexler (1994, footnote 60). Given the high frequency of the phenomenon in French, German, etc. (for example, Pierce's 1989 French corpus at T1 includes 534 finite root clauses and 498 non-finite root clauses) its extreme rarity in Italian calls for an explanation.

Let me sketch out a possible approach which deals with these peculiarities. Two ingredients are needed: an idea on the nature of the structural truncation that appears to be possible in the early systems, and an analysis of the peculiarity of Italian infinitives, which I will express by using the checking technology of Chomsky (1993).

3 Root null subjects and clausal truncation

Starting from the first point, I would like to capitalize on the analysis of the early null subject phenomenon presented in Chapter 11. Early null subjects attested in the acquisition of non Null Subject Languages appear to be confined to the specifier of the root: learners of English (Valian

1991) or French (Crisma 1992) typically don't produce them after a Wh phrase in Comp; learners of Dutch (de Haan and Truijman 1988) and German (Poeppel and Wexler 1993, footnote 11; but see Hamann 1992 and Weissenborn 1992) typically exclude them from the post V-2 subject position. The following examples are taken from Crisma (op. cit.):

(4) a ___ est perdu xxx celui-la.
 '___ is lost that one.'
b Où il est le fil?
 'Where it is the wire?'
(5) a ___ va sous le tabouret.
 '___ goes under the stool.'
b Où elle va maman?
 'Where she goes mummy?'

Just to give some figures, in the Philippe files from 2;1 to 2;3, Crisma found 407 declaratives with a null subject out of a total of 1002 declaratives, and only one null subject out of a total of 114 Wh questions (Valian had found only nine null subjects out of 552 Wh questions in her corpus of natural production from 21 learners of English ranging from 1;10 to 2;8).

The idea is the following: the null subject is licit only in the specifier of the root; the reason is that null elements in general must be identified clause internally, but this requirement holds only if it is satisfiable in principle, i.e., if there is a potential identifier c-commanding the null element. The Spec of the root is not c-commanded by any other position, hence a null element can fail to be identified clause internally exactly in this position. The Spec of the root is then the only position available for direct discourse identification. Such examples as (4)b and (5)b necessarily involve the CP layer to integrate the Wh element, so the null subject in Spec IP could not be licensed. Why are (4)a and (5)a excluded in adult French? I assume that the following principle is operative:

(6) CP = root

Principle (6) ensures that a sentential structure always starts from the CP layer, which precludes the possibility of a root null subject in the IP Spec in adult French (English, etc.). It is then assumed that (6) is not operative in the early stages, under the guidelines of hypothesis (ii') in the Introduction of this chapter. The clausal structure can then start from the IP layer in early French, and a root null subject is legitimate in the Spec of IP (or of the AgrS projection, under the Split Infl hypothesis). As soon as (6) becomes operative, some time between the second and third birthday, the root null subject option is lost (see Chapter 11 for detailed presentation and discussion of this approach).

One noticeable feature of this theory of the early null subject is that it also automatically provides a theory of clausal truncation in the early phases. I will assume that the sequence of functional heads and projections is determined by UG according to the following hierarchy (Belletti 1990):

(7)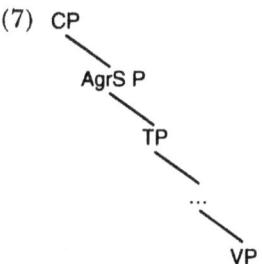

Principle (6), in the terminology of early work in generative grammar, defines the 'axiom' of the system, the point of departure of syntactic derivations (alternatively, (6) defines the necessary 'end point' of derivations, if the generalized transformation approach of Chomsky 1993 is adopted). Principle (6) makes it compulsory to take the whole of representation (7) in the generation of a well-formed structure (with the exception of special environments, such as question–answer pairs, in which isolated chunks of sentences can be appropriately used). But if (6) is not operative initially, this makes it possible to take other categories as legitimate 'axioms', in addition to CP; the choice of AgrS P is what underlies root null subjects (at least in tensed clauses), but other choices corresponding to lower maximal projections of (7) are possible as well. That's how, in this system, truncated structures are ruled in.

We then predict, among other things, a wider range of root categories than in the adult systems: small clauses (Radford 1990), lexical maximal projections, functional maximal projections different from CP are expected to be possible root categories. A very rough measure of the empirical adequacy of this prediction may be provided by the sudden growth of utterances containing a verb in the course of the third year of life. For instance, Valian (1991) reports that only 27% of the utterances produced by the first group in her study (1;10–2;2) contain a verb, a proportion that rises to 70% in her third and fourth group (2;3–2;6 and 2;6–2;8): since the selection of (7) with CP as the axiom inevitably leads to a structure with a verb, we may take this sudden growth as signalling the beginning of the operativity of (6).

Root infinitives may then be viewed as arising in this way: if the selected starting point is a category lower than TP in (7), then one will get the root infinitive, or a root construction exhibiting whatever unmarked non-finite form the language possesses. So, a root infinitive can be a bare VP in a language like English, in which the infinitival form is the bare stem (as

Wexler 1994 argues); or the maximal projection of the head corresponding to the infinitival morpheme (-r in French, -en in German, etc.), the Infin(itive) P(hrase) of Kayne (1991); or any other clausal projection lower than TP. Since there is no T position, there is no tense variable to bind, hence the root infinitive at this stage will not incur in the violation of the binding requirement which bans this construction in the adult systems (ultimately, Full Interpretation). In a sense, the truncated structure approach to root infinitives converges with Wexler's proposal in that it identifies the key factor in the admissibility of tenseless clausal representations in the early stages (even though such tenseless representations would not be a primitive property of early systems: they would arise because of the non-operativeness of (6), and would be consistent with an early knowledge of tense differences). Notice that there is no real optionality of tense in this approach, as T is an obligatory component of representation (7). What is optional is the choice of the axiom, the selected point of departure to generate a structure. Three major properties of root infinitives are immediately explained under this hypothesis.

First of all, the Crisma–Weissenborn observation on the non-occurrence of Wh root infinitives now follows directly. If root infinitives involve the stripping off of structural layers from the TP on in (7), *a fortiori* they will not include the CP layer, hence they will contain no structural host for a Wh element (on Wh *in situ*, see footnote 2).

Secondly, consider the fact that subject clitics tend not to occur in root infinitives in early French production (Pierce 1989: 45). If Pierce is right in analysing subject clitics as AgrS markers (at least) in the early stages of French, then their near absence straightforwardly follows from the clausal truncation approach: root infinitives never include the relevant head. If, on the other hand, subject clitics in (Early) French are distinct from AgrS but cliticize onto it (Kayne 1984 and Rizzi 1986), or are licensed as 'weak pronouns' by it (Cardinaletti and Starke 1993), their near absence is also explained, under the clausal truncation approach, by the lack of the host/licensing head. Pierce's finding is now corroborated cross-linguistically by Haegeman's (1995a) observation that Early Dutch also shows a selective lack of subject clitics in root infinitives, a fact which is amenable to the same explanation under the truncation hypothesis, as Haegeman argues.

Thirdly, it has been repeatedly noticed in the acquisition literature that root infinitives generally involve lexical verbs; in particular, one does not find such forms as the following, with root infinitival auxiliaries (Wexler 1994):

(8)a *Avoir mangé.
  'To have eaten.'
 b *Être venu.
  'To have come.'

c   *Gekauft haben.
    'Bought to have.'

In her analysis of the causative construction, Guasti (1993) has proposed that aspectual auxiliaries are intimately related to T; so, if causative verbs select a reduced clausal complement, one can explain the non-occurrence of auxiliaries in causative complements, Guasti argues. Suppose that auxiliaries are generated in T (alternatively, they are base-generated as heads of their own VPs, but inherently specified with respect to abstract T features, under the checking approach discussed in the next section). Under this hypothesis and the proposed approach to root infinitives, one directly explains the non-occurrence of forms like (8) in the early systems: the presence of the auxiliary implies the T projection, hence an ill-formed tense variable if the non-finite verbal form is selected. The non-occurrence of infinitival forms of modals in the acquisition of German, etc. (see references cited) may be amenable to the same kind of explanation.

What does the truncation hypothesis predict about the occurrence of negation in root infinitives? It all depends on the position of the negative phrase in scheme (7). If NegP is lower than TP, we would expect to find negated root infinitives, all other things being equal; if NegP is higher than TP, we would not. Moreover, if the position of NegP is parametrized, lower than TP in some languages and higher in others, we would expect the cross-linguistic occurrence of negated root infinitives to vary accordingly. Various further complicating factors should be taken into account (for instance, if there is a selection relation between T and Neg, as proposed by Zanuttini (1991, 1997), we would expect negated root infinitives to tend not to occur, regardless of the respective position of T and Neg). For relevant discussion, see Haegeman 1995a, but these are the straightforward predictions. The empirical evidence bearing on these issues is quite complex, though.

Consider early French productions. Examples involving negated root infinitives are frequently discussed in the literature, and in fact play a crucial role in the argument for an early mastery of functional categories (e.g., in Déprez and Pierce 1993). But this is a point in which quantitative considerations become crucial. Friedemann (1992) observes that in the Philippe and Grégoire corpuses, only six out of 137 negated sentences are construed with root infinitives (none of which involves a preverbal subject; Friedemann also counted ten negated non-finite root clauses whose verbal head is a past participle). He interprets this as suggesting that such fairly rare examples are instances of constituent negation, not genuine manifestations of the NegP (i.e., as in the adult form *Un homme pas capable de faire cela*, 'A man not capable of doing this'). If the observed rarity of negation (in comparison to tensed roots) is a general property of French root infinitives, we would thus have evidence for the conjunction of the truncation approach to root infinitives and the hypothesis that NegP is higher than TP in French (see Belletti 1990 for relevant discussion). But the point is complex, and more robust quantitative evidence is desirable.[1]

A thorough cross-linguistic investigation of this topic is not possible here, but we would like to report a suggestive observation in this context. Hoekstra and Jordens (1991) observed in the natural production of a child acquiring Dutch that two distinct forms of negation were used in the early phases. The regular adult form *niet* occurred with finite verbs and modals, while the special form *nee* (corresponding to the anaphoric negation = 'no' in the adult system) regularly occurred with root infinitives. This pattern is immediately consistent with the truncation approach and the assumption that NegP is higher than TP in Dutch. If so, the regular clausal negation involving the NegP layer would not be available in root infinitives; the child would then have to revert to another way of expressing negation in infinitives, say constituent negation, and it would not be surprising to find out that this structural difference may also be reflected in the choice of a morphologically different negative marker (even though there would be no necessity for that, so we wouldn't necessarily expect a neat complementary distribution *niet/nee* in the early productions of all learners of Dutch). Hoekstra and Jordens assume that *nee* is a kind of adverbial adjoined to the non-finite VP (or InfinP) in the early grammar of the child they have studied, a proposal which is consistent with the assumptions discussed.

Pursuing this topic for a moment at a speculative level, suppose that we were to find a language in which negative root infinitives are fully productive in the early stages. The natural conclusion would be such that a language would allow a NegP lower than TP in a fully productive way. This sort of developmental evidence would then bear directly on the question of whether the hierarchical order of the functional projections constituting the clausal structure is universally fixed or not, an important question of theoretical and comparative syntax. The complex theoretical and empirical facets of this issue are now being extensively investigated (see Haegeman 1995a on Dutch; Hamann 1994 on German).

If tenable, the truncation approach has the advantage of explaining some major structural properties of root infinitives while relating the phenomenon to other properties of the early stages, the root null subject and the possible occurrence of categories different from CP as the root.[2] Let me now mention, in passing, another property that may be connected: all other things being equal, we are led to expect the possibility of a stage in the acquisition of a V-2 language in which a V-final finite root clause would be allowed. The reason is that if the CP layer can fail to be projected, a tensed IP (AgrS) can be the root, hence V-2 can fail to apply. Such cases are occasionally reported in the literature; Déprez and Pierce (1993: 51), for example, discuss examples like the one below.[3]

(9) Da Bela Kuche-backe macht. (Katrin, 2;2)
    'There Bela cake-baking does.'

As the phenomenon is not clearly quantified yet, I prefer to leave the topic at that.

I will conclude this section with a brief comment on the Case issue. Overt subjects are generally possible with root infinitives, as the examples in (1) show. How can they be Case-marked? Under the truncation hypothesis, Agr and T (the usual Case assigners/checkers for subjects) are not available there; all other things being equal, we would then expect to find some peculiarity in the Case properties of subjects of root infinitives. Two properties of early French productions are suggestive in this context:

1   Postverbal subjects in adult French (possible in the so-called Stylistic Inversion construction) must be adjacent to the verb, a subcase of the familiar adjacency constraint on Case assignment under government (see Chapter 9; Friedemann 1992 and references quoted there). On the other hand, no adjacency constraint is operative on postverbal subjects in early French, which freely allows V O S (and, more generally, V XP S) order (Pierce 1989; Friedemann 1992).

2   The pronominal forms *moi* and *toi*, inherently non-nominative, typically appear as subjects of root infinitives.

As for the question of what makes lexical subjects of root infinitives possible, various hypotheses entertained in the literature can be relevant. It has been argued that the Case Filter is not (fully) operative in the early stages (Radford 1990; Friedemann 1992), so that overt NPs can occur in caseless positions (as complements of Ns, etc.). It has also been argued that the early stages manifest a process of inherent (non-nominative) Case assignment to VP-internal subjects (see Vainikka 1993 on English) which may be involved here. It may be the case that at least some overt subjects of root infinitives occupy an A' position, as topicalized or dislocated elements (Friedemann 1992); the issue for such cases would then reduce to the general question of the Case properties of overt NPs in A' position. A further variant of the latter approach would be that whatever default Case mechanism is operative in adult grammars for (some) NPs in A' position, it may be over-generalized in early grammars to other NP positions. I will not be able to explore these alternatives here. Suffice it to say that French provides some indication that overt subjects of root infinitives do not share significant morphosyntactic properties of Nominative marked NPs in finite clauses, as the truncation hypothesis would lead us to expect.[4]

4 AgrS features in infinitives

Let us now turn to the extreme rarity of root infinitives in Early Italian. Guasti (1992, footnote 27) puts forth the conjecture that this property may be related to the special behaviour of Italian infinitives with respect to the other languages considered. As observed by Belletti (1990), Italian infinitives appear to rise as high as finite verbs in the clausal structure (and in any event to a position higher than NegP, hence *a fortiori* higher than TP). Let me now sketch out a cross-linguistic analysis of verb movement by adapting the feature-checking technology put forth by Chomsky (1993) to the case of infinitives. This will give us the essential ingredient to understand the near absence of root infinitives in Italian.

Consider the following cross-linguistic paradigm illustrating the properties of V to I movement across languages with auxiliaries and main verbs in finite and non-finite clauses; examples *a* illustrate the case in which the verbal element has raised to the inflectional head higher than negation, examples *b* are the cases in which raising did not occur:

English:

(10) a John has not read the book.
    b *John not has read the book.
(11) a *John reads not the book.
    b John does not read the book.
(12) a to have not read the book.
    b to not have read the book.
(13) a *to read not the book.
    b to not read the book.

French:

(14) a Jean n'a pas lu le livre.
    b *Jean ne pas a lu le livre.
(15) a Jean ne lit pas le livre.
    b *Jean ne pas lit le livre.
(16) a n'avoir pas lu le livre.
    b ne pas avoir lu le livre.
(17) a *ne lire pas le livre.
    b ne pas lire le livre.

Italian:

(18) a Gianni non ha più letto il libro.
      'Gianni not has anymore read the book.'
    b *Gianni non più ha letto il libro.
      'Gianni not anymore has read the book.'
(19) a Gianni non legge più il libro.
      'Gianni not reads anymore the book.'
    b *Gianni non più legge il libro.
      'Gianni not anymore reads the book.'

(20) a Non aver più letto il libro.
  'Not to have anymore read the book.'
 b *Non più aver letto il libro.
  'Not anymore to have read the book.'
(21) a Non leggere più il libro.
  'Not to read anymore the book.'
 b *Non più leggere il libro.
  'Not anymore to read the book.'

Danish:

(22) a (*) ... at John har ikke laest bogen.
  ... that John has not read the book.
 b ... at John ikke har laest bogen.
  ... that John not had read the book.
(23) a (*) ... at John laeser ikke bogen.
  ... that John reads not the book.
 b ... at John ikke laeser bogen.
  ... that John not reads the book.
(24) a *... at have ikke laest bogen.
  ... to have not read the book.
 b ... ikke at have laest bogen.
  ... not to have read the book.
(25) a *... at laese ikke boegen.
  ... to read not books.
 b ... ikke at laese boegen.
  ... not to read books.

The parenthesized asterisks on (22)–(23) refer to the fact that the order V-neg is possible in certain environments as a consequence of embedded verb second; see Vikner (1990, 1995) for discussion; thanks are due to Sten Vikner for help with the Danish data.

According to the system of Chomsky (1993), lexical features can be strong or weak (on this distinction see also Pollock 1989 and Belletti 1990); if strong, lexical features must be checked in the overt syntax (so that they can disappear by PF). Therefore, a verb must raise in the syntax to AgrS if the AgrS feature is strong; if AgrS is weak, verb movement can (and by the Procrastinate Principle must) be delayed until LF, so there is no visible verb movement to check weak AgrS features.

As verbs behave differently with the tensed and untensed paradigm in some languages (and the verbal morphology obviously differs in the two cases), I believe it is natural to assume that AgrS features can have a different status in the two paradigms in the same language (while holding the clausal architecture constant for finite and non-finite clauses). We can describe the pattern illustrated by (10)–(25) if we assume the following assignments for the languages in question:

(26)

AgrS paradigm	Tensed	Untensed
Italian	S	S
French	S	(W)
English	W	(W)
Danish	–	–

Italian verbs have strong AgrS paradigms both in the tensed and untensed form, hence the verb, no matter whether lexical or functional, uniformly raises to AgrS in the syntax. Therefore, only the a examples are well-formed in (18)–(21). The symmetric case is Danish (and the other major continental Scandinavian languages): verbs, no matter whether lexical or functional, tensed or untensed, have no AgrS features at all (a fact directly reflected in the lack of any morphological manifestation of subject agreement), hence they do not raise at all to AgrS (or whatever functional head higher than the negative phrase has the surface subject position as its specifier), even though they may transit through this position in V-2 structures (Vikner 1990, 1995 and references cited there). So, only the b examples are acceptable in (22)–(25).

On the other hand, English and French manifest asymmetric assignments for the tensed and untensed paradigm. The tensed paradigm in English follows from the assumption that the AgrS features are weak: lexical verbs cannot raise in the syntax because of the Procrastinate Principle (see (11)); as for auxiliaries in the tensed paradigm, Chomsky's proposal is that they are invisible to LF processes due to the lack of semantic content. Since they can't be raised in LF, the Procrastinate Principle is overridden and they can and must move to AgrS in the syntax, as in (10).[5]

A problem is raised for this system by the apparent optionality of Aux movement in the infinitive paradigm (as in (12)), as optional movement is not expected in an economy framework: if movement is a 'last resort', avoided if not necessary, movement should be either compulsory or impossible.

One possible way to go is to observe that it remains possible in this system to shift the optionality from derivations/representations to the inventory of elements entering the computational system. Suppose that an infinitival verb can be specified as possessing weak AgrS features in English, but does not have to (this is the sense of the notation '(W)' in (26)). For lexical verbs this move has no visible consequences: if the infinitive verb has weak AgrS it will move to have its feature checked only in the syntax of LF by Procrastinate; if it has no such feature, it won't move at all. In either case, no overt movement of the lexical verb will occur (as in (13)). For auxiliaries there are visible consequences, though: if the infinitive Aux has no AgrS feature, it won't move at all, as in the corresponding Danish case; if it has a weak AgrS feature, it will have to move in the syntax, not being accessible to LF movement because of the lack of lexical content. In this way the apparent optionality of movement illustrated by (12)a–b can be reduced to the option of a certain morphological specification, the presence or absence of a weak AgrS specification. So, in the untensed paradigm English has the option of the tensed paradigm, or the Mainland Scandinavian option.

Consider now the French case. In the tensed paradigm (14)–(15), French is like Italian: AgrS is strong, verb movement is compulsory for lexical and auxiliary verbs. In the untensed paradigm (16)–(17) it is like English: the higher verb of the VP, whether lexical or not, may or may not be specified with weak AgrS features; if it is, the untensed Aux will move in the syntax due to its LF 'invisibility', while the untensed lexical verb will have to move at LF by Procrastinate.[6]

We are now in a position to straightforwardly account for the extreme rarity of main clause infinitives in Early Italian. As the infinitival verb must check its strong AgrS features, the AgrS head must be present to ensure proper checking and morphological well-formedness. If the structure is truncated at any layer under AgrS (say, at Kayne's 1991 InfinP), then the strong AgrS feature associated to the non-finite verb will not be checkable, and PF ill-formedness will ensue. If the structure containing a non-finite verb is truncated at AgrS (or extends all the way up to the CP system), no problem arises for morphological checking at PF, but the structure now includes an unbound tense variable, and it is excluded by Full Interpretation at LF. So, root infinitives cannot arise as truncated structures in Early Italian, due to the strength of the AgrS feature in the untensed paradigm.[7]

As for the rare cases of root infinitives produced in Early Italian, different hypotheses are conceivable. The first is that they could be analysed as involving an incorrect assumption on the feature specification of infinitives in the target language. After all, the relevant line of table (26) must be learned, and this may involve some mistakes and oscillations. For instance, Verrips and Weissenborn (1990) report some cases like the following in French, involving non-raising of a tensed verb:

(27) Pas joue le chat.   (Fabienne, 2,0)
    'Not plays the cat.'

In terms of Chomsky's feature system, as adapted in (26), this could be interpreted as involving the incorrect assignment of the weak feature to the French tensed verb. So, it could be the case that the rare root infinitives produced by some Italian children involve an oscillation in the assignment of AgrS features to the infinitival form. This approach would predict that the child should incorrectly place the infinitive verb lower than an element signalling the NegP (*più*, etc.). No evidence of this sort is available at the moment.[8]

Alternatively, it could be that some of such rare cases involve a null modal. A detailed inspection of the discourse contexts in which the rare root infinitives are uttered in Early Italian could shed light on whether a modal interpretation is intended.[9]

Conclusion

The existence of root declarative infinitives in the early linguistic production is amenable to the option of taking as a 'starting point' a category different from CP, an option which we have assumed to hold in early grammars. Root infinitives can be analysed as truncated clausal structures, starting from a categorial layer lower then TP. The following basic properties of the construction can be deduced via reasonable auxiliary assumptions:

a   incompatibility with Wh preposing;
b   incompatibility with subject clitics in Early French;
c   incompatibility with auxiliaries;
d   extreme rarity in Early Italian.

Other properties of early grammars can be unified in part with the root infinitives under the truncation approach:

1   Early Null Subjects;
2   Sudden growth of the ratio verbal utterances/total of utterances;
3   and, possibly, Verb-final structures with finite verbs in V-2 languages.

Some of these properties are relatively well-established, others still require in-depth investigations and could only be discussed at a very tentative level here. All in all, the basic hypothesis presented here makes clear predictions, open to empirical verification, about the existence and developmental correlation of various apparently unrelated properties of early grammars.

The goal of this paper was to try to extend the approach of comparative syntax to aspects of language development, in line with much current work on acquisition. The analogy with adult comparative syntax is that, given the tight deductive structure of UG, a single abstract difference between grammatical systems can be shown to govern quite diverse observable patterns. The special feature of the proposed extension is that the abstract difference we focused on between early and adult systems is arguably located in the (mild) underspecification of early UG, rather than in its parametric structure. More generally, if this approach is tenable on a larger scale, we may expect the study of development to provide a qualitative enrichment of the standard comparative evidence bearing on the structure of UG.

Notes

1 Pierce (1989) reports a relatively high proportion of negated root non-finite clauses in the acquisition of French. She counted 79 cases of negated root non-finite clauses versus 196 negated finite clauses in her corpus based on three children's early productions (Nathalie, Philippe, Daniel); but 50 of these cases come from a single file, Nathalie's first file, apparently reflecting a stage in which the child lacks tensed verbs altogether (Pierce, op. cit: 50). If this file is removed, and the distinction between infinitival and participial clauses is taken into account, we are back to a proportion comparable to the one observed by Friedemann. We leave open the question of what the significance and interpretation of Nathalie's first file may be.

2 Moreover, Crisma (1992) notices that Wh *in situ* is absent from the early files of the Philippe corpus, which show a number of cases of syntactic Wh movement. Crisma argues that this surprising delay of the *in situ* strategy (very common in ordinary spoken French) can be related to the initial non-operativeness of (6) through plausible auxiliary assumptions.

3 Similarly, Clahsen, Penke and Parodi (1993) report a number of examples in which the finite verb is in final (non V-2) position. This is particularly clear in cases in which the finite verb follows the negative marker (the second case involves a modal, which only occurs in its finite form):

i a Der Hahn nich macht. (Katrin)
   The rooster not do.
   'The rooster doesn't do (something).'
 b Julia Schere nicht darf. (Mathias)
   Julia scissors not may.
   'Julia isn't allowed the scissors.'

I am indebted to Harald Clahsen and Martina Penke for pointing out the relevance of their findings in the present context. As Andrew Radford points out, a truncation approach to finite V-final declaratives makes the interesting prediction that one should find no finite V-final Wh question in Early German, if Wh movement necessarily involves the CP layer, which should activate compulsory V-2.

4 As for the question of why (6) is not operative initially, it does not seem plausible that such an abstract principle should (or could) be learned from experience. A maturational approach, in the sense of Borer and Wexler (1987), seems to be more promising. Pursuing a plausible path within the guidelines of ii', Haegeman (1995a) argues that the operativeness of (6) can be related to the maturation of the temporal system analysed along Reichenbachian lines, an approach which unites the structural properties of the truncation hypothesis with Wexler's (1994) initial intuition on the fundamental role of tense. Alternatively, we could observe that (6) appears to be non-operative in adult systems under certain special discourse conditions, such as question–answer pairs (which allow root null subjects, isolated clausal chunks, etc.), and possibly in some special registers, such as Haegeman's (1990) diary style, etc. So, (6) is operative in adult systems, unless P (a set of special pragmatic conditions) are met. Then, it could be that children 'possess' the principle from the very beginning, but initially disregard the pragmatic conditions on its (non-)operativeness (the learning versus maturation issue would arise again in connection with the acquisition of P, rather than the principle itself – as is the case in all the recently discussed instances of delayed pragmatic knowledge). It should be noted that the latter variant of the analysis still provides a formal

5   syntactic explanation of the cluster of properties that go with root infinitives, root null subjects, etc., and should not be confused with purely pragmatic approaches to these phenomena.

5   As modals cannot be assumed to lack semantic content and still pattern with auxiliaries, the relevant distinction may be more appropriately drawn by *lexical* content: elements lacking lexical content (hence, such functional verbal elements as auxiliaries and modals) cannot undergo LF raising.

6   Do clitics attach to root infinitives in early French? Judging from some cases listed in Friedemann (1992), the answer seems to be positive. If so, the truncation analysis of root infinitives has a direct implication for the analysis of (Romance) clitics: if root infinitives lack T, there must be a valid clitic host lower than T, possibly the head carrying AgrO features, distinct from and higher than Agr Past Participle according to Friedemann and Siloni (1997). See Chapter 4 for discussion.

As for the optional 'short' movement of infinitival verbs in French (Pollock 1989), (optional movement to T in terms of structure (7): 'Souvent parler de linguistique' – 'Parler souvent de linguistique'), it can now be described as involving an optional specification w.r.t. strong T features.

7   Early German and Early Dutch show a high proportion of root infinitives. Given the logic of the proposed approach, we would be lead to expect that OV Germanic languages should pattern with English–French in keeping infinitival forms lower in the tree than finite forms (in non-V-2, non-V-raising structures). A clue that this may be correct is offered by the fact that the affixal negation *en-* optionally affixes to finite forms, but not to infinitives in West Flemish (Haegeman 1995b):

i a ... da ze nie (en-)zingt.
       '... that she not (en-)sings.'
  b ... nie te (*en-)zingen.
       '... not to (*en-)sing.'

It may be the case that the infinitive form does not raise to the head of the NegP, hence it cannot pick up the affixal negative head *-en*.

8   I will not address here the important learnability question of how the different values of (26) are acquired for non-finite forms (as the crucial evidence involving adverbial positions may be scarce in the primary linguistic data), and in particular of how the learner of Italian decides that infinitives have strong AgrS features in the target language. Belletti (1990: 140) puts forth the conjecture that this may be related to the capacity of AgrS to license *pro*, hence to the Null Subject Parameter. See also Guasti (1993). Another possible trigger for assuming obligatory verb movement in infinitives could be provided by the obligatory V-cl order (*vederlo* = to see + it) under the analysis of enclisis of Kayne (1991). See Chapter 4.

9   Incidentally, it should be noted that the rarity of root infinitives in Italian seems to argue against a generalized null modal approach for root infinitives across languages (thus converging with the arguments given by Poeppel and Wexler 1993 for German): why should a null modal be only marginally available in Italian? Consider also that a null modal construction has been argued to exist in adult Italian in negative imperatives (Kayne 1992). Kayne crucially assumes that the null modal is a possible host for object clitics (*non lo+M fare* = don't do it). Then, under a generalized null modal approach to root infinitives, the lack of co-occurrence of root infinitives with subject clitics in French would remain mysterious.

We do not analyse here other root clauses with non-finite verbal forms, present and past participial forms in particular (*Mummy reading, Train broken,* etc.). These appear to be more naturally amenable to an analysis involving a null auxiliary (many adult natural languages have such constructions: Slavic, Semitic). Notice that the null Aux hypothesis would predict free occurrence of such forms also under the CP layer (*What mummy doing?, What broken?*).

References

Abney, S. (1987) *The English Noun Phrase in its Sentential Aspects*, PhD Thesis, MIT.
Aboh, E. (1997) *From the Syntax of Gungbe to the Grammar of Gbe*, Doctoral Thesis, Université de Genève.
Acquaviva, P. (1989) 'Aspetti della complementazione frasale', Tesi di laurea, Università di Pisa.
Adams, M. (1987) 'From Old French to the Theory of Pro-drop', *Natural Language and Linguistic Theory*, 5: 1–32.
Akmajian, A. (1977) 'The Complement Structure of Perception Verbs in an Autonomous Syntax Framework', in Culicover, P., Wasow, T, Akmajian, A. (eds) *Formal Syntax*, New York: Academic Press.
Akmajian, A., Demers, R. and Harnish, R. (1984) *Linguistics*, Cambridge, Massachusetts: MIT Press.
Anderson, M. (1977) 'Transformations in Noun Phrases,' ms. University of Connecticut, Storrs.
Anderson, S. (1982) 'Types of Dependency in Anaphors: Icelandic (and other) Reflexives', *Journal of Linguistic Research* 2: 1–22.
Antinucci, F. and Cinque, G. (1977) 'Sull'ordine delle parole in italiano: l'emarginazione', *Studi di grammatica italiana* 6: 121–46.
Aoun, J. (1981) *The Formal Nature of Anaphoric Relations*, PhD Dissertation, MIT, Cambridge, Massachusetts.
Aoun, J. (1985) *Generalized Binding*, Dordrecht: Foris Publications.
Aoun, J., Hornstein, N. and Sportiche, D. (1981) 'Aspects of Wide Scope Quantification', *Journal of Linguistic Research* 1: 67–95.
Aoun, J. and Sportiche, D. (1981) 'The Domain of Weak Crossover Restrictions', in Borer, H. and Aoun, J. (eds) *Theoretical Issues in the Grammar of Semitic Languages*, MIT Working Papers in Linguistics 3.
Bach, E. (1979) 'Control in Montague Grammar', *Linguistic Inquiry* 10: 533–81.
Baker, C. L. (1970) 'Notes on the Description of English Questions', *Foundations of Language* 6: 197–219.
Baker, M. (1985) *Incorporation: The Syntax and Morphology of Changing Grammatical Functions*, PhD dissertation, MIT, Cambridge, Massachusetts.
Baker, M. (1988) *Incorporation*, Chicago: the University of Chicago Press.
Baker, M. and Hale, K. (1990) 'Relativized Minimality and the Incorporation of Pronouns', *Linguistic Inquiry* 21: 289–97.
Baltin, M. (1982) 'A Landing Site for Movement Rules', *Linguistic Inquiry* 13: 1–38.

Barss, A. (1986) *Chains and Anaphoric Dependence*, PhD dissertation, MIT, Cambridge, Massachusetts.
Bayer, J. (1984) 'COMP in Bavarian', *The Linguistic Review* 3: 209–74.
Belletti, A. (1982) 'On the Anaphoric Status of the Reciprocal Construction in Italian', *The Linguistic Review* 2: 101–37.
Belletti, A. (1986) 'Unaccusatives as Case Assigners', Lexicon Project Working Papers 8, MIT, Cambridge, Massachusetts.
Belletti, A. (1988) 'The Case of Unaccusatives', *Linguistic Inquiry*, 19: 1–34.
Belletti, A. (1990) *Generalized Verb Movement*, Torino: Rosenberg & Sellier.
Belletti, A. (ed.) (1993) *Syntactic Theory and the Dialects of Italy*, Torino: Rosenberg & Sellier.
Belletti, A. (1994) 'Case Checking and Clitic Placement: Three Issues in (Italian/Romance) Clitics', *GenGenP* 1.2: 101–18.
Belletti, A. and Rizzi, L. (1981) 'The Syntax of *ne:* Some Theoretical Implications', *The Linguistic Review* 1: 117–54.
Belletti, A. and Rizzi, L. (1988) 'Psych-Verbs and Theta Theory', *Natural Language and Linguistic Theory* 6,3: 291–352.
Belletti, A. and Shlonsky, U. (1995) 'The Order of Verbal Complements: A Comparative Study, *Natural Language and Linguistic Theory* 13: 489–526.
Benincà, P. (1985–6) 'L'interferenza sintattica: un aspetto di sintassi ladina considerato di origine tedesca', *Quaderni Patavini di Linguistica* 5: 3–15.
Benincà, P. (1988) 'Costruzioni con ordine marcato degli elementi', in Renzi, L. (ed.) *Grande grammatica italiana di consultazione*, Volume I, Bologna: Il Mulino, 129–45.
Benincà, P. (ed.) (1989) *Dialect Variation and the Theory of Grammar*, Dordrecht: Foris Publications.
Benincà, P. (1994) *La variazione sintattica. Studi di dialettologia romanza*, Bologna: Il Mulino.
Benincà, P. (1995) 'La struttura della frase esclamativa alla luce del dialetto padovano', ms., University of Padua.
Benincà, P. and Cinque, G. (1990) 'On Certain Differences between Enclisis and Proclisis', ms., Università di Padova, Università di Venezia.
Berwick, R. (1982) *Locality Principles and the Acquisition of Syntactic Knowledge*, PhD dissertation, Department of Computer Science and Electrical Engineering, MIT, Cambridge, Massachusetts.
Bhatt, R. and Yoon, J. (1991) 'On the Composition of Comp and Parameters of V-2', *WCCFL* 10: 41–52.
Bianchi, V. (1995) *Consequences of Antisymmetry for the Syntax of Headed Relative Clauses*, doctoral dissertation, Scuola Normale Superiore, Pisa; published in 1999, Berlin: Mouton De Gruyter.
Bianchi, V. and Figueiredo-Silva, C. (1993) 'On Some Properties of Object Agreement in Italian and in Brazilian Portuguese', ms., Scuola Normale Superiore, Pisa and Université de Genève.
Bloom, P. (1990) 'Subjectless Sentences in Child Language', *Linguistic Inquiry*, 21.4: 491–504.
Bordelois, I. (1974) *The Grammar of Spanish Causative Complements*, Ph.D. dissertation, MIT, Cambridge, Massachusetts.
Borer, H. (1983) *Parametric Syntax*, Dordrecht: Foris Publications.
Borer, H. (1984) 'The Projection Principle and Rules of Morphology', in Jones, C.

and Sells, P. (eds) *Proceedings of the Fourteenth Annual Meeting of NELS*, GLSA, University of Massachusetts, Amherst.

Borer, H. (1986) 'I-subjects', *Linguistic Inquiry* 17.3: 375–416.

Borer, H. and Wexler, K. (1987) 'The Maturation of Syntax', in Roeper, T. and Williams, E. (eds) *Parameter Setting*, Dordrecht: Reidel.

Boser, K., Lust, B., Santelman, L. and Whitman, J. (1991) 'The Syntax of CP and V-2 in Early German Child Grammar', paper presented at NELS 22, University of Delaware.

Bottari, P., Cipriani, P., Chilosi, A. M. (1992) 'Proto-syntactic Devices', *GenGenP* 0, 1–2: 83–101.

Bouchard, D. (1983) *On the Content of Empty Categories*, Dordrecht: Foris Publications.

Brandi, L. and Cordin, P. (1981) 'Dialetti e italiano: un confronto sul parametro del soggetto nullo', *Rivista di Grammatica Generativa* 6: 33–87.

Brandi, L. and Cordin, P. (1989) 'Two Italian Dialects and the Null Subject Parameter', in Jaeggli, O. and Safir, K. (eds) (1989).

Bresnan, J. (1977) 'Variables in the Theory of Transformations', in Culicover, P. et al. (eds) *Formal Syntax*, New York: Academic Press.

Bresnan, J. (1982) 'Control and Complementation', in Bresnan, J. (ed.) *The Mental Representation of Grammatical Relations*, Cambridge, Massachusetts: MIT Press.

Brody, M. (1985) 'On the Complementary Distribution of Empty Categories', *Linguistic Inquiry* 16.4: 505–46.

Brody, M. (1990a) 'Some Remarks on the Focus Field in Hungarian', *UCL Working Papers*, Vol. 2, University College of London.

Brody, M. (1990b) 'Case Theory and Argumenthood', *GLOW Newsletter* 24: 14–15.

Brody, M. (1995a) *Lexico-Logical Form: A Radically Minimalist Theory*, Cambridge, Massachusetts: MIT Press.

Brody, M. (1995b) 'Focus and Checking Theory', in Kenesei, I. (ed.) *Levels and Structures (Approaches to Hungarian, Vol. 5)*, Szeged: JATE, 30–43.

Bromberg, H. and Wexler, K. (1995) 'Null Subjects in Wh Questions', *MIT Working Papers* 26.

Brown, R. (1973) *A First Language: The Early Stages*, Cambridge, Massachusetts: Harvard University Press.

Burzio, L. (1981) *Italian Auxiliaries and Intransitive Verbs*, PhD dissertation, MIT, Cambridge, Massachusetts.

Burzio, L. (1982) 'D-structures Conditions on Clitics', *Journal of Linguistic Research*, 2.2: 23–54.

Burzio, L. (1986) *Italian Syntax*, Dordrecht: Reidel.

Burzio, L. (1992) 'The Role of the Antecendent in Anaphoric Relations', in R. Freidin (ed.), *Current Issues in Comparative Grammar*, Dordrecht: Kluwer.

Calabrese, A. (1982) 'Alcune ipotesi sulla struttura informazionale delle frase in italiano e sul suo rapporto con la struttura fonologica', *Rivista di Grammatica Generativa* 7: 3–78.

Calabrese, A. (1985) 'Focus and Logical Structures in Italian', ms., MIT.

Campos, H. (1986) 'Indefinite Object Drop', *Linguistic Inquiry* 17: 354–9.

Cardinaletti, A. (1983) 'Lo status dei pronomi d- e la ricostruzione nella dislocazione a sinistra in tedesco', *Rivista di Grammatica Generativa* 8: 111–25.

Cardinaletti, A. (1990) *Pronomi nulli e pleonastici nelle lingue germaniche e romanze*, doctoral dissertation. Università di Venezia.

Cardinaletti, A. (1991) 'On Pronoun Movement: The Italian Dative *Loro*', *Probus* 3: 127-53.
Cardinaletti, A. and Roberts, I. (1991) 'Clause Structure and X-second', ms., Università de Venezia, Université de Genève.
Cardinaletti, A. and Starke, M. (1993) 'On Dependent Pronouns and Pronoun Movement', paper presented at the 1993 GLOW Conference, Lund.
Cardinaletti, A. and Starke, M. (1994) 'The Typology of Structural Deficiency', ms., Università de Venezia, Université de Genève.
Cecchetto, C. (1994) 'Clitic Left Dislocation and Scrambling: Towards a Unified Analysis', ms., DIPSCO, Fondazione San Raffaele, Milano.
Cheng, L. (1991) *On the Typology of Wh Questions*, PhD dissertation, MIT.
Chierchia, G. (1984) *Topics in the Syntax and Semantics of Infinitives and Gerunds*, PhD dissertation, University of Massachusetts, Amherst.
Choe, Y. S. (1985) 'Syntax Generals Paper', MIT, Cambridge, Massachusetts.
Chomsky, N. (1955/1975) *The Logical Structure of Linguistic Theory*, New York: Plenum.
Chomsky, N. (1957) *Syntactic Structures*, The Hague: Mouton.
Chomsky (1965) *Aspects of the Theory of Syntax*, Cambridge, Massachusetts: MIT Press.
Chomsky, N. (1973) 'Conditions on Transformations', in Anderson, S. and Kiparsky, P. (eds) *A Festschrift for Morris Halle*, New York: Holt Rinehart and Winston.
Chomsky, N. (1976) 'Conditions on Rules of Grammar', *Linguistic Analysis* 2: 303-51.
Chomsky, N. (1977a) 'On Wh Movement', in Akmajian, A., Culicover, P. and Wasow, T. (eds) *Formal Syntax*, New York: Academic Press, 71-132.
Chomsky, N. (1977b) *Essays on Form and Interpretation*, New York: North Holland.
Chomsky, N. (1980) 'On Binding', *Linguistic Inquiry* 11: 1-46.
Chomsky, N. (1981) *Lectures on Government and Binding*, Dordrecht: Foris Publications.
Chomsky, N. (1982a) 'On the Representation of Form and Function', in Mehler, J., Walker, E. T. C. and Garrett, M. (eds) *Perspectives on Mental Representation*, Hillsdale, New Jersey: Lawrence Erlbaum.
Chomsky, N. (1982b) *Concepts and Consequences of the Theory of Government and Binding*, Cambridge, Massachusetts: MIT Press.
Chomsky, N. (1986a) *Knowledge of Language: Its Nature, Origins and Use*, New York: Praeger.
Chomsky, N. (1986b) *Barriers*, Cambridge, Massachusetts: MIT Press.
Chomsky, N. (1991) 'Some Notes on the Economy of Derivations and Representations', in Freidin, R. (ed.) *Principles and Parameters in Comparative Grammar*, Cambridge, Massachusetts: MIT Press, 417-54.
Chomsky, N. (1993) 'A Minimalist Program for Linguistic Theory', in Hale, K. and Keyser, S. J. (eds) *The View From Building 20*, Cambridge, Massachusetts: MIT Press.
Chomsky, N. (1995) *The Minimalist Program*, Cambridge, Massachusetts: MIT Press.
Chomsky, N. and Lasnik, H. (1977) 'Filters and Control', *Linguistic Inquiry* 8: 425-504.
Chomsky, N. and Lasnik, H. (1991) 'Principles and Parameters Theory', in Jacobs, J., von Stechow, A., Sternefeld, W. and Vennemann, T. (eds) *Syntax: an International Handbook of Contemporary Research*, Berlin: De Gruyter.

Chung, S. (1982) 'Unbounded Dependencies in Chamorro Grammar', *Linguistic Inquiry* 13: 39–78.
Chung, S. (1984) 'Identifiability and Null Objects in Chamorro', in *Proceedings of the Tenth Annual Meeting of the Berkeley Linguistic Society*, University of California, Berkeley.
Cinque, G. (1979) *Studi di sintassi e pragmatica*, Padova: CLESP.
Cinque, G. (1982a) 'On the Theory of Relative Clauses and Markedness', *The Linguistic Review* 1: 247–96.
Cinque, G. (1982b) 'Constructions with Left-Peripheral Phrases, Connectedness, Move Alpha and ECP', unpublished ms., University of Venice.
Cinque, G. (1984) 'A-bar Bound *pro vs* Variable', ms., University of Venice.
Cinque, G. (1986) 'Bare Quantifiers, Quantified NP's and the Notion of Operator at S-structure', *Rivista di grammatica generativa* 11: 33–63.
Cinque, G. (1990) 'Pseudo-relatives and Small Clauses', paper presented at the Gargnano workshop.
Cinque, G. (1990) *Types of A' Dependencies*, Cambridge, Massachusetts: MIT Press.
Cinque, G. (1993) 'A Null Theory of Phrase and Compound Stress', *Linguistic Inquiry* 24: 239–98.
Cinque, G. (1995) *Italian Syntax and Universal Grammar*, Cambridge: Cambridge University Press.
Cinque, G. (1999) *Adverbs and Functional Heads*, New York: Oxford University Press.
Cipriani, P., Chilosi, A. M., Bottari, P. and Pfanner, L. (1992) *L'acquisizione della morfosintassi in italiano: Fasi e processi*, Padova: UniPress.
Clahsen, H. (1991) 'Constraints on Parameter Setting – A Grammatical Analysis of some Acquisition Stages in German Child Language', *Language Acquisition* 1.4: 361–91.
Clahsen, H., Penke, M. and Parodi, T. (1993) 'Stage I in German Child Language: Evidence for Functional Categories in Early Grammars', ms., University of Dusseldorf.
Clark, R. (1988) 'Minimality and Verbal Small Clauses', ms., Carnegie Mellon University.
Clements, G. N. (1984) 'Binding Domains in Kikuyu', *Studies in the Linguistic Sciences* 14: 37–56.
Cole, J. (1985) 'Null Arguments in Hindi', ms., MIT, Cambridge, Massachusetts.
Contreras, H. (1989) 'Closed Domains', *Probus* 1.2: 163–80.
Coopmans, P. (1985) *Language Types: Continua or Parameters?*, doctoral dissertation, University of Utrecht.
Corver, N. and Delfitto, D. (1993) 'Feature Asymmetry and the Nature of Pronoun Movement', ms., University of Tilburg, University of Utrecht.
Cottell, S. (1994) 'The Representation of Tense in Modern Irish', ms., Université de Genève.
Couquaux, D. (1979) 'Sur la syntaxe des phrases predicatives en français', *Linguisticae Investigationes* 3: 245–84.
Crain, S. (1992) 'Language Acquisition in the Absence of Experience', *Behavioral and Brain Sciences*, 14: 597–611.
Crain, S. and Nakayama, M. (1987) 'Structure Dependence in Grammar Formation', *Language*, 63: 522–43.
Crisma, P. (1992) 'On the Acquisition of Wh Questions in French', *GenGenP*, 0, 1–2, 115–22.

Culicover, P. (1992) 'Topicalisation, Inversion and Complementizers in English', *OTS Working Papers*, Delfitto, D. et al. (eds) *Going Romance and Beyond*, University of Utrecht, Utrecht.

Culicover, P. (1993) 'The Adverb Effect: Evidence against ECP accounts of the that-t effects', *NELS* 1993, 97–110.

de Chenes, B. (1995) 'Towards an Explanatory Account of the that-trace Effect', ms., Université de Genève.

de Haan, G. and Truijman, K. (1988) 'Missing Subjects and Objects in Child Grammar', in Jordens, P. and Lalleman, J. (eds) *Language Development*, Dordrecht: Foris Publications, 101–21.

den Besten, H. (1977/1983) 'On the Interaction of Root Transformations and Lexical Deletive Rules', in Abraham, W. (ed.) *On the Formal Syntax of Westgermania*, Amsterdam: Benjamins, 47–131.

Déprez, V. and Pierce, A. (1993) 'A Cross-linguistic Study of Negation and Functional Projections in Early Grammar, *Linguistic Inquiry* 24: 25–67.

Dobrovie-Sorin, C. (1994) *The Syntax of Romanian: Comparative Studies in Romance*, Berlin: Mouton De Gruyter.

Dotson Smith, B. R. (1984) *Infinitival NP Constructions in Italian: A Study of the Projection Principle*, doctoral dissertation, University of Utrecht.

Epstein, S. D. (1984) 'Quantifier-*pro* and the LF Representation of PRO_{arb}', *Linguistic Inquiry* 15: 499–505.

Everaert, M. (1988) 'Nominative Anaphors in Icelandic: Morphology or Syntax?', ms., University of Tilburg.

Everett, D. (1986) 'Piraha Clitic Doubling and the Parametrisation of Nominal Clitics', *MIT Working Papers in Linguistics* 8: 85–127.

Falkenberg, G. (1990) 'A Semantic Hierarchy in the Complements of German Perception Verbs', paper presented at the Gargnano Workshop.

Fiengo, R. (1974) *Semantic Conditions on Surface Structure*, PhD dissertation, MIT, Cambridge, Massachusetts.

Fiengo, R. (1980) *Surface Structure: The Interface of Autonomous Components*, Cambridge, Massachusetts: Harvard University Press.

Figueiredo-Silva, M. C. (1994) *La position sujet en portugais brésilien*, doctoral dissertation, Université de Genève; published in 1996, Campinas: Editora da Unicamp.

Frampton, J. (1991) 'Relativized Minimality: A Review', *The Linguistic Review* 8.1: 1–46.

Friedemann, M.-A. (1990) 'Le pronom interrogatif que', *Rivista di grammatica generativa* 15: 123–39.

Friedemann, M.-A. (1992) 'The Underlying Position of External Arguments in French: A Study in Adult and Child Grammar', *GenGenP*, 0, 1–2: 123–44.

Friedemann, M.-A. (1995) *Sujets syntaxiques: positions, inversions et pro*, doctoral dissertation, University of Geneva; published in 1997, Bern: Peter Lang.

Friedemann, M.-A. and Rizzi, L. (eds) (2000) *The Acquisition of Syntax*, London, New York: Longman.

Friedemann, M.-A. and Siloni, T. (1997) 'AgrObject is not AgrParticiple', *The Linguistic Review* 14,1: 69–96.

Fukui, N. (1993) 'A Note on Improper Movement', *The Linguistic Review* 10, 2: 111–26.

Gee, J. P. (1977) 'Comments on the Paper by Akmajian', in Culicover, P., Wasow, T. and Akmajian, A. (eds) *Formal Syntax*, New York: Academic Press.

George, L. and Kornfilt, J. (1981) 'Finiteness and Boundedness in Turkish', in Heny, F. (ed.) *Binding and Filtering*, London: Croom Helm, 105–27.

Georgopoulos, C. (1985) 'Variables in Palauan Syntax', *Natural Language and Linguistic Theory* 3: 59–94.

Georgopoulos, C. (1991) *Syntactic Variables – Resumptive Pronouns and A' Binding in Palauan*, Dordrecht: Kluwer Publications.

Giorgi, A. (1984) 'Toward a Theory of Long Distance Anaphors: A GB Approach', *The Linguistic Review* 4: 307–72.

Giorgi, A. and Pianesi, F. (1994) 'Extraction from Subjunctive Clauses and Clausal Architecture', talk presented at the University of Geneva, November 1994.

Graffi, G. (1980) 'Su alcune costruzioni "pseudorelative"', *Rivista di grammatica generativa* 5: 117–39.

Grewendorf, G. and Sternefeld, W. (eds) (1990) *Scrambling and Barriers*, Amsterdam: Benjamins.

Grimshaw, J. (1979) 'Complement Selection and the Lexicon', *Linguistic Inquiry* 10: 270–326.

Grimshaw, J. (1991) 'Extended Projections', ms., Rutgers University.

Grimshaw, J. (1993) 'Minimal Projections, Heads and Optimality', ms., Rutgers University.

Grimshaw, J. (1997) 'Projection, Heads and Optimality', *Linguistic Inquiry*, 28.3: 373–422.

Grosu, A. (1975) 'The Position of Fronted Wh Phrases', *Linguistic Inquiry* 6: 588–99.

Gruber, J. (1965) *Studies in Lexical Relations*, PhD dissertation, MIT, Cambridge, Massachusetts.

Guasti, M. T. (1988) 'La pseudorelative et les phénomènes d'accord', *Rivista di grammatica generativa* 13: 35–57.

Guasti, M. T. (1992) 'Verb Syntax in Italian Child Grammar', *GenGenP* 0, 1–2: 145–62.

Guasti, T. (1993) *Causative and Perception Verbs*, Torino: Rosenberg and Sellier.

Guasti, T. (1996) 'On the Controversial Status of Romance Interrogatives', *Probus* 8, 2: 161–80.

Guilfoyle, E. and Noonan, M. (1991) 'Functional Categories and Language Acquisition', ms., MIT & McGill.

Gundel, J. (1974) *The Role of Topic and Comment in Linguistic Theory*, Indiana University Linguistic Club, Bloomington, Indiana.

Haegeman, L. (1985) 'The Interpretation of Inherent Objects in English', ms., Université de Genève.

Haegeman, L. (1986) 'INFL, COMP and Nominative Case Assignment in Flemish Infinitivals', in van Riemsdijk, H. and Muysken, P. (eds) *Features and Projections*, Dordrecht: Foris Publications, 23–137.

Haegeman, L. (1990) 'Understood Subjects in English Diaries', *Multilingua*, 9–2: 157–99.

Haegeman, L. (1991) 'Scrambling, Clitic Placement and Agr Recursion in West Flemish', ms., Université de Genève.

Haegeman, L. (1992) *Theory and Description in Generative Syntax*, Cambridge: Cambridge University Press.

Haegeman, L. (1995a) 'Root Infinitives, Tense and Truncated Structures in Dutch', *Language Acquisition*, 4,3: 205–55.

Haegeman, L. (1995b) *The Syntax of Negation*, Cambridge: Cambridge University Press.
Haegeman, L. (1996a) 'Root Infinitives and Initial Null Subjects in Early Dutch', *GALA Proceedings*, 1996, 239–50.
Haegeman, L. (1996b) 'Verb Second, the Split CP and Null Subjects in Early Dutch Finite Clauses', *GenGenP* 4: 133–75.
Haegeman, L. and Zanuttini, R. (1991) 'Negative Heads and the Negative Criterion', *The Linguistic Review* 8: 233–51.
Haider, U. (1986) 'Affect Alpha', *Linguistic Inquiry* 17,1: 113–26.
Haïk, I. (1990) 'Anaphoric, Pronominal and Referential Infl', *Natural Language and Linguistic Theory* 8: 347–74.
Haïk, I., Koopman, H. and Sportiche, D. (1985) 'Infl in mooré et le liage dans le système A'', *Rapport de recherche du groupe de linguistique africaniste*, année 1985–86, Montréal.
Haiman, J. (1988) 'From V-2 to Subject Clitics: Evidence from Northern Italian', ms., University of Manitoba, Winnipeg.
Hamann, C. (1992) 'Late Empty Subjects in German Child Language', *Technical Reports in Formal and Computational Linguistics*, 4, Université de Genève.
Hamann, C. (1994) 'Negation, Infinitives and Heads', ms., Université de Genève.
Hamann, C. (1997) *From Syntax to Discourse. Children's Use of Pronominal Clitics, Null Subjects, Infinitives, and Operators*, Habilitation Thesis, University of Tübingen.
Hamann, C and Plunkett, K. (1997) 'Subject Omission in Child Danish', *BU Conference on Language Development* 21: 220–31, Somerville: Cascadilla Press.
Heim, I. (1982) *The Semantics of Definite and Indefinite Noun Phrases*, PhD dissertation, University of Massachusetts, Amherst.
Heim, I, Lasnik, H. and May, R. (1988) 'On the Logical Form of Reciprocal Sentences', *GLOW Newsletter* 20: 27–8.
Henry, A. (1995) *Belfast English and Standard English: Dialect Variation and Parameter Setting*, Oxford: Oxford University Press.
Higginbotham, J. (1980) 'Pronouns and Bound Variables', *Linguistic Inquiry*, 11.4: 679–708.
Higginbotham, J. (1983) 'The Logic of Perceptual Reports: An Extensional Alternative to Situation Semantics', Center for Cognitive Science, MIT, Occasional Paper 21.
Higginbotham, J. (1985) 'On Semantics', *Linguistic Inquiry* 16: 547–93.
Higginbotham, J. (1987) 'Indefiniteness and Predication', in Reuland, E. and Ter Meulen, A. G. B. (eds) *The Representation of Indefinites*, Cambridge, Massachusetts: MIT Press, 43–70.
Hoekstra, T. and Jordens, P. (1991) 'From Adjunct to Head', ms., University of Leiden.
Holmberg, A. (1986) *Word Order and Syntactic Features*, PhD dissertation, University of Stockholm.
Holmberg, A. and Platzack, C. (1988) 'The Role of Inflection in Scandinavian Syntax', *Working Papers in Scandinavian Syntax* 42: 25–43.
Hornstein, N. and Weinberg, A. (1981) 'Case Theory and Preposition Stranding', *Linguistic Inquiry* 12: 55–91.
Horvath, J. (1985) *Focus in the Theory of Grammar and the Syntax of Hungarian*, Dordrecht: Foris Publications.
Huang, J. (1982) *Logical Relations in Chinese and the Theory of Grammar*, PhD dissertation, MIT, Cambridge, Massachusetts.

Huang, H. J. (1984) 'On the Distribution and Reference of Empty Pronouns', *Linguistic Inquiry* 15: 531–74.
Hyams, N. (1983) *The Acquisition of Parametrized Grammars*, PhD dissertation, CUNY.
Hyams, N. (1986) *Language Acquisition and the Theory of Parameters*, Dordrecht: Reidel.
Hyams, N. and Sano, T. (1994) 'Agreement, Finiteness and the Development of Null Arguments', paper presented at NELS, 24.
Hyams, N. and Wexler, K. (1993) 'On the Grammatical Basis of Null Subjects in Child Language', *Linguistic Inquiry*, 24,3: 421–59.
Iatridou, S. (1991) 'Clitics and Island Effects', ms., MIT.
Jackendoff, R. (1972) *Semantic Interpretation in Generative Grammar*, Cambridge, Massachusetts: MIT Press.
Jaeggli, O. (1982) *Topics in Romance Syntax*, Dordrecht: Foris Publications.
Jaeggli, O. (1984) 'Passives, Middles and Implicit Arguments', ms., USC, Los Angeles, California.
Jaeggli, O. (1985) 'Arbitrary Subjects', *SCOPIL* 10, Department of Linguistics, USC, Los Angeles, California.
Jaeggli, O. and Safir, K. (eds) (1989) *The Null Subject Parameter*, Dordrecht: Kluwer.
Jakubowicz, C. (1985) 'Do Binding Principles Apply to INFL?', Proceedings of NELS, 15.
Johnson, K. (1985) 'Some Notes on Subjunctive Clauses and Binding in Icelandic', *MIT Working Papers in Linguistics* 6: 102–32.
Kayne, R. (1975) *French Syntax: The Transformational Cycle*, Cambridge, Massachusetts: MIT Press.
Kayne, R. (1984) *Connectedness and Binary Branching*, Dordrecht: Foris Publications.
Kayne, R. (1991) 'Romance Clitics, Verb Movement and PRO', *Linguistic Inquiry*, 22: 647–86.
Kayne, R. (1992) 'Italian Negative Infinitival Imperatives and Clitic Climbing', in Tasmowsky, L. and Zribi-Hertz, A. (eds) *Hommages à Nicolas Ruwet*, Ghent: Communication and Cognition.
Kayne, R. (1994) *The Antisymmetry of Syntax*, Cambridge, Massachusetts: MIT Press.
Kazman, R. (1990) 'The Acquisition of Functional Categories and the Lexicon: A Psychologically Plausible Model', ms., CMU, Pittsburg.
Kempchinsky, P. (1985) 'Operators and Binding in Subjunctive Clauses', WCCFL Proceedings 4: 139–51.
Kempchinsky, P. (1986) *Romance Subjunctive Clauses and Logical Form*, PhD dissertation, UCLA.
Kenstowicz, M. (1989) 'The Null Subject Parameter in Modern Arabic Dialects', in Jaeggli, O. and Safir, K. (eds) (1989).
Keyser, S. J. and Roeper, T. (1984) 'On the Middle and Ergative Constructions in English', *Linguistic Inquiry* 15: 381–416.
Kiss, K. (1987) *Configurationality in Hungarian*, Dordrecht: Reidel.
Kiss, K. (1990) 'Against LF Movement of Wh Phrases', ms., University of Budapest.
Koopman, H. and Sportiche, D. (1982) 'Variables and the Bijection Principle', *The Linguistic Review* 2: 139–60.
Koopman, H. and Sportiche, D. (1991) 'The Position of Subjects', *Lingua* 85: 211–58; republished in Sportiche (1999).
Koster, J. (1978a) 'Why Subject Sentences Don't Exist', in Keyser, S. J. (ed.) *Recent*

Transformational Studies in European Languages, Cambridge, Massachusetts: MIT Press.
Koster, J. (1978b) *Locality Principles in Syntax*, Dordrecht: Foris Publications.
Koster, J. (1984) 'On Binding and Control', *Linguistic Inquiry* 15: 417–59.
Kroch, A. (1989) 'Amount Quantification, Referentiality, and Long Wh Movement', ms., University of Pennsylvania.
Kuroda, Y. (1988) 'Whether we Agree or not: Remarks on the Comparative Syntax of English and Japanese', in Poser, W. (ed.) Papers from the Second International Workshop on Japanese Syntax, Stanford: CSLI.
Laenzlinger, C. (1993) 'A Syntactic View of Romance Pronominal Sequences', *Probus*, 5,3: 241–70.
Laenzlinger, C. (1998) *Comparative Studies in Word Order Variation: Adverbs, Pronouns and Clause Structure in Romance and Germanic*, Amsterdam: John Benjamins.
Laka, I. (1990) *Negation in Syntax: On the Nature of Functional Categories and Projections*, PhD dissertation, MIT, Cambridge, Massachusetts.
Larson, R. (1988) 'On the Double Object Construction', *Linguistic Inquiry* 19: 335–91.
Lasnik, H. (1972) *Analyses of Negation in English*, PhD dissertation, MIT, Cambridge, Massachusetts.
Lasnik, H. (1976) 'Remarks on Coreference', *Linguistic Analysis* 2: 1–22.
Lasnik, H. and Saito, M. (1984) 'On the Nature of Proper Government', *Linguistic Inquiry* 15: 235–89.
Lasnik, H. and Saito, M. (1992) *Move Alpha*, Cambridge, Massachusetts: MIT Press.
Lasnik, H. and Stowell, T. (1991) 'Weakest Cross-over', *Linguistic Inquiry* 22: 687–720.
Lebeaux, D. (1983) 'A Distributional Difference between Reciprocals and Reflexives', *Linguistic Inquiry*, 14: 723–30.
Lebeaux, D. (1984) 'Anaphoric Binding and the Definition of PRO', in Jones, P. and Sells, C. (eds) *Proceedings of the Fourteenth Annual Meeting of NELS*, GLSA, University of Massachusetts, Amherst.
Lebeaux, D. (1988) *Language Acquisition and the Form of the Grammar*, PhD dissertation, University of Massachusetts, Amherst.
Lees, R. and Klima, E. (1963) 'Rules for English Pronominalisation', *Language* 39: 17–28.
Levow, G. (1995) 'Tense and Subject Position in Interrogatives and Negatives in Child French', MIT Working Papers 26.
Lightfoot, D. (1989) 'The Child's Trigger Experience: Degree-0 Learnability', *Behavioral and Brain Sciences*, 12.2: 321–34.
Lightfoot, D. (1991) *How to Set Parameters: Arguments from Language Change*, Cambridge, Massachusetts: MIT Press.
Longobardi, G. (1980) 'Connectedness, complementi circostanziali e soggiacenza', *Rivista di Grammatica Generativa* 5: 141–85.
Longobardi, G. (1994) 'Reference and Proper Names: A Theory of N-movement in Syntax and Logical Form', *Linguistic Inquiry* 25: 609–65.
MacWhinney, B. (1999) *The CHILDES Project: Tools for Analyzing Speech*, second edition, Hillsdale: Lawrence Erlbaum Associates.
MacWhinney B. and Snow, C. (1985) 'The Child Language Data Exchange System', *Journal of Child Language* 12.
Maling, J. (1984) 'Non-Clause-Bounded Reflexives in Modern Icelandic', *Linguistics and Philosophy* 7: 211–41.

Manzini, M. R. (1983a) 'On Control and Control Theory', *Linguistic Inquiry* 14: 421–46.
Manzini, M. R. (1983b) *Restructuring and Reanalysis*, PhD dissertation, MIT, Cambridge, Massachusetts.
Manzini, M. R. (1992) *Locality*, Cambridge, Massachusetts: MIT Press.
Manzini, M. R. (1995) 'From "Merge and Move" to "Form Dependency"', *University College London Working Papers in Linguistics* 7: 205–27.
Manzini, M. R. and Wexler, K. (1986) 'Parameters, Binding Theory and Learnability', *Linguistic Inquiry* 18: 413–44.
Maracz, L. (1990) 'V-movement in Hungarian: A Case of Minimality', in Kenesei, I. (ed.) *Approaches to Hungarian*, Vol. 3, Szeged: JATE.
May, R. (1985) *Logical Form: Its Structure and Derivation*, Cambridge, Massachusetts: MIT Press.
McCloskey, J. (1991) 'Clause Structure, Ellipsis and Proper Government in Irish', *Lingua* 85: 259–302.
McCloskey, J. (1992) 'Adjunction, Selection and Embedded Verb Second', Working Paper LRC-92-07, Linguistics Research Center, University of California, Santa Cruz.
McCloskey, J. and Hale, K. (1984) 'On the Syntax of Person–Number Inflection in Modern Irish', *Natural Language and Linguistic Theory* 1: 487–533.
McDaniel, D. (1989) 'Partial and Multiple Wh-Movement', *Natural Language and Linguistic Theory* 7.4: 565–604.
Meisel, J. (1990) 'Infl-ection: Subjects and Subject-verb Agreement in Early Child Language. Evidence from Simultaneous Acquisition of two First Languages: German and French', ms., University of Hamburg.
Melvold, J. (1985) 'Getting PRO under Control', ms., MIT, Cambridge, Massachusetts.
Milsark, G. (1985) 'Which Is Rich', ms., Temple University, Philadelphia, Pennsylvania.
Mohanan, K. P. (1983) 'Functional and Anaphoric Control', *Linguistic Inquiry* 14: 641–74.
Moritz, L. (1989) 'Syntaxe de la négation de phrase en français et en anglais', Mémoire de licence, Université de Genève.
Moro, A. (1993) 'Heads as Antecedents: A Brief History of the ECP', *Lingua e stile* 28: 31–57.
Moro, A. (1997) *The Raising of Predicates*, Cambridge: Cambridge University Press.
Motapanyane, V. (1989) 'La position du sujet dans une langue à l'ordre SVO/VSO', *Rivista di grammatica generativa* 14: 75–103.
Motapanyane, V. (1991) *Theoretical Implications of Romanian Complementation*, doctoral dissertation, Université de Genève.
Motapanyane, V. (1995) *Theoretical Implications of Complementation in Romanian*, Padova: Unipress.
Muller, G. and Sternefeld, W. (1993) 'Improper Movement and Unambiguous Binding', *Linguistic Inquiry* 24: 461–507.
Nakajima, H. (1993) 'Topic Phrases and Complementizers', ms., Tokyo Metropolitan University.
Noonan, M. (1985) 'Complementation', in Shopen, T. (ed.), *Language Typology and Syntactic Description*, Vol. II, Cambridge: Cambridge University Press, 42–140.
Obenauer, H.-G. (1976) *Etudes de syntaxe interrogative du français*, Tübingen: Niemeyer.

Obenauer, H.-G. (1984) 'On the Identification of Empty Categories', *The Linguistic Review* 4, 2: 153–202.

Oshima, S. (1985) 'Control, Case-marking and ECP', ms., MIT, Cambridge, Massachusetts.

Otero, C. (1985) 'Arbitrary Subjects in Finite Clauses', ms., UCLA, Los Angeles, California.

Otsu, Y. (1981) *Universal Grammar and Syntactic Development in Children*, PhD dissertation, MIT, Cambridge, Massachusetts.

Perlmutter, D. (1978) 'Impersonal Passives and the Unaccusative Hypothesis', in *Proceedings from the 4th Annual Meeting of the Berkeley Linguistic Society*, Los Angeles, California.

Perlmutter, D. (ed.) (1983a) *Studies in Relational Grammar 1*, Chicago and London: The University of Chicago Press.

Perlmutter, D. (1983b) 'Personal vs. Impersonal Constructions', *Natural Language and Linguistic Theory*, 1: 141–200.

Pesetsky, D. (1982) *Paths and Categories*, PhD dissertation, MIT, Cambridge, Massachusetts.

Pesetsky, D. (1987) 'Wh *in situ*: Movement and Unselective Binding', in Reuland, E. and ter Meulen, A. (eds) *The Representation of (In)definiteness*, Cambridge, Massachusetts: MIT Press, pp. 98–129.

Pesetsky, D. (1995) *Zero Syntax*, Cambridge, Massachusetts: MIT Press.

Picallo, C. (1985) *Opaque Domains*, PhD dissertation, CUNY, New York.

Pierce, A. (1989) *On the Emergence of Syntax: A Cross-linguistic Study*, PhD dissertation, MIT, Cambridge, Massachusetts.

Pierce, A. (1992) *Language Acquisition and Syntactic Theory*, Dordrecht: Kluwer.

Platzack, C. (1987) 'The Scandinavian Languages and the Null Subject Parameter', *Natural Language and Linguistic Theory*, 5: 377–401.

Platzack, C. (1990) 'A Grammar without Functional Categories: A Syntactic Study of Early Swedish Child Language', *Working Papers in Scandinavian Syntax* 45: 13–34.

Poeppel, D. and Wexler, K. (1993) 'The Full Competence Hypothesis of Clause Structure in Early German', *Language* 69: 1–33.

Poggi, L. (1983) 'Implicazioni teoriche della sintassi dei pronomi clitici soggetto in un dialetto romagnolo', Tesi di Laurea, Università della Calabria.

Poletto, C. (1993) 'Subject Clitic – Verb Inversion in North-Eastern Italian Dialects', in Belletti, A. (ed.) *Syntactic Theory and the Dialects of Italy*, Torino: Rosenberg and Sellier, 204–51.

Pollock, J. -Y. (1986) 'Sur la syntaxe de *en* et le paramètre du sujet nul', in Couquaux, D. and Ronat, M. (eds) *La grammaire modulaire*, Paris: Éditions de Minuit.

Pollock, J. -Y. (1989) 'Verb Movement, Universal Grammar and the Structure of IP', *Linguistic Inquiry* 20: 365–424.

Prévost, P. (1997) 'Truncation in Second Language Acquisition', PhD Thesis, McGill University, Montréal.

Puskas, G. (1992) 'The Wh Criterion in Hungarian', *Rivista di Grammatica Generativa* 17: 141–86.

Puskas, G. (1996) *Word Order in Hungarian: The Syntax of A' Positions*, doctoral dissertation, Université de Genève.

Radford, A. (1988) *Transformational Grammar*, Cambridge: Cambridge University Press.

Radford, A. (1990) *Syntactic Theory and the Acquisition of English Syntax*, Oxford: Blackwell.
Raposo, E. (1985a) 'Case Theory and INFL to COMP: A Study of the Inflected Infinitive in European Portuguese', ms., University of California, Santa Barbara.
Raposo, E. (1985b) 'Some Asymmetries in the Binding Theory in Romance', *The Linguistic Review* 5: 75–110.
Raposo, E. (1986a) 'The Null Object in European Portuguese', in Jaeggli, O. and Silva-Corvalan, C. (eds) *Studies in Romance Linguistics*, Dordrecht: Foris Publications, pp. 373–90.
Raposo, E. (1986b) 'Romance Infinitival Clauses and Case Theory', in Neidle, C. and Nunez-Cedeno, R. (eds) Linguistic Studies in Romance Languages, Dordrecht: Foris Publications.
Raposo, E. (1987) 'Case Theory and Infl-to-Comp: The Inflected Infinitive in European Portuguese', *Linguistic Inquiry*, 18,1: 85–109.
Rappaport, M. (1983) 'On the Nature of Derived Nominals', ms., MIT, Cambridge, Massachusetts.
Rasetti, L. (1999) 'Null Subjects and Root Infinitives in the Child Grammar of French', in Friedemann, M. -A. and Rizzi, L. (eds) (1999).
Reinhart, T. (1981) 'Two Comp Positions', in Belletti, A., Brandi, L. and Rizzi, L. (eds) *Theory of Markedness in Generative Grammar*, Pisa: Scuola Normale Superiore.
Renzi, L. and Vanelli, L. (1982) 'I pronomi soggetto in alcune varietà romanze,' in *Studi in onore di G. B. Pellegrini*, Padova.
Rivero, M. -L. (1991) 'Exceptional Case Marking Effects in Rumanian Subjunctive Complements', in Wanner, D. and Kibbee, D. A. (eds) *New Analyses in Romance Linguistics*, Amsterdam: Benjamins, 273–98.
Rizzi, L. (1976) 'Ristrutturazione', *Rivista di grammatica generativa* 1: 1–54.
Rizzi, L. (1978a) 'A Restructuring Rule in Italian Syntax', in Keyser, S. J. (ed.) *Recent Transformational Studies in European Languages*, Cambridge, Massachusetts: MIT Press.
Rizzi, L. (1978b) 'Violations of the Wh Island Constraint in Italian and the Subjacency Condition', *Montreal Woking Papers in Linguistics*, 11: 155–90.
Rizzi, L. (1979) 'C-comando e condizioni sull'anafora', in *Atti del Convegno sull'Anafora*, Firenze: Accademia della Crusca.
Rizzi, L. (1982) *Issues in Italian Syntax*, Dordrecht: Foris Publications.
Rizzi, L. (1986) 'On the Status of Subject Clitics in Romance', in Jaeggli, O. and Silva-Corvalan, C. (eds) *Studies in Romance Linguistics*, Dordrecht: Foris Publications, 391–419.
Rizzi, L. (1990a) *Relativized Minimality*, Cambridge, Massachusetts: MIT Press.
Rizzi, L. (1990b) 'Speculations on Verb Second', in Mascaró, J. and Nespor, M. (eds) *Grammar in Progress. GLOW Essays for Henk van Riemsdijk*, Dordrecht: Foris Publications, 375–86.
Rizzi, L. (1991) 'Proper Head Government and the Definition of A Positions', *GLOW Newsletter*, 26.
Rizzi, L. (1993) 'A Parametric Approach to Comparative Syntax: Properties of the Pronominal System', *English Linguistics*, Tokyo 10: 1–27.
Rizzi, L. (1995) 'A Note on Do Support', ms., Université de Genève.
Rizzi, (1998) 'Remarks on Early Null Subjects', *Proceedings of the 22 BU Conference on Language Development*, Somerville: Cascadilla Press.

Rizzi, L. and Roberts, I. (1989) 'Complex Inversion in French', *Probus* 1: 1–30.
Roberge, Y. (1986) *The Syntactic Recoverability of Null Arguments*, doctoral thesis, University of British Columbia; published in 1990, Montréal: McGill–Queen's University Press.
Roberts, I. (1988) 'Some notes on VP Fronting and Head Government', ms., Université de Genève.
Roberts, I. (1991a) 'NP Movement, Crossover and ChainFormation', in Haider, H. and Netter, K. (eds) *Representation and Derivation in the Theory of Grammar*, Dordrecht: Kluwer.
Roberts, I. (1991b) 'Excorporation and Minimality', *Linguistic Inquiry*, 22: 209–18.
Roberts, I. (1993a) *Verbs and Diachronic Syntax*, Dordrecht: Kluwer.
Roberts, I. (1993b) 'The Nature of Subject Clitics in Franco-Provencal Valdotain', in Belletti, A. (ed.) (1993), 319–53.
Rochemont, M. (1989) 'Topic Islands and the Subjacency Parameter', *Canadian Journal of Linguistics* 34: 145–70.
Rochemont, M. and Culicover, P. (1990) *English Focus Constructions and the Theory of Grammar*, Cambridge: Cambridge University Press.
Roeper, T. (1985) 'Implicit Arguments and the Head-Complement Relation', ms., University of Massachusetts, Amherst.
Roeper, T. (1991) 'Why a Theory of Triggers Supports the Pro-drop Analysis', ms., University of Massachusetts, Amherst.
Roeper, T. and Rohrbacher (1994) 'True pro-drop in Child English and the Principle of Economy of Projection', ms., University of Massachusetts, Amherst.
Roeper, T. and Weissenborn, J. (1990) 'How to Make Parameters Work', in Frazier, L. and de Villiers, J. (eds) *Language Processing and Language Acquisition*, Dordrecht: Reidel.
Rooryck, J. (1992) 'Romance Enclitic Ordering and Universal Grammar', *Linguistic Review* 9: 219–50.
Rosenbaum, P. S. (1967) *The Grammar of English Predicate Complement Construction*, Cambridge, Massachusetts: MIT Press.
Ross, J. R. (1967) *Constraints on Variables in Syntax*, PhD dissertation, MIT, Cambridge, Massachusetts.
Ross, J. R. (1982) 'Pronoun Deleting Processes in German', paper presented at the annual meeting of the LSA, San Diego, California.
Ross, J. R. (1983) 'Inner Islands', Proceedings of the Tenth Meeting of the Berkeley Linguistics Society, 258–65.
Rothstein, S. (1983) *The Syntactic Forms of Predication*, PhD dissertation, MIT, Cambridge, Massachusetts.
Rouveret, A. (1992) 'Clitic Placement, Focus and the Wackernagel Position in European Portuguese', in Rizzi, L. (ed.) *Clitics in Romance and Germanic*, Eurotyp Working Papers, 3, European Science Foundation, Tilburg, The Netherlands.
Rouveret, A. and Vergnaud, J.-R. (1980) 'Specifying Reference to the Subject', *Linguistic Inquiry* 11: 97–202.
Rudin, C. (1988) 'On Multiple Questions and Multiple Wh Fronting', *Natural Language and Linguistic Theory* 6: 445–501.
Ruwet, N. (1982) *Grammaire des insultes et autres études*, Paris: Seuil.
Ruwet, N. (1984) '*Je veux partir/*Je veux que je parte*. A propos de la distribution des complétives à temps fini et des compléments à l'infinitif en Français', *Cahiers de grammaire*, 7, Toulouse-le-Mirail.

Ruzicka, R. (1983) 'Remarks on Control', *Linguistic Inquiry* 14: 309–24.
Safir, K. (1985) 'Missing Subjects in German', in Toman, I. (ed.) *Linguistic Theory and the Grammar of German,* Dordrecht: Foris Publications.
Safir, K. (1992) 'Structural Economy', ms., Rutgers University.
Saito, M. (1985) *Some Asymmetries in Japanese and their Theoretical Implications,* PhD dissertation, MIT, Cambridge, Massachusetts.
Schein, B. (1981) 'Small Clauses and Predication', ms., MIT, Cambridge, Massachusetts.
Schmerling, S. (1973) 'Subjectless Sentences and the Notion of Surface Structure', CLS 9.
Shlonsky, U. (1988) 'Complementizer–cliticization in Hebrew and the ECP', *Natural Language and Linguistic Theory* 6.2: 191–206.
Shlonsky, U. (1991) 'Strategies of Wh Movement in Palestinian Arabic', ms., Université de Genève.
Shlonsky, U. (1994) 'Agreement in Comp', *The Linguistic Review* 11: 351–75.
Shlonsky, U. (1997) *Clause Structure and Word Order in Hebrew: An Essay in Comparative Semitic Syntax,* New York: Oxford University Press.
Sigurdsson, O. (1989) *Verbal Syntax and the Case in Icelandic,* PhD dissertation, University of Lund.
Siloni, T. (1996) 'Hebrew Noun Phrases: Generalized Noun Raising', in Belletti, A. and Rizzi, L. (eds) *Parameters and Functional Heads,* New York and Oxford: Oxford University Press.
Siloni, T. (1997) *Noun Phrases and Nominalisations: The Syntax of DPs,* Dordrecht: Kluwer.
Smits, R. J. C. (1989) *Eurogrammar – The Relative and Cleft Constructions of the Germanic and Romance Languages,* Dordrecht: Foris Publications.
Solà, J. (1992) *Agreement and Subjects,* doctoral dissertation, Universitat autònoma de Barcelona.
Speas, P. (1994) 'Null Arguments in a Theory of Economy of Projections', in Benedicto, E. and Runner, J. (eds) *Functional Projections,* UMOP 17.
Sportiche, D. (1983) *Structural Invariance and Symmetry in Syntax,* PhD dissertation, MIT, Cambridge, Massachusetts.
Sportiche, D. (1988a) 'A Theory of Floating Quantifiers and its Corollaries for Constituent Structure', *Linguistic Inquiry,* 19.3: 425–49; republished in Sportiche (1999).
Sportiche, D. (1988b) 'Conditions on Silent Categories', ms., UCLA.
Sportiche, D. (1996) 'Clitic Constructions', in Roorick, J. and Zaring, L., *Phrase Structure and the Lexicon,* Dordrecht: Kluwer; republished in Sportiche (1999).
Sportiche, D. (1999) *Positions and Atoms of Clause Structure,* London and New York: Routledge.
Starke, M. (1993) 'En deuxième position en Europe centrale', Mémoire de licence, Université de Genève.
Starke, M. (1994) 'On the Format for Small Clauses', *GenGenP* 2: 79–97.
Stowell, T. (1978) 'What Was There before There Was There', in Farkas, D. et al. (eds) *Chicago Linguistic Society* 17: 457–71.
Stowell, T. (1981) *Origins of Phrase Structure,* PhD dissertation, MIT, Cambridge, Massachusetts.
Stowell, T. (1983) 'Subjects across Categories', *The Linguistic Review* 2: 285–312.
Suñer, M. (1982) 'Big PRO and little *pro*', ms., Cornell University, Ithaca, New York.

Suñer, M. and Padilla-Rivera, J. (1984) 'On the Subjunctive and the Role of the Features of Infl: Evidence from a Null Subject Language', ms., Cornell University, Ithaca, New York.
Suppes, P., Smith, R. and Léveillé, M. (1973) 'The French Syntax of a Child's Noun Phrases', *Archives de Psychologie* 42: 207-79.
Szabolcsi, A. and Zwarts, F. (1991) 'Weak Islands and Algebraic Semantics', ms., UCLA - University of Groningen.
Taraldsen, T. (1986) '*Som* and the Binding Theory', in Hellan, L. and Christensen, K. K. (eds) *Topics in Scandinavian Syntax*, Dordrecht: Reidel, 149-84.
Tomaselli, A. (1989) *La sintassi del verbo finito nelle lingue germaniche*, doctoral dissertation, Università di Pavia.
Tomaselli, A. (1990) 'Cases of V-3 in Old High German', ms., Université de Genève.
Torrego, E. (1984) 'On Inversion in Spanish and some of its Effects', *Linguistic Inquiry* 15: 103-29.
Torrego, E. (1985) 'Some Theoretical Implications of Spanish Datives', ms., University of Massachusetts, Boston.
Travis, L. (1984) *Parameters and Effects of Word Order Variation*, PhD dissertation, MIT, Cambridge, Massachusetts.
Trigo, L. (1985) 'Syntax Generals Paper', MIT, Cambridge, Massachusetts.
Tsimpli, I. M. (1994) 'Focussing in Modern Greek', in Kiss, K. (ed.) *Discourse-configurational Languages*, New York: Oxford University Press.
Tuller, L. (1982) 'Null Subjects and Objects in Hausa', ms., Université de Paris VIII/UCLA, Los Angeles, California.
Tuller, L. (1985) 'Tense Features and Operators in Hausa', in *Rapport de recherche du groupe de linguistique africaniste*, année 1985-86, Montréal, 493-516.
Turano, G. (1993) 'Subjunctive Constructions in Arberesh and Standard Albanian', *Rivista di Grammatica Generativa* 18: 101-33.
Turano, G. (1995) *Dipendenze sintattiche in albanese*, Padova: Unipress.
Uriagereka, J. (1995) 'Aspects of the Syntax of Clitic Placement in Western Romance', *Linguistic Inquiry* 26: 79-123.
Vainikka, A. (1993) 'Case in the Development of English Syntax', ms., University of Massachusetts, Amherst.
Valian, V. (1991) 'Syntactic Subjects in the Early Speech of American and Italian Children', *Cognition* 40: 21-81.
van Riemsdijk, H. (1983) 'Correspondence Effects and the Empty Category Principle', in Otsu, Y. et al. (eds) *Studies in Generative Grammar and Language Acquisition: A Report on Recent Trends in Linguistics*, Editorial Committee, Tokyo, pp. 5-16.
Vanelli, L., Renzi, L. and Benincà, P. (1985) 'Typologie des pronoms sujets dans les langues romanes', *Actes du XVIIème Congrès International de Linguistique et Philologie Romane*, Université de Provence.
Verrips, M. and Weissenborn, J. (1990) 'Finite Verbs in the Acquisition of German, Dutch and French', ms., Max-Planck Institute, Nijmegen.
Vikner, S. (1985) 'Parameters of Binding and Binding Category in Danish', *Working Papers in Scandinavian Syntax*, University of Trondheim.
Vikner, S. (1990) *Verb Movement and the Licensing of NP Positions in the Germanic Languages*, doctoral dissertation, Université de Genève.
Vikner, S. (1991) 'Relative der and other C Elements in Danish', *Lingua* 84, 109-36.

Vikner, S. (1995) *Verb Movement and Expletive Subjects in the Germanic Languages*, Oxford and New York: Oxford University Press.

Vikner, S. and Sprouse, R. (1988) 'Have/Be Selection as an A-Chain Membership Requirement', *Working Papers in Scandinavian Syntax* 38: 1–48.

Visser, F. Th. (1963) *An Historical Syntax of the English Language*, Vol. 1, Brill, Leiden.

Visser, F. Th. (1969) *An Historical Syntax of the English Language*, Vol. 2, Brill, Leiden.

Wang, Q., Lillo-Martin, D., Best, C. and Levitt, A. (1991) 'Null Subjects vs. Null Objects: Some Evidence from the Acquisition of Chinese and English', *Language Acquisition*, 2,3: 221–54.

Watanabe, A. (1993) 'The Notion of Finite Clauses in Agr-based Case Theory', *Papers on Case and Agreement I: MIT Working Papers* 18: 243–96.

Wehrli, E. (1983) 'Remarks on Cliticization in French Causatives', in Haik, I. and Massam, D. (eds) *Papers in Grammatical Theory: MIT Working Papers in Linguistics* 5.

Weinberg, A. and Hornstein, N. (1981) 'Case Theory and Preposition Stranding', *Linguistic Inquiry* 12: 55–91.

Weissenborn, J. (1992) 'Null Subjects in Early Grammars: Implications for Parameter Setting Theory', in Weissenborn, J., Goodluck, H. and Roeper, T. (eds) *Theoretical Issues in Language Acquisition*, Hillsdale, NJ.: Lawrence Erlbaum.

Weissenborn, J. (1994) 'Constraining the Child's Grammar: Local Well-formedness in the Development of Verb Movement in German and French', in Lust, B., Suñer, M. and Whitman, J. (eds) *Syntactic Theory and First Language Acquisition: Cross-linguistic Perspectives*, Vol. 1, Hillsdale: Lawrence Erlbaum Associates.

Wexler, K. (1994) 'Optional Infinitives, Head Movement and the Economy of Derivations in Child Grammar', in Lightfoot, D. and Hornstein, N. (eds) *Verb Movement*, Cambridge University Press.

White, L. and Prevost, P. (2000) 'Truncation and Missing Inflection in Second Language Acquisition', in Friedemann, M.-A. and Rizzi, L. (eds) (2000).

Whitman, J., Lee, O. and Lust, B. (1991) 'Continuity of the Principles of Universal Grammar in First Language Acquisition: The Issue of Functional Categories', in *Proceedings of NELS 21*, GLSA, University of Massachusetts, Amherst.

Williams, E. (1983) 'Against Small Clauses', *Linguistic Inquiry* 14: 287–308.

Woolford, E. (1999) 'More on the Anaphor Agreement Effect', *Linguistic Inquiry*, 30,2: 257–87.

Zanuttini, R. (1991) *Syntactic Properties of Sentential Negation: A Comparative Study of Romance Languages*, PhD dissertation, University of Pennsylvania, Philadelphia.

Zanuttini, R. (1997) *Negation and Clausal Structure: A Comparative Study of Romance Languages*, New York and Oxford: Oxford University Press.

Zribi-Hertz, A. (1984) 'Prépositions orphelines et pronoms nuls', *Recherches Linguistiques* 12: 46–91.

Zubizarreta, M. L. (1985) 'The Relation between Morphophonology and Morphosyntax: The Case of Romance Causatives', *Linguistic Inquiry* 16: 247–89.

Zucchi, A. (1989) *The Language of Propositions and Events: Issues in the Syntax and Semantics of Nominalization*, PhD dissertation, University of Massachusetts, Amherst.

Author index

Abney, S. 7, 98, 340
Aboh, E. 247, 340
Acquaviva, P. 198, 340
Adams, M. 91, 340
Akmajian, A. 198, 206, 340
Akmajian, A., Demers, R. and Harnish, R. 319, 340
Anderson, M. 52, 340
Anderson, S. 164, 340
Antinucci, F. 247, 340
Aoun, J. 88, 152, 156, 173, 222, 340

Bach, E. 21, 22, 66, 67, 301, 337, 340
Baker, C. L. 238, 241
Baker, M. 50, 66n, 78, 231, 233, 240n, 340
Baker, M. and Hale, K. 233, 340
Baltin, M. 237n, 260, 267, 340
Barss, A. 66n, 205, 340
Bayer, J. 244, 341
Belletti, A. 4, 6, 40, 66n, 67n, 71n, 98, 100, 102, 103, 104, 105, 106, 108, 110, 121n, 151n, 152n, 163, 172n, 176, 193, 200, 201, 208n, 209n, 225, 231, 234, 236, 240n, 247, 254, 287n, 316n, 327, 330, 332, 333n, 338n, 341, 351, 352, 353, 354
Belletti, A. and Rizzi, L. 6, 40, 163, 341, 354
Belletti, A. and Shlonsky, U. 247, 341
Benincà, P. 4, 83, 84, 90, 92, 107, 108, 117, 250, 291n, 341, 355
Benincà, P. and Cinque, G. 107, 108, 117, 341
Berwick, R. 41, 78n, 341
Best, C. 356
Bhatt, R. 289n, 341
Bianchi, V. 253, 290n, 291n, 341
Bianchi, V. and Figueiredo-Silva, C. 100, 341

Bloom, P. 301, 341
Bordelois, I. 154n, 341
Borer, H. 37, 50, 77n, 88, 148, 340, 341, 342
Borer, H. and Wexler, K. 11, 312, 322, 337n, 342
Boser, K., Lust, B., Santelman, L and Whitman, J. 311, 342
Bottari, P., Cipriani, P., Chilosi, A. M. 313, 342, 344
Bouchard, D. 60, 151n, 342
Brandi, L. and Cordin, P. 80, 112, 342, 352
Bresnan, J. 21, 66n, 271, 342
Brody, M. 221, 243, 246, 318n, 342
Bromberg, H. and Wexler, K. 13, 342
Brown, R. 300, 342
Burzio, L. 5, 6, 40, 66n, 67n, 74n, 75n, 78n, 129, 131, 132, 137, 138, 151n, 152n, 153n, 154n, 156n, 172n, 192, 196, 342

Calabrese, A. 234, 247, 342
Campos, H. 31, 342
Cardinaletti, A. 99, 120n, 287n, 290n, 305, 308
Cardinaletti, A. and Roberts, I. 105, 342
Cardinaletti, A. and Starke, M. 99, 292n, 328, 343
Cecchetto, C. 246, 343
Cheng, L. 243, 343
Chierchia, G. 21, 66n, 343
Choe, Y. S. 58, 343
Chilosi A. M. 344
Chomsky, N. 1, 2, 3, 4, 7, 9, 14, 20, 24, 31, 35, 43, 50, 72n, 73n, 89, 90, 94, 97, 98, 102, 103, 104, 116, 121n, 125, 126, 128, 134, 136, 137, 149, 151n, 152n, 155n, 157n, 158, 159, 160,

Chomsky, N. *continued*
  161, 162, 166, 167, 169, 170, 171,
  172n, 173n, 182, 184, 186n, 190,
  191, 194, 197, 200, 213, 214, 219,
  221, 224, 228, 236n, 237n, 238n,
  242, 243, 244, 245, 246, 247, 248,
  251, 253, 259, 260, 261, 265, 274,
  275, 284, 285, 290n, 291n, 292n,
  308, 309, 316, 324, 325, 327, 332,
  333, 334, 335, 343
Chomsky, N. and Lasnik, H. 2, 3, 265, 343
Chung, S. 77n, 216, 343
Cinque, G. 6, 8, 66n, 69n, 71n, 79n, 98,
  107, 108, 117, 151n, 152n, 174, 177,
  184, 185n, 208n, 221, 223, 237n,
  246, 247, 249, 250, 251, 252, 253,
  254, 260, 287n, 289n, 316n, 318n,
  340, 341, 344
Cipriani, P., Chilosi, A. M., Bottari, P
  and Pfanner, L. 302, 325, 342, 344
Clahsen, H. 316n, 334, 344
Clahsen, H., Penke, M. and Parodi, T
  337n, 344
Clark, R. 191, 208n, 318n, 344
Clements, G. N. 216, 344
Cole, J. 72n, 344
Contreras, H. 232, 238n, 239n, 344
Coopmans, P. 75n, 344
Cordin, P. 80, 342
Corver, N. and Delfitto, D. 97, 98, 99, 344
Cottell, S. 244, 344
Couquaux, D. 138, 344, 351
Crain, S. 11, 344
Crain, S. and Nakayama, M. 321, 344
Crisma, P. 13, 275, 316n, 325, 326, 328, 337n, 344
Culicover, P. 245, 250, 271, 274, 276,
  277, 279, 287n, 290n, 292n, 293n,
  340, 342, 343, 344, 345, 353

de Chenes, B. 287n, 293n, 345
de Haan, G. 316n, 326, 346
Delfitto D. 97, 98, 99, 344
den Besten, H. 213, 244, 341n, 345
Déprez, V. and Pierce, A. 323, 329, 330, 345
Demers, R. 319n, 340
Dobrovie-Sorin, C. 100, 345
Dotson Smith, B. R. 70n, 345

Epstein, S. D. 32, 345
Everaert, M. 172n, 345
Everett, D. 66n, 231, 345

Falkenberg, G. 210n, 345
Fiengo, R. 52, 208n, 345
Figueiredo-Silva, M. C. 100, 263, 341, 345
Fisher, S. 68
Frampton, J. 185, 345
Friedemann, M.-A. 9, 99, 113, 219, 259,
  313, 314, 316n, 321, 325, 329, 331,
  337n, 345, 352, 356
Friedemann, M.-A. and Rizzi, L. 15, 345
Friedemann, M.-A. and Siloni, T. 104,
  105, 338n, 345
Fukui, N. 271, 345

Gee, J. P. 196, 198, 345
George, L. and Kornfilt, J. 288n, 345
Georgopoulos, C. 185n, 216, 307, 345
Giorgi, A. 172n, 346
Giorgi, A. and Pianesi, F. 275, 346
Goodall, G. 287
Graffi, G. 192, 346
Grewendorf, G. 223, 346
Grimshaw, J. 66n, 102, 190, 245, 273,
  275, 276, 346
Grosu, A. 289n, 346
Gruber, J. 68n, 346
Guasti, M. T. 100, 103, 192, 193, 198,
  208n, 259, 287n, 288n, 302, 313,
  314, 316n, 325, 329, 331, 337n,
  338n, 346
Guilfoyle, E. and Noonan, M. 313, 346
Gundel, J. 245, 346

Haegeman, L. 9, 13, 15, 68n, 105, 185n,
  187n, 234, 242, 244, 247, 262, 287n,
  292n, 303, 304, 316n, 319n, 328,
  329, 330, 337n, 338n, 346, 347
Haegeman, L. and Zanuttini, R. 238n,
  278, 347
Haider, U. 94, 347, 353
Haïk, I. 216, 217, 224, 347
Haiman, J. 93, 347
Hale, K. 7, 77n, 233, 340, 343
Hamann, C. 13, 306, 316n, 326, 330,
  337n, 347
Hamann, C. and Plunkett, K. 15, 347
Harnish, R. 319n, 340
Heim, I. 324, 347
Heim, I., Lasnik, H. and May, R. 172n, 347
Henry, A. 276, 347
Higginbotham, J. 25, 66n, 187n, 191,
  196, 198, 202, 208n, 209n, 318n, 347
Hoekstra, T. and Jordens, P. 154n, 330, 347

Holmberg, A. 309, 347
Holmberg, A. and Platzack, C. 244, 347
Hornstein, N. 69n, 149, 222, 340, 347, 356
Horvath, J. 246, 347
Huang, J. 30, 58, 77n, 94, 171, 215, 300, 305, 347
Hyams, N. 10, 72n, 299, 314, 321, 347, 348
Hyams, N. and Sano, T
Hyams, N. and Wexler, K. 300, 301, 348

Iatridou, S. 246, 348
Igria, B. 74

Jackendoff, R. 195, 348
Jaeggli, O. 52, 71n, 88, 348, 352
Jaeggli, O. and Safir, K. 3, 299, 342, 348
Jakubowicz, C. 172n, 348
Johnson, K. 66n, 172n, 348
Jordens, P. 330, 346, 347

Kayne, R. 1, 2, 5, 66n, 69n, 73n, 80, 84, 88, 90, 91, 95, 99, 100, 102, 103, 107, 109, 110, 115, 116, 117, 120n, 121n, 129, 135, 140, 143, 145, 147, 151n, 152n, 155n, 162, 168, 172n, 192, 206, 208, 209n, 217, 224, 241, 242, 246, 248, 255, 270, 280, 290n, 328, 335, 338n, 348
Kazman, R. 300, 313, 348
Kempchinsky, P. 172n, 233, 348
Kenstowicz, M. 318n, 348
Keyser, S. J. 52, 343, 348, 352
Keyser, S. J. and Roeper, T. 52, 348
Kiss, K. 239n, 246, 348, 355
Klima, E. 158, 349
Kornfilt J. 288, 345
Koopman, H. and Sportiche, D. 5, 138, 209n, 217, 308, 347, 348
Koster, J. 21, 45, 65, 290n, 348, 349
Kroch, A. 174, 187n, 317n, 349
Kuroda, Y. 5, 227, 349

Laenzlinger, C. 105, 283, 285, 292n, 349
Laka, I. 246, 349
Larson, R. 241, 349
Lasnik, H. 2, 3, 70n, 155n, 172n, 244, 265, 343, 347, 349
Lasnik, H. and Saito, M. 222, 229, 237n, 238, 260, 267, 268, 290n, 349
Lasnik, H. and Stowell, T. 251, 252, 253, 300, 306, 349
Lebeaux, D. 32, 172n, 313, 349

Lee, O. 301, 356
Lees, R. 158, 349
Levitt, A. 356
Levow, G. 13, 349
Léveillé, M. 355
Lightfoot, D. 3, 209n, 349, 356
Lillo Martin, D.356
Longobardi, G. 98, 260, 349
Lust, B. 301, 311, 342, 356

MacWhinney, B. 13, 349
Maling, J. 164, 349
Manzini, M. R. 50, 66n, 68n, 243, 349, 350
Manzini, M. R. and Wexler, K. 170, 350
Maracz, L. 239n, 350
May, R. 32, 116, 172n, 214, 220, 237n, 248, 261, 347, 350
McCloskey, J. 218, 219, 234, 236n, 261, 276, 287n, 291n, 350
McCloskey, J. and Hale, K. 77n, 350
McDaniel, D. 179, 180, 186n, 237n, 350
Meisel, J. 316n, 350
Melvold, J. 65, 350
Milsark, G. 77n, 350
Mohanan, K. P. 67n, 350
Moritz, L. 225, 350
Moro, A. 247, 318n, 350
Motapanyane, V. 232, 239n, 350
Muller, G. and Sternefeld, W. 287, 350

Nakayama, M. 273, 287n, 350
Noonan, M. 190, 207, 313, 346, 350

Obenauer, H. 71n, 223, 350
O'Neil, W. 74
Oshima, S. 59, 351
Otero, C. 71n, 351
Otsu, Y. 321, 351, 352

Padilla-Rivera, J. 171, 354
Parodi, T. 337, 344
Parry, M. 82
Penke, M. 337, 344
Perlmutter, D. 2, 131, 163, 351
Pesetsky, D. 190, 237n, 280, 324, 337n, 351
Pianesi, F. 275, 346
Picallo, C. 165, 166, 167, 351
Pierce, A. 11, 12, 299, 313, 314, 316n, 321, 323, 324, 325, 328, 329, 330, 331, 337n, 345, 351
Platzack, C. 54, 58, 93, 244, 313, 314, 347

Poeppel, D. and Wexler, K. 11, 311, 313, 326, 338n, 351
Plunkett, K. 347
Poggi, L. 86, 87, 351
Poletto, C. 240n, 291n, 351
Pollock, J.-Y. 8, 54, 104, 176, 216, 225, 231, 241, 324, 333, 338n, 351
Prévost, P. 15, 351
Puskas, G. 239n, 246, 351

Radford, A. 301, 310, 312, 313, 327, 331, 337, 351
Raposo, E. 30, 76n, 102, 166, 172n, 311, 352
Rappaport, M. 52, 352
Rasetti, L. 15, 263, 352
Reinhart, T. 287n, 352
Renzi, L. 80, 81, 90, 341, 352, 355
Renzi, L. and Vanelli, L. 80, 81, 352
Rivero, M.-L. 288n, 352
Rizzi, L. 1, 3, 4, 6, 13, 15, 40, 56, 59, 72n, 74n, 80, 81, 85, 100, 108, 113, 143, 148, 163, 172n, 174, 176, 177, 185n, 194, 203, 206, 214, 216, 217, 218, 219, 222, 224, 230, 237n, 240n, 242, 248, 250, 254, 260, 263, 266, 267, 270, 271, 272, 275, 288n, 291, 292n, 299, 301, 307, 309, 310, 318n, 328, 331, 341, 345, 352, 353, 354, 356
Rizzi, L. and Roberts, I. 114, 168, 226, 231, 287n, 352
Roberge, Y. 86, 88, 353
Roberts, I. 6, 93, 100, 105, 114, 118, 120n, 168, 185n, 191, 209n, 216, 217, 218, 226, 231, 240n, 263, 287n, 293n, 342, 352, 353
Rochemont, M. 245, 260, 273, 290n, 353
Rochemont, M. and Culicover, P. 245, 353
Roeper, T. 52, 62, 66n, 67n, 300, 342, 348, 353, 356
Roeper, T. and Rohrbacher, 13, 301, 353
Roeper, T. and Weissenborn, J. 301, 353
Rohrbacher, B. 13, 301, 353
Rooryck, J. 106, 353
Rosenbaum, P. S. 134, 353
Ross, J. R. 2, 69n, 174, 237n, 305, 353
Rothstein, S. 25, 353
Rouveret, A. 101, 353
Rouveret, A. and Vernaud, J. R. 48, 50, 139, 148, 353

Rudin, C. 237n, 353
Ruwet, N. 78n, 172n, 348, 353
Ruzicka, R. 65, 353

Safir, K. 3, 54, 188n, 275, 299, 342, 348, 354
Saito, M. 58, 66n, 78n, 222, 223, 229, 237n, 238n, 260, 267, 268, 290n, 349, 354
Sano T. 356
Santelman, L. 311, 342
Schein, B. 24, 73n, 354
Schmerling, S. 319n, 354
Shlonsky, U. 106, 112, 185n, 238, 244, 247, 281, 287n, 292n, 341, 354
Sigurdsson, O. 319n, 354
Siloni, T. 98, 104, 105, 207, 234, 238n, 337, 338n, 345, 354
Smits, R. J. C. 184, 354
Smith, R. 13, 70, 325, 345, 355
Snow, C. 300, 325, 349
Solà, J. 233, 239n, 318n, 354
Speas, P. 275, 354
Sprouse, R. 6, 356
Sportiche, D. 5, 9, 72n, 92, 93, 97, 105, 108, 138, 209n, 217, 222, 243, 308, 340, 347, 348, 354
Starke, M. 99, 106, 120, 287n, 288n, 292n, 312, 328, 337, 343, 354
Sternefeld, W. 223, 287n, 343, 346, 350
Stowell, T. 24, 25, 26, 74n, 138, 199, 251, 252, 253, 280, 300, 306, 310, 349, 354
Suñer, M. 71, 354
Suñer, M. and Padilla-Rivera, J. 172, 354
Suppes, P. 13, 325, 355
Szabolcsi, A. 174, 355

Taraldsen, T. 309, 355
Tomaselli, A. 236n, 355
Torrego, E. 66n, 78n, 107, 238n, 355
Travis, L. 54, 355
Truijman, K. 326, 346
Trigo, L. 67n, 355
Tsimpli, I. M. 246, 355
Tuller, L. 77n, 217, 355
Turano, G. 246, 288n, 355

Uriagereka, J. 101, 106, 112, 117, 355

Vainikka, A. 331, 355
Valian, V. 13, 299, 300, 301, 312, 317n, 325, 326, 327, 355

Vanelli, L. 80, 81, 90, 352, 355
Vanelli, L. Renzi, L. and Benincà, P. 90, 355
Van der Does, J. 68
van Riemsdijk, H. 346, 352
Verrips, M. 335, 355
Vergnaud, J.-R. 48, 50, 148, 151n, 353
Vikner, S. 58, 172n, 223, 236n, 289n, 333, 334, 355, 356
Vikner, S. and Sprouse, R. 6, 356
Visser, F. Th. 46, 356

Wang, Q., Lillo-Martin, D., Best, C and Levitt, A. 299, 356
Watanabe, A. 265, 356
Wehrli, E. 153n, 356
Weinberg, A. and Hornstein, N. 69n, 149, 347, 356
Weissenborn, J. 11, 301, 316n, 325, 326, 328, 335, 353, 355, 356

Wexler, K. 11, 12, 13, 170, 299, 300, 301, 311, 312, 313, 314, 322, 323, 324, 325, 326, 328, 337n, 338n, 342, 347, 350, 351, 356
White, L. and Prévost, P. 15, 356
Whitman, J. 301, 311, 342, 356
Williams, E. 24, 342, 356
Woolford, E. 6, 356

Yoon, J. 289n, 341

Zanuttini, R. 110, 111, 238n, 278, 329, 347, 356
Zribi-Hertz, A. 36, 70n, 77n, 289n, 348, 356
Zubizarreta, M. L. 75n, 356
Zucchi, A. 202, 356
Zwarts, F. 174, 355

Subject index

accusative with infinitive 191, 193, 197, 199, 202, 203, 205, 207, 208n, 210
adjacency 213, 230, 239n, 242, 248, 286, 293n
   anti-adjacency 242, 248, 266, 270ff, 290n, 293n, 294n, 295n
   with negative preposing 276ff
   string adjacency 75
   with Case assignment 74n, 234, 235, 260, 261, 262, 331
   with PRO licensing 264–5
   with trace licensing 266ff
adjective 23, 24, 56, 67n, 75, 99, 138–41, 149, 155, 155n
adjunct 46, 224, 283, 293n, 347
   argument/adjunct asymmetries 174ff
adjunction 9, 114–17, 121n, 242, 255, 256, 261, 268, 284, 294n, 350
   left-adjunction 87
   to IP 237n, 238n, 242, 248, 260, 261, 269, 286
adverb 74, 82, 118, 119, 121n, 187n, 231, 235, 236, 240n, 260, 261, 262, 263, 269, 271, 272, 274, 279, 281, 282, 283, 286, 287, 293n, 294n
   adverb preposing 260
   adverbial positions 8, 288n, 338n
affectedness 47, 50–4, 76, 78
affix 37, 109, 110, 114, 280, 281, 287, 289n, 338n
   affix hopping 219
Agr 38, 56–60, 71n, 72n, 76n, 77n, 81, 82, 84, 86, 105–7, 225, 231, 240n, 262, 263, 267, 268, 272, 274, 280, 281, 282, 284, 285, 287, 288n, 290n, 294n, 310, 318n, 331, 356
   AgrC 106, 110ff, 219, 267, 269, 287n, 290n, 292n, 354

AgrCl 105–6, 110, 119
AgrFin 268, 272, 273, 274, 278, 281, 293n, 294n
AgrO 103–6, 109ff, 120n, 252, 281, 338n, 345
Agr Past Participle 105–6, 110, 120n, 338n, 345
AgrS 97–8, 104, 105, 110–19, 121n, 281, 284, 287n, 326, 327, 328, 330, 338n
   recursion of Agr 105–6, 112, 290, 346
agreement 6, 7, 9, 23–4, 35ff, 57, 67n, 80, 97, 102, 110, 113–15, 119, 170, 172, 173n., 199, 201–5, 209n, 219, 227–8, 238, 240n, 241 243–4, 268, 273, 282, 347, 350
   agreement as +N 203
   dynamic agreement 227, 238n
   pronominal agreement 167–70
   strong 20, 35, 58
   weak 56, 58, 77n
Albanian 246, 288
anaphor 5, 6, 22, 61, 63, 67n, 68n, 97, 126, 130–9, 142ff, 152n, 158ff, 318n, 340, 345, 346
   anaphor–agreement effect 6, 158ff, 164ff, 172, 356
   anaphoric prepositional object 142
   long distance anaphor 164ff, 170, 346
antecedent 4, 20, 22, 23, 27, 35, 69n, 74n, 126, 129, 138, 142–4, 146–7, 149, 151, 153n, 154, 155n, 158, 161ff, 172n, 175, 176, 252, 253, 254, 306, 311, 350, 315
   antecedent-government relation 176ff, 185n, 264, 318n
   designated 147 ff

Subject index

AP 24, 61, 136, 140, 141, 142, 312
A-position 108, 150, 155n, 156n, 252, 254, 310
A'-position 155n, 156n
Arabic
  Lebanese 88
  Levantine 318
  modern arabic dialects 348
  Palestinian 354
arbitrary interpretation 22–6, 28–30, 34–5, 38, 47, 53, 59, 63, 67–8n, 71n
arguments 73n, 74n, 76n, 81, 89–90, 96, 97, 126–7, 129–30, 134–5, 168, 174–7, 182, 184, 185n, 194–5, 198ff, 235, 250, 257, 261, 280, 283, 285, 305, 321, 338, 344, 345
  referential arguments 54ff, 56
Aux to Comp 56, 108, 234, 263
auxiliary 30, 56, 86, 100, 108–9, 116ff, 132, 138, 191
  – to Comp 56
  aspectual 99, 102, 103, 105, 131, 138
avoid structure 275
axiom 327

Bach's generalization 21, 22, 66n, 67n
barrier 3, 268, 343, 346
Bijection Principle 308, 348
binding 6, 14, 22–3, 27, 32, 35–7, 42, 45, 56–8, 60, 63, 66, 67n, 70n, 71n, 73, 75, 77n, 144ff, 153n, 159ff, 173n, 177ff, 186n2, 219, 251, 304, 316, 318n, 328, 340ff
  A'-binding 45, 251–2, 306–7
  A-binding 78n, 151n, 307
    antecedent binding 143, 155n, 318n
    binding principles 27, 144, 147, 149, 160, 164, 168, 254
    Binding Theory 3, 21, 129–30, 138, 145–6, 150–1, 153n, 158–9, 162, 165, 169, 170, 249
    local binder 126, 145–6, 148, 152n, 153n
    local binding 151, 152, 168, 219
    non-local binding relations 6
    principle A 23, 49, 158
    principle B 27, 30, 160–1
    principle C 30
Brazilian Portuguese 100, 238n, 262, 341
Burzio's generalization 137

Case 5, 6, 7, 9, 39, 40, 41, 43, 55, 59, 61, 72n, 73n, 74n, 78n, 79, 87, 88, 89, 90, 93, 97, 120, 137, 152n, 165, 187n, 198, 203, 204, 205, 208n, 209n, 210n, 219, 232, 241, 260–263, 269, 270, 286, 291n, 292n, 331, 341, 342, 346, 347, 350, 351, 352, 354, 355
  abstract 151
  accusative or objective 61, 74n, 89, 103–106, 192, 197, 200, 207
  case assignment under agreement 56, 59
  case assignment under government 48, 54, 201, 234, 236, 331
  case filter 231, 239n, 331
  dative 61, 62, 79
  exceptional case marking 228n, 352
  inherent 66, 79n, 200, 331
  nominative 36, 40, 56, 89, 163, 231, 235, 236, 240, 244, 262–263, 288n
  null case 3, 265, 286
  partitive 71n, 200, 201
  quirky 164
Catalan 190, 213, 233, 239n
causative construction 48, 67n, 147, 288n, 329
c-command 27, 45, 92, 126, 134, 137, 138, 142, 143, 144, 145, 151n, 154n, 156n, 172n, 175, 185n, 193, 309, 315, 316, 319, 326
  asimmetric c-domain 143, 144, 147
  asymmetric c-command 143, 144, 147
  c-domain 143, 154n
  local c-command 93
Celtic 244
chains 4–6, 37, 40, 41, 71, 75n, 89–90, 103, 114, 125ff, 167ff, 186n, 205, 210n, 216, 219–20, 242, 243, 247, 254, 260, 270, 278, 281ff, 294n, 295n, 307, 308, 318n, 337n, 340, 353
  A chain 5, 6, 60, 90, 174ff, 186n, 269, 318n, 356
  A' chain 6, 35, 60, 174ff, 185n2, 237n, 252, 269
  CHAIN 186
  chain formation algorithm 5, 126, 128, 130, 151, 153n
  chain structure 127ff
  derivational 151
  NP-chain 176
  representational 278–9
  Wh-chain 176, 181

Subject index

Chamorro 216, 343
Chinese 58, 77n, 77, 171, 172, 173n, 179, 215, 347, 356
clausal reduction 192, 207, 208n
Clause Mate Condition 158
cleft 181ff, 289n, 247, 289n, 295
  negative cleft 181–2, 187n
  pseudo-cleft 192, 198, 203, 204, 205
clitic 4, 5, 40, 42, 49, 50, 54, 60, 70n2, 75n, 81, 84, 86, 93, 96ff, 120n, 126, 129, 130, 138, 149, 150, 154n, 162, 231, 249, 250, 252–3, 283, 287, 289n2, 338n, 341, 342, 348, 353, 354, 355, 356
  anaphoric 5, 129–33, 141–4, 135, 147, 148, 153n, 304
  chain 42, 285
  climbing 1, 120n, 121n, 348
  Clitic Left Dislocation (CLLD) 246, 287, 343
  cluster 82, 105
  doubling 80, 88, 95, 345
  impersonal, 37, 71n, 131, enclitic position 4, 87, 96, 106ff. 121n, 353
  landing site 96, 99ff, 104–106, 109ff
  locative 71n
  Ne 40, 97, 111, 120n, 176, 254, 341
  object 72n, 80, 88, 89, 95, 104, 112, 113, 116
  proclitic position 4, 87–9, 96, 106ff, 120n2
  reflexive clitic 5, 129, 130, 133–4, 140, 142, 146, 153n, 156n
  Romance cliticization 4, 96ff, 338n
  subject 4, 7, 37, 60, 62, 80ff, 95, 110, 112–14, 116, 117, 208n, 214, 226, 231, 328, 336, 338n, 347, 351, 352, 353
  trace 5, 49, 50, 130, 138, 139, 146–8, 152n, 154n3, 252, 254
comment *see* topic–comment articulation
Comp or C 7, 8, 30–32, 56, 69n, 74n, 86, 108, 191, 198, 203, 206, 207, 214, 216, 220, 234, 237n, 238, 247, 257, 263, 326, 341, 346, 352, 354
  affixal 280
  assigning Case 260–4
  Doubly Filled Comp effect 69
  licensing pro 264
  null 280
  split-C 241ff, 287
  syncretic 272ff

comparative syntax 15, 80, 330, 336, 349, 352
conjunction 85
connectedness 162, 172n, 344, 348, 349
connectivity effects 205
continental Scandinavian languages 81, 334
continuity 11, 12, 287
control 21, 23, 28, 34, 36–37, 44, 46, 51, 55, 61, 62ff, 66n, 67n, 68n, 73n, 74n, 77, 91, 92, 108, 134, 163, 191, 264, 269, 270, 288n, 292n, 340, 342, 343, 349, 350, 351, 353
  object control 21, 22, 24, 62, 63, 66n, 67n, 74n, 198
  subject control 134, 162
  theory of control 3, 35, 60, 65
coordination 121n
  conjunctive coordination 108
  disjunctive coordination 108
coreference 154n, 155n, 160, 165, 166, 167, 209n, 317n, 349
CP 7, 8, 14, 15, 176, 188, 191, 192–4, 199, 203, 206–207, 208n, 209n, 214, 244, 245, 261, 265, 270, 287n, 305, 310–12, 319n, 325–8, 330, 335, 336, 337n, 339, 342, 346
  recursion 226, 237, 291n
  split-cp 241ff, 287n, 346
crossover 290
  strong 30
  weak 138, 290

Danish 15, 172n, 289n, 323, 333, 334, 347, 353
diachrony 46, 47, 59, 73n, 74n, 236n, 353
dialect 4, 72n, 80, 81, 83–5, 93, 110, 112, 116–17, 120n, 240, 341, 342, 347, 348, 351
definitess effect 8, 71n, 85
delearning 317n, 319n
determiner 7, 96, 97, 98, 99, 313
development 310, 321
diary register 303ff
disjoint reference 29
  with subjunctive 6, 165, 166, 167, 170, 171
do support 217, 232, 275
DP 4, 5, 7, 97, 98, 104, 105, 242, 250, 252, 254, 255, 283, 290n, 295n
D-structure 71n, 74n, 128, 129, 150, 150n, 152n, 153n, 157n, 184, 208n, 216, 342

Subject index 365

Dutch 13, 15, 76n, 154n, 316n, 319n, 323, 326, 328, 330, 338n, 346

Easy to please construction 90, 101, 103, 120n, 149, 285
economy 103, 228, 243, 274, 287, 293n, 294n, 334, 343, 353, 354, 356
  economy of representations 243, 275, 290n
  reference set for economy 275, 276
Empty Category Principle (ECP) 4, 8, 35, 45, 59, 60, 69n, 70n, 73n, 74n, 87, 35, 109, 116, 118, 159, 162, 164, 170, 172n, 174, 207, 215, 218, 237n, 254, 264, 267, 268, 270ff, 292n, 293n, 294n, 307, 309, 316, 318n, 344, 350, 351, 354
  Generalized ECP (GECP) 35, 59, 70n
empty elements 308–10
  functional characterization, 152n-3n
English 54, 58ff, 81, 86, 91, 93, 98, 133, 134, 149, 158, 159, 171ff, 186, 190, 196, 201ff, 250
  Belfast English 347
  Early Modern English 46
  Hiberno English 218, 236n, 276
  Middle English 46
  Modern English 46, 47, 75n, 91
  Old English 46
ergative 131–3, 154n, 155n, 156n, 348
  marker of ergativity 154n, 156n
  see also unaccusative
exclamatives 236n, 237n
explanatory adequacy 9
expletive 36, 37, 41–8, 53, 54, 59, 60, 73n–6n, 88, 89, 95, 126, 152n, 157n, 179, 180, 186n, 187n, 188, 196, 198, 237, 275, 355
  expletive operator 179, 180, 184, 186n, 187n
  expletive replacement 186
  non-argument 41, 48, 54ff
  quasi argument 43, 54ff
  root expletive subjects 314ff
extended projection 24, 42, 102, 245, 346
event 177, 191, 193, 202, 205, 207, 208n, 209n

Faroese 54, 77
features
  feature checking 9, 97–9, 103, 104, 105, 114, 115, 120n, 282, 294n, 329, 332
  gender- 34, 37, 56, 68n, 120n
  interpretable 9, 242
  number- 4, 34, 37, 56–7, 60, 68n, 76n, 77, 78n, 81, 82, 92, 119, 120n, 350
  person- 4, 34, 37, 56, 57, 60, 68n, 76n, 77, 78n, 81, 82, 92, 93, 97, 119, 120n, 244, 288, 305, 350
  Phi or φ-34–8, 57–9, 60, 76n
  strong- 121
  weak- 121n
finiteness 8, 243ff, 345, 347
Fiorentino 82, 83, 85, 87, 112
focus 182–4, 187n, 188n, 239n, 246ff, 342, 347, 353
  contrastive focus 246
  focus or Foc-Criterion 247, 259
  focus–presupposition articulation 245, 246, 286, 289n
  new information focus 245, 246
Foc 8, 242, 245, 247, 251, 255, 256, 257, 258, 259, 260, 278, 279, 281, 286, 289n, 290n, 291n, 292n, 294n
force 8, 243, 245, 248, 249, 257, 258, 261, 262, 264, 269, 272, 273
French 1, 11, 13–15, 29, 36, 48, 54, 59, 70n, 77n, 78n, 80ff, 121n, 129, 135, 147, 155n, 168, 176, 181, 183, 189, 190, 203, 204, 208n, 214, 217, 219, 222–4, 226–31, 237n, 238n, 246, 266, 267, 269, 279, 280–283, 286, 289n, 291n, 292, 293n, 294n, 299, 303, 310, 311, 313, 315, 316n, 317n, 323–329, 331–6, 337n, 338n, 340, 344–50, 352, 355, 356
  Literary French 101
  Old French 90–3, 340
  Québec French 86
full interpretation 14, 90, 182, 182n, 251, 252, 255, 324, 328, 332
functional elements 7, 275, 313, 314, 319n

Galician 101
Gardenese 92, 93
generalized transformation 327
German 6, 11, 13, 29, 54, 69n, 75n, 77n, 91, 93, 94, 118, 176, 179, 180, 208, 219n, 223, 236n, 242, 244, 253, 275, 290n, 304, 305, 308, 310, 313, 316n, 323, 325, 326, 328, 329, 330, 337, 338n, 342

366 Subject index

Germanic 6, 75n, 118, 208, 238, 242, 244, 253, 290n, 304, 338n, 342, 349, 353–5
government 7, 35, 37, 39, 40, 43, 48, 54, 59, 70, 92, 93, 94, 174, 175, 178, 180, 182, 183, 185, 186, 187, 189, 192, 194ff, 208n, 218, 231, 234–6, 240, 267–9, 283, 331, 343
  antecedent government 69n, 74n, 172n, 175–7, 180, 181, 185n, 264, 318n
  canonical government 91
  Government Transparency Corollary, 240n
  head government 4, 176, 218, 242, 243, 265, 286, 291n, 292n, 318n, 352, 353
  proper government 45, 172n, 285, 292n, 349, 350
Government and Binding Theory 20, 125, 158, 343
governing category 27, 28, 50, 138, 139, 140, 144, 147, 148, 150, 155n, 160, 165–7, 169, 170, 309, 318n
governor 50, 59, 66, 139, 140, 144, 147, 148, 150, 155, 160, 165, 166, 167, 169, 170, 267, 268, 272
  potential governor 175, 185n, 208n
Greek 246, 355
  ancient greek 190
Gungbe 247, 340

Hausa 217, 355
head 4ff, 36ff, 50, 54, 56–60, 66, 70n, 71n, 72n, 74n, 77n, 86, 88, 91, 93ff, 166, 173–6, 185n, 186n, 191, 196, 199, 203, 205, 207, 208n, 213, 214ff, 242–7, 249, 252, 256ff, 309, 310, 313, 316, 318nff, 327ff, 341, 346, 347, 350
head movement constraint 9, 116, 174, 176, 264
heavy NP shift 45, 73n, 75n, 206, 209n, 217, 224, 288n
Hebrew 88, 181, 190, 238n, 354
Hungarian 239n, 246, 290, 342, 347, 348, 350, 351

Icelandic 93, 164, 170, 275, 319n, 340, 345, 348, 349, 354
identification 4, 12, 96, 97, 128, 152n, 153n, 254, 307, 309, 350
  discourse identification 309, 316, 326

idioms 135, 175, 185
imperative 106, 110, 111–13, 116, 120n, 121n, 312, 313, 338, 348
  imperative criterion 110
implicit arguments 19ff, 35, 65–6, 348
incorporation 108, 114, 231, 319n, 340
  excorporation 118, 335
index 26, 27, 69n, 71n, 147, 150, 177ff, 185n, 186n-188n, 199ff, 238n, 318n
  coindexing 45, 65, 71n, 201, 209
  referential index 6, 29, 69n, 71n, 177, 178, 180, 183, 184, 185n-8n, 318n
indirect negative evidence 319, 320n
infinitive 11ff, 25, 76n, 78n, 100, 104, 106, 111, 112, 114, 120n, 121, 147, 155, 189, 191, 192, 193, 196ff, 232, 239n, 240, 244, 248, 262, 264, 265, 269, 288n, 292n, 313, 319n, 320ff, 343, 346, 352, 356
  naked 205ff
InfinP 330, 335
Infl 7, 10, 36–41, 54ff, 167, 170, 172n, 173n, 219, 227, 228, 233, 310, 346–8, 352, 354
  I to C movement 8, 112, 116, 210, 213–215, 218, 220, 224, 249, 259, 263, 276, 277–9, 290n-292n, 319
  Infl recursion 105ff
  Split-Infl 102, 216, 231, 326
information
  old, new 245, 246
interface
  lexicon-syntax 190
  morphology-syntax 11
IP 4, 8, 9, 80, 81, 94, 110, 112, 113, 191, 193, 199, 203, 207, 219, 237n, 238n, 241–8, 256, 257, 259–61, 264ff, 288n, 309, 311, 326, 330, 351
Irish 77n, 234, 244, 344, 350
island 2, 69, 158, 174, 179, 182, 185n, 187n, 348, 353
  strong 182
  weak 6, 174, 175, 176, 178, 184, 185, 355
  Wh-island 2, 6, 174, 176, 178, 180, 181, 182, 218, 352
Italian 1, 3, 4, 8, 12, 19, 20–25, 27–29, 31, 35, 36–39, 43, 45, 46, 53–56, 58–61, 63, 64, 67n, 68n, 70n, 72n 74n, 77n, 78n, 80, 81, 85, 86, 88,

Subject index 367

91, 92, 95, 97, 99, 100, 103, 106, 107, 108, 109, 110, 111, 112, 114, 115, 116, 118, 120n, 121n, 129, 131, 138, 148, 160, 163, 165, 166, 172n, 176, 181, 183, 184, 189, 190, 198, 200, 203, 208n, 213, 229, 230, 231, 239, 239n, 240, 242, 246–249, 252–255, 258, 259, 263, 264, 266, 269, 270, 286, 289n, 290n, 292, 300, 302, 303, 313, 317n, 323, 331, 332, 334, 335, 336

Japanese 58, 77n, 179, 215, 223, 229

Kayne's generalization 80, 88ff
Kikuyu 216, 344
Korean 58, 77

language acquisition 1, 9, 10, 12, 15, 72n, 73n, 104, 299, 300, 302, 303, 313, 316n, 323ff, 344–56
language faculty 1, 9
language development 1, 11, 14, 320, 336, 346, 347, 352
Latin 244
learnability 41
Left Dislocation 83
  Clitic Left Dislocation 246, 287, 343
LF 5, 32, 33, 72n, 83, 89, 90, 96, 98, 99, 102, 128, 162, 172n, 176, 178, 179, 186n, 214, 215, 220, 221–3, 227–9, 237n, 238n, 247n, 248, 254, 255, 292n, 312, 324, 333, 335, 338n, 345, 348
  LF movement 72, 99, 162, 222, 237n, 238n, 248, 334, 348
locality 2, 3, 5–7, 49, 147, 174, 175, 177, 178, 184, 185n, 208, 215, 243, 256, 268, 270, 291n, 341, 348, 350
  theory of locality 1, 2

maturation 11, 337n, 342
  maturational processes 11
  maturational schedule 312, 319n
middle 52, 53, 348
minimalist program 4, 97, 343
minimality 136, 174, 208n, 233, 344, 350, 353
  relativized 6, 8, 109, 116, 174, 175ff, 242, 262, 268, 286, 340, 345, 352
modal 261, 277, 329, 330, 335, 336, 337n, 338n

null modal 120, 121n, 335, 338n
morphologically complete 109, 110, 112–16
movement
  as 'last resort' 242, 247, 260, 274, 286, 334
  head to head movement 173n, 213, 225, 273, 280
  improper 114, 115, 345, 350n
  move features 292
  NP-movement 39, 140, 162, 200, 209n, 353
  partial Wh-movement 178ff
  Wh-movement 6, 140, 152, 162, 179, 180, 182, 184, 185n, 186, 187n, 188, 206, 215–17, 227–9, 236n, 239n, 311–13, 337n, 343, 349, 350, 354

negation 32, 33, 82, 97, 102, 103, 110, 112, 119, 174, 176, 179, 180, 182, 183, 184, 186n, 187n, 188n, 224, 244, 323, 329, 330, , 332, 338n, 345, 346, 347, 349, 356
  affixal negation 338
  constituent negation 329
negative concord 238
Negative Criterion 185, 225, 238n, 278, 347
negative inversion 224ff
negative islands 174ff
negative polarity items 276
negative preposing 226, 276ff
NegP 103, 104, 108, 119, 121n, 176, 185n, 187n, 225, 329, 330, 332, 335, 338n
nominative island condition 158
northern italian dialects 4, 72n, 80, 110, 116–17
NP 21, 22, 25, 27, 28, 31–33, 39, 40, 42–45, 56, 57, 59, 71n, 73n, 74n, 75n, 79n, 80, 81–84, 87, 88, 92, 94, 97, 98, 101, 103, 117, 125, 126, 130, 131, 133, 134, 137, 139, 140, 141, 145, 146, 149, 151, 151n, 152n, 153n, 155n, 158, 159, 161, 162, 168, 171, 176, 177, 178, 186n, 187n, 191, 192, 193, 198, 200, 204, 205, 206, 209n, 210n, 217, 218, 223, 224, 288n, 292, 307, 309, 310, 312, 313, 331, 344, 345, 353, 355
  determinerless NP's 313
null complement anaphora 68n

368 Subject index

null costant 251, 252, 253, 290n, 306–12, 314–15, 316n, 319n
null elements 3, 12, 13, 19, 20, 27, 35–37, 60, 94, 153, 254, 268, 300, 306, 307, 308, 310, 316, 318n, 326
null subject languages 4, 12, 324, 325
null subject parameter 2, 3, 4, 10, 12, 80, 85, 90, 266, 269, 303, 317, 338n, 342, 348, 351
    early null subjects 11–15, 299ff, 336, 352
numeration 275, 276

operator
    anaphoric 253, 260
    discourse bound null operator 305
    negative 174, 176
    null or empty 20, 30–2, 69n, 73n, 94, 182n, 252, 253, 268, 286, 289n, 293n, 295, 300, 304ff
    quantificational 253
optimality theory 276
optionality 68n, 69n, 78n, 283, 334
ordering 255ff, 353
    extrinsic 129, 143

Padovano 83, 84, 341
Palauan 345
parameters 39, 41, 55, 57, 60, 241, 321, 322, 343, 344, 347, 349, 350, 353, 354, 355
    parameter resetting 73n, 299, 321
    parameter setting 10, 12, 36, 38, 39, 41, 43, 45, 57, 74n, 299, 317n, 342, 344, 347, 356
parasitic gap 31, 76n, 137, 224, 308
participle 100, 103, 120n, 190, 198, 345n
    passive 40, 71n, 119, 200
    past 56, 106, 230, 231, 239, 240n, 244, 281, 282, 338
    present 118–19, 190
particular grammars 1, 2, 20
    as systems of rules 2
passive 5, 37, 39, 40, 52, 53, 54, 67n, 71n, 72n, 99, 100, 127, 129, 131, 132, 133, 142, 146, 155, 194, 195, 200
    impersonal passive 131, 132, 133, 155n, 351
perception 7, 52, direct vs indirect 190ff
performance 10, 321
PF 81, 85, 87, 333, 335

Piedmontese 83, 100, 106, 117
pied piping 237
Polish 244
Portuguese 30, 56, 76, 100, 101, 238n, 262, 288n, 311
possessive 159, 161, 172n
poverty of stimulus 10, 321
PP 66, 79, 88, 134, 154, 187n, 254, 271, 283, 285, 290n, 293n, 294n, 295n, 312
predication 21, 25, 42, 185n, 187n, 247
preposition 59, 61, 66, 70n, 77, 79, 99, 133, 140, 149, 198, 262, 263, 289n, 347, 356
    licensing *pro* 36, 70
presupposition *see* focus-presupposition articulation
principles and parameters approach 2ff
PRO 3, 13, 20, 24, 27, 28, 29, 31, 34, 35, 36, 44, 55, 60, 63–65, 67n, 68n, 70n, 73n, 90–92, 94, 108, 126, 127, 134, 147, 148, 150, 152n, 153n, 168, 169, 170, 190, 191, 242, 252, 264, 265, 269, 270, 286, 288n, 292n, 307, 310, 318n, 348, 349, 350, 354
    PRO gate effects 318n
    PRO Theorem 3, 36, 60, 70n, 168, 170, 265
Pro 3, 4, 10, 19, 20, 27, 29, 30, 32, 34–49, 53–62, 64, 70, 71n, 72n, 74n, 75n, 76n, 77n, 78n, 79n, 81, 84, 89, 91–95, 121n, 192, 252, 289, 307, 316, 317n, 319n, 338n, 344, 345, 353, 354
    formal licensing 35–6
    interpretation, or identification 3
procrastinate 333, 334, 335
projection principle 20, 24–6, 37–9, 42, 60, 65, 79n, 89, 128, 136, 197, 198, 199, 216, 227–9
    extended pp 24, 42
pronouns 20, 22, 30, 34, 37, 40, 43, 49, 59, 60, 69n, 72n, 81, 82, 92, 93, 96, 97, 118, 131, 133, 138, 139, 143, 154, 159, 160, 165, 166–8, 171, 188n, 192, 196, 229, 231, 241, 245, 247, 253, 255, 258, 286, 289n, 302, 305, 317n, 318n, 319, 340, 342, 344, 347, 349, 353
    D-pronouns 253
    resumptive pronoun 185n, 246, 307, 345
    weak 120, 292n, 328
psych verbs 1, 6

Puter 93

Q-float 92, 231, 354
QR 32–33, 83, 254, 255, 261, 313
quantificational 22, 32, 237, 242, 250–4, 306, 308
quantifiers 31–3, 69n, 92, 99, 138, 162, 176, 235, 251, 252, 255, 306–8, 344, 345
question 12, 79, 110, 113, 116, 117, 183, 186n, 191, 213–6, 218, 220, 224, 226, 229, 232, 233, 237n, 238n, 249, 251, 257, 260, 261, 266, 277, 278, 280, 290n-292n, 300, 306, 311, 319n, 325, 326, 337n, 340, 342–4, 353
  echo questions 238n, 301, 317n, 319n
  indirect 191, 183, 232, 236n, 288n
  multiple 214, 221, 222, 353
  operator 215, 249, 258, 259, 307, 309, 258

raising 5, 127, 132–8, 148, 154n, 155n, 162, 200, 201, 269, 270, 292, 332, 338n, 350, 354
  super raising 174–8
range 307
reanalysis 48, 69
reciprocal 67, 129ff
reflexives 6, 23, 142, 156, 165, 239, 340, 349
  intrinsic reflexives 156
relational grammar 2, 351
relative clause 186, 192, 193, 342, 344
  appositive 251, 252, 290n, 306n
  pseudo-relatives 192ff, 344
  relative operator 249, 251, 258, 290n
restructuring 100, 120n, 139, 148, 149, 155n, 156n, 350
Rhaeto-romance 92
River Plate Spanish 88
Romagnolo 82, 86, 87, 351
Romance 89, 90, 92, 93, 96, 97, 98, 99, 101, 102, 104, 106, 107, 109, 115–118, 126, 140, 148, 149, 159, 160, 162, 165, 172n, 189, 192, 196, 205–210, 213, 214, 232–234, 238n, 242, 244, 246, 248, 253, 268, 270, 282, 286, 291n, 295n, 338, 341, 344, 345, 348, 349, 352–356
  Western Romance 112, 117, 355
Romani 180, 181, 185n, 186n, 237n
Romanian 100, 101, 213, 352

root 104, 121n, 216, 218, 227–9, 232, 243, 299ff, 341
root infinitives 11–15, 320ff, 346, 352
root null subjects 11, 15, 300ff
Russian 207, 208, 210n

scrambling 187, 223, 343, 346
second language acquisition 15, 351, 356
selection 26, 66, 75n, 79, 207, 226, 227, 229, 233, 275, 285, 288n, 289n, 327, 329, 346, 350, 356
  categorial, 190
  semantic 197
sisterhood 7
Slovac 106
small clauses 21, 24, 25, 41, 43–47, 50, 53, 55, 60, 61, 68n, 136, 138, 148, 149, 155n, 201, 204, 209, 265, 288n, 312, 327, 344, 354, 356
  adverbial 288
  causative 24, 25
  epistemic 47, 201, 204, 209
Spanish 31, 36, 67n, 81, 88, 91, 154n, 176, 213, 232, 234, 238n, 239n, 246, 341
specificity 97
Specified Subject Condition 147, 158
specifier 7–9, 97, 104, 171, 191, 199, 203, 215, 222, 223, 228, 236, 239n, 242, 243, 247, 249, 255–8, 268, 272, 278, 282, 283–5, 286n, 294, 300, 310, 334
  a-176–178
  a'-175, 176, 185n, 222, 224
  of the root 12, 13, 303, 309, 311, 317n, 325, 326, 300
  optionality of specifiers 315
  Spec/head configuration 98, 120, 247, 259, 278
spell-out 80, 82, 86, 185n, 259, 277, 314
S-structure 5, 32, 39, 40, 71n, 89, 98, 113, 125, 126, 128, 130–2, 136, 137, 150, 152n, 157n, 162, 179, 180, 184, 186n, 214–17, 219, 220, 222, 229, 254, 259, 264, 277, 344
structural cartography 8
structure preservations 236n, 238n
stylistic inversion 331
subjacency 2, 283, 290n, 291n, 293n–5n, 321, 352, 353
subject–auxiliary inversion 213, 214
subject clitic inversion 95, 226

370 Subject index

subject inversion 4, 44, 45, 85, 91
   superordinate subject 77n, 160, 164, 165
subjunctive 6, 54, 106, 159, 164–7, 170, 171, 232–4, 240n, 244, 288n, 346, 348, 352, 354, 355
Subset Principle 41
substitution 114, 115, 117, 121n
superscript 50, 139, 140, 149, 151n, 286n, 294, 300, 310, 334

tense 97, 107, 110, 115, 166, 167, 170, 191, 193, 216, 225, 232, 239n, 244, 281, 282, 288n, 313, 328–9, 337n, 344, 346, 349, 355
   tense variable 324
Tensed S Condition 158
that-t effect 8, 85, 267–8, 344
Theta or θ-theory 175–8, 182, 185n, 205, 220, 341
   argumental Theta roles 177
   experiencer 133, 156
   individual vs propositional theme 202ff
   thematic sharing 190ff
   theme 163
   Theta Criterion 5, 26, 90, 182, 187n, 197, 199, 200n, 209n
   Theta-grid 25, 197, 199, 200, 202
   Theta roles 25, 51–4, 186n, 187n, 197, 199, 200, 202, 203, 209
top 8, 237, 242, 246, 247, 251, 255, 256, 257, 258, 259, 260, 261, 262, 264, 265, 267, 268, 270, 273, 274, 280, 281, 282, 284, 285, 286, 290n, 291n, 292n, 293n, 294n
   recursion of Top 256
topic
   topic–comment articulation 84, 172, 182, 222, 241, 245ff, 268, 346, 350
   topic-drop 304ff
   topic or top-criterion 247
topicalization 29n, 237, 245, 253, 260, 267, 268, 271, 274, 344
TP 14, 113, 225, 327, 328–30, 332, 336
trace 4, 5, 8, 20, 27, 35, 42, 45, 50, 59, 67n, 70n, 72n, 83, 94, 103, 125, 126, 130ff, 217, 266ff
   spell-out 185
Trentino 80, 82, 85, 86
truncation 14, 15, 320, 325, 328–31, 336, 337n, 338n, 351, 356
   in second language acquisition 15

unaccusative *see also* ergative 5, 131, 341
Universal Grammar (UG) 1, 2, 10, 11, 15, 321
unspecified object deletion 68
utterances 104, 324, 327, 336
   non verbal 312

Valdôtain 100, 353
variables 30, 73n, 126, 177, 188n, 221, 251, 252, 254, 306, 307, 308, 318n, 342
verbs
   aspectual 100, 102
   auxiliary 100, 102, 335
   causative 24, 47–49, 62, 100, 103, 189, 208
   copulative 138, 140, 142
   epistemic 47, 49, 55, 202–4, 270
   modal 120, 187n, 261, 277
   perception 7, 49, 189 ff, 340, 345, 346
   restructuring 148
   tensed 224, 334, 335, 337n
   untensed 334
verb-second 80, 90ff, 333, 346, 350, 352
   embedded V-2 236, 333, 350
   full V2 289
   residual V-2 213 ff
VP 19, 21, 71, 78n, 85–8, 120n, 132, 137, 143, 145, 154n, 156n, 191, 195, 196, 199, 206, 219, 222–4, 235, 236, 241, 245, 254, 261, 272, 277, 311, 312, 321, 325, 327, 329–31, 335, 353
VP bare 67n, 75n 209n
VP preposing 156n, 209n
VP small clauses 209n
VP internal subject hypothesis 5, 6, 219

West Flemish 105, 176, 181, 187n, 234, 262, 328n
Wh
   association with focus 239
   discourse-linked 237
   Wh Criterion 9, 179, 180, 181, 213ff, 278, 290n, 319n, 351
   Wh *in situ* 186n, 214, 221, 226–8, 238n, 301, 312, 313, 328, 337n, 351
   Wh-operator 179, 180, 214–17, 274
   functional definition 221
Williams's Predication Principle 24

X-bar theory 7, 191, 236n, 255

Yiddish 54

For Product Safety Concerns and Information please contact our EU representative GPSR@taylorandfrancis.com
Taylor & Francis Verlag GmbH, Kaufingerstraße 24, 80331 München, Germany

www.ingramcontent.com/pod-product-compliance
Lightning Source LLC
Chambersburg PA
CBHW071144300426
44113CB00009B/1082